THE MAN OF THE MOMENT

Narendra Modi

The Man of the Moment

Narendra Modi

M V Kamath
Kalindi Randeri

2013 Enriched and Enlarged New Edition

Wide Canvas
(An Imprint of Vikas Publishing House Pvt Ltd)

Vikas® Publishing House Pvt Ltd
E-28, Sector-8, Noida-201301 (UP) India
Phone: +91-120-4078900, Fax: +91-120-4078999
Regd. Office: 576, Masjid Road, Jangpura, New Delhi-110014. India
E-mail: helpline@vikaspublishing.com • www.vikaspublishing.com

© 2013 M V Kamath & Kalindi Randeri
Photo Source: Authors, Private Collections

All rights reserved. No part of this publication may be reproduced, stored in a retrieval system or transmitted, in any form or by any means electronic, mechanical, photocopying, recording or otherwise without first seeking written permission of the publisher.

First Published by Rupa Publications Pvt. Ltd. as
Narendra Modi: The Architect of a Modern State

Marketed and Distributed exclusively in India & subcontinent by:

Times Group Books
(A division of Bennett, Coleman and Company Limited)
Times Annexe, Express Building
9-10, Bahadur Shah Zafar Marg, New Delhi-110 002

ISBN 978-93-259-6838-7

Published by Vikas® Publishing House Pvt Ltd
Printed at Gopsons Papers Ltd.

Dedicated to
Today's Youth
and
Gen X

Contents

Preface ix

SECTION I
From Grass Roots to Gujarat's Helmsman

1. Beginnings of a Quest — 3
2. Rites of Passage — 14
3. The Threshold and Beyond — 22
4. The Interregnum — 29
5. The Power of Retreat — 37
6. The Man and His Mission — 48
7. History and Hysteria — 63
8. The Secular Gossamer — 77
9. Of Commissions and Reality — 88
10. Test of Faith — 103
11. Renaissance Outside the Labyrinth — 132
12. The General in Command — 149
13. The View Beyond the Prism — 172
14. No Full Stop; Not Yet — 181

SECTION II
FROM GOVERNMENT TO GOVERNANCE

	Open letter to Narendra Modi from Prof. B M Hegde	219
15.	Focus on Governance	221
16.	Women, Tribal Welfare and Skill Development	236
17.	Novel Developments	254
18.	Economic and Industrial Growth	269
19.	Beyond the Shores of Gujarat	281
20.	Spreading Sadbhavana	303
21.	Modi and the Media	313
22.	Vibrant Gujarat 2013	335
23.	Pinpricks	342
24.	The Elections of 2012	358
25.	The Press Post-Mortem after Election 2012	372
26.	Will He or Won't He?	382
27.	At Close Quarters: The Man and His Persona	388
	Afterword	399
	Annexure I	403
	Annexure II	406
	Bibliography	409
	Index	411

Preface

As two concerned and committed citizens of India, we have observed the unfolding panorama of political, social and economic life in the country post-Independence. We have witnessed and shared in the hope that flowed through India after being freed from the shackles of imperial colonialism. Leaders have come and gone, each leaving behind a mixed legacy of reform and growth on the one hand, but stymied by either divisive politics or the greed for personal gain on the other. Consequently, it would not be an exaggeration to say that every time the country has moved forward in a certain direction, it has slipped back in other areas. Of course, prudence also steps in wisely to admit that that is the greatness of democracy – change is the only constant!

However, during the last decade or so, India seems to have lost its growth momentum: astounding levels of corruption, scams in numerous fields and governance have hit an all-time low. Amidst these disturbing phenomena, the emergence of a strong leader is what Indian citizens have been praying for. There is one hopeful contender – Narendra Modi.

Narendra Modi was born in a lower middle-class family in the historic town of Vadnagar in Gujarat, and spent his formative years there prior to setting off for the Himalayas, without so much as a paisa in his pocket, in search of the Supreme. How he spent those years in exile, how he was attracted to the Hindu nationalist organization, Rashtriya Swayamsevak Sangh (RSS), how, in the course of time, he took a shaky step into the river of politics and its muddy waters, and then went on to emerge as a fearless achiever, is a story in itself.

Nominated as the Chief Minister of Gujarat in 2001, the Godhra carnage and subsequent riots blackened his image with devastating effect. With the accusing fingers of the entire country being pointed at him and being branded as a near-fanatical *Hindutva* follower,

The Man of the Moment: Narendra Modi

every manner of allegation and hatred was flung at Modi. And then came the findings of the Special Investigative Team (SIT) set up by the Supreme Court to inquire into the carnage and riots. Modi was given a clean chit. It has been over eleven long years since the horrific event took place and things have changed beyond imagination.

With peace restored in Gujarat, a vibrant state has risen from the ashes. Its current economy stands unmatched, its prosperity is self evident, its stature unchallenged. Modi's achievements, against many odds, as a manager of progress and possessing the ability to man economic forces that have turned Gujarat into the number one state in India, especially in the areas of industrial growth and economic development, have ensured him three consecutive wins to continue as Chief Minister of Gujarat. His victory in the 2012 state elections removed the last thread of doubt, if any, that Narendra Modi is here to stay. Importantly, Modi has won over the hearts of the Muslims in the state – the proof of that being the fact that BJP candidates have scored victories in districts with substantive Muslim populations.

That Modi has won worldwide recognition is evident from the tremendous support he has received at all the biannual conferences of Vibrant Gujarat. Britain has now made up with him, as has the European Union. Even China and Japan, not to speak of Russia, want to have a close association with him in matters of trade, commerce and investment.

Such has been his success that there is now open talk that he would make an ideal candidate for the Prime Ministership of India, should the BJP-led NDA coalition get elected in the general elections to be held in 2014, barely a year away. The National Executive Meet of the BJP held in Goa in June 2013, has officially named him 'Chairman of the Campaign Committee', a move that makes Modi the de facto PM nominee of the BJP.

Modi, let it be admitted, continues to have his critics, a fact that cannot be wished away, though their credibility is being watered down with every passing day. The point often made by other political parties is that if Gujarat under his direction has done remarkably well in several fields of administration, more notably in agriculture, at least a few other states have done just as well, if

Preface

not better, meriting equal praise. The fact remains, however, that in all his years as Chief Minister, Modi has concentrated on his task with singular devotion. It has paid him rich dividends. The Congress, for all its efforts, has not been able to destabilize him, as the results of the latest municipal elections in the state as well as the bagging of the two Lok Sabha by poll seats and four assembly by poll seats, have so clearly demonstrated.

In poll after poll, Narendra Modi has emerged as the candidate most favoured to be named India's Prime Minister, with even citizens of Bihar voting heavily in his favour. What has remained constant is that in spite of acquiring name and fame, Narendra Modi continues to be truly and effectively a *janapratinidhi* – people's representative. He is his own master who does not dance to the pull of anyone else's strings. The projects he has conceived, devised and promoted are all his own. Of how many chief ministers can it be said that they have travelled widely and received the praise, appreciation and approbation of governments, industrialists and entrepreneurs?

This book, first published in 2009, was titled *Narendra Modi: The Architect of a Modern State*. This is an enlarged and enriched edition more suitably titled *The Man of the Moment: Narendra Modi*. This updated and revised edition is richly endowed with information of major relevance that we hope earnestly meets the citizen's desire to know him well.

Narendra Modi stands out as a fearless, determined visionary who can be trusted to hold the nation's flag high, even under the most trying circumstances. His definition of secularism is putting India *first* above everything else. And that tells it all!

As for the rest, we leave it to history.

M V Kamath
Kalindi Randeri

SECTION I

From Grass Roots to Gujarat's Helmsman

Beginnings of a Quest

Narendra Modi was born on 17 September 1950 in Vadnagar, an unpretentious town in north Gujarat. The Modi family originally hailed from the Navdotra village in Banaskantha district. In the later years of the nineteenth century, a person by the name of Maganlal Ranchhoddas left home to set up a grocery store in Vadnagar. Maganlal had a son, Mulchand, who took over his father's small shop. Mulchand's son, Damodardas, was born in 1915. Damodardas's third child was Narendra.

All the Modi children were born in Modi *Ol* – a neighbourhood in Vadnagar, where many other families belonging to the Modi community lived. The eldest son, Som, born in 1944, completed his school education, a diploma course in sanitary inspection, and then became a sanitary inspector in the Public Health Department. The second son, Amrit, born in 1946, finished his schooling, did a course at the Industrial Training Institute (ITI), and became a turner in a private company in Odhav. Narendra's only sister, Vasanti, was born after him in 1955. His two younger brothers, Prahlad and Pankaj, were born in 1955 and 1958, respectively. Neither of them went in for higher studies. After completing his studies at the school level, Pankaj did a course in journalism and joined the information department of the Gujarat government.

The house Narendra was born in was very basic. Built of brick and mud, it was forty feet long and twelve feet wide, and had three rooms. The front room served as a bedroom and sitting room. The same room, partitioned off with a sheet, doubled up as a bathing area. The room next to it served as a kitchen and prayer room where the idols and photos of the household gods were kept in a little niche. Drinking water was stored in a corner in the kitchen. The third and adjacent room, about eight by twelve feet, was used to store dung cakes and wood that fired the hearth and it was not unusual for the three rooms to be filled with smoke when the

Modi household began cooking for the day. As none of the three rooms had windows, the house was dark and dingy. A kerosene lamp had to be kept lit throughout the day, which only added to the smoky atmosphere within the house. The only opening was the main door that led out to an extremely narrow lane.

As the family grew, Modi senior built an additional floor and had it roofed with corrugated iron sheets. During summer, the heat was unbearable. The flooring was made of bamboo which Narendra's mother covered with mud and cow dung. There were no bathing or toilet facilities. The family had to go out into the fields to relieve themselves. In subsequent years, a small toilet was built outside the house, close to the door and the bathing area was reasonably covered. The male members, including Narendra, went to a nearby lake to bathe, wash their clothes and enjoy swimming. Water for cooking and drinking had to be fetched from a well some distance away. Even though all these daily activities made life a struggle for the Modi family, they emerged unscathed.

Narendra did his primary school-level education at a government-run institution and then enrolled in the Bhagavatacharya Narayanacharya High School (BN High School). His classmates remember him as a bright student, good at English and social studies. Jasood Khan Pathan, who studied with Narendra from standard I to XI, was a close friend. He lived in an adjacent *mohalla* (neighbourhood), and has fond memories of his classmate. He cannot recall even a single instance when he had a quarrel with his bench-mate. Nor, does he say, was there any social tension between the two communities living cheek by jowl. Hindus and Muslims mixed freely and were invited to each others' weddings and social get-togethers. In fact, Vadnagar never experienced any communal conflict.

Narendra had a huge friends' circle and was known to them as ND (Narendra Damodardas). Another friend remembers Narendra as fair skinned, stockily built with a round face and a sparkle in his eyes. As soon as classes were over, he would rush to his father's tea shop (which, at best, could hold some thirty customers) to help him out.

Narendra loved reading books and spent a lot of time at the Vadnagar library. He frequently helped his science teacher, Mistry

Sir, in setting up experiments at the lab. The school had a debating society and Narendra, though shy, was a regular participant in the debates. One of his teachers, Dr P G Patel, remembers Narendra as a lad with a strong will and firm, clear views on everything – a fact that won him the admiration of his friends and teachers. Besides, he had a strong sense of right and wrong. Once the Sanskrit teacher asked the class to write the declensions of the word *nadi* (river) in grammatical sequence and show it to the class monitor. Narendra refused to do so on the grounds that the only person to correct his copy would be his teacher and not a mere class monitor. He would not budge from his decision and was satisfied only when the teacher himself went through his work. Another time, an additional class in Sanskrit was fixed for students who were weak in that subject but Narendra would not attend it, saying: 'Even Brahma cannot teach a boy who doesn't want to learn!' It wasn't that Narendra did not want to learn; he read widely. Children's magazines such as *Bal Sandesh, Bakor Patel Chakho-Mako* and *Miya Phuski* were available at the Vadnagar library, and Narendra would read them avidly.

Dr Sudhir Joshi, now a practising physician in Vadnagar, and Narendra's classmate in school, remembers him as being outspoken, never afraid of anyone or anything, ready to face any problem and getting it resolved by talking it over with the principal of the school. His argumentative skills and power of persuasion were evident on many occasions.

Yet another friend, Harish Patel, remembers Narendra as being both ingenious and resourceful. Patel recalls an incident when four boys were beating up another lad who seemed helpless. Narendra was watching the fight and knew that the boy was no match for the four bullies who were physically much stronger than he was. Moving towards them swiftly, he sprayed ink from his fountain pen on the four boys and fled. When the headmaster learnt about the fight, he reportedly went to the class and asked the culprits to stand up. No one did. Seeing this, Narendra told the headmaster: 'Sir, the boys who were involved have ink stains on their shirts.' That did it! The bullies were appropriately punished.

Even when he was six or seven years old, the desire to serve was obvious to others. Rasikbhai Dave, an old Congressman now in

The Man of the Moment: Narendra Modi

his eighties, who was influenced greatly by Jayaprakash Narayan, remembers Narendra as a curious child who always offered to help Dave in any way possible. Sometime in 1956, when the Maha Gujarat movement[1] was at its height, Narendra walked into Dave's office and offered to distribute badges to those who asked for them. Later too, whenever the Congress party held a meeting or arranged a function, Narendra was there with his friends as a volunteer. By then he had joined the Rashtriya Swayamsevak Sangh (RSS), but that did not deter him from volunteering his services to the Congress. What was important for him was not party affiliation but service to his fellow men.

Narendra suffered from no political biases. Rasikbhai's wife, Sarlaben, recalled that Narendra visited Vadnagar in 1999, after thirty-two years, to attend the golden jubilee celebrations of his school. Although Rasikbhai was then the leader of another party, Narendra respectfully touched the feet of the couple, and fondly enquired about their four children, even recalling their names. This gesture moved them to tears.

In his everyday life, Narendra was spartan. Born into a lower middle-class family, he never had more than two pairs of clothes which he maintained meticulously. He did household chores happily, and if his mother fell sick, he would even cook for the family. According to his eldest brother Sombhai, Narendra conditioned himself to a rigorous life. He gave up eating salt, chillies and oil, but he liked his jaggery. Eventually he gave that up too. Another astonishing fact was that the young Narendra never quarrelled with his siblings. If he felt that he had been wronged in any way by a member of the family, he would go into a sulk and maintain *maun* (silence) for hours, refusing to speak to anyone till he got over his anguish and anger.

Even from his school days, it was obvious that he was bound to grow up as a man who would work with plans and ensure their

---

1 In 1947, after Independence, the former princely and Deccan states in Gujarat were merged with former Bombay province and it was renamed as the state of Bombay. Soon, the Marathi and Gujarati linguistic movements began, both seeking to create separate linguistic states. On 1 May 1960, the state of Bombay was partitioned into the states of Gujarat and Maharashtra.

execution. His school needed a compound wall, but lacked the funds to build it. Narendra organized a play to raise funds, with help from his teachers and fellow students. It was an ambitious task to undertake for a youngster, but he succeeded in his self-appointed goal, and ended up acquiring far more than he had anticipitated.

In September 1959, there were floods in the Tapi River at Surat due to a dyke-burst. There was a lot of damage and about five hundred people died. All over the state, people were busy raising funds for rehabilitation and offering their personal services. As a nine-year-old student, Narendra gathered a group of friends and organized a food stall at the annual fair in their town on Janmashtami (the festival that celebrates Lord Krishna's birthday). The enthusiastic, hard-working boys managed to sell all the different food items they had put up for sale and the entire profit was contributed to the Relief Fund.

At his school in Vadnagar, Narendra is especially remembered for a one-man play of which he was the writer, director and lead actor. It was called *Piloo Phool* (Yellow Flower) and dealt with the social problem of untouchability. In staging this show, Narendra had a simple message to convey – God's *prasad* was like a flower, over which everyone had a right.

Narendra loved to swim and his favourite haunt was Lake Sharmistha, not far away from his *Ol*. In the centre of the lake was a small rocky outgrowth, over which there was an idol. On certain auspicious days, it was customary to change the flag on top of that tiny temple. On one occasion, it rained heavily. As a result, the lake was full and the crocodiles were moving about freely. Swimming over to the rock to hoist a new flag would have been a daring act. But the twelve-year-old Narendra volunteered. Without much ado, he and his two friends – Mahendra and Bachu – jumped into the water, while some people who had gathered on the bank started to beat drums in the hope that the crocodiles would be frightened away. Narendra made it to the mandir where he reverentially changed the flag and swam back to the cheers of the multitude.

Narendra was religious right from his childhood. There was a temple of Giripur Mahadev at the end of the lane where he lived, which he visited every day. He did the ritual circumambulation and then chose a spot to do his *jap* (chanting).

He observed the Navaratri fasts twice a year, during which time he only ate lemons. Around 1962-63, when Narendra was barely twelve years old, an interesting event took place. A holy man chanced to visit Vadnagar. As per tradition, he stopped at various homes for food and alms. He called on the Modi home in due course and casually asked whether any horoscopes of the family members were available. Narendra's mother had just two with her – Sombhai's and Narendra's. The holy man analysed the horoscopes carefully and then announced that life for Sombhai would be normal. About Narendra, he stated: 'If this boy gets into politics, he will be as powerful as an emperor, or else he may become a *sanyasi* (mendicant) and eventually turn out to be like Shankaracharya.'

The family was aware of the fact that Narendra was beginning to show an inclination towards becoming a *sanyasi*. His mother Heeraba recounted that 'Narendra was happily engaged in spiritual activities and associated with sadhu-*sants*. We noticed that his devotion was growing with every passing day. We were constantly afraid that one day Narendra would run away, leaving behind this home, town and *sansar* (worldly activities).' Indeed, Narendra seemed to be disinterested in *grihasthashram* (role of a householder).

Narendra was tremendously influenced by the life and work of Swami Vivekananda. He read almost everything that the latter had written – Vivekananda's views on patriotism and his political philosophy. Quite early on, Narendra had begun to save money to buy books, and proudly showed off his small personal library. Dr Vasantbhai Parikh, a great devotee of Vivekananda, provided him with the books written by the author he so admired.

When he was seventeen, Narendra joined college in Visnagar. But after a year or so, he decided to quit both home and studies to set off for the Himalayas in search of the supreme truth and spiritual knowledge. For two years Narendra was incommunicado. He had left home with practically no money. All he wanted was to roam through the countryside. During his travels, he went to the Ramakrishna Mission in Rajkot. His earnestness must have impressed the head of the Mission for he was invited to stay at the Mission for a while. But the stay did not last for more than a week. Narendra was a restless soul. As he put it: 'I wanted to do something, but did not know what exactly it was that I wanted to do.'

Glamour, power, money meant nothing to him; all he wanted to do was serve. Actually, when he was in the fifth standard, he had applied for admission to the Sainik School and wanted to serve the country through the armed forces. His father objected and Narendra had to drop the idea. He thought he would join the Ramakrishna Mission. He went to Calcutta (now Kolkata) and stayed at the Belur Math for some time. But the Mission admitted only graduates, and as a result, he had to move out. He had heard from someone that Swami Vivekananda had spent some time in the Himalayas. There, in a remote jungle, he met an ascetic. In Narendra's words, 'He (the ascetic) was alone, all by himself. Not a single human being was to be seen in the vicinity of four to five kilometres. He must have been about ninety years old. Very thin, it seemed that he had transparent skin. He looked like some kind of a spiritual person. He insisted that I stay with him. I agreed and stayed with him for about a month. People would occasionally bring him some food and he shared it with me. He would do some work in the garden and I would help him. Sometimes he would sit and chant *bhajans* (devotional songs). There were times when we would have a discussion on spiritual matters. Then, one day I decided to leave.'

For almost two years, Narendra wandered aimlessly. When he returned from the Himalayas after two years, he had chosen the course of his life. He had decided to be a *pracharak* (full-time official appointee in charge of several responsibilities) in the RSS which meant he had to remain single and render full-time service to the organization.

Some time between 1970 and 1971, Narendra came back to his roots in Gujarat and to Vadnagar for a tantalisingly brief period, as if just to show his face to the family. His mother, Hira Ba recounts the event: 'For two years we had no news of him. I had almost gone mad. Then suddenly he came home one day, with a small bag on his shoulders. I was in the kitchen and my daughter was outside. Suddenly she started shouting, "Bhai has come, bhai has come!" I started crying. I asked him where he had been. He said he had been in the Himalayas. I asked him whether he had eaten. "I have made *rotla* and vegetables. Let me make some *sev* (sweet dish) for you." He insisted that I was not to do anything special for him and that he was perfectly happy with *rotla* and vegetables. He stayed only one night and one day. Then he left.'

After he left home for the second time, Narendra went to Ahmedabad to his uncle, Babubhai, who ran a canteen at the State Transport office. Narendra served there for a while, determined to be of some use. In his spare time, he attended discourses on social, political and spiritual matters. However, they did not impress him much. It was at this point in his life that he became fully inclined towards the RSS, with which he was familiar. Though the RSS had come into existence in 1925, it had not spread its wings in Gujarat. The Vadnagar *shakha* (branch) was set up only in 1944. The *shakha* ran very well from 1944 to 1948, but following the assassination of Mahatma Gandhi in 1948, its reputation took a nose dive. Narendra says that while growing up, he never heard anyone in the RSS discuss the Mahatma's murder. He had read about Gandhiji – things that children of his age read. He had not heard anything negative about the Mahatma even once. The most talked about name within the RSS was that of Chhatrapati Shivaji.

The Vadnagar *shakha* was started by Babubhai Nayak who had begun his career as a primary school teacher. From 1942 to 1944, Babubhai went to Baroda to work as a *swayamsevak* (volunteer) at Yukudpura. He came to Vadnagar in 1944 and soon attracted a considerable following among the township's young people; Narendra was one of them. In one of his interviews, Narendra recalled that when he was seven or eight years old, he had a sitting with Vakil Saheb, (as Laxmanrao Inamdar was known) at Vadnagar. He was inducted as a *balswayamsevak* (child volunteer). This involved Vakil Saheb guiding him to take certain vows which amounted to dedicating his spare time to the activities of the RSS organization specially designed to train children. Narendra clearly remembered that the meeting took place on the day of Diwali because much to the disappointment of his family, he could not celebrate the festival with them.

The Congress too was active and Dwarkadas Joshi was busy with *sarvodaya* (universal uplift). Gandhiji had used this term for his own political philosophy based on peace and non-violence. Later, Vinoba Bhave, a Gandhian activist, adopted the name for the social movement he led to ensure that self-determination and equality reached all stratas of Indian society. Amongst all these activities, it was the RSS that received greater support because of its ideological appeal. In a sense, it was Baroda that was the epicentre of the RSS in the late 1930s. Several Maharashtrian RSS activists had deliberately enrolled in educational institutions outside Maharashtra, hoping to enrol new adherents to the organization. The names of followers, like Gopalrao Zinzarde and Nanubhai Bhosale can be mentioned in this connection. But it was in Saurashtra that the RSS found fertile ground to spread its ideology. Rajabhau Nene from Bombay, who had laid the foundation of the RSS in Surat around 1940, was shifted to Rajkot after a year.

In 1943, the RSS sent Bapurao Lele to Ahmedabad to work as a *pracharak*. He became so successful that the first officers' training camp for the RSS activities was organized in Ahmedabad in 1945. At about the same time, the RSS sent Madhukarrao Bhagwat to Gujarat as their *prant-pracharak* (a full-time worker for a specifically designated region consisting of several districts) for six years and he truly laid the foundation of the RSS in the state. Rajpal Puri, a doyen of the RSS from Sindh, succeeded Bhagwat in the wake of Partition. But Puri did not last long. He was succeeded by Laxmanrao Inamdar who led the RSS in Gujarat for three long decades and made it a force to reckon with. It was Inamdar who came to be known as Vakil Saheb and trained Narendra in the early years of his apprenticeship in the RSS hierarchy. Indeed, being influenced by the ideas and philosophy of Vakil Saheb, Narendra went on to become his *manas putra,* (literally, a son born out of the mind). Though Narendra was already familiar with the RSS even before Inamdar entered his life, it was Inamdar who turned out to be a decisive influence in Narendra's life.

In 1971, when Narendra was twenty-one, he proved his sense of commitment to values by offering *satyagraha* (the force of truth) as a possible solution to major problems, as in the case of Bangladesh and the struggle of East Bengali Muslims and Hindus against the

The Man of the Moment: Narendra Modi

tyranny and genocide by the Pakistani army. He was arrested and sent to Tihar jail, but released soon after. In 1972, he started working as an RSS *pracharak* formally.

Narendra explained in an interview why he left his uncle's house. He said, 'I met Vakil Saheb and I talked to him. He said, "Okay, come and stay with me." I was working in the Sangh office then, and decided that that was where I belonged. There were about twelve to fifteen people living together when Vakil Saheb invited me to join them. My daily routine was as follows: waking up at 5.00 am, fetching milk, waking everybody up, participating in *pratah-smaran* (morning prayers), making tea and serving everyone. It was followed by cleaning utensils, going to the *shakha*, returning and making snacks for everyone. Then I served breakfast from 8.30 am to 9.00 am, after which I had to clean up the entire building, consisting of eight to nine rooms. I swept and mopped the whole place, and washed both Vakil Saheb's clothes and mine. Initially, Vakil Saheb would not let me wash his clothes but I insisted that I wanted to do so out of respect for him. For lunch, I used to go to the *swayamsevaks*' homes by rotation. After returning to Hedgewar Bhavan, I got to work again and made tea for everyone. This was my routine for at least a year and this was the time when I met many people. I was very close to two people: Eknathji Ranade, who established Vivekananda Rock Memorial in Kanyakumari and Dattopantji Thengadi, the renowned labour leader who had established the Bharatiya Mazdoor Sangh (BMS). With them I had a spiritual relationship or intellectual connection, howsoever you define it. They loved me. There was a time when Eknathji strongly desired that I should look after the Vivekananda Rock Memorial along with him, while Dattopantji wished me to go with him and help him with his work. But somehow, I continued working as a *pracharak* with the organization.'

It was around this time that Narendra started developing an interest in studying. One day, Vakil Saheb told him, 'God has given you so much, study something! Study history and Sanskrit!' Narendra took that advice seriously, got admitted as an external student at Delhi University and graduated in due course.

Meanwhile, he was assigned additional duties of looking after the correspondence of the Sangh at its *prantik prant* (certain assigned regions in the RSS organization) office. That took a lot of Narendra's time. After a year, he was given the responsibility of helping the families of *swayamsevaks* who came to Ahmedabad from all over the country for medical treatment. This was work right up Narendra's alley. He was there when people needed him. A workaholic, Narendra was then assigned the duty of arranging the reservation of seats in buses and trains for Sangh officials who had to go on tours regularly. This called for constant communication with rail and bus transport officials and soon, Narendra was on the friendliest of terms with all of them. In the meanwhile, he learnt one of the most important lessons – how to get things done!

By then, a fresh development had taken place. The Vishwa Hindu Parishad (VHP) was to hold its Gujarat *Sammelan* (convention) in Siddhapur, under the guidance of Dr Vanikarji. Inevitably, the task of planning and organizing the *sammelan* fell on Narendra's shoulders. He got one more opportunity to gather experience in organizational work.

For Narendra, every type of work was a learning experience. He observed, analysed and added to his valuable study of human nature. He was always ready to lap up any new responsibility, especially if it was challenging, because he loved to work, interact with people, and find ways to make life easy for others. At that point in time, when he was cooking, washing clothes, cleaning toilets and serving his RSS colleagues in various ways, Narendra could not possibly have been remembering what an astrologer had predicted about his being a *sanyasi* or a person 'as powerful as an emperor'. As time proved, the *'sanyasi'* element was soon in ascendance and the apprenticeship in 'emperorhood' had begun!

Rites of Passage 2

In 1948, the RSS had launched the Akhil Bharatiya Vidyarthi Parishad (ABVP) under the leadership of Prof. Balraj Madhok. Three years later, on 21 October 1951, the Jan Sangh was formed. Though nobody from Gujarat was present at its founding conference, the party was to play an important role in the years to come, especially after Vasant Gajendragadkar took charge as the party's state organizing secretary.

As long as the British ruled, there were two Gujarats: one was ruled by petty princes and the other was a part of the larger Bombay Presidency. It seems odd, but when linguistic groups from all over the country demanded separate states, Gujaratis were practically the only group to eschew any such desire.

A small group of citizens had formed a party called the Maha Gujarat Janata Parishad (MGJP), but it had neither the voice nor the muscle to play any role in public life. The MGJP was dominated by Leftist forces such as communist, socialist and some independent radicals. The Jan Sangh did not join the MGJP but supported the agitation from outside. As long as Gujarat was divided and foreign rule prevailed, the Congress party dominated the political scene in 'British' Gujarat. Parties in Gujarat proliferated and within parties, factions became common. The first to enter the Congress fortress was the Swatantra Party, which was to become a force to be reckoned with in Gujarat politics in the 1960s. It started withering in the early 1970s and went into oblivion in the 1980s to make way for the Jan Sangh.

Then there was the Praja Socialist Party (PSP) that had limited support and like the Swatantra Party, was also to go into oblivion. Where the RSS took the lead was the fact that it had a distinct ideology which went beyond the immediacy of gaining independence from the British, which is why it survived. Other parties withered on the vine, but the RSS and organizations like

Rites of Passage

the ABVP that it sponsored, thrived along with the Jan Sangh with its own vision of a strong and self-sustaining Hindu society.

Narendra's interest in social activism was evident quite early. In 1967, Narendra had participated in the *Gau-Raksha* (cow protection) movement which was followed by his participation in movements against price rise, inflation and other issues that affected common people. By the early 1970s, Narendra was still to make his mark as a *pracharak*. Meanwhile, the Jan Sangh was gaining ground in Gujarat under the leadership of Vasant Gajendragadkar. Vasantbhai had built a team of youthful Jan Sangh activists like Nathalal Zagda, Shankersinh Vaghela, Kashiram Rana, Narasinha Padiyar, Kasambhai Achhva and Dattaji Chirandas. There were also others like Chimanbhai Shukla, Keshubhai Patel, Arvind Maniar, Harisingh Gohil, Suryakant Acharya, Suresh Mehta and Makarand Desai who were working hard to popularize the Jan Sangh.

The formation of Bangladesh in 1971 gave tremendous fillip to the fortunes of Congress (I) whose leader, Indira Gandhi, was hailed by Atal Bihari Vajpayee as goddess Durga. Pakistan had been effectively defeated and Indira Gandhi reigned supreme. But nemesis awaited the Congress: Gujarat fell into the grip of a severe famine. The severe shortages of food grains, edible oil and sugar took the situation from bad to worse till nearly two-thirds of Gujarat was stricken by famine.

By October 1972, things were getting out of hand and public opinion seemed to be turning against the Congress. Chief Minister Ghanshyambhai Oza proved to be ineffective in dealing with the crisis. Factional quarrels arose within the Congress and the atmosphere deteriorated so quickly that charges of corruption began to fly thick and fast. The Jan Sangh, then under the leadership of Chimanbhai Patel, was perhaps the first party to smell the rot in Gujarat. To gauge the mood of the people, the Jan Sangh held its National Working Committee meeting in Rajkot on 3-4 November 1973. In his presidential address, Lal Krishna Advani, the then president of the Bharatiya Jan Sangh, urged the local cadre to be vigilant and help build the protest movement into a massive one.

And so it happened. By the end of 1973, several groups coalesced into a virulent mass movement. This was *Navnirman* – a movement calling for total revolution that had the support of Jayaprakash Narayan. The movement triggered off a recrudescence of the smouldering factional hatreds against Chimanbhai Patel and several other Congress leaders. The *Navnirman* movement organized an anti-price rise conference in tune with popular sentiment. Fomented and fanned by leading political figures, the *Navnirman* agitation pushed Gujarat into anarchy, and continuous rioting was witnessed across the state. As many as forty-two lives were lost in police firing. The Army had to be called into Baroda and Ahmedabad.

The arrival of Jayaprakash Narayan (JP) in Ahmedabad gave Narendra an opportunity to meet and understand the charismatic leader, who was to return to Bihar in order to launch a *Navnirman* movement there too. Narendra held several talks with him and holds that period of time that he spent with such a magnetic personality as very precious.

Jayaprakash Narayan returned to Bihar, enthused by what he had seen in Gujarat, and launched a protest movement against Bihar's corrupt Congress government. The ABVP merged with the Chhatra Sangharsh Samiti (CSS) and joined the JP movement.

In the latter part of 1974, the movement was to change its character to target Indira Gandhi. JP's concept of *total revolution* was endorsed by the RSS. The ABVP, too, supported Jayaprakash. At a rally in Delhi, Balasaheb Deoras called JP 'a saint' who had come to rescue society 'in dark and critical times'. JP reciprocated the compliment in ample measure. He attended the twentieth all-India session of the Jan Sangh where he declared: 'If the Sangh is fascist, then I too am a fascist.'

So massive was the *Navnirman* movement that in the end, Chimanbhai had to abdicate office. His resignation came on 9 February 1974 after being in power for barely six months. Gujarat came under President's rule. The Vidhan Sabha was suspended. Rumours circulated that Chimanbhai had fallen out of favour with the Government of India, that is the Congress (I), the ruling party at the Centre. Perhaps it was that, or maybe it was the factionalism that hounded him while in power. But such was his frustration, that at one go he resigned from the leadership of the Congress (I) Legislative Party, the membership of the Vidhan Sabha and even the membership of Congress (I) itself.

The Government of India should have called off President's rule at the end of six months, but that did not happen. Instead, it extended the rule for another six months. The extension infuriated the already agitated masses of Gujarat. Morarji Desai, who had chosen to remain with Congress (O) at the time of its bifurcation and stood as a leader of the Opposition, went on an indefinite fast on 7 April 1975 to press for fresh Vidhan Sabha elections. Prime Minister Indira Gandhi gave in. President's rule was finally called off and fresh elections were ordered. Congress (O) and the Jan Sangh arrived at an electoral adjustment and came up with a common election manifesto. In the elections that followed, of the 182 Vidhan Sabha seats, the strength of Congress (I) was reduced from 140 to 79; Congress (O), a breakaway faction of the Congress party, won 56 seats, and Jan Sangh – 18. Chimanbhai's Kisan Mazdoor Lok Paksh (KMLP) bagged fifteen seats. With the aid of other parties like the PSP, Bharatiya Lok Dal (BLD), and the National Labour Party (NLP), the newly formed Janata Front formed the first ever non-Congress (I) government in Gujarat on 18 June 1975 with Babubhai Jashbhai Patel as the chief minister. The Jan Sangh ministers in the government comprised Keshubhai Patel, Makrand Desai and Hemabehn Acharya.

And then the bomshell fell! On 26 June 1975, Indira Gandhi clamped the 'Emergency' on the entire country. All hell broke loose in the country! Leading Opposition politicians – Jayaprakash Narayan, Morarji Desai, Charan Singh, LK Advani and Atal Bihari Vajpayee – were arrested. The RSS had to gear up to fight against the odds. This resulted in the formation of the Gujarat Lok Sangharsh Samiti (GLSS). At a meeting held under the chairmanship of the Sangh *kshetra-pracharak* Laxmanraoji Inamdar, it was decided that an underground movement should be mobilized to fight the Emergency. The main RSS workers would ensure that they did not fall into the hands of the police. 'Safe' residences had to be located for RSS workers. A list of activities was drawn up and the RSS *swayamsevaks* spread themselves throughout the state with the message of non-violent resistance.

Like all RSS workers, Narendra too had gone into hiding and his whereabouts were known only to a limited few. One day, towards the end of July 1975, Narendra received a message following which he had to go to the house of Prabhudas Patwari, a prominent lawyer and activist, around 10.30 pm. When he arrived there, he was told that George Fernandes, the chairman of the Socialist Party, was expected shortly. Fernandes was unrecognizable. He was wearing an un-ironed Lucknavi kurta, a checkered lungi and had a green cloth tied on his head. Besides, he had grown a long beard and looked like a Muslim fakir. Narendra and Fernandes hugged each other and exchanged news.

Narendra had been assigned the job of taking care of *swayamsevaks* and others in the Sangh *parivar*, of receiving people from other states and arranging for their safe accommodation. There were other jobs like organizing meetings at short notice, collecting news, making arrangements for their printing and distribution, and constantly changing meeting venues to outsmart the police. Narendra excelled. When Indira Gandhi called an international conference of parliamentary representatives from Commonwealth countries, it was Narendra who managed to get five booklets printed and despatched to Delhi for distribution to the delegates. The booklets were titled: *Indian Press Gagged; Facts vs Indira's Lies; 20 Lies of Mrs Indira Gandhi; When Disobedience to Law is a Duty;* and *A Decade of Economic Chaos.*

How hundreds of these booklets were despatched secretly to Delhi by train and then delivered to the right persons there, constitutes a thriller by itself. When Nanaji Deshmukh, secretary of the GLSS, who was working in hiding, was arrested, there were fears that the address book he had with him might fall into the hands of the police. Narendra had to quickly arrange for scrapping all pre-arranged addresses!

Towards the end of October 1975, there was a covert meeting of the Lok Sevak Sangh officials. It was decided to hold a *satyagraha* on 14 November, Jawaharlal Nehru's birthday. All care was taken to ensure that the government did not come to know of it in advance. The code was: 'Marriage Date Fixed'. Phone calls to all party workers were made announcing that the wedding was fixed for 14 November. The underground members in Rajasthan wanted two lakh pamphlets printed in Hindi for distribution throughout the state. Narendra's first job was to find someone to agree to do the printing in Hindi. Once that was taken care of, the challenge lay in the logistics of despatching them to Rajasthan without the police getting wind of it. Two *swayamsevaks* from each district in Rajasthan were summoned to Ahmedabad and asked to bring with them bags and 'hold-alls'. These were used to carry the pamphlets to their respective destinations. Sometimes, innocent-looking women were used as couriers. The *satyagraha* went according to plan.

As an underground worker, Narendra had to don various disguises frequently. On one occasion, he donned the garb of a sanyasi, wearing saffron clothes; on another, he grew a beard and looked like a proper Sikh with long hair and a turban. He played safe and familiarized himself with the role he would assume beforehand. On one such occasion, it became necessary for him to meet Shankersinh Vaghela and Vishnu Pandya, who were in the Bhavnagar jail at that time. For an underground worker to dare to visit someone in jail was equivalent to inviting trouble. But he managed to act as a consort to a lady who was a regular visitor to the jail and succeeded.

But Narendra's toughest task was to raise funds to help the families of the RSS men who were jailed. Rich people were unwilling to give money for the cause, but many common folk came forward to help. Apart from the members of the Sangh *Parivar*, Narendra often found that many apolitical people opposed to the Emergency were willing to make small donations on a regular basis.

Apart from bringing out *Muktwani* – a small underground newspaper – Modi also published full-length commentaries on the Emergency and the philosophy of democracy. Some titles which created ripples in the political world, were published under great risk to everyone involved. These include *Story of two Emergencies* (in English and Gujarati); *Twenty-two point Deception; Emergency X-rayed; Proposed Constitutional Reforms; Review of a Decade; When Disobedience to Law is a Duty; Indian Press Gagged; Anatomy of Fascism;* and *Nail Indira's Lies.*

Meetings were organized at all levels – from wards to districts to provinces – for collective thinking among the underground workers. These meetings were attended by fifteen or twenty people at a time and each attendee was scrupulously investigated and cultivated. Narendra had calculated that for every full-time underground worker, the support of at least ten families who had no fear of the consequences was needed. He identified such families throughout Gujarat. It was an experience which, he says, stood him in good stead later. Those who came forward to help were firm believers that the real cause was a struggle for values. People trusted leaders like Jayaprakash Narayan, Sarvodaya workers, and the RSS and its leaders, who they believed were above political ambitions. Significantly, during those twenty-one months of the Emergency, the distance between the Sarvodaya and the Sangh had shrunk. The process that had begun with the *Navnirman* movement gathered momentum during the Emergency.

In fact, it was during the Emergency that many non-RSS people who were opposed to the Emergency came to Gujarat to escape the police net; they had to be given shelter by the families of the RSS workers. Living with the RSS workers and sharing their thoughts made the outsiders appreciate the purity of motive and patriotism of the RSS workers.

Narendra remembers 1 January 1976, when he was invited to meet Ravindra Varma at Ramlal Parikh's house, the latter being the vice-chancellor of Gujarat Vidyapeeth. 'Happy New Year!' said Narendra to Varma, who was taken aback. In reply to his greetings, Varma said, 'Narendraji, I too, was about to greet you likewise, but then I thought you are a *Hindutvawadi* and might feel offended if I did so!' Narendra laughed and said, 'See, that is the greatness of *Hindutva* – it does not permit narrow-mindedness!' The two struck up an instant rapport. Varma was able to see the RSS and its leaders and workers in a new light. Old prejudices gave way to new opinions.

Babubhai Patel had been formally elected leader of the Janata Front government and his ministry was supported from outside by Chimanbhai Patel's KMLP with fifteen members and five independent candidates. Though dependent upon their support, Babubhai had scrupulously avoided the inclusion of any of them in his 'quadruple' ministry, every member of which enjoyed cabinet rank. But none of them except Babubhai himself had any previous experience as ministers. The KMLP was bitterly disappointed at being kept out of power and was to later ditch the government.

The Janata Front government was an interesting experiment and served as a model to a similar government at an all-India level in 1977. It was not a party because its constituent units had fought the elections as separate entities with their own resources and symbols. Yet, they had jointly elected Babubhai as the leader of the Front. It wasn't a federation of parties because while the legislative wings of the parties merged, their organizational wings continued with their separate independent existence. Under the circumstances, it was a miracle that the Janata Front government survived for as long as nine months!

For Chief Minister Babubhai, it was an exercise in tight-rope walking. He avoided internal bickering wherever possible, but fought any unnecessary encroachment upon his legal powers. When the Emergency was declared, he assured the Union government that he would comply with whatever directives were issued by it and even extended his full cooperation to the 20-Point Programme. The reality, however, was that he complied with the Union directives in principle, but dragged his feet or sought cover behind administrative snags while trying to implement the more unpalatable ones.

The Babubhai Patel ministry might have lasted, but trouble was brewing in the KMLP that could not be contained. The party was wound up. Freed of constraints, the majority of its members joined the Congress (I), raising its strength to eighty-seven, exactly equal to that of the Janata Front. The Congress (I) then managed to engineer a couple of defections. When a vote was taken on budgetary demands, the Janata Front government lost by two votes (87 to 89). Babubhai Patel resigned on 13 March 1976 and several other Janata leaders were detained under MISA (Maintenance of Internal Security Act).

Eight months passed. The Congress (I) was itching for power but factionalism within the party delayed the formation of a Congress (I) government. Finally, in December 1976, a Congress ministry was formed under the chief ministership of Madhavsinh Solanki. However, the ministry, the tenth in a series, survived barely for a hundred days and that too, to pave the way for the formation of yet another Janata Front government under the same leader as the chief minister – Babubhai Patel.

THE THRESHOLD
AND BEYOND   3

While all these events were taking place in rapid succession, Narendra was doing what he was asked to do by the RSS like a disciplined soldier. The twenty-one months between 26 June 1975, when the Emergency was first declared, and 22 March 1977, when it was finally lifted, were significant by all accounts.

The RSS held its first emergency meeting on 2 July 1975 and soon after, an underground paper *Janata Chhapu* came to be widely circulated. Within two days, several RSS workers were arrested and the government took over the Sangh office. Events followed one after another. An article titled 'Katokati Vishe Punarvicharna Karo' was published in *Sadhana* magazine which was promptly censored by the authorities. A writ petition was lodged in the Gujarat High Court. The case went in favour of those representing *Sadhana*.

Being the opposition party during the period of the Emergency, the Jan Sangh's leaders were either put behind bars or went underground. Hence, it was not possible to have a meeting of the All India Executive Committee. Leaders of the Gujarat Jan Sangh used a ploy and came up with the idea of organizing the Citizens' Freedom Conference or the *Nagarik Swatantrya Sammelan* (NSS) on 12 October 1975 at Ahmedabad. They invited as many members and like-minded people as possible, including Jan Sangh workers who did not have warrants issued in their names. A week later, a general body meeting of the Gujarat High Court Advocates' Association moved a resolution against the Emergency. On 5 November, demonstrations against the Emergency were held in the presence of members attending a Commonwealth Conference. Many people were arrested during the demonstration. Towards the end of the month, an appeal was submitted to Vice President

B D Jatti requesting him to help lift the Emergency. On 3 December, underground leader Dattopantji Thengdi arrived in Gujarat to meet labour leaders and on 7 December, RSS *Sarsanghchalak* Balasaheb Deoras's birthday was celebrated in Ahmedabad. At about the same time, several prayer meetings were held throughout Gujarat to wish for the long life of Jayaprakash Narayan.

As the year 1976 was ushered in, it saw a rapid increase in, and heightening of, political activity. It began with a 'Save the Constitution' conference attended by several leading lawyers. On 2 January, underground workers of the Jan Sangh's organizing committee from all over India met in Ahmedabad. Sadly, on 16 February, Vasantbhai Gajendragadkar passed away. Arrests of leading leaders continued. Whereas Bhogilal Gandhi was arrested in Bombay on 19 June, C T Daru was nabbed on 26 June, under MISA. On the same day, a large *morcha* (gathering) made its way to Raj Bhavan to submit a petition. This led to the arrest of twelve underground leaders; one of them was Babubhai. On 2 July, Sadhana Press was confiscated and its employees arrested under MISA. On 9 August, *Kranti Din* (Revolution Day) was celebrated. (The date was chosen in deference to the date on which Mahatma Gandhi had given a call for the Quit India movement from Bombay's Gowalia Tank maidan in 1942.) Some fifty-one people were arrested for being a part of it. On 14 November, a People's Union for Civil Liberty was set up and on 21 November, a Youth Conference was held in Barejadi where around a hundred participants were arrested. It was one long tale of repression. The death of Vasantbhai came as a major blow to Narendra and all Jan Sangh activists in Gujarat.

After all these ups and downs came the startling announcement on 18 January 1977 of the Lok Sabha polls. On 21 March, the election results were formally declared. The Congress party was effectively defeated. The very next day, the Emergency was formally lifted and hundreds of RSS workers all over the country were freed. It was during the decade of 1970-80 that Narendra was to experience *sangharsh* (hardship). This was the period when for the first time, the Jan Sangh became a partner in forming a government in Gujarat. In the forefront were three leaders – Keshubhai Patel, Makrandbhai and Hemabehn. In the background were Nathabhaijagda, Vasantbhai Gajendragadkar and Narendra. This was the first decade of Narendra's public life and the third decade of Gujarat as a state. Narendra had written a book on the history of Gujarat titled *Sangharsh maa Gujarat* (Gujarat in Hardship) during the Emergency. What was revealing was that Narendra never wrote in the first person singular. The authorial voice was detached. Reading it, nobody would identify him as one of the agitators in the anti-Emergency movement. During the Emergency, one of the duties allocated to Narendra had been to maintain links between Indians abroad, and at home. Makarand Desai, in his book, *Smuggling of Truth*, refers to a newsletter *Satyavani*, which was published from both the United Kingdom and the United States. It was Narendra's task to see that copies of it reached *satyagrahis* jailed in Ahmedabad, Baroda and other places.

Narendra became a *vibhaag pracharak* in 1978, at a relatively young age. The *vibhaag* consisted of six districts, namely rural Vadodara, Panchmahal, Dahod, Anand, Kheda and Vadodara city. At about the same time, he was appointed as a *praant padadhikari* (regional head) and was allocated the responsibility of *praant sabha vyavastha pramukh* (joint president of regional organizations). Narendra's talents as an organizer were being recognized. Within two years, he was appointed *sambhaag pracharak*, with jurisdiction over the *vibhaags* of Surat and Vadodara, while his field extended from central and south Gujarat's Kheda district to Valsad's Umergaon.

Following the death of the *praant pracharak* Keshavrao Deshmukh on 2 March 1981, Narendra was asked to stay at Gujarat's *praant* headquarters at Ahmedabad to maintain close liaison with various organizations of the Sangh, namely the Akhil Hind Vidyarthi Parishad, Bharatiya Kisan Sangh, Vishwa Hindu Parishad, Samutkarsh and its publications wing, and the weekly *Sadhana*.

The Sangh was very pleased with the thirty-one year old Narendra's dedication and efficiency. Whatever task he undertook, he completed with full vigour and zeal. On 11 August 1979, a dam on the Machchhu river in Morbi broke down. Nearly 1,800 people died and the whole city was devastated. The Sangh started relief work on a massive scale which lasted for almost a year. Narendra ensured that the rehabilitation work was completed satisfactorily.

The Threshold and Beyond

Indira Gandhi's defeat in the 1977 general elections and the consequent rise of the Janata Party were hailed by most Indians, especially those who had suffered greatly during the Emergency, as a 'revolution by the ballot box'.

However, not only did the Janata government destroy itself with astonishing rapidity, but also, in some way, helped and hastened Indira Gandhi's return to power. By supporting Morarji Desai for prime ministership, Charan Singh, the *kisan* (farmer) leader with a strong following in Uttar Pradesh, successfully elbowed out Jagjivan Ram. But Charan Singh wanted the prime ministership for himself. His BLD contingent of seventy-one members of parliament (MPs) was the second largest among the Janata Party's MPs, but he had to reckon with the Jan Sangh that was committed to keeping Morarji firmly in power. Charan Singh turned out to be an embarrassment for the new government. He had Indira Gandhi arrested on 3 October 1977, allegedly for campaigning in that year's elections in jeeps owned by an industrial house. The court released her the next day on the grounds of insufficient evidence. This helped Mrs Gandhi to gain public sympathy.

Charan Singh then made charges of corruption against Kanti Desai, Morarji Desai's son. That further served to erode public sympathy for the Janata government. This was not all: there was the maverick Raj Narain, who had to be suspended from the Janata Party for one whole year for gross indiscipline.

Meanwhile, early in June 1977, Charan Singh shot off an angry letter to Morarji Desai describing the Cabinet as 'a collection of impotent men' incapable of bringing Indira Gandhi to justice. Desai had to ask Charan Singh to resign; however, he returned again and was made the finance minister and deputy prime minister. But even this did not last for long. Charan Singh's party ratted on Morarji Desai, whose government fell. Charan Singh was invited by President Sanjiva Reddy to form a new government. He had been promised help by Indira Gandhi who had by then been elected to Parliament and was leading her party. But when Charan Singh formally became the prime minister, Indira Gandhi betrayed him and withdrew her party's support to him. He didn't even have time to face the Lok Sabha. His prime ministership lasted for a mere twenty-four days!

The Man of the Moment: Narendra Modi

Though the infighting in the Janata Party at the Centre led to its fall, in Gujarat the intra-party feuds rarely came to the fore. There was not even a breath of scandal against any top-ranking Janata leader in Gujarat. But having captured power in Delhi, Indira Gandhi took her revenge against the Janata Party and ordered the dissolution of assemblies in nine states – Bihar, Gujarat, Madhya Pradesh, Maharashtra, Orissa, Punjab, Rajasthan, Tamil Nadu and Uttar Pradesh. When elections were held for the Gujarat Assembly in May 1980, the Congress (I) emerged triumphant, capturing 142 out of 182 seats. The Janata Party barely managed to get twenty-two seats. On 5 April 1980, the Jan Sangh decided to retain its identity under a new name – Bharatiya Janata Party (BJP). Keshubhai Patel was nominated president of the Gujarat BJP.

The Congress party then decided to project itself as the representative of the exploited and oppressed at the Chandod-Karnali Conference. Such downtrodden sections were identified on the basis of social, rather than economic or political affiliations. The Gujarat Congress virtually endorsed casteism as a weapon to fight elections. The Chandod Conference identified four communities that they could court: *Kshatriyas*, Harijans, *Adivasis* and Muslims (KHAM). This caste-based politics aroused the resentment of the RSS.

The Madhavsinh Solanki Congress ministry introduced a Reservation Policy. Eighty-two castes and communities were classified as socially and educationally backward. It recommended five steps for their advancement, including reservation of ten per cent seats in educational institutes and government jobs. The fact that people from backward classes were being given the benefits was not the problem; the major trouble was the manner in which the policy was incorporated. Non-availability of suitable candidates in a given year led to a carry over of those quotas in the following years; that resulted in a blockage of seats, so much so that in any one year, all the seats would have to be allocated only to backward caste candidates. The upper castes became highly agitated that due to this policy, they would be effectively barred from all seats of learning. The result: agitation and riots.

Price rise further aggravated the tense situation. A prolonged strike by government employees against the Roster System led to a vertical split in the administrative cadre. The second Backward Class Commission headed by Justice Rane added another sixty-three occupational groups to the backward castes listed by the Reservation Quota Commission. The Rane Commission recommended the enhancement of the reservation quota from 10 per cent to 27 per cent which brought reservations to a total of 48.5 per cent. Furious riots erupted from one end of Gujarat to another.

Amidst all this, a major tragedy took place – the assassination of Indira Gandhi on 31 October 1984 by one of her own Sikh bodyguards. The country was convulsed with grief and anger. According to one report, more than five thousand Sikh men, women and children were massacred by Congress mobs across the country, more so in New Delhi. Many believe even today that it put to shade the Godhra riots in Gujarat in 2002.

Fresh elections followed. As if condoning the killing of innocent Sikhs, Rajiv Gandhi commented: 'When a big tree falls, the earth is bound to shake.' The earth was shaken indeed. A tremendous sympathy wave for the Congress party, now under the leadership of Rajiv Gandhi, brought the party to power. The Congress captured twenty-four out of twenty-six seats to the the Lok Sabha, while the BJP succeeding in winning merely two seats.

The anti-reservation agitation was resumed in full fury. The agitation was soon converted into an anti-Muslim conflagration. There was 'a complete breakdown of law and order across the state, while educational activities were disrupted for six months … The Gujarat language press turned virulent to malign the police force. Maddened by the press denunciations, the Ahmedabad police rose in revolt and in a premeditated and planned attack, smashed and burnt down the entire establishment of the most widely circulated daily, *Gujarat Samachar,* inflicting damage that was estimated at ₹3.50 crores ….' (*Gujarat: A Political Analysis by Nagindas Sanghavi*).

Sanghavi went on to say: 'The total collapse of government control was demonstrated when police failed to prevent the *Rath Yatra* being taken out in defiance of curfew regulations ….'

The Man of the Moment: Narendra Modi

In the end, Solanki had to resign under orders from Rajiv Gandhi. By the end of his rule, 237 people had been killed, a thousand injured, and production loss and property damages of over ₹2,200 crores were reported.

Communal hatred, which had resurfaced in history periodically, was expected to disappear after Independence. However, instead of disappearing, it has continued with unabated fury to be a barrier in the country's progress. According to an official report, there have been more than thirty thousand riots in India, both major and minor. The Congress party was the ruling party in the country most of the time.

Madhavsinh Solanki was succeeded by Amarsinh Chowdhary in July 1985, the first *Adivasi* to become the chief minister. From 1985 to 1989, Gujarat was hit by communal rioting, bomb explosions, police revolt and a breakdown in the administration. Casteism ran riot; Hindu society stood divided, and corruption ruled the roost. In May 1990, the Congress party lost heavily and the Janata Dal-BJP coalition headed by Chimanbhai Patel formed a new government.

The years of Congress rule in Gujarat were marked by inefficiency and recklessness of the rulers. At the end of everything, the man who was to bring peace and normalcy to Gujarat was one who has been most reviled by the English media in recent history – Narendra Modi.

The Interregnum 4

The riots that took place in Ahmedabad in 2001 have been much talked about; a lot has been said and written about the incident. But people forget some of the most horrendous riots that had engulfed the city in October 1969 when Congress was in power. The riots were preceded by the elections of 1967 which, according to Nagindas Sanghavi, constituted 'a watershed of Indian politics, a point of departure from where began the decline of political organizations and political processes.'

Following the elections of 1967, Hitendra Desai became chief minister. His government was to pass through a series of crises. What kept the government in Gujarat alive was the fact that the mutual hostilities amongst the opposition parties were far more intense than their revulsion against the Congress. The Left parties declined to cooperate with the Swatantra Party while three independent legislators were ready to go 'where their snouts would lead them'. Hitendra Desai was smart enough to adjust himself to every emerging situation and consult the Opposition on every issue. At about the same time, Gujarat took a few hits at the international level. In February 1968, the proclamation of the Kutch Award by the International Tribunal awarded a part of Kutch to Pakistan. India was committed to abide by the award, and although there were several popular outbursts in Kutch, the agitation was not to last too long. India and Pakistan agreed to a new frontier in March 1969 and tempers cooled not long after.

The political stability in Gujarat had been reinforced by a policy decision taken by the Swatantra Party, debarring all state units from pulling down stable ministries. An event took place at this time which set communal feelings ablaze. Muslims in Gujarat went into a frenzy over the reported dismantling of the Al-Aqsa Mosque in Jerusalem, some four thousand kilometres away. The government of India proclaimed that the right to protest must not be stretched to encompass any anti-Islamic activity occurring outside India as it would have a negative effect on the lives of Indians. In April 1969, the Union government also warned all the states about the deteriorating communal situation, but Gujarat took the warning lightly. The chief secretary wrote to the Union Government that the state was traditionally free from all such communal tensions. He was to pay dearly for his complacency.

The immediate cause of the 1969 Ahmedabad riots – the first since Independence – was no different from the provocations witnessed elsewhere in the country. Details of the riot are furnished by Ashutosh Varshney in his book *Ethnic Conflict and Civic Life*:

'On 18 September 1969, a large number of Muslims had assembled for *Urs* (celebration at the tomb of a Muslim saint). The tomb was located near the Jagannath Temple, a place of considerable importance for the local Hindus. At about 3.00 pm, the sadhus of the temple were returning with their cows, as they did every single day at that time. When the cows tried to make their way through the crowd, a skirmish issued. A few cows as well as some Muslims were hurt. In the confusion that followed, the sadhus were apparently attacked for being unmindful of Muslim religious sentiment. Windows of the temple were also damaged. Realizing that an attack on the sadhus was unnecessary, some Muslim leaders issued an apology the same evening, blaming thoughtless and unduly excitable Muslim youths for the attacks.

'The next morning, the local newspapers reported in detail how the temple was attacked but did not report the apology. Later in that day, angry that a nearby grave had been desecrated, some Muslims gathered in front of the temple and shouted slogans. At about the same time, a false rumour began to circulate in the town that the head priest (*mahant*) of the Jagannath Temple had been attacked.

'By the afternoon of 19 September, rioting and killings began .... The violence worsened immeasurably. The next day the police admitted their complete failure to restore order, despite the fact that a curfew had been imposed, and the army was called in. By 23 September, the rioting had ceased ...

'The number of deaths was staggering. Since India's Partition, no other riot in the country had led to so many deaths, nor indeed has any single riot in a city caused such a large number of casualties since 1969 ...

'More than six hundred lives lost in just a few days of uncontrolled rioting would be an awful development for any government responsible for law and order. What made the riots symbolically more chilling was that 1969 was also the centenary year of Gandhi's birth. The rioters also damaged Gandhi's ashram and assaulted its Muslim inmates ....'

In his biography of Shankersinh Vaghela, *Portrait of a Charismatic Leader*, Atmaram Kulkarni says that the riots left 'about two thousand dead, four thousand injured and fifty thousand homeless.'

The Congress government had failed. Varshney expresses his views as follows:

'When the riots broke out in September 1969, Congressmen were nowhere to be seen. Neither the leaders nor the cadres were active in containing communal violence. Morarji Desai, Gujarat's main leader after Gandhi and Patel ... arrived in the city (Ahmedabad) only on the fourth day of the riot when nearly four hundred lives had been lost ... In more activist and committed times, they would have resigned for having failed to save hundreds of lives in the state capital. In 1969, they hung on to power. There is, of course, no evidence that Congress cadres were actively involved in killing. But the acts of omission were all too obvious.'

When a gang armed with axes, rods and stones stormed Gandhiji's Sabarmati Ashram, both leaders and cadres were entirely missing from the scene.

Varshney lays the blame on the Congress party. The BJP was of no consequence. The Jan Sangh was then an insignificant party. Who incited the people to riot in 1969? The 306-page report of the Justice Jagannath Reddy Commission noted the following:

9.2: Even according to the chronological printed statements filed by the government relating to the Ahmedabad commissioner, there were about 750 incidents of violence to property and person within the period of 19 September to 30 September, involving damage or destruction of more than six thousand properties, about sixty religious places, injury to more than 350 persons and death of more than five hundred people.

9.4: The Commissioner of Police admits that he cannot say that no offence which had not been reported to the police station had been committed. There is also a serious allegation made on behalf of the Muslim organizations that several Muslim complainants who had gone to file oral complaints at the police stations were turned away and their complaints not recorded.

'The Commissioner of Police admits that the damage done (at the Shabe Burani dargah) was massive ... The Police Inspector Vyas in his first statement sought to indicate that a crowd of only 50 to 60 persons did the damage but under pressure of cross-examination, admitted that even if 2,000 to 4,000 persons together were to cause the damage that was actually caused, it would take a minimum of two to three hours.'

22.97: (Well-to-do people taking part in the loot on the main road) is indeed a very disgraceful feature of the riot in Baroda ... Both Hindus and Muslims of the respective areas took part in the looting ....

After reading this report, if one thought that one was reading the report of riots in Ahmedabad in 2002, one should be pardoned for it. Whatever the media has said about Narendra Modi applies verbatim to Hitendra Desai. If the Commission Report is to be believed, in many places the Ahmedabad police did not – or could not – take action.

What about the curfew being imposed then? Here is a part of the report dealing with that:

11.88: The question of delay may, in retrospect, be academic because it is clear from the evidence that the curfew, even after it was imposed, was not strictly enforced or implemented ....

A fact that comes into question again and again is also with respect to the time when the Border Security Force (BSF) was summoned by the government. The riots began on 18 September 1969. The BSF arrived on 20 September 1969, that is, two days after the riots had started. In contrast, Narendra Modi summoned the force in

The Interregnum

2002 within twenty-four hours. He hardly got any credit for that from the 'secular' media.

Contrast this with 1969. The Government Counsel giving evidence before the Reddy Commission was sparing of the truth. The report says:

11.25: A suggestion was made by the learned Government Counsel to some of the private witnesses to show that life in the suburban area was normal on the 20th and curfew would have disturbed that life by compelling mills to close. As for the 20th – day time, a glance at the course of incidents from 0600 hours to 1800 hours is sufficient to show how abnormal the law and order position was.

11.32: The manner in which the curfew passes were issued goes to show how haphazard was the implementation of the curfew.

More revealing is the Commission's comment on shoot-at-sight orders. It says:

11.30: The shoot-at-sight orders, which were issued simultaneously with the curfew orders on the 19th at 2200 hours, postulated the issue of necessary firearms. But in the matter of issue of firearms, there has been an economy which is not easy to understand, particularly when the situation was deteriorating so fast.

In light of these and other observations, contrast Narendra Modi's reaction to the riots following the gruesome Godhra killings and the manner in which he sought to control them.

On 27 February 2002, he ordered a state-wide alert directing the law enforcement agencies to take all necessary steps to maintain law and order. Steps were taken to see that the dead bodies of Hindu pilgrims killed in the fire in the Sabarmati Express were *not* brought to the Ahmedabad Civil Hospital but, instead, taken to a civil hospital away from the city at Sola to prevent any aggravation of the situation. Curfew was imposed in Godhra the same day. Starting from the morning of 28 February, curfew was imposed at places like Vadodara, Ahmedabad city, Sabarkantha and several other sensitive places. The Rapid Action Force was summoned and deployed from 27 February.

The Man of the Moment: Narendra Modi

One might well ask: How can anyone say that the government under Narendra Modi did not function or that it was ineffective in the light of how the post-Godhra riots were handled?

The truth of the matter is that from the very start, the so-called secular English press was prejudiced against Narendra Modi, irrespective of how well he sought to control the riots. It was like giving the dog a bad name in order to hang it.

Major events were taking place all over India and Narendra had to watch from the sidelines. But the year 1987 turned out to be especially challenging for him as he conceived the idea of holding a *Nyay* Yatra (Journey for Justice), the first of its kind ever to be undertaken in Gujarat. It was Narendra's own brainchild and he conducted it with his usual élan.

Four leaders were chosen, each to head one yatra from different parts of the state. These yatras went around the famine-affected areas of Panchmahal, Sabarkantha, Mehsana, Ahmedabad, Banaskantha, Kutch, Surendranagar, Rajkot, Jamnagar, Amreli and Bhavnagar districts covering 115 *talukas* and approximately 15,000 villages. For Narendra, who organized the entire operation, it was a coup of a kind. What made the difference was that he had taken the party to the people.

This was followed by yet another yatra – the *Lok Shakti Rath* Yatra – to extend the influence of the BJP and to awaken the people. The yatra was organized by Narendra once again, and was led by Keshubhai Patel. It was to take place in five stages, from 31 January 1989 to 1 May 1989. It started from Ambaji and passed through *talukas* covering approximately ten thousand villages; in the process, contacts were established with over a million people.

One might mention two other yatras that Narendra helped organize – the Somnath Ayodhya Yatra and the *Ekta* Yatra from Kanyakumari to Kashmir. The Somnath Ayodhya Yatra, led by L K Advani, started on 25 September 1990 from the famed Somnath Mahadev temple. Narendra Modi accompanied Advani, but only upto Mumbai. In Gujarat, the yatra received terrific response.

The other yatra, which intended to unify the common people, was the *Ekta* Yatra and was led by the then president of the BJP, Dr Murli Manohar Joshi. It started from Kanyakumari on

The Interregnum

11 December 1991 and made its way to Srinagar on 26 January 1992. The responsibility of planning this elaborate yatra fell on Narendra, who by then had come to be accepted as having achieved considerable expertise in this particular department.

Prior to undertaking the long journey, Narendra travelled the entire route on his own to see if all arrangements were in place. He had to reckon with, among other things, possible missile attacks from terrorists. The *Ekta* Yatra culminated in Srinagar, where the Indian national flag was hoisted with great ceremony and under tight security.

The debacle of Congress (I) in the Lok Sabha elections in Gujarat took its toll and Amarsinh Chowdhury was replaced by Madhavsinh Solanki in January 1990. Meanwhile, a Janata Dal Ministry had been formed in Delhi with the support of the BJP; in Gujarat, Narendra was raring to fight the assembly elections without support from any other party. But those involved in state politics were in favour of striking an understanding with Chimanbhai Patel whereby the BJP was allotted 143 seats. Chimanbhai reserved 148 seats for his party for an Assembly total of 182. He fancied himself as an elder brother, but that did not work well with everyone. There was noticeable acrimony between the two opposition parties, with the JD refusing to withdraw its nominees from several constituencies. Nevertheless, the BJP won sixty-seven seats to the JD's seventy. The Congress party lost heavily. A coalition government was formed under Chimanbhai's leadership, which was sworn in on 3 March 1990.

For Chimanbhai, it was a victory to be savoured. The last time he had been chief minister was in 1973 and his government had not lasted even for a year. This time he intended to be the boss and that too with a vengeance; he dominated the cabinet. Keshubhai was informally named 'Number Two' in the state government. The rest of the BJP ministers were all new to office.

The Chimanbhai government was in the process of settling down when two major events took place and shook the country. Firstly, L K Advani was arrested on his *rath* yatra to Ayodhya.

After covering over eight thousand kilometres from Somnath, Advani was scheduled to enter Uttar Pradesh on 24 October

The Man of the Moment: Narendra Modi

1990, but even while he was still in Bihar, he was unexpectedly arrested and detained near Dumka, a small town bordering West Bengal. The news spread like wild fire. In Delhi, the JD split on 5 November, with Chandrashekhar deserting it with his fifty-eight MPs to form a separate party. Two days later, V P Singh stepped down as prime minister. In Gujarat, the BJP chose to opt out of the government and sit in the opposition. That did not bother Chimanbhai. He sought the support of Congress (I), which he easily received. But when the Congress (I) withdrew its support to Chandrashekhar in March 1991, Chimanbhai broke away from JD to form a regional party – the Janata Dal (Gujarat) – and continued to rule. Finally, when P V Narasimha Rao became the prime minister, Chimanbhai merged his JD(G) with the Congress (I) to keep going.

At this point in time, Narendra was named a member of BJP's All-India Election Committee. For him, it became a matter of pride to be one of the seventeen members of the BJP National Election Committee. He went on to shoulder heavier responsibilities. In subsequent years, Narendra was to become an important part of every working committee of the BJP at the all-India level.

In Gujarat, the BJP was itching for a political showdown with the Congress (I) and it humbled its opponent in the tenth general elections for the Lok Sabha held in May 1991. Had Rajiv Gandhi not been assassinated in the midst of the elections, it would probably have won all twenty-six seats. For all that, it still won twenty, polling over fifty per cent of the votes. L K Advani, who won from the Gandhinagar constituency, polled over fifty-seven per cent votes.

It can never be forgotten that it was Narendra who had organized the *Ekta* Yatra and had busied himself in its preparation from August 1991 onwards. After the successful completion of the yatra, Narendra returned to Ahmedabad on 30 January 1992 to a rousing reception. It was to be his undoing temporarily. His very success turned out to be his nemesis. It stirred jealousy among his seniors and the new state BJP President Shankersinh Vaghela declined to include Narendra in his team. Overnight, as it were, he found himself unwanted. It was then that the service-minded Narendra involved himself in educational activities.

The Power of Retreat

Samskardham, located on the outskirts of Ahmedabad, is a secondary school with a difference. It is a residential school, affordable to the Gujarati middle class, contemporary in standards but traditional in concept. It inculcates India's ancient cultural values in its students. Set amidst sylvan surroundings, Samskardham is the perfect example of an idea being materialized at the right time, with the right force, and in the right spirit. Narendra was deeply interested in such an institution. A school based on these thoughts and practices was Vakil Saheb's dream. Narendra, being his *manas putra*, wanted to be a part of this venture. Even now, whenever Narendra can, he likes to spend time with the children at the school. He says that being in a pious environment of a modern *gurukul* like Samskardham is a source of great satisfaction for him. Admission to the school starts from the fifth grade; children from rural areas get preference. Any candidate who wants to apply to this premier institution has to be above the age of eleven. The reason for such a clause is indicated in the prospectus:

'According to modern science, a child needs love and care during his tender age. It is rightly said that the mother is the best teacher, especially at a young age. We at Samskardham believe that only after the basic lessons are learnt from one's family, should a child be admitted to Samskardham.'

Samskardham school offers a comprehensive training and development programme for the students according to which, skills are not taught in isolation but in a holistic way. Everything is planned and designed in such a manner that there is a lot of room for a child to learn to be expressive.

Students are divided into batches of twenty-five. Each batch is presided over by an *abhibhavakacharya* (guardian teacher) who is involved in resolving every problem that a student may face ... The *abhibhavakacharya* is not only a trouble-shooter but a guide as well. Each and every student gets personal attention which, in turn, helps in his overall development. There are game sessions: some are specially designed to increase bonding between people from different backgrounds.

Apart from the prescribed curriculum, there are other activities that keep the students active – yoga, karate, music, moral education, horse riding, computer skills, and so on. The student's daily regime begins at sharp five in the morning and ends at ten at night. Within these hours, the students get instruction in music, *shramdaan* (manual work) and environmentalism. Regular group discussions are held, often with teacher-parent participation, which iron out differences that arise because of differences in perspectives. Then there are weekly meetings for news-analysis and knowledge tests while birthdays are celebrated in the form of a *yajna*, a pure Samskardham specialty. Right from the very first day, when the foundation stone was laid, Narendra was involved with the growth and operation of the school. The school is an inseparable part of his being, so much so that whenever he travels abroad, he brings gifts for the school – new equipment for the laboratory or something equally meaningful.

Both Samskardham and Laxman Jnanpeeth were inaugurated on Rishi Panchami Day in June 1992 (it falls on the fifth day of the waxing moon – *shukla paksha* – of Bhadrapad month (August-September). It is the day to show respect to the *sapta rishis* – seven sages). From then on, Narendra was available to the staff on any matter concerning the functioning of the school. He would give the minutest of instructions on how to receive and entertain visitors; how to hold exhibitions, and how to see that chauffeurs of VIPs, who were visiting the school, were fed and not left to fend for themselves. No detail was too insignificant for him to attend to. Once, when a staffer fell dangerously ill, he made haste to attend to his needs and did not leave his side, realizing that he might be breathing his last any moment. He had to go to Delhi on summons, but when he was told over the phone that his friend had died, he took the next flight to Ahmedabad and was in Samskardham, in time to attend the funeral.

Essentially, Samskardham was Narendra's tribute to his guru and preceptor, Vakil Saheb. For the inaugural function, he even wrote two inspirational songs that were set to music and sung on the occasion.

By 1992, people had started taking note of Narendra as a political force to reckon with in Gujarat, and this fact was recognized by the US government that invited him to the country as a youth leader. The party, too, had come to recognize his organizational skills and Narendra was summoned to Delhi and asked to take over the responsibility of organizing party affairs as Secretary. In a sense, Narendra had come of political age. He took over his duties in right earnest. Assembly elections were to be held in five states – Uttar Pradesh, Madhya Pradesh, Rajasthan, Himachal Pradesh and Assam. Outside Gujarat, this was Narendra's first political task. It was a great learning experience for him; it exposed him to the geopolitical leadership of different states. Every task that he was given, he converted into a capacity-building exercise for the party.

In Gujarat, Chimanbhai was the chief minister. He enjoyed the support of over a hundred members in the house of 182. His relations with the Union government led by Congress (I) under the prime ministership of P V Narasimha Rao were quite cordial. For the Congress (I), he was like a bulwark blocking BJP's avalanche. It was during Chimanbhai's rule that the Babri Masjid was demolished in 1992.

Repercussions in Gujarat were terrible. Widespread and maniacal Hindu-Muslim riots broke out all over the state. According to one account, Surat was the worst affected by the gruesome carnage. Chimanbhai could do little except organizing fire-fighting operations. But he was a changed man. He went on to display rare maturity and was prepared to respond to any situation. Writer Nagindas Sanghavi describes his experiences in the following words: 'He faced the wildcat operations of Narmada Bachao Andolan at Ferkuva and refused to yield to the pressure tactics of Baba Amte and Medha Patkar. Unfortunately for Chimanbhai, he came to be widely suspected of being in league with shady characters. There were allegations of corruption against him. In the wake of growing lawlessness, a senior Congress (I) worker,

The Man of the Moment: Narendra Modi

M P Rauf Waliullah, was murdered in broad daylight in one of the localities in Ahmedabad, prompting a senior Congress (I) politician, C D Patel, to resign from Chimanbhai's cabinet.'

Then the inevitable happened which changed the flow of things. In February 1994, Chimanbhai died of a massive heart attack. The seniormost among his ministers, Chhabildas Mehta, took over as chief minister. The Congress (I) continued its support to the new administration, but insisted on saddling him with a jumbo ministry of forty-five members, a scandalous thing to do. Chhabildas had no option. To stay in power, he had to give in to Congress (I) pressures. But he also knew that he was merely holding the fort till the impending assembly elections scheduled for February-March 1995, when he expected the situation to normalize. Narendra was ready to face the elections. To gain the upper hand at the elections, the BJP had decided to train workers at every level. In a large-scale training programme, about 1.5 lakh workers, who had to handle about 28,000 polling booths, were given rigorous training on how to handle voters and other problems that might crop up at the time of elections. The programme was highly successful. 'Organization Centred Elections' also turned out to be a uniquely successful experiment. Most of it was Narendra's handiwork.

After the poor performance of the BJP in various states, the 1995 Gujarat assembly elections turned out to be a major event. The Congress (I) entered the electoral fray with several handicaps. In the first place, it had no leader of the calibre of Chimanbhai Patel. Intense factionalism had widened, following the merger of the JD(G) into its fold. Within the Congress (I), there were four factions: one led by Chimanbhai's widow, Urmilabehn; another led by Chhabildas Mehta, the outgoing chief minister; a third led by Prabodh Rawal, and a fourth led by Madhavsinh Solanki, a Congress elder who had been chief minister once in the late 1970s and thereafter in the late 1980s. The entry of the Bahujan Samaj Party (BSP), led by Mayawati, did not make it any easier for the Congress, which felt that it stood to lose the Dalit vote.

Of a total of 182 seats, the BJP won 121. The Congress (I) barely managed to get forty-five seats. In the first general elections in 1952, the BJP's predecessor party had the support of barely 4,000 citizens; four decades later, in 1995, the BJP's tally was 6,624,711 votes! It was a quantum jump in popularity. Never before in history had any party made such sensational progress. The BJP won in almost ninety-eight per cent of units. In some district panchayat elections, the party's victory was hundred per cent. Media and political analysts named Narendra 'the architect of BJP's victory' in Gujarat, thus giving him credit for victory in both the assembly and the local elections. But BJP's very success turned out to be a problem. In *Portrayal of a Charismatic Leader*, Kulkarni stated:

'The revival of the post of Organizing Secretary some time in the 1980s in the party set-up of BJP proved to be a stumbling block in Gujarat's implementing the Open Door Policy. The Organizing Secretary, usually a *pracharak* of the RSS, tried to steer the BJP. In his unique position, he wields considerable influence. When the BJP was formed in 1980, this post, considered to be a legacy of the Jan Sangh, was abolished. The post was revived to strengthen the party. Narendra Modi, the organizing secretary of the Gujarat BJP, being a *pracharak*, wielded considerable clout in the party. An able organizer, he streamlined the party machinery.'

There were apparently personality clashes. When Kashiram Rana got elected as president of the Gujarat BJP, he refused to re-nominate Narendra as state party general secretary, since he preferred Suresh Mehta. The RSS took it as an affront to its authority and compelled Rana to nominate Narendra. BJP's all-India president L K Advani also favoured Modi.

Following the victory, Keshubhai was elected chief minister of Gujarat. He took the oath of office and secrecy on 14 March 1995 at a function which was thrown open to the public. But it was not going to be plain sailing for Keshubhai. There was trouble right from the start. Ministry-making turned out to be painful. It took a whole week for Keshubhai to get it together. Everybody wanted to be a minister. Under such circumstances, Keshubhai was forced to form a jumbo ministry comprising thirty-three members! There were charges that Saurashtra had been over-represented, that good men did not receive berths, but above all that, it was not Keshubhai but Narendra who was responsible for naming the ministry. Shankersinh claimed that he had not been consulted.

It is unique to the BJP that important decisions are collectively taken by the senior leaders. But Keshubhai's rival group led by

The Man of the Moment: Narendra Modi

Shankersinh wanted to target him and the party. It tried to project Narendra in a bad light. The government was formed in March, and for the months of April and May, Narendra got extremely busy with training party workers for the upcoming local self-government elections. During this period, Narendra did not even have the time to look at the government and how it was working as he was training party workers as a part of the organization work of the party. As many as ten thousand elected representatives received training. When elections were held in June 1995, BJP won six Municipal Corporations and eighteen of the nineteen Zilla Panchayat Boards (district local self-government bodies). In the elections to the Surat Municipal Corporation, the BJP won all the seats.

According to a rule laid down by the BJP for its members, the organization secretary is not expected to have a say in the working of the party. This weakness of the system was fully exploited by Shankersinh. Narendra's silence was taken advantage of by Keshubhai's rival group. In its quest for power, this rival group led by Shankersinh wanted to make Narendra the *bali ka bakra* (the sacrificial lamb). But such discipline was of no concern to Keshubhai's rivals. Shankersinh wanted to be consulted on all important matters, such as the appointment of the forty-two chairmen of the various state government boards and corporations. The relationship between Keshubhai and Shankersinh became more strained with each passing day. On 8 September 1995, Keshubhai was to leave for a month-long visit to the UK and US to mobilize funds from Non-Resident Indians (NRIs) for the development of Gujarat. He was to be accompanied by a large team, but Keshubhai refused to make Shankersinh a part of the entourage. On the eve of his visit to the US, when the two arch rivals met, Keshubhai is reported to have told the other not to poke his nose in the matter of appointments to which Shankersinh is reported to have replied, 'You may not be the chief minister when you return.'

Before leaving, Keshubhai announced the names of people appointed as chairmen in various government corporations. Shankersinh was incensed and raised the banner of revolt. It was primarily a clash of egos; no ideology was involved in the revolt. On 24 September, Shankersinh organized a convention in Ahmedabad, which was to fight 'authoritarianism, nepotism, corruption and *goondaism* (hooliganism)' in the Gujarat BJP. Shankersinh could have called upon the BJP high command to vent his anger. But he did not.

The members of the BJP in Gujarat met on 26 September, two days after the Shankersinh convention, but the meet was attended by just sixty MLAs or a little more than half the BJP strength in the Vidhan Sabha. In such a situation, where their egos clashed head-on, Shankersinh took a chance to materialize the opportunity to quench his thirst for power. He mobilized the leaders against Keshubhai and as usual, the blame fell on Narendra. But in order to save the party, Narendra tendered his resignation to the then state party president, Kashiram Rana. His letter was as follows:

Respected Shri Kashirambhai,

Respectful salutations.

Today there are several question marks facing the people, of Gujarat's hopes and aspirations. Our party made by the hard toil of thousands of workers has been blatantly robbed of its reputation after continuous debate. Now the 'truth' has come out in its complete form. The events of the last two days bear witness to it. I have been silent for long in the interests of the party. In the past, I have often met you personally and requested you to free me from the responsibilities.

Today the situation is very delicate. The events of the last two days have proven my innocence. Yet my *sanskar* is to think in terms of my role as a worker.

I remember a story. A fight was going on in a court between a 'real mother' and a stepmother' over a child. The judge suggested that the child be cut into two so each claimant can have one part. At that, the *real* mother pleaded against the child being cut into two. Yes, on the same premises, I have come to this decision.

To be a *bali* for the sake of the Party means to resign from the post of the general secretary. I shall always work for the party as a worker.

I trust that henceforth no one will have to do anything in my name. I am earnestly requesting you to accept my resignation unlike in the past when you have refused it.

On this occasion, through you I thank the thousands of BJP workers to whom I feel obliged.

My very special thanks to you.

In the service of Mother India, always I remain

Yours

Narendra Modi.

The letter was dated 28 September 1995.

On the same day, Shankersinh addressed a press conference to reiterate his claim to a majority in the Gujarat State Assembly. He severely criticized the Gujarat BJP leadership for nepotism and corruption and laid the blame squarely on L K Advani, the party chief, for his indifference towards the growing rift within the party. In order to keep his followers with him, he first took all of them to a village called Vasan, some thirty kilometres away from Gandhinagar and then secretly arranged for his followers to be flown to Khajuraho, in Madhya Pradesh, under the protection of the Congress government. They were thereafter to be identified as 'Khajurias'.

At this, the BJP high command decided to take action. On the evening of 5 October, Vajpayee flew to Gandhinagar and spent hours discussing the situation with local members of the party. He had consultations, especially with Keshubhai, and persuaded him to step down as chief minister, which the latter reluctantly agreed to, even while warning Vajpayee that it would be like a reward offered to Shankersinh for his indiscipline. But they arrived at an understanding of sorts. The rebels were to return to Ahmedabad and would have to express their confidence in Keshubhai by voting for him on a motion of confidence. This was achieved on 7 October. Having won the vote of confidence, Keshubhai resigned the next day and Shankersinh rejoined the party. But there was no way in which Shankersinh could get elected as the next chief minister. That post went to a compromise candidate, Suresh Mehta.

Shankersinh may have rejoined the party but he must have known that he had no future in it. By rebelling, he had burnt his boats. The high command nominated Keshubhai, Shankersinh and Narendra, respectively, to the posts of all-India Vice-President, Member of the National Executive and all-India General Secretary of the party. But the anger between the ex-rebels (Khajurias) and the old-time loyalists (Hajurias) was not to be easily put down. In the Lok Sabha elections held in May 1996, the Hajurias settled scores with the Khajurias and even had Shankersinh defeated. The infighting, with no holds barred, was suicidal.

First, Shankersinh announced the formation of a farmers' organization, the Maha Gujarat Kisan Sena. Then, on 18 August 1996, he broke away from the parent party to form the Maha Gujarat Janata Party (MGJP). On 19 August, the newly formed MGJP demanded that it be recognized as a separate party in the Gujarat legislature as it allegedly enjoyed the support of more than one-third of the total number of BJP legislators. On 20 August, the Rashtriya Janata Party (RJP) was formally launched at the huge Ram Lila grounds in Ahmedabad. In this way, Shankersinh broke all his bonds with the BJP with a vengeance. But 18 out of the 46 BJP MLAs, who had supposedly defected to the RJP, rejoined the parent organization. Just as importantly, on 2 September 1996, some ninety-four BJP legislators visited Gandhiji's Sabarmati Ashram to take a pledge to strengthen party unity. But uncertainty about the Suresh Mehta ministry persisted. When the Legislative Assembly was convened on 18 September, followers of Shankersinh behaved atrociously and the session had to be adjourned.

The governor thereupon understandably recommended the imposition of President's rule in Gujarat which was carried out the very next day. The Suresh Mehta government thus lasted from 21 October 1995 to 19 September 1996. One wonders how Vaghela, who had 'personal clout, political skills and enviable public relations', failed to abide by party discipline.

Shankersinh's action proves that it was hunger for power that was the reason for all his revolts, and blaming Narendra was only a tactic adopted by him. Dragging Narendra's name was just a ploy by Shankersinh to achieve his own goal. In effect, Shankersinh turned out to be a snake in the grass!

On 22 October 1996, Gujarat's Governor, Krishna Pal Singh, who had succeeded Naresh Chandra, invited Shankersinh to form the new government. Shankersinh now had the support of the Congress (I) and mustered the strength of 102 MLAs out of 182. But of the 102 who voted for him, only forty-two belonged to his party and forty-five belonged to the Congress (I). The rest were independent candidates. In effect, Shankersinh's strength lay not in his own party but in the support lent to him by the Congress (I). His weakness became evident when in a by-election in the Sarkhej constituency, the BJP candidate Amit Shah defeated the Congress (I) candidate by an impressive margin of over twenty-four thousand votes.

The Congress was now confused and in deep thought. In reality, its members outnumbered those of the RJP. Moreover, the defeat of the RJP in Sarkhej showed how weak Shankersinh's party was at the grass-roots level. There was much wrangling in the Congress (I) circles over the issue whether it should continue to support Shankersinh or withdraw from the coalition. Shankersinh was no saint and in no time there were charges of corruption against him; the charges were made by Congress (I) itself. Inevitably, Shankersinh had to resign. He had been in power for just about a year when he was forced to bow out. On 27 October 1997, his second-in-command, Dilipbhai Parikh, succeeded him. Parikh, however, could not last long. His rule, such as it was, lasted for about seventy days before Keshubhai took over as the chief minister once again.

In the meantime, Narendra had been appointed National Secretary of the BJP on 20 November 1995. From then on, Delhi became his centre of work. In 1996, under Advani's leadership as party president, a team was formed in which Narendra was assigned the responsibility of organizing the BJP in Haryana, Himachal Pradesh, Chandigarh, Punjab and Jammu & Kashmir.

It was a tough assignment. But being a workaholic, Narendra enjoyed it. He kept moving from place to place, meeting people at all levels. He says that by working with people in terrorism-affected Punjab and Jammu & Kashmir, he came to understand several issues that he was but dimly aware of till that time. Not long after that, elections were held in all the states. The party gave him the task of preparing the workers for the same. In all the states, the BJP was to succeed beyond its dreams. When the summons from Delhi had come to Narendra asking him to quit his job in Gujarat and take over responsibilities at the party headquarters in the capital, he had obeyed it without the slightest hesitation. Narendra was quite clear about one thing – the need for discipline. In Delhi, he stayed in a colleague's house in the room assigned to him. He neither wanted nor sought anything more by way of comfort. His stand had been vindicated when the very people who wanted to make him a scapegoat revolted against Shankersinh and brought him down.

Such was his devotion to his work that in a short period of two years, he was assigned the responsibility of General Secretary (Organization) at the all-India level – Maha Mantri of the All India Bharatiya Sangathan on 19 May 1998. His predecessors in this position had been luminaries like Pandit Deendayal Upadhyaya, Sundersinh Bhandari and Kushabhau Thackeray. Narendra became the fourth to occupy this prestigious post.

The Man and His Mission 6

As always, Narendra was a disciplined worker of the party. He dedicated himself fully to the task assigned to him. He was effective and functioned daringly. As the national secretary of BJP, he worked diligently at organizing the BJP in Haryana, Himachal Pradesh, Chandigarh, Jammu and Kashmir, and Punjab. He was not afraid of terrorists or any other anti-social force. He went ahead to work in ways he thought fit.

Jammu and Kashmir did not boast of any significant presence of the BJP. When former US President Bill Clinton was on a visit to India, some thirty-six Sikhs were killed in Chhatisingpura in Kashmir. Narendra, as the Party-in-Charge of that area, decided to visit the town. The then Chief Minister, Farooq Abdullah, complained to Advaniji that Modi went anywhere not bothered about security.

One suspects that this attitude was based on a fatalistic approach to life where nothing mattered except doing one's duty. While doing party work in Haryana and Himachal Pradesh, Narendra kept his eyes and ears open to what was happening in Punjab and he spent about six months there. Elections were due for the 20 seats of the Chandigarh Municipal Corporation. Thanks to Narendra's quiet political work, the BJP won 17 of them. An MP from Chandigarh, Pavan Kumar, commented: 'In this belt, the Jan Sangh did not have a foothold before.'

Narendra's obsession with doing his duty motivated him to make and carry out unusual plans. He happened to be in Kargil when war broke out there. He decided to stay put. 'The Army needed volunteers to carry baggage; I organized it. There was a man who didn't have enough warm clothes but was moving about with agility, saying: "Come, let's do something!" People would join him. I was not giving any leadership, I was simply a colleague.'

When asked about the whole situation at Kargil, his remarks were the centre of every listener's attention: 'Chicken *biryani nahi*, bullet *ka jawab* bomb *se diya jayega'* (Not with chicken *biryani*, bullets will be answered by bombs).

In Delhi, when the National Democratic Alliance (NDA) formed its first government, it was left to Narendra to invite the chief ministers of all BJP-ruled states to come to Delhi for the oath-taking ceremony. 'When the BJP-led NDA government was formed under Atalji's leadership, people from all over the world, diplomats and journalists wanted to know what the decision-making process in the BJP and NDA was. They were interested to know BJP's relationship with the RSS and the system. They seemed familiar with the Congress party but the BJP was something new for them.'

With the BJP having performed well in the elections, Narendra was sought after by many international capitals. A foreign minister of a Commonwealth country inviting the general secretary of the BJP was an unusual act in any case.

In 2000-01, at the invitation of foreign Minister Alexander Donner, Narendra visited Brisbane in Australia where the Commonwealth Heads of Government Meeting (CHOGM) was going to be held later in the year. Narendra met leaders of the Liberal Party and the Labour Party, and discussed the working of the political system in Australia with them. He discussed prospects of joint ventures between the two countries with Donner. The latter appreciated the growing power of India in Information Technology (IT), bio-technology and yoga. Australia had made a lot of progress in the field of eco-tourism and Narendra took the opportunity of his visit to make a study of Frazer Island.

In July 2001, Narendra visited Malaysia at the invitation of Dr Mahathir Mohammad, Prime Minister of Malaysia and president of the United Malays National Organization (UMNO), the ruling party in the country. In a rare gesture, Narendra was invited to the national assembly of UMNO. Earlier, when the Prime Minister of India, Atal Bihari Vajpayee, had visited Malaysia, a Memorandum of Understanding (MoU) had been signed for the construction of a railway line in the country. Narendra reminded Dr Mahathir about the same. Immediately, Dr Mahathir gave the work order amounting to eighteen billion US dollars.

The Man of the Moment: Narendra Modi

The Gujarati society in Malaysia organized a vegetarian food fair in Malacca for raising relief funds for the earthquake victims of Gujarat. A sum of 40,000 Malaysian ringgit was raised on the occasion and it was donated to the Chief Minister's Relief Fund in Gujarat.

Meanwhile, in the RSS, Narendra had graduated from being a *pracharak* to becoming the organizing secretary in Gujarat and then moved to the national level. Traditionally, *pracharaks* and organizing secretaries remain away from the media and Narendra was no different. But during the Kargil war, he was given the responsibility of addressing the media on behalf of the party. For a person who had stayed away from the media, this was a big challenge and Narendra shone. He appeared as the party representative in various TV debates and made a mark with his points of view.

By 1999, Narendra had won the full confidence of Prime Minister Vajpayee and was acting as the party spokesperson. Following the 2001 Agra Summit between Vajpayee and Pakistan's President General Pervez Musharraf, Narendra was in demand. The responsibility of providing the details of the party's position vis-á-vis Musharraf to the media fell on him and he carried out his duty responsibly. He was at his best in an exclusive interview to Rediff.com's senior correspondent Onkar Singh on 19 July 2001.

Onkar Singh wanted to know if Vajpayee was on the defensive after his meeting with Musharraf. Narendra was sharp. He said, 'Defensive and offensive are subjective terms. Atalji is not merely a politician but also a statesman. He was very clear about what he was doing before extending an invitation to the Pakistan president. The very fact that Musharraf had to go back without signing any agreement clearly shows that Atalji was not on the defensive, but on the offensive.'

And then there was one final probing question. Singh asked, 'Did Musharraf's breakfast meeting with senior editors annoy the Indian government?' Modi was frank. He replied, 'It was not proper on the General's part to have played games with the media. We have been told by some editors that they were not even aware that it was being telecast live on Pakistan television. When two heads of state hold talks, you do not go to the media to score a point or two. If General Musharraf thought he could solve the

Kashmir problem through press conferences, then he is welcome to hold 1,000 press meets. He would still be at square one.'

In an interview to the party journal *BJP Today*, Narendra stressed: 'This meeting is more important for Pakistan. Its policy makers have to utilize this opportunity. In the last fifty years, whether at Tashkent, Shimla or Lahore, Pakistan has got a lot of opportunities to project itself as a peace-loving nation. But it has lost all these opportunities. Since an anti-terrorism mood has been sweeping the nations of the world, Pakistan has become isolated. It has still to establish its credibility in the international community.'

As general secretary of the BJP in Delhi, Narendra was catching the attention of the media. He was invited, for instance, by Sify. com to talk about his understanding of a roadmap towards the India of his dreams on the country's fifty-fifth Independence Day. Narendra made some remarkable observations. He said:

'Unfortunately, it is being increasingly perceived now that the sense of service and duty to the nation that had permeated the freedom movement has now lost its sheen. Now the citizens are more concerned about their rights, almost to the total neglect of their duties and responsibilities towards the nation.

'I appeal to my friends in the media that they work out a system where at least every two days in a week, they will desist from reporting the activities of politicians in the newspapers.

'I propose that a moratorium of ten years be imposed on the practice of naming a government building or street or road after a politician who dies in harness. We are living in the IT age. For me, it does not mean only Information Technology, it also means "India Tomorrow".'

Narendra further put forward a point to highlight India's prowess. He said: 'The Mahakumbh[1] is a pristine example of what India can

---

1 It is considered the most auspicious religious event. The Kumbh Mela is held at Allahabad in January every twelve years at the confluence (*sangam*) of the rivers Ganga, Yamuna and the mythical Saraswati. The Mahakumbh Mela is held every 144 years at Allahabad. Bathing in these rivers during the Kumbh Mela is considered a meritorious act that cleanses the body and the soul.

do when motivated and inspired in the right way. It is a miracle of organizational acumen. It is the largest gathering of people on the planet. Over twenty million people attend the Mahakumbh. Everyday, the number of people who assemble at the banks of the Ganga equals the entire population of Australia ... It is a pristine example of human management. Cannot we extend this prowess we show at Mahakumbh to all walks of life in the nation? The Mahakumbh demonstrates that we are quite capable of meeting any challenge provided we are motivated and inspired.'

And he added, somewhat dramatically: 'As far as I am concerned, nothing is impossible. After all, the word "impossible" itself contains "I'm possible"!'

At a conference of the Modi community held in Phalna, Rajasthan, among other things, Narendra said: 'I am the son of this *samaj* (society). I have been a member of the RSS since my childhood. RSS taught me *Hindutva* and it has been a part of me since then. 'A person becomes great on the strength of the *samaj*. If the *samaj* is not with him, he cannot be great. But to use the *samaj* for purposes of politicking does not help. The platform of the *samaj* should be used to enhance the *samaj's* strength ...

'If we resolve to become strong economically, educationally and socially, we will forge ahead, taking all along with us ... There is a proverb in Chinese: "Those who think for one year do farming. Those who think for ten years, grow trees that will bear fruits in the years to come. But those who think for a generation nurture good human beings." We have to nurture good human beings to create a good society ...

'If we educate our girls, we educate our entire *samaj*. Meanwhile, if you want to succeed in politics, work for those who are left out, who are neglected. There lies power.'

From 1995 to 2001, except during the 1999 elections, Modi remained in Delhi since he was the party's general secretary. But events were happening that were sure indications of things to come. On 28 June 2000, when Narendra returned to Gujarat to attend a function organized in Ahmedabad to felicitate MISA detainees during the period of the Emergency, he received a standing ovation. At the function, Narendra was given the last

The Man and His Mission

chair on the dais, in spite of perceived objections from the state BJP leaders.

Politically, Gujarat was in the doldrums. The BJP government and the party were acting and working like two exclusive entities, passing the buck to each other when they failed to deliver. The people of Gujarat who had given the BJP an absolute majority felt cheated. And while the people felt cheated, the ministers and leaders seemed to continue working for personal stakes. The BJP in Gujarat needed someone to re-inculcate a sense of discipline and unity towards the organization.

Indeed, matters had come to such a pass that in 2000-01, the party could not win a single by-election in the state. Losing the prestigious Sabarmati assembly seat, Sabarkantha Lok Sabha seat, and all local self-government, *taluka*, *nagarpalika* (Municipal Corporation) elections to the Congress came as a wake-up call for the BJP. It decided to act. And the only man, according to the senior party leaders, who could set matters right was Narendra. He was peremptorily told to proceed to Ahmedabad to take over the reins of power as chief minister from Keshubhai Patel.

This happened in a somewhat unexpected – even amusing – manner. Narendra recounted the event in an interview. He said, 'This was in October 2001. Madhavrao Scindia had died. So had a few journalists (in an air crash), among them a cameraman of Aaj Tak, Gopal, whom I knew well. He was to be cremated in Delhi and I went for the cremation. I felt I had to. He had often come to the party office to see me. At the cremation I received a call from Atalji's office. Atalji was on the line. He said, "Where are you?" I told him I was at the crematorium. He said, "What are you doing there?" I told him. He asked me to see him later in the evening.

When I met him, he said, "You have become fat eating all that Punjabi food. You must slim down. Go away from here. Vacate Delhi." I asked, "Go where?" "Go to Gujarat," he replied, "you have to work there." So I said, "Would I be in charge only of Gujarat or of some other state as well?" I did not know then that Atalji wanted me to be the chief minister of Gujarat. I thought I was to be in charge of party organizational work and was somewhat concerned that now I was being given just one state to handle. But then Atalji said, "No, no, you will have to contest elections.

You have so far helped others fight. Now you will have to fight for yourself." I told him that I would not do it. I said, "I will go to Gujarat for ten days in a month and do organizational work." As I came to know that I was being marked out for chief ministership, I told Atalji, "That is not my work. I have been away from Gujarat for six long years. I am not familiar with the issues. What will I do there? It is not a field of my liking. I don't know anyone."

'To that Atalji said, "When I came here (Delhi), whom did I know?" But I kept on saying "No". At night, Advaniji called me to meet him and asked me, "What did you tell Atalji?" I said, "Why?" He said, "Look, everybody has decided about you." I told him, "I will not fit into the job."

'Five or six days passed and finally I had to concede to what the party wanted me to do. So I came over and since then, I have been involved here.'

It is possible that he did not particularly relish the idea of taking over the chief ministership of Gujarat. But then he was not given any option. He had to go to Gujarat, and he went. Keshubhai, the then Chief Minister, put on a brave face and articulated his ouster philosophy by telling his friends: 'My political journey will continue as an MLA and party worker.'

What tipped the scales in favour of Narendra can only be guessed. According to one source, it was the example set by Rajnath Singh (the now BJP president), in Uttar Pradesh. When Rajnath had taken over the state responsibilities, the BJP's fortunes were at a low there. His decisive no-nonsense style had then strengthened his party position. Soon after reaching Gandhinagar, Narendra had a one-to-one meeting with Keshubhai who, thereafter, submitted his resignation to Gujarat's governor, S S Bhandari. The fourth of October was a major day in Narendra's life. On that day, in the presence of the national party president, a meeting of BJP legislative members was held at Gandhinagar. Narendra was elected leader of the BJP Legislative party at the same. The outgoing Chief Minister Keshubhai Patel proposed Narendra's name for the post, which was seconded by Suresh Mehta. Also present at the meeting was senior party member Madan Lal Khurana and the state BJP president Rajendrasinh Rana. On 5 October 2001, the *Express News Service National Network* carried the following report:

> National BJP General Secretary and RSS strongman Narendra Modi, who is scheduled to be sworn in as chief minister on Sunday, appears all set to make sweeping changes in the ministry to resurrect the party's image in Gujarat.
>
> Modi is said to have received a clear mandate from the party high command to ensure that the BJP and its government's prestige is redeemed, and to pull it out of the deep morass it has been in, since the debacle in the recent elections ... he made his priorities clear soon after he arrived here from Delhi on Wednesday. 'I have come here to play a one-day match. I need fast and performing batsmen to score runs in the limited-overs game,' Modi was quoted as saying. Top party sources said on Wednesday that while effecting changes, Modi would have three criteria – efficiency, discipline and integrity. Ministers accused of corruption and incompetence may get the boot ... The signal is clear – he has little time, just over a year, to face assembly elections in March 2003.

For Narendra, his election as chief minister was a very emotional occasion. He touched the feet of his predecessor and Kushabhau Thackeray and warmly embraced Madan Lal Khurana, Rajendrasinh Rana and others. He told his party colleagues that he had to keep the run rate fast. 'We have only 500 days and 12,000 hours before the next election for the State Assembly,' he said and added that within this short period, the team would have to strive hard to fulfill the expectations of the people and ensure victory for the BJP. He raised a new slogan for the state – *Aapanu Gujarat Aagavu Gujarat* (Our Gujarat, unique Gujarat).

Three days later, on 7 October, Governor Sundersinh Bhandari swore in Narendra Modi as the state's fourteenth chief minister. This was the first time that a Sangh *pracharak* had become a chief minister – a record of its kind.

BJP Today, the party's journal, stated the following about the emerging leader:

'Modi's return to Gujarat has electrified the spirit of BJP youths and the state party leaders are confident that his charismatic leadership will benefit the party.'

The Man of the Moment: Narendra Modi

Within a month of being elected the chief minister of Gujarat, Narendra got an opportunity to visit Russia with Prime Minister Atal Bihari Vajpayee. He signed a protocol of cooperation with the Astrakhan region of Russia at the Kremlin in the presence of Prime Minister Vajpayee and Russian President Vladimir Putin. With this initiative, Gujarat and Astrakhan further strengthened their bilateral cooperation in different areas including trade, commerce, service and culture. It was expected that ports in Gujarat such as Kandla and Okha would be revived to mutual benefit.

During his time in office so far, Narendra has donated every gift that he has received from people. He deposits all the gifts and the money so collected for encouraging plans about the education of the girl child. He swears, 'I am willing to go to any extent in earnestly pleading for the education of girls.' One of the first things that Narendra did on being elected the chief minister of Gujarat was to call on his mother to seek her blessings. She had just one bit of advice to give. She said: 'My son, never take bribes.'

The statement made by Narendra on the occasion of his election as leader of the party in the Gujarat Legislative Assembly that he had come to play a one-day match elicited wide interest and became the subject of much debate. He was questioned by the media on it. Narendra had to explain that one-dayers are usually played keeping the run rate and speed of achieving targets in mind. Further, in a one-day match, what counts is not the number of balls faced by the batsman, but the number of balls in which he scores runs. Similarly in governance, efficiency has to be measured not by the number of files disposed of, but by the number of problems effectively solved.

Narendra, who is ever capable of turning an adversity into an opportunity, made use of his inexperience to start afresh, on a clean slate without the burden of the past and prejudices. Immediately after the swearing-in ceremony, he swung into action. He refused felicitation programmes for two months and spent time with ministers and bureaucrats to understand the problems and issues that were bogging the state down. The first few weeks sent signals about how things would be during his tenure. It was the beginning of a new political culture, all without making any announcement to the media about his plans.

Progress at every stage had to be reported after the task was accomplished. People's participation became the axis around which the wheel of administration started moving. Lok Kalyan melas (People's Welfare Festivals) were organized to introduce transparency. In November 2001, all the ministers celebrated Diwali in the homes of the earthquake-affected people. Narendra quickly understood that for the government to perform, it was necessary to motivate the bureaucrats. When Narendra took over as chief minister, the bureaucracy was generally demotivated. Frequent transfers, instability, petty political interference in day-to-day administration had resulted in cynicism and apathy. In Narendra's regime, frequent transfers were put to a halt; performing officers were identified and appropriate tasks were assigned to them. The honesty and integrity of officers was taken into consideration apart from their capability. Stable tenures were assured to bureaucrats, which in turn provided scope for long-term planning and implementation. Petty interference in day-to-day administration became history.

The first step towards a paradigm shift was to transform the chief minister's office into an office where issues were dealt with in a professional manner. Those whose contribution was nil were removed from their positions. For the first time, midnight lamps burned in the secretariat and many a person who saw this, expressed disbelief.

Narendra worked out a plan for the implementation of the Vision 2010 documents, prepared by his predecessor Keshubhai Patel, for infrastructure development within three months. The tech-savvy Narendra saw no reason why Gujarat, which leads the country in industrial and economic development, should also not lead the country in IT. Extending his vision to the future development of the entire country, he coined the slogan 'IT (Indian talent) + IT (Information Technology) = IT (India Tomorrow).'

He also focussed on rural development, improvement of education, education of the girl child, social justice, agricultural development, science and technology and disaster management.

On 26 January 2001, Kutch was hit by a high-intensity earthquake causing unbelievable loss of life and damage not only there but also in Jamnagar, Rajkot, Surendranagar and Patan districts of

Gujarat. It was the most calamitous natural disaster to strike Gujarat in two hundred years in terms of scaled intensity. The earthquake was unsparing. Houses, schools, hospitals, business centres, and many such organizations came down like a pack of cards causing unimaginable devastation. As many as 13,805 people lost their lives and 1,67,000 were injured. Over a million houses were damaged. In a mere ten minutes, entire townships tumbled down leaving everything in disarray. The Government of Gujarat swung into action.

The earthquake left the educational system completely shattered with over 8,000 classrooms totally destroyed and over 42,000 rooms damaged. It destroyed or damaged 11,39,193 houses in 7,633 villages and urban areas. As many as ninety major and minor bridges were put out of service. It disrupted water supply and sewerage systems causing health hazards that needed immediate attention. The Government of Gujarat responded swiftly to the challenges. Rescue and relief measures were started on a war footing. Power, health care facilities, water supply and transportation were restored in a remarkably short time. The injured were treated immediately and 19,000 orthopaedic operations were done in the first few weeks. The government immediately went into top gear. A Gujarat State Disaster Management Authority (GSDMA) was quickly set up to coordinate all construction and rehabilitation activities efficiently. For long-term disaster management capacity building in Gujarat, the government started a comprehensive rehabilitation and reconstruction programme.

When Narendra had taken over as the chief minister in October 2001, the biggest challenge was to speed up reconstruction and rehabilitation activities. It is amazing, but by January 2002, as many as 8,00,027 housing units or about 2,200 houses were built each day. Some 6.6 lakh bank accounts were opened within three months and ₹1,100 crore paid to over ten lakh beneficiaries as housing assistance. Over one crore bags of cement were sold at subsidised prices. Narendra's bottom line was the involvement of the community in decision making as well as implementation of the programme. His prime focus was on attaining long-term results without losing sight of immediate needs. In order to involve the communities in the reconstruction programme, the repair of schoolrooms was entrusted to the village civil works committees. These committees, by their active involvement, repaired all the 42,678 damaged schoolrooms in record time. Not only were old schoolrooms repaired, but new ones were simultaneously built. Schools were built with hazard-resistant materials. No child lost an academic year. The government went a step further. In order to make disaster preparedness a way of learning, the syllabi of engineering colleges and polytechnics were revised to incorporate seismic engineering as a subject in the civil engineering courses. Lessons on disaster preparedness and natural disasters were introduced even at the school level.

Such was the speed with which the government undertook repair and reconstruction that by 2005, as many as 9,08,710 out of 9,17,158 damaged houses had become fully ready for occupation. As many as 2,42,120 houses, that had completely collapsed, were reconstructed. Displacement or relocation of houses was minimal. In the process, as many as 6,500 engineers and 29,679 masons were trained.

The first and foremost task in the earthquake-affected areas was to restore the healthcare system. All the health units were made immediately functional through 4,134 temporary and alternative arrangements. More than 17,000 orthopaedic operations were performed during the course of four years and nearly 1,67,000 injured were treated immediately. A proof of the remarkable functioning of the health system was that there was no outbreak of any epidemic even after such a massive disaster. Both preventive and curative aspects of rehabilitation were taken care of. What was more, a unique surveillance system was launched to check all communicable and water-borne diseases. Information, education and communication campaigns were carried out for public awareness and vaccination drives were conducted on a large scale.

There was no problem of any significance that was not attended to. Attention was especially given to those who were rendered jobless. The government evolved a three-pronged approach for sustainable livelihood:

- Enhancing the skills of artisans
- Empowering artisans to market their skills and wares
- Immediate restoration of livelihood

Assistance to artisans included free distribution of kits, working capital assistance, provision for loans and interest subsidy, and marketing linkages and establishment of sales outlets. Immediate restoration of livelihood took care of the situation in the following ways: Over 58,000 farmers were provided tarpaulins, spray pumps, farming tools, storage bins, seeds, chemical fertilizers and pesticides. Nearly 47,000 farmers were given assistance to set up farm utilities like engine rooms; over 3,400 handloom weavers were provided with new looms, while 1,629 owners of kiosks and shops were given cash. The mantra of the day was infrastructural development. Roads, bridges and associated structures were repaired and reconstructed; dams and irrigation works, severely damaged, were taken up for reconstruction on an emergency basis. Twenty water supply schemes were launched while 222 tube wells were drilled in 152 villages. Power was restored to Bhuj town by 28 January and to eight other towns by 30 January 2001. All the 465 transmission equipment in the districts of Kutch, Rajkot, Surendranagar, Jamnagar and Banaskantha were repaired and put back in service.

As a government notification stated: The Government of Gujarat has done everything to rehabilitate the orphans, widows, aged and handicapped by declaring financial assistance, death compensation, residential facilities, provision for education and skill upgradation, medical aid, therapy and counselling.

The list of things that the government did for its people is long: understandably, the GSDMA received the Gold Award established by the Commonwealth Association for Public Administration and Management (CAPAM). Even more importantly, GSDMA received the UN Sasakawa Award 2003 for outstanding work in the field of disaster management and risk reduction. The citation read:

> *The Sasakawa Jury wishes to recognize the inclusive and innovative approach adopted by GSDMA in disastrous situations, in which many partners and their stakeholders, both inside and outside India, provided knowledge and resources to formulate effective policies and legislation and prepare disaster management plans ... Created in the wake of the powerful and deadly Bhuj earthquake of January 2001 in Gujarat, India, GSDMA has acquired a solid reputation in the massive reconstruction and rehabilitation work following the disaster.*

The Man and His Mission

GSDMA's Emergency Reconstruction and Rehabilitation Programme also received the prestigious Green Award from the World Bank.

Undoubtedly, a large number of Non-Governmental Organizations (NGOs) also made substantial contributions towards rehabilitation of the earthquake victims. But such were the efforts that Modi and his government had put in that many found their achievements hard to believe. In the field of rehabilitation, for instance, three *Bal Kutirs* (Children's Homes) and three *Balika Kutirs* (Homes for Girls) were set up in record time; 998 widows were sanctioned pensions, and economic livelihood restoration projects covering 35,000 women at the cost of ₹35 crore were made operational.

The GSDMA became a model organization for all the states to follow. Expert teams from various countries such as Iran, Afghanistan, Sri Lanka and Bangladesh visited Gujarat to study the rehabilitation and reconstruction programme. It became a model programme for many tsunami and earthquake-affected countries to follow. Narendra also conceived the Gujarat Institute of Disaster Management (GIDM), which will be a nodal agency for imparting training to all stakeholders on various aspects of disaster management. Setting up of the Institute of Seismological Research (ISR) is another milestone in the earthquake reconstruction programme. It is the first of its kind to focus on pure and applied research of seismology for reducing seismological risk not only in Gujarat but in the entire country.

Today, one does not see any symptoms of large-scale destruction. There is a welcome change in the civic amenities and the infrastructure. Due to the right policies that Narendra banked upon at that time, the worst affected areas, including the district of Kutch, have seen massive industrialization after the earthquake. This industrialization has further resulted in the creation of large-scale employment opportunities and spreading of economic benefits to the people through ancillary works. As a step ahead, Narendra also undertook the work of developing and highlighting tourism spots in Kutch, including the white Rann. Sharadotsav and Ranotsav which were started in 2003-04, continue till today. Another major work was accomplished by undertaking to supply the waters of the Narmada to far-off areas. He organized people's

The Man of the Moment: Narendra Modi

committees to manage this precious resource. The experiment of people's participation earned him the Prime Minister's Award for Excellence in Public Service for 2006-07.

The villages and towns of Gujarat have been re-built with modern plans and a futuristic vision. Narendra used to say that what was needed was to convert the adversity of the earthquake into an opportunity, and indeed, events took shape in that way on account of the resilience of the people of Gujarat and the vision, planning and execution of *their* leader – Narendra Modi.

While Gujarat and the entire country were all praise for the spontaneous manner in which Narendra addressed himself to the people's problems, there was hardly a whisper of admiration from the English 'secular' media. The media, it seemed, was unaccustomed to seeing an ordinary RSS *pracharak* share the sufferings of his fellow men and women, and also acting on the spot. Narendra, it was apparent, baffled them with his ways of working. Here was a man, reportedly without any experience in the art of government, responding to events with a professionalism that just took one's breath away. That man was Narendra Modi!

HISTORY AND HYSTERIA

No other communal incident has been discussed and analysed more than the Godhra carnage and the riots that erupted in its aftermath. When thousands of incidents of communal violence have been erased from memory as soon as normalcy was restored, the dark memories of the 2002 communal riots in Godhra have been kept alive even after over a decade of peace in Gujarat. However, there are many questions that arise and remain unanswered. When the people of Gujarat are ready to move on, then why are there those who do not allow the wounds to heal? It is necessary to look at the entire episode objectively to understand the harsh reality between truth and mere propaganda.

Narendra was sworn in as chief minister of Gujarat on 7 October 2001. He was not yet a member of the state legislative assembly. In consonance with the rules, he stood for elections from the Rajkot constituency on 19 February 2002 as the BJP candidate and was declared elected on 24 February. Three days later, on 27 February, the Sabarmati Express running from Faizabad to Ahmedabad was attacked and torched at Godhra, resulting in the death of fifty-eight innocent passengers, mostly women and children.

All this happened in broad daylight and in the presence of many onlookers. A great deal has been written and said about the outrage and what followed. But nobody paid attention to the fact that this incident took place within three days of Narendra's confirmation as Gujarat's chief minister. No questions were raised, and thus, no answers were provided.

Was it just an accident or was there some organization behind it? Could it just be that someone – or some anti-BJP organization – was determined to see that Narendra would not get time to settle down and become a model chief minister?

The Man of the Moment: Narendra Modi

Could it just be the fact that someone was determined to give the RSS a bad name right from the start of Narendra's taking over as chief minister? Considering how much flak Narendra has received since then in his handling of the riots that ensued, such doubts seem only natural.

What is significant is that no one has pursued these questions to find the answers. In his book, *Gujarat: The Making of a Tragedy*, well-known journalist Siddharth Varadarajan writes:

The Ghanchis of Godhra are known as an aggressive, impulsive community, descendants of Afghan soldiers and Bhil women. They were initially harvesters and traders of oil, and later became farmers. Today, they are in the transport business. They are largely illiterate and poor, though the number of educated among them is growing. *The Ghanchis have had a long history of violent conflicts with Godhra's Hindus,* both pre and post-Independence.'

The Ghanchi community has been associated with an aggressive attitude since the very beginning. It is not surprising that in 1948, the then government (incidentally a Congress government that ruled from Bombay before linguistic states were set up) even had to order the police to set fire to Ghanchi settlements in Godhra in order to scatter them. Most of them fled to Pakistan, though, reportedly, many returned, impoverished, and were therefore easily drawn to crime.

To return to 2002, however, it is important to know the actual sequence of events that took place in Godhra on that fateful morning. This is the sequence of events provided by the Railway Protection Force (RPF):

26.02.2002: Train number 9166 UP left Muzzafarnagar for Ahmedabad.

27.02.2002, 07.43 am: Train reached Godhra four hours later than the scheduled time.

Kar sevaks returning from Ayodhya step down for tea and snacks. Scuffle between *kar sevaks* and Muslim vendors.

07.48 am: Train started for Vadodara, chain pulling from four bogies simultaneously, train halted on platform.

While railway authorities were restoring the ACP dish, a mob of Muslims start pelting stones on the train.

07.55 am: Train restarts.

07.58 am: Another chain pulling from four compartments simultaneously.

Train halted near A' cabin.

Mob comprising 900-1,000 Muslims attacked bogey number S-6 and S-5 with deadly weapons and inflammable liquids. Fifty-eight persons died while forty-eight were injured.

Hundreds of self-styled secularists and so-called activists, organizations, fact-finding missions, and self-appointed commissions visited Godhra after the incident. Every one has a theory and a conclusion and claims its findings to be *the* truth. An account by one such mission says that there was an altercation at the station between the *kar sevaks* who alighted from the train for tea and snacks and the local hawkers of the minority community. Another version spoke about the 'molestation and abduction of a girl'. Was a Muslim girl really molested? Nobody, to this day, has identified the girl who was allegedly molested or raped.

Another version that did the rounds was that the Hindu pilgrims insisted that the Muslim tea vendors pay obeisance to Lord Rama. Yet another version stated that the pilgrims refused to pay for the tea which they bought from the vendors at the station. Are these reasons enough for killing as many as fifty-eight human beings by torching them to death? Which court of justice would accept this?

In his book, *Godhra: The Missing Rage,* the author S K Modi says:

> *There was some stone pelting while the train was still at the station. Passengers of many coaches were forced to close their windows. The train started, but the emergency chain was pulled by some people and it stopped about a hundred metres away from the platform. The emergency chain is directly linked to the brakes. The chain, provided in each coach, is not a signal to the driver to halt the train. The chain itself halts the train when pulled. A fairly large crowd was pelting stones at the train when it halted but the railway police managed to disperse the crowd. The train resumed its journey. Within minutes, the emergency chain was pulled again, this time simultaneously from*

several coaches. It halted at a distance of a few hundred metres from the station. A crowd of over 1,000 surrounded the train. The leaders of this crowd had at least 140 litres of gasoline that had been bought the previous night.

The presence of over a thousand people – some reports put the figure at over two thousand – surrounding the train and pelting stones at it has never been denied or questioned. The story continues thus:

Windows of the train coach were too high for anyone to throw the fuel inside the coach while standing at the ground-level. At a platform, it is possible. Outside the platform, the windows are too high … So the culprits mounted the vestibule connecting the S-6 coach with other coaches of the train. They cut the cloth covering of the vestibule and threw the fuel inside the coach and burnt it. Passengers in that coach were not even given time to contemplate an escape route from the coach, though some did manage to escape. The whole coach was cindered. Fifty-eight passengers were burnt alive … All this happened over a period of about twenty minutes …

The television news channels showed the pictures of the burning S-6 coach and the dead bodies throughout the day. On the morning of 28 February, Godhra was the first-page story in all the leading newspapers, in English and in regional languages. The pictures, the stories, and the comments were all quite extensive …

But something was missing. The rage was missing. There was no sense of rage in the reports. There was no trace of indignation … Nobody was feeling pained or hurt. Nobody was feeling anguished at such a ghastly incident having taken place. Nobody was furious at the sheer brazenness of the gory massacre. And this applied to the elite of the society as a whole. Besides the media, no political leader, no social activist, no thinker, no analyst, no policy think tank displayed a sense of despair …

Only fifty-odd women and children killed in the blaze? As long as they happened to be the wives and children of Ram *sevaks*, our Hindu secular intellectuals couldn't have cared less. A few days after the event, Jaya Jaitley, a part of the Samata Party, wrote: '… on Godhra there was stubborn silence when the Treasury benches begged the Opposition to join in a unanimous condemnation of the event.' That shouldn't have come as a surprise to Ms Jaitley.

History and Hysteria

Not even Sonia Gandhi felt the need to call on the prime minister on 27 February. Were the RSS members, also known as Ram *sevaks*, expendable?

S K Modi further noted in *Godhra: The Missing Rage*:

> *The silence on 27 February 2002 was deafening. The indifference was complete. The insensitivity was infuriating ... But the English language media did not stop at indifference. Its attitude was outright callous. Everybody knew that only Muslims lived in Signal Falia, where the train was stopped and the S-6 coach, along with 58 human beings, was burnt. Yet, the media refused to say that it was a Muslim mob that attacked Hindu pilgrims. Some called the attackers just a mob; some called them unidentified people. The standard dictum that 'naming names creates problems' prevented the media from pointing an accusing finger at a particular community.*

The *Asian Age* on 28 February 2002, for instance, stated:

> *A mob of 1,500, reportedly belonging to a minority community, attacked a bogie of the Sabarmati Express ferrying VHP activists ... using iron rods and swords, and hacked to death over 50 passengers ... Inflammable substances were thrown into the coach which led to a fire in a portion of the bogie and several passengers were charred to death.*

These words give the whole story an unimaginably vague aspect. The mob 'reportedly' belonged to a minority community. Reportedly? Was it a Hindu mob or Muslim?

The Hindu story went thus:

> *Fifty-seven persons, mostly women and children, were killed and 43 sustained burn injuries when a coach carrying Ram sevaks was set afire by a group of people on the outskirts of the Godhra railway station ...*

For *The Hindu*, it was simply 'a group of people', not a 'mob' that set the coach afire.

What *NDTV* said on the day of the incident was equally *revealing*. It reported:

> *At least 57 people are feared killed and 43 injured, as unidentified persons attacked and set on fire four bogies of an Express train carrying hundreds of kar sevaks near Godhra railway station in Gujarat.*

The Man of the Moment: Narendra Modi

Some fifty-seven people were mentioned without specifying the number of women and children who were a part of the dead; they were feared killed, not really killed. To say that would be adding fuel to fire. In fairness to the English-language media, note must be taken of the first report that appeared in the *Times of India* under the by-line of Sajid Shaikh on 28 February 2002. It read:

> Godhra: In a ghastly incident which has shocked the collective conscience of the entire nation, at least 58 people were burnt alive and many injured when the Ahmedabad-bound Sabarmati Express was stoned and set on fire by a mob at Godhra junction Wednesday morning. The victims were mostly VHP volunteers returning from Ayodhya with their families after participating in a religious ceremony for the construction of the Ram Mandir.
>
> The dead included 25 women and 14 children, most of whom were in the S-6 coach which was completely charred as the mob put petrol cans to deadly use. About 36 persons were rushed to the Godhra Civil Hospital with burn injuries. Survivors said the train was first pelted with stones and petrol bombs around 7.30 am, a couple of hundred metres from Godhra Junction. As it left the railway station, the train was stopped near Signal Falia, a notorious area of Godhra, as someone apparently pulled the chain. A mob rushed towards the two coaches (S-6 and S-7) pelting stones initially. Once the windows were broken, they threw petrol bombs inside. Later, said the survivors, the S-6 coach was doused with petrol and diesel from outside and set on fire even as passengers looked on helplessly, screaming for help ... The Panchmahal's Raju Bhargava said that the police have identified five persons who may have masterminded the attack ... At 11 am the coach stood badly burnt, with a heap of bodies strewn across ....

Shaikh quoted a first-hand account by a survivor, Hirabhai Ummed Das:

> About 500 to 1,000 people started pelting stones. They broke the railings, threw petrol bombs inside. We tried to climb the upper berths, but soon smoke engulfed the coach and there was panic. I was pulled out from a window ....

Notes S K Modi:

> It is the self-righteous rage of the English language media and the elite, immediately following the complete lack of concern for the

incendiary deaths, that enraged the masses as much as, if not more than, the Godhra carnage itself.

Because of what had happened at Godhra, because of the complete lack of empathy on the part of the English language media and the elite, and because of the hideous attempts at protecting the perpetrators of the inhuman carnage and the veiled threats of recurrence of similar incidents of terrorism hinted at by the media, Gujarat went into a frenzy on the afternoon of February 28, 2002 ....

When communal riots had taken place in earlier times during Congress regimes, the English media did not seem unduly bothered. But how could the media ignore the fact that an RSS *pracharak*, and an exceedingly effective one at that, who had the good of the people in his heart, and was at the helm of the state, be let off!

The documents pertaining to the actions taken by the government are in great detail, but for our purpose, we will highlight a few vital steps taken. Apart from what happened, the general public does not know about the steps taken by the government after the Godhra carnage to prevent violent reactions from the enraged public and maintain peace. The steps inter alia included:

- A state-wide alert was issued on 27 February, directing the law enforcement agencies to take all possible steps to maintain law and order.
- It was ensured that the dead bodies of the Godhra victims were not brought to Ahmedabad Civil Hospital but were taken to a Civil Hospital away from the city at Sola to prevent any vitiation of the atmosphere in Ahmedabad and elsewhere. It was also decided that a mass funeral be held in order to prevent tension in many areas.
- A curfew was imposed in Godhra instantly on 27 February. Starting from the morning of 28 February, a curfew was imposed at places like Vadodara, Ahmedabad city, Sabarkantha and other several sensitive places. Many other urban areas came under curfew on 1 March. The chief minister held a high-level meeting to review the situation and appeal for peace.

- The government mobilized the entire state police force and the Reserve Police to meet the emerging situation.
- The Rapid Action Force (RAF) was called and deployed instantly at Ahmedabad City, Vadodara and Godhra from the afternoon of 27 February.
- Paramilitary forces were called and deployed at sensitive places.
- Several repeat alert messages were sent on 28 February calling for preventive steps to ensure security of all religious places, including mosques.
- On 28 February, the government of India was requested for the help of the armed forces. There were no armed forces stationed in Ahmedabad and those stationed in border areas had to be airlifted to Ahmedabad, Vadodara and Rajkot.
- Two brigades were deployed at sensitive places in Ahmedabad city on the morning of 1 March 2002.
- Police authorities were asked to monitor the situation round the clock. Shoot-at-sight orders were issued.

Does one seriously believe – as the secular critics would want us to – that a chief minister who, on learning that fifty-eight women and children had been burnt alive in a railway coach in broad daylight, kept quiet, when what he actually did was to promptly call for the help of the RAF and the Army! In fact, Narendra Modi had rushed to Godhra on the very day, winding up the proceedings of the Gujarat Legislative Assembly. But the 'secular' press was determined to launch a full-blast attack against him.

There is no doubt, however, that large-scale riots followed the Godhra carnage. But what is interesting to note is that no one had bothered to make a study of the riots that had taken place in the past when the Congress party had been in power. This time, no one tried to question what it was that had made the otherwise peace-loving people go mad. The whole effort of the English media was to damn Modi. There was no division in the matter of Godhra between BJP Hindus and Congress Hindus. The viciousness of the English media only served to rouse deep anger among all Gujaratis, barring professional secularists.

History and Hysteria

During the Mumbai riots in the past, the *Times of India* had put the figure of those killed at 872 in an article titled 'The X Files: Where the Mob Goes Scot-free' (13 July 2003). Following the assassination of Indira Gandhi on 31 October 1984, the paper gave the number of those killed as 2,733. They were mostly Sikhs and the figure included women and children as well. Nobody called it a 'genocide' though Sikhs were killed in the most gruesome manner. A report written by the leading Indian journalist M J Akbar in the *Telegraph* (2 November 1984) makes for sickening reading. Describing the killing of Sikhs and the looting of Sikh shops, Akbar wrote: 'The police simply looked the other way ... The looters were totally unembarrassed. The desire for revenge was the controlling theme of the day ....'

True, Muslims were killed in Gujarat following the gruesome burning of two coaches by a Muslim crowd of about five hundred to two thousand. When Sikhs were killed in Delhi and elsewhere following the assassination of Indira Gandhi, it was called 'an act of revenge'. In this situation, the coaches were full of Hindu pilgrims returning from Ayodhya. They had not killed anybody in Ayodhya, so there is no question of 'revenge', which went to the extent of burning innocent women and children alive, along with the *kar sevaks*. And yet, Muslim crowds openly set fire to coaches that carried Hindu pilgrims. The reaction was terrible because not one but as many as fifty-eight people, mostly women and children, had been incinerated. But to call it 'genocide' shows a sense of imbalance for which secularists are notorious.

The BJP Executive met in Goa in April 2002. By that time, Narendra Modi had been barraged with the full blast of 'secular' criticism that had been aimed at him beyond the scope of all reason. Out of disgust, Narendra offered his resignation from the post of chief minister. But his offer was rejected. At a public meeting held on 12 April in Goa, Prime Minister Vajpayee said:

'... If a conspiracy had not been hatched to burn alive the innocent passengers of the Sabarmati Express, then the subsequent tragedy in Gujarat could have been averted. But this did not happen. People were torched alive. Who were the culprits? The government is investigating. Intelligence agencies are collecting information. But we should not forget how the tragedy of Gujarat started. The subsequent developments were no doubt condemnable, but who lit the fire? How did the fire spread?

'Ours is a multi-religious country, a multilingual country; we have many different modes of worship. We believe in peaceful and harmonious coexistence. We believe in equal respect for all faiths. Let no one challenge India's secularism ... We do not believe in religious extremism. Today, the threat to our nation comes from terrorism.

'... Now, other nations in the world have started to realize what a great mistake they made by neglecting terrorism. Now they are waking up and organizing themselves. They are putting together an international consensus against terrorism.

'We tell them through our own example that a large number of non-Hindus live in our country, but there never has been religious persecution here. We have never discriminated between "our people" and "aliens". The modes of worship may differ, but God is one. It is for this reason that India's prestige is growing.'

The most shocking part of the Gujarat riots was that self-styled Gandhians, Congressmen and 'secularists' did nothing to stop the killings. The Ahmedabad Municipal Corporation had a Congress majority, but did any Congressman come out into the streets to protest against the killings and protect those who were getting killed and whose shops were being looted? To the best of one's knowledge, not one dared.

Wasn't it the immediate duty of the Congress president, Sonia Gandhi, to call on the Gujarat Pradesh Congress Committee chief and order him to organize a riot-fighting operation in the affected areas? Similarly, shouldn't she have ordered every Congress MP to rush to Ahmedabad to organize and provide immediate succour to the distressed? Nothing of the kind was done. The secularists stayed comfortably in their homes as did Congressmen, while the killings and looting were going on. It was easier to stay at home and put the blame on Narendra Modi and the VHP. It made them feel morally very superior.

To say that the riots were organized is absurd. However, there is evidence that setting fire to the coaches was an organized act.

History and Hysteria

The riots were a consequence. At such times, logic, reason and humanitarianism are thrown out of the window and passion rules. Narendra was reported as quoting Newton's law that every action has an equal and opposite reaction; he denied having said that. In an emotion-charged atmosphere, reaction is often more volatile than expected, howsoever much it is condemnable.

It would be necessary to recall what Rajiv Gandhi said about the killing of Sikhs following the assassination of Indira Gandhi in 1984. Author Inder Malhotra writes in his book *Dynasties of India and Beyond*:

'He [Rajiv Gandhi] had been slow to control the shameful anti-Sikh riots in Delhi and some surrounding areas that had begun immediately after Indira was killed. More disgracefully, there was also evidence to show that several Congress (I) leaders had joined in engineering the pogrom. To make matters worse, Rajiv insensitively told a public meeting that "when a big tree falls, the earth is bound to shake". If this statement was regrettable, as it certainly was, some of Rajiv's tactics during the subsequent election campaign were downright deplorable ... He played very heavily on the anti-Sikh sentiment, appeased Hindu chauvinism much like Indira had tried to do during the early 1980s, and attacked his political opponents as virulentely as she had often done. Being a modern-minded man, enthusiastic about hi-tech, he also used newspaper and TV advertising on a much bigger scale than she had ever done. Some of the advertisements were in very poor taste, hurtful and divisive. . . .'

Rajiv Gandhi, considered to be a secular icon, behaved the way most human beings would have behaved. Where he should have played the part of a responsible leader of a secular country, he arguably misguided many people.

Consider what Inder Malhotra said about Rajiv Gandhi. He was 'slow to control' the riots. Was the delay purposeful? Were the riots an act of genocide? And what was said of 'several' Congress (I) leaders – that they joined in 'engineering the pogrom'? There are times, alas, when passions are roused and idealism goes overboard. This happened in 1948 when Nathuram Godse assassinated Mahatma Gandhi. As a result of that, Congressmen went in search of Brahmin houses in Pune to kill and loot. Under extraordinary circumstances, people – even those who are otherwise good and devoid of extremely violent tendencies – respond in unusual ways.

In Delhi, in 1984, the mobs were led not by the VHP, but by Congressmen. Nobody described the riots as genocide. The case in Gujarat after the deliberate incineration of fifty-eight innocent Hindus by a Muslim crowd was similar. A Gujarat government report did not minimize what happened. It stated:

'In the cities and towns, a thoroughly provoked cross-section of people, rich and poor, educated and illiterate, businessmen, labourers, came out on the streets in their thousands. It was high-pitched mob frenzy. Villagers, including tribals, went on a rampage in Gujarat against the Muslims. It was seen that certain traditional and old socio-economic exploitative factors played a role in provoking tribals against the minority community.'

The report did not play down the riot-proneness of Gujarat either. It maintained:

'Gujarat's history is beset with communal flare-ups on the slightest pretext, including kite-flying. Riots on account of communal and socio-political reasons are a known phenomenon in the state. In the communal riots of 1969, 660 persons were killed; 208 died in the 1985 riots; 219 in the 1990 riots, and 441 in the 1992 riots ... In fact, since 1970, 440 riots have taken place in Gujarat. The above-mentioned ones were the most severe.'

The report went on to mention:

'However, this time (2002), because of the mass burning of the innocent *kar sevaks*, the provocation was extreme, the anger was at its maximum and directed towards an identified community. There was already an accumulated anger against the fundamentalist forces because of the attack on Parliament, the controversy regarding Ayodhya and the situation on the border with Pakistan.

'Most of the violent incidents occurred between 27 February and 5 March 2002. Out of the total of 741 deaths reported till 5 March, 611 occurred in that one week when mass anger was at its peak. After a period of relative normalcy of about fifteen days,

History and Hysteria

the situation deteriorated again; this time it happened because Muslim forces were mobilized for retaliatory action. Secular writers are reticent about what happened during this period. In Bharuch, Muslim mobs burnt shops and wagons belonging to the majority community. Curfew had to be imposed quickly. The next day at Modasa in Sabarkantha district in north Gujarat, a thousand Muslims gathered and went on a rampage. Innocent people were targetted; the son of a police inspector was stabbed, but quick action brought the situation under control.'

It is stated that the second phase of violence, during which the Muslim community took the lead, was well organized. What happened to a scheduled caste employee in the Sales Tax Department is beastly beyond description. He was first reported as 'missing'. But after twenty-five days, his body, brutally cut into twenty-five pieces, was discovered buried near a relief camp of riot-affected Muslims. There was no explanation available as to why he was killed.

The third phase of the disturbances started when the Gujarat government decided to hold the annual board examinations. During this period, the so-called 'secular' media played a dirty role. An analysis of the events published by the *Hindu Vivek Kendra*, an academic branch of the *Hindutva* movement, stated:

'The exams in Gujarat to be held in early March were postponed due to riots in the state. When the Gujarat government decided to hold the exams according to a revised schedule, the English media termed it irresponsible, claiming that the situation was still not normal. As an expression of its sincerity, the government made special transport arrangements for the students, especially those living in the refugee camps and in the sensitive areas of the city.'

A concerted effort was made by various Muslim leaders and 'secularists' to create a sense of insecurity amongst the students. The English media reported instances of some of the local Muslim leaders in Ahmedabad forcibly taking the children out of the buses.

According to a report in The *Indian Express* (19 March 2002), at some points from where Muslim students were to be bussed under police guard to centres in the city's riot-free western parts, some Muslim leaders stood by trying to coerce candidates to boycott the exams. Some of the students, who were already in the bus, were forced to get off. The newspaper report says that the family members had to make their own private arrangements for transporting their wards to the examination centres. While The *Indian Express* reported that nine thousand out of fourteen thousand students took the exams on the first day of the revised schedule, The *Times of India* said that only 10 per cent did so. The latter in its editorial dated 20 April termed the 10 per cent figures as 'predictable'.

The fourth phase of the riots began on the morning of 5 May 2002, when organized and aggressive attacks by the minority community at Parikshitnagar in Ahmedabad city let loose a chain of violent incidents and group clashes.

The fundamentalist forces were disappointed that examinations were going on peacefully and most of the students, including those from the minority community, had appeared for the examinations, defying a fatwa. The minority students had set an excellent example by attending the examinations in overwhelming numbers.

What surprised many was the flexibility shown by the government towards students to facilitate them in appearing for the examinations. Examination centres were earmarked on a need-to-need basis, late entries were permitted and students were given more time. Students who had lost their entry slips were accommodated. Finally, the government also decided that the students who were not able to appear in the examinations for the last three days would be separately provided with an opportunity to take them, which it did.

The Secular Gossamer 8

Undeniably, the fallout of the Godhra incident was ugly violence by both Hindus and Muslims. However, the deliberate attempts made by the secularists to exaggerate certain incidents undoubtedly raise questions of credibility.

Reports were spread about a pregnant Muslim woman whose stomach was allegedly ripped open and her foetus taken out and burnt. A film of doubtful authenticity showing the incident was circulated. That anybody would attempt to undertake such a heinous act and let the whole incident be filmed calls for questioning.

This was first mentioned on 6 March 2002 in a BBC report. The reporter, however, stated that the story was uncorroborated, but he felt 'duty-bound' to mention it. The next reference to it was in an article by Harsh Mander in The *Times of India* on 20 March. Meanwhile, a report appeared on the Tehelka website on 19 April which stated that one Saira Banu had spoken about her sister-in-law being the victim of the gory incident. The narration gave an indication that Saira Banu was a witness to the tragic incident and also that it actually happened. In the very next paragraph, the report acknowledged that the story had been heard from many others, but that the details varied. For an event, which was fully filmed, it has never been clarified how the details could be so different.

Then there is the instance of the writer and social activist, Arundhati Roy, talking of a story where a Muslim woman was caught by a mob, which ripped open her stomach and then stuffed it with burning rags. Balbir Punj, a Rajya Sabha MP, immediately got in touch with the Gujarat police to verify the story, only to be told that no such incident had been reported to them. When the police sought Roy's help to identify the victim and seek access to witnesses who could lead them to those guilty of the crime, her response through her lawyer was that the police had no powers to issue summons to her.

In a lengthy article in *Outlook,* Roy had reported about the daughters of Ehsaan Jaffri, the ex-MP from the Congress party, being killed along with him in Ahmedabad. Jaffri's son replied by writing that his sisters were not in the city at the time of the riots and that, in fact, one of them was living in the United States. When the discrepancy was pointed out to Roy, her reply was that she had got the information from two other sources, one a report in the *Time* magazine and another an 'independent fact-finding mission' that consisted of a former inspector general of police of Tripura and a former finance secretary, Government of India. In her reply she is quoted as having written: 'This and other genuine errors in recounting the details of the violence in Gujarat in no way alters the substance of what journalists, fact-finding missions, or writers like myself are saying.'

Malicious Myths

The media may have immense power in our country, but it may not always be truthful. It propagated many myths.

Myth No 1: The Entire State Was Burning

It is to be remembered here that violence took place not in the entire state, but in about forty locations out of a total of 248 towns and 18,000 villages. Many of them have a history of communal riots. Unlike past riots, these riots in Gujarat were strictly confined to a limited number of areas in the state and did not spread to other states. But the impression created by the media was that the entire state was burning. In Ahmedabad, though initially the violence occurred in historically non-sensitive areas, the later phase of violence took place in sensitive areas only, and the last three phases were limited to historically the most-sensitive areas alone.

Myth No 2: Only Muslims Were Killed!

Another myth propagated by the media was that only Muslims were killed in these riots. The various phases of riots left 254 Hindus and 790 Muslims dead as mentioned in a report given by the Union Minister of State for Home, Shriprakash Jaiswal of the Congress party, in the Parliament on 11 May 2005[1]. As many

---

1 From www.indiya.com

as 104 Muslims and 80 Hindus died in police firing[2]. During the riots, about 1,180 Hindus and 1,164 Muslims were injured.

Myth No 3: Gujarat's Economy Was in Shambles

The next myth that did the rounds was about the economy of the state. It was said that the economy in Gujarat suffered a great deal due to the riots. But facts were to prove these reports wrong. According to the Gujarat Chamber of Commerce and Industry (GCCI), some fifteen per cent of small, medium and tiny units were affected by the riots. But by and large, industry remained untouched. According to the GCCI, around 600 hotels, restaurants and parlours incurred losses to the tune of some ₹200 crore. However, the figures were later corrected and it was found that around 220 hotels or so were affected with losses amounting to ₹10 crore. Insurance claims were made by 4,767 persons for an aggregate sum of ₹168 crore.

A good indicator of the state of the economy was the functioning of banks in Ahmedabad, the worst-affected city. According to the available data, 47.74 lakh cheques were cleared for an aggregate amount of ₹25,531 crore between 1 March 2002 and 15 April 2002. In January 2002, as many as thirty-five lakh cheques had been cleared for an amount of ₹17,724 crore, whereas in February, thirty-two lakh cheques were cleared for an amount of ₹16,754 crore. That is a clear indication that cheque clearances during the time of the riots were quite normal.

It was also said that as a result of the riots, foreign investors would shy away. Nothing of that sort happened. An important agreement was signed at Gandhinagar indicating how misleading the media had been. The agreement, involving an investment of ₹5,200 crore, was between the Royal Dutch Shell Company and the port authorities for the development of the Hajira Port. At the same time, General Motors declared its plans for expanding its plant at Halol, near Godhra, with an additional investment of ₹500 crore.

Despite communal riots, the state maintained its share of 16.73 per cent of the total investment in the country. This goes to show that there was no adverse impact on the investment climate in

---

[2] As published by the Concerned Citizens Tribunal in Gujarat in 2002.

the state. According to official figures, out of a total investment of ₹10,85,383 crore in the country, Gujarat bagged ₹1,80,577 crore despite all attempts to malign the state. Within just three months of the riots, foreign companies went to Gujarat with huge projects amounting to ₹7,58,000 crore.

In 2002, Gujarat ranked number two in industrial investments in the country. Its share in the country was 16.73 per cent as stated above, and its share of industrial production was 13 per cent. Due to these positive indicators, the Resurgent Gujarat Meet-2002, held from 8-10 February 2002 at Ahmedabad, and jointly organized by the Federation of Indian Chambers of Commerce and Industry (FICCI), GCCI, the Ministry of External Affairs, GOI and the Government of Gujarat, was attended by delegates from the US, UK, Japan, China, Germany and Singapore. Sixty-two projects involving investments of crores of rupees were discussed. Under the circumstances, the efforts of some of India's leading national newspapers to malign the state only sounded ridiculous!

Myth No 4: The Police Forces and the Government Took No Real Action

A full-scale statewide alert was sounded on 27 February 2008 for taking precautionary and preventive measures and to deal with anti-social and hardcore communal elements firmly. There are many indicators to tell us that most of Gujarat was unaffected and things returned to normalcy due to the efforts of the state government. Some of these indicators include:

- From 18-28 March 2002, the SSC and HSC Board examinations were conducted smoothly. More than nine lakh students took the examinations in about one thousand centres. On an average, the attendance was ninety-eight per cent which was at par with previous records. For students of Ahmedabad and Vadodara, and others who could not sit for the first part of the Board examinations, fresh examinations were held from 18 April 2002.
- University examinations and all internal examinations in schools were conducted peacefully.
- In a Special Civil Application (SCA) number 3389 of 2002 (Prakash B Zaveri vs State of Gujarat), the honourable

judges observed that there was no reason to assume that the situation in the places where examinations were being held was not conducive to holding examinations, and the state government had made adequate arrangements to hold the examinations.

In SCA number 373 of 2002 (Mukti Anvar Ahmed Siddiqui vs State of Gujarat), the honourable High Court observed that the report submitted by the state government clearly showed that minute details were furnished about the facilities given to the inhabitants of the relief camps. Reading the report, *prima facie*, the high court felt that more than reasonable care had been taken by the administration to look after the inhabitants of the camps.

- Within six months of the Godhra incident, 1,700 village panchayats went to elections from 11 March 2002 and the election process was completed without any unfavourable incident. In fact, thirty-seven per cent of the panchayats were elected unanimously. Polls were peaceful.
- Moharram passed off peacefully and around two thousand *tajias* (replicas of the mausoleum of Iman Hussain) were taken out in March 2002 (The *Daily Pioneer*, 25 April 2002).
- Around six thousand Haj pilgrims returned to the state and were warmly welcomed in the villages during March 2002 (The *Daily Pioneer*, 25 April 2002).

Riots and post-riot rehabilitation efforts are not new activities for Gujarat administration, but the efforts made by Narendra Modi's government to provide relief and rehabilitation were swift and noteworthy. All efforts were undertaken to provide temporary shelter, food and recovery of livelihood, business and housing rehabilitation.

Initially, the state government announced a package of uniform benefits to be given to all affected industrial units, large shops, showrooms, hotels and warehouses as under:

- Four per cent interest subsidy on term loans, working capital loan requirements for restoration limited to ₹1 lakh per annum for a period of three years.

- Sales tax deferment for a period of five years limited to seventy-five per cent of the quantum of damage minus the insurance claim received, repayable in thirty-six monthly instalments thereafter.
- Deferment of electricity duty for a period of one year, repayable in six monthly instalments thereafter.
- After the announcement of the prime minister's package of ₹150 crore, a component of twenty per cent capital subsidy to be given on the total cost of the project was introduced, subject to a maximum ceiling of ₹50,000 per unit. This was in addition to the benefit already announced by the state government.
- Twenty per cent subsidy for the purchase of commercial vehicles subject to a maximum of ₹50,000.

At the same time, the Reserve Bank of India (RBI) announced certain relief measures that turned out to be more liberal than similar packages implemented in the past under similar circumstances:

- Cash doles were increased threefold from ₹5 per day to ₹15 per day per person.
- Household assistance was doubled from ₹650 to ₹1,250 and was then further raised to ₹2,500 in the wake of the Prime Minister's Relief Fund.
- Ex gratia assistance of ₹1 lakh for death, later increased to ₹1.5 lakhs.
- Assistance for injury and incapacitation up to ₹50,000.
- Provision of shelter, free sanitary and health services.
- Regular health check-up by the different teams attached to the refugee camps.

No deadline was set for closing the relief camps. Contrary to the information spread by certain interested parties, the chief minister was constantly monitoring relief and rehabilitation measures.

A World Health Organization (WHO) report dated 22 April 2002 on medical and health services provided at Gujarat relief camp sites mentioned:

- Mobile medical teams equipped with medical officers, trained para-medical staff, medicines, vaccines and other logistics have been visiting various campsites regularly under the supervision and direction of additional director (Public Health) and other senior health officials camping at SIHEW, Sola and Ahmedabad.
- Chlorination of water, sanitation and personal hygiene are being addressed in consultation with the Ahmedabad municipal health authorities.
- Specialist services have been made available for needy patients at these relief campsites.
- Mental health problems are addressed by providing psycho-social support services at the campsites.
- There is no epidemiological incidence of water-borne, vector-borne or vaccine-preventable diseases reported from the campsites.

Routine immunization services were made available. Measles immunization was provided to 7,792 children in these campsites during the second and third weeks of March 2002 which prevented a measles outbreak in the state of Gujarat during the otherwise favourable season for the virus. Due care (in terms of diet, vitamin A, antibiotics) was given to unprotected children with symptoms of measles.

The above healthcare and welfare activities were undertaken uniformly for people from different backgrounds under the leadership of Narendra Modi, as even the WHO report verifies. Why did the secular press then shoot all their cannons at the chief minister?

What really triggered the Godhra incident? What really happened? What is the truth and what are the rumours? Rumours, half-truths and lies were paraded in the form of truth. The media, particularly the electronic media, played an important role in fanning the violence. In the first communal violence of the satellite TV era, naming communities and showing dead bodies repeatedly aggravated the feelings of anger and hatred and abetted in prolonging the riots. The report *of Outlook's* correspondent in Ahmedabad read:

The Man of the Moment: Narendra Modi

> On Wednesday, 27 February, groggy passengers were waking up to a warm, sunny morning as the Ahmedabad-bound Sabarmati Express pulled into the Godhra railway station off Baroda at 7.20 am. Slogans of Jai Shri Ram rent the air as the train carrying a sprinking of kar sevaks came to a halt. With thoughts of getting home uppermost in their minds, weary passengers alighted for tea and bhajias. Nothing seemed out of the ordinary ... Even a confrontation between two vendors and some passengers over a petty matter seemed routine and no one spared it a thought as the train left Godhra after a brief halt.
>
> It must have proceeded barely a kilometre when it stopped in its tracks – someone had pulled the emergency chain ... Suddenly, a fusillade of stones smashed into the windowpanes of the second class sleeper coach S-6 in which VHP volunteers were travelling. In coach S-6 as in other bogies, passengers panicked and pulled down window shutters and bolted the doors. Soon burning rags and acid bulbs landed inside the compartments while the mob rained petrol from outside. Within minutes the coach was blazing and the fire spread to the adjoining coaches. Innocent passengers in S-6 were roasted alive ...
>
> The news of the torching set all of Gujarat on fire. The situation became even more volatile as rumours that the mob had attacked the Sabarmati Express, kidnapped Hindu women and raped them, spread like wildfire. Vernacular newspapers duly splashed the news prominently the next day. Though subsequently scotched by the government, the damage had already been done ...' All hell broke loose on February 28 ...

The extent to which rioting spread can be gauged from the fact that twenty-six cities and towns including Ahmedabad, Baroda, Rajkot and Surat had to be placed under curfew. Hitherto an urban phenomenon, communal riots this time spread to the smaller towns and rural areas.

Although taken by surprise, the government acted fast and called for help from the armed forces. The *Hindu* reported on 2 March 2002:

> The army began flag marches in the worst affected areas of Ahmedabad, Baroda, Rajkot and Godhra cities and 'shoot-at-sight' order was extended to all 34 curfew-bound cities and towns in Gujarat ...'

The media ran amok and began a campaign against the Gujarat chief minister. It broke all rules of civilized journalism. The TV media was as much, if not even more guilty, of fanning violence. Sevanti Ninan, writing her column on the media in The *Hindu* on 10 March 2002 said:

> *Two things stood out in the media conduct during the communal riot which is rather tiredly being logged as the first communal riot for the satellite TV era.* One *was the naming of the communities which the media has been circumspect about doing in the past. One STAR TV report by Rajdeep Sardesai talked of a mob identifying Muslims and then setting them alight. The Government's case is that such reporting was watched in the villages and reacted to by further violence. The other was the live filming of pitched battles as well as attacks on cars, including that of George Fernandes, as well as those used by the channels. Violence was carried live.*
>
> *Certainly, Barkha Dutt's reporting on a 90-kilometre rural stretch where she said violence was taking place and there was not even a single constable in sight along the entire stretch, irked the government. Graphic pictures of violence and pitched battles were also shown at another point. Dutt's reports and those of Rajdeep Sardesai alarmed those who watched. Some fellow journalists thought Dutt was being hysterical ....*

What Sevanti Ninan's above article says is – though not unambiguously – that the media behaved most irresponsibly. Not only did it prolong the riots, it was in a way responsible for the death of many innocents too.

The Gujarat police was condemned for not acting on time, and sometimes for not acting at all. But R K Raghavan, a distinguished senior police commissioner, wrote in *Frontline* on 16 March 2002:

> *In Gujarat, by their own admission, the police were clearly outnumbered. I have no reason to disbelieve them. I have seen this happening again and again whenever a major calamity took place. This was one major complaint that was levelled against the entire Gujarat administration during last year's earthquake too. In a country of India's proportion, there is definitely a need for more than the two million policemen (including those in the paramilitary forces) that we now have. But then, can we afford to keep on adding numbers?*

Raghavan was critical of the failure of the intelligence agencies, for not having discovered the plot behind the Godhra incident early enough, especially because this was a crime that bore signs of elaborate preparation. He took note of the fact that there was a 'gap of nearly 24 hours between the incident (setting the coach on fire) and the commencement of the *bandh*.'

Raghavan wrote something worth noting about the media:

> Most people mention the undiplomatic response of the Ahmedabad police commissioner to a television reporter's comment that the police could not remain uninfluenced by the milieu in which they lived, to be an unexceptionable statement. What the reporter said was 100 per cent true. The only quarrel: should he have been so blunt during a live and developing situation? From my own experience, I know how difficult an art this is, especially when you are quizzed by the likes of Rajdeep Sardesai and Barkha Dutt ...

That is the trouble with the media, especially television, which believes in indulging in heroics to show how brave and committed they are and how concerned they are to establish justice in the world – even if that only adds to incitement and thus, more killings.

But what Raghavan said at the end deserves to be digested fully by all concerned. He wrote:

> In sum, the Gujarat police have not exactly distinguished themselves in recent weeks ... The question, however, is whether they alone are blameworthy. Everyone of us knows that when a seething sea of humanity pours out into the streets, neither the police nor the army can be equal to the situation. The entire polity will have to bear the responsibility for having brought about this mess. What we need today are opinion leaders in the community who firmly believe in the wisdom and the ethics of burying religious differences and putting up a credible front of harmony before the common man. If they themselves appear to dither, a wrong message gets disseminated, with disastrous consequences to public peace. I believe that this is what happened in Gujarat. I am not sanguine that we will be able to get rid of the canker of communalism in the near future.

In this, the media has a singularly large responsibility. TV reporters should be forbidden to show killings or to identify victims. More damage was done in inflaming public opinion than was suspected, when a leading English weekly put the picture of a frightened Muslim on the cover page.

To make a study of media reportage, India First Foundation conducted a research on news and views published in six national dailies: The *Times of India, Hindustan Times,* The *Indian Express,* The *Statesman,* The *Hindu* and The *Telegraph.* The nationwide survey was presented at the seminar on 'Godhra and After: The Role of Media' on 6 April 2002 by the C-Voters Team. The survey, conducted in twenty-four cities (including seventeen state capitals) between 26 and 31 March 2002, revealed not only prejudiced and partisan reporting on the riots in Godhra and other parts of Gujarat, but also exposed their provocative nature. The survey results said that 44 per cent people out of a total of 2,203 respondents felt that the coverage by the TV channels was biased, against thirty-one per cent who termed it as fair. In western India, sixty-nine per cent respondents believed that the coverage by TV channels was biased. In the national dailies, soft words were used to describe the killings of Hindus in reports, editorials and commentaries. But the killings of Muslims were described through hard expressions such as 'hacked', 'butchered' and 'murdered'.

Immediately following the torching of the Sabarmati Express coaches, when it became evident that riots had started, the help of the Army was requested. Additional help from neighbouring states was also sought. A state-wide alert was sounded and curfew (prohibitory orders) was imposed wherever required. In the clashes, both communities had to suffer. The severity of the situation can be understood by the fact that out of a total of 1,037 deaths, 611 occurred during the very first three days. The police action was strong and can be seen from the fact that out of 196 deaths in police firing, 101 deaths occurred during the same period of three days. Out of these, 61 were Hindus. People's Committees were formed to maintain peace. 4,260 offences were registered and appropriate action taken. At several places, the police and other local officials saved thousands of lives and a large number of properties of the minority community. This aspect was conveniently forgotten by the media! The National Human Rights Commission (NHRC) took note of the good work done by the officials in handling the law and order situation as well as the rescue and relief operations at many places.

OF COMMISSIONS AND REALITY 9

At this point, it may be relevant to take note of the reports on the Gujarat riots, one brought out by the NHRC and another by a Committee headed by Justice D S Tewatia. Interestingly, they all but contradict each other.

At the time of the NHRC report, Justice J S Verma was its chairperson. Other members who were a part of that team were Secretary General P C Sen, Special Rapporteur Chaman Lal, and Y S R Murthy, Personal Secretary to the chairman. The second and final report submitted by the NHRC on 31 May 2002 held the state government squarely responsible for the riots and said that the facts indicate 'a complicity that was tacit if not explicit'. The report recommended handing over of the cases for investigation to the Central Bureau of Investigation (CBI) to ensure impartiality.

The NHRC's fifty-three-page report concluded that 'there is no doubt in the opinion of this Commission that there was comprehensive failure on the part of the State Government to control the persistent violation of the rights to life, liberty, equality and dignity of the people of the state.'

Quoting the central principle of administration of criminal justice, the report said:

> Those against whom allegations are made should not themselves be entrusted with the investigation of these allegations ... It would be a travesty of the principles of criminal justice if such cases were not transferred to the CBI.

The report urged the Centre to intervene under Article 355 of the Constitution and 'go beyond a mere invocation of the existing rules' in cases where the CBI should take up a case against 'politically connected persons named by the victims of the crimes committed' and who 'remained at large, many defying arrest.' The report added that 'these are grave matters that must not be allowed to be forgiven or forgotten.'

Reiterating intelligence failure as the cause for the violence, the report stated that 'the response of the State Government (in its official report) has been unable to rebut this presumption.' The report added:

> Till 10 May 2002, of 16,245 persons arrested for substantive offence, all but 2,100 have been granted bail. Of the 11,363 Hindus arrested for such offences, 8 per cent remain in custody, while 20 per cent of the 4,882 Muslims arrested remained in custody.

On the matter of attacks on women and children, the report read:

> That report (of the Gujarat government submitted on 12 April 2002) also testifies to the assault on the dignity and worth of the human person, particularly of women and children, through acts of rape and other humiliating crimes of violence and cruelty.

Further, the report maintained that victims of atrocities, including rape, were having difficulties in 'having First Information Reports (FIRs) recorded, in naming those whom they had identified and in securing copies of their FIRs.' The report said that many women were not coming forward for recording FIRs because often there were no policewomen at relief camps or due to insensitive questioning and too few police desks that worked only for a few days in a week and stayed open for just two hours on those days.

Significantly, the NHRC report itself fails to understand the nature of Muslim intolerence and the excessive use of violence time and again. The report is totally one sided and fails to understand, let alone accept, the nature of the majority community's angst in the face of constant and arrogant bullying by the minority community. The report has nothing to say about the role of the Pakistani Inter-Services Intelligence (ISI) in provoking violence.

As the NHRC went into action, another body led by Justice D S Tewatia, former Chief Justice of the Calcutta, Punjab and Haryana

The Man of the Moment: Narendra Modi

High Courts, was looking into the Godhra outrage and the riots that followed. Justice Tewatia was appointed by the Delhi-based Council for International Affairs and Human Rights (CIAHR).

The Justice Tewatia team spent four days interviewing a large number of people and examining such evidence as it could collect. It came to the conclusion that 'there is a strong logic supported by direct and circumstantial evidence that enables the team to assert without an iota of doubt, that the entire action was carried out at the behest of the Government of Pakistan.'

The Tewatia Report, which is a dispassionate analysis of what happened in Godhra, has divided the facts relating to the incident into four categories: (a) indisputable; (b) that appear to be true but need verification; (c) that appear to be untrue; and (d) mysterious.

(a) Indisputable facts:
- On 27 February 2002, the Sabarmati Express from Faizabad reached Godhra more than four hours late.
- There were more than two thousand Hindu pilgrims on this train.
- No serious dispute took place at the platform at Godhra between the passengers and the vendors.
- The train was pelted with stones right after it left the platform at Godhra. The stoning continued even after it was stopped at Signal Faliya.
- Firebombs, acid bulbs and highly inflammable liquids were used to set the coaches on fire. These may have been already stored for the purpose.
- The conspirators did not allow the fire-fighting staff to reach the burning train expeditiously.
- The iron grills of the windows of S-6 coach were broken from the outside.
- Fifty-eight passengers of S-6 were burnt to death by a Muslim mob and one of the conspirators was Congress Councillor, Haji Bilal.
- The train was stopped by pulling the chain and the vacuum pipe was cut.

- Someone used the public address system exhorting the mob to kill *kafirs* and the enemies of Bin Laden.
- The attack on Sabarmati Express on 27 February 2002 was pre-planned and pre-meditated. It was the result of a criminal conspiracy hatched by a foreign power with the help of local jihadis.

(b) Facts that need verification:

- There was a conspiracy to reduce the effectiveness of the fire-fighting system of the Godhra Municipal Committee.
- The mob that burnt the coach included Muslims from outside the town as well.
- Firearms were used by the mob.
- Police could have caught some of the miscreants on the spot.
- Local politicians and elected representatives took active part in instigating the mob.
- The Railway Police at Dahod sent a message to Godhra Railway Police that some Muslim youths on board Sabarmati Express were likely to create mischief at Godhra.
- A passenger on S-6 coach was beheaded when he tried to get out of the window. The passenger's head was later thrown back into the coach to burn.

(c) Information that appears to be untrue:

- Some women passengers are missing.
- Some women passengers were raped or molested.
- Passengers had pulled the beard of a vendor at the Godhra Railway Station.
- Passengers carried weapons with them.
- Railway staff connived with the miscreants.
- The pilgrims had taunted certain Muslims of Godhra while returning from Ayodhya.
- Police firing, while the miscreants were burning the coach, killed two Muslims.

The Man of the Moment: Narendra Modi

(d) Some mysteries:
- Assistant collector, Godhra (a young Muslim from eastern UP), goes on leave two days before the incident and does not return till the middle of March while the district of his posting is aflame with communal riots.
- Absence of information with the district officials about the number of arms licenses issued.
- An abnormally large number of passports issued to residents of Godhra.
- Presence of a very large number of persons without ration cards in Signal Falia and Polan Bazaar areas of Godhra.
- A large number of unemployed Muslims in Godhra with mobile phones.
- Very high traffic of telephone calls from Godhra to Pakistan (mainly Karachi) before 27 February 2002.
- Holding of *istema* – religious gatherings – at Godhra, that were attended by foreigners in large numbers.

The Tewatia Report came to the following conclusions:
- The burning of fifty-eight Hindu pilgrims at Godhra on 27 February 2002 was an act of international terrorism carried out with the evil objective of pushing the country into a communal cauldron.
- The plan was to burn the entire train with more than two thousand passengers in the wee hours of 27 February 2002.
- It was a terrorist action plan that partly failed. The perpetrators of the terrorist acts received support from jihadi elements operating from Godhra. These included some Congress members of the Nagarpalika.
- Preparations for enacting the Godhra carnage were made in advance.
- There were no quarrels or fights between Hindu and Muslim passengers in the train.
- The intention of the mob was to put to death *all* the pilgrims travelling by the Sabarmati Express.

Of Commissions and Reality

- The fire-fighting system available in Godhra was weakened and its arrival at the place of the incident wilfully delayed by the mob with the open participation of a Congress Councillor, Haji Bilal.
- The Army was requisitioned and deployed in time.
- The police was on many occasions overwhelmed by the rioting mobs that were heavily armed.
- Barring a few exceptions, the police was not found to be communally motivated.
- The local administration and police at Godhra did not take adequate and prompt action even after the receipt of information about the attack on the train by an armed mob.
- The English language media, particularly the Delhi press, was perceived by Gujaratis as biased. The information disseminated by it was neither balanced nor impartial.
- By converting half-baked news stories into major headlines, both the print and the electronic media widened the psychological hiatus between Muslims and Hindus.
- By disseminating half-truths and lies, the media played no mean role in distorting the country's image in the world.
- Adverse media reports about the role of officials affected their performance and demotivated them. Several officials were reluctant to take firm action.
- Communal violence in Gujarat has become politicized and instead of treating it as a human tragedy, it was being used to get political mileage by political parties.
- There are elements within the country that help and collaborate with the forces inimical to India.
- The governing class in India was ignorant or was wilfully blind to the threat posed by the jihadi forces.

One wonders what the NHRC will have to say, following the serial blasts in Ahmedabad and Surat in July 2008, when over forty people were killed and several more injured. Credit for the blasts was taken by an organization called Indian Mujahideen (IM). It needs to be stressed that there had been no riots in Ahmedabad or Surat to serve as a provocation to the Mujahideen. The blasts in Gujarat were preceded by blasts in Bengaluru and in Jaipur, all capitals of states ruled by the BJP.

It is in this context that an article that appeared in The *Hindu* on 1 August 2008 is highly revelatory. Written by correspondent Praveen Swami, it spoke of the terrorist calls in Ahmedabad and of Maulana Sufiyan Patangia, who runs the Lal Masjid seminary in Ahmedabad's Kalupur area. According to Swami, following the February 2002 riots in Gujarat, Patangia decided to seek revenge and turned to one Abdul Bari, who is among the Lashker-e-Taiba's (LeT) top financiers, for help. Bari apparently put in ₹3,75,000. Two Saudi Arabia-based Jaish-e-Mohammad (JeM) fundraisers, Farhatullah Ghauri and Abdul Rehman, threw in another ₹5 lakh.

Patangia reportedly made contacts with Rasool Khan, a contractor working for top Gujarat mafioso Abdul Latif Sheikh and his boss Dawood Ibrahim based in Pakistan. In May 2002, Khan and his brother Idris met Patangia in Mumbai to discuss how vengeance might be planned. First, Gujarat's former Home Minister Haren Pandya was shot by a hit-team directed by Patangia.

Swami mentioned names, including that of Maharashtra-based SIMI bomb maker Zulfikar Fayyaz Kagzi, who had built a sophisticated suitcase bomb that was planted on the Mumbai-Ahmedabad Express train in February 2006.

Minutes before the Ahmedabad serial explosions, the IM, according to Swami, sent out a manifesto which said that it was 'raising the illustrious banner of jihad against the Hindus and all those who fight and resist us, and here we begin our revenge with the help and permission of Allah – a terrifying revenge of our blood, our lives and our honour that will, Insha-Allah, terminate your survival on this land.' The manifesto called on Hindus to 'realize that the falsehood of your 33 crore dirty mud idols and the blasphemy of your deaf, dumb, mute and naked ram, krishna and hanuman (names written in lower case) are not at all going to save your necks from being slaughtered by our hands.'

Swami wrote: 'No great effort is needed to locate the intelluctual genesis of this body of ideas: it draws heavily on long-standing LeT polemic.'

According to The *Hindu* (1 August 2008): 'Gujarat has been targetted by jihadis half a dozen times since 2002 in a little-understood war and our secularists have not once raised their voice against the LeT, whose chief, Hafiz Mohammad Saeed, has often made it clear that "the Hindu is a mean enemy and the proper way to deal with him is the one adopted by our forefathers [who] crushed them by force".'

The Banerjee Committee that had been appointed vide a Government of India notification dated 2 September 2004, was declared illegal on 13 October 2006 by the Gujarat High Court in a historic judgement. The Government of Gujarat had already appointed the Justice Nanavati Commission to inquire into the events which led to the Godhra carnage and its aftermath. The terms of reference for the Inquiry Commission were laid down in the government notification dated 6 March 2002. Subsequently, the terms of reference were extended on 20 July 2004. These terms were very vast and there was literally no need and no scope for any committee to be constituted again. A cursory reading of the terms of reference of both the committees shows that the Banerjee Committee was just duplicating the scope of work of the Nanavati Commission.

The Justice U C Banerjee Committee submitted its report on 3 March 2006. The Gujarat High Court passed an order on 7 March 2006 directing the railway ministry and all others not to give any further publicity to the High Level Committee and not to implement or take any further action on the basis of its report. Aggrieved by this order, the Railway Ministry approached the Supreme Court, which, in turn, directed the Gujarat High Court to decide the matter expeditiously. The court passed the final order on 13 October 2006, quashing the notifications constituting the high level committee by the Union Railway Ministry. The High Court, in its order, clearly mentioned that declaring an interim report before the Bihar elections showed mala fide intentions.

On 14 October 2006, The *Times of India* (Ahmedabad) carried the news item: 'Bannerjee Panel is illegal: HC'. On the same day, The

Indian Express carried a story quashing the appointment of the committee as 'unconstitutional, illegal and null and void'.

What happened in Gujarat following the torching of the coach of the Sabarmati Express in Godhra on 27 February 2002? This question has been boggling the minds of many people. No wonder it took the Justice Nanavati Commission almost six years to submit its report which literally took the wind out of the pseudo-secularists' sails.

The Commission had been appointed under the provisions of the Commission of Inquiry Act, 1952. The appointment of Justices G T Nanavati and Akshay Mehta was validated by the Gujarat High Court and the Chief Justice of the Hon'ble Supreme Court. The terms of reference were broad, covering all aspects of the Godhra incident.

During the six-year-long inquiry, the Commission examined a large number of eyewitnesses, documentary evidence, forensic reports and also acquired the facts and figures that were gathered by the investigating officers. It received applications and affidavits from 44,475 persons and another 2,019 statements and affidavits filed by government officers. All the witnesses were duly cross-examined by lawyers. The first part of its report was tabled in the Gujarat Assembly on 25 September 2008.

The Commission's findings leave no doubt as to the modus operandi followed by the Muslim mob. According to the Commission, the Godhra train carnage was a 'pre-planned conspiracy' hatched by some local Muslims at the Aman Guest House in Godhra a day prior to the carnage. The recorded evidence of over a hundred witnesses noted that a crowd of about one thousand Muslims that had gathered near the station was shouting, 'Set the train on fire and kill the Hindus'. Provocative slogans were being shouted over loudspeakers from a nearby mosque to attack Hindus.

The 168-page report of the Commission claimed that a mob of Muslims attacked the train and stoned the coaches so heavily that the passengers could not come out. This was to ensure maximum casualties when the S-6 coach of the Sabarmati Express caught fire.

The Muslim conspirators had made arrangements for collecting 140 litres of petrol from a nearby pump on the night of

Of Commissions and Reality

26 February 2002. According to the report, Maulvi Umerji of the local mosque was the 'mastermind' of the conspiracy. Among those who participated in what turned out to be a mass murder, the following were named: Rajak Kurkure, Salim Panwala, Saukatlal, Imran Sheri, Rafiq Batuk, Salim Jarda, Jabbir and Siral Lala. Their aim was to 'cause harm to the *kar sevaks* travelling' in the train. It was Hassan Lala who opened the vestibule between coaches S-6 and S-7, entered S-6 and threw burning rags into it.

The report said that setting fire to the train was a part of the 'larger conspiracy' to instil a sense of 'fear' in the administration.

The Commission disagreed with the contentions of the Banerjee Committee and the Jan Sangharsh Manch which represented the riot victims before the commissions, that alarm chains could not be operated from outside under the modified system introduced by the railways in 1995. The Commission quoted a railway officer of the carriage and wagon department as saying that the alarm chain could still be pulled from outside.

The Sabarmati Express was attacked twice, the second time some three hours after the stone-throwing and burning incident, when the train was being shunted to detach the two affected coaches. The second time, two Muslims mobs had resumed throwing stones on the passengers waiting in the yard for the train to resume its onward journey.

Significantly, the Commission specifically claimed that there was no evidence to justify the contention that the *kar sevaks* had been fighting with Muslims vendors at the stations before Godhra. There were minor scuffles at Godhra, but the Commission found no 'reliable evidence' to show that the *kar sevaks* had made any effort to abduct a Muslim girl. As the Commission saw it, it was Salim Panwala who had spread these 'false rumours' to arouse Muslim sentiments to a degree that the latter pelted stones at the coaches.

Another significant finding of the Commission was the fact that the fire was not the result of any 'short circuit'. In such an event, according to the Commission, the passengers would not have climbed up to the upper berths to protect themselves as the electric lines went through the top of the coaches.

The Man of the Moment: Narendra Modi

In reporting the presentation of the Commission's report before the Gujarat State Assembly, The *Times of India* (27 September 2002) said that the 'conspiracy' theory hinged on the proof that the accused had purchased petrol the previous day. Putting the word conspiracy in quotes suggests that The *Times of India*, as usual, had doubts about the accuracy of the Nanavati Commission's findings! However, the paper said that Justice Nanavati relied on police witnesses who spoke about the influential Muslim cleric, Maulvi Husain Haji Ibrahim Umerji, as being the brain behind the attack on the train. Witnesses had also named a former CRPF (Central Reserve Police Force) constable, Nanu Miyan, a native of Assam who used to frequent Kurkure's house and incite Muslims.

According to The *Times of India* (27 September 2008), 'the account of Ajay Baria, a young tribal boy, which was recorded before a magistrate in July 2002, was critical to establish the conspiracy theory'. The paper mentioned: 'The boy's 8-page statement is significant because he was a member of one of the four Hindu families staying in Signal Falia and knew all the Ghanchi Muslims in the neighbourhood.' Police sources are quoted as saying that the boy's statement 'was the best part of the investigations carried out so far'.

The most significant part of the Commission's report was its reference to Chief Minister Narendra Modi. It said in plain words: 'There is absolutely no evidence to show that either the chief minister or any of the ministers in his council or police officers had played any role in the Godhra incident.' As minister of state for home affairs, Amit Shah tabled the Commission's report on the first day of the three-day monsoon session of the assembly. It predictably created a furore, with Congress as the Opposition party crying foul and walking out.

The so-called liberal media also went on the attack mode. An excellent example of the 'Hate-Modi' media was the editorial in the Bengaluru-based *Deccan Herald* (21 September 2008) which went wild with fury against Modi. It stated: 'Unfortunately, commissions of inquiries are often instituted in our country to delay the truth of a matter of public import from coming out, to

Of Commissions and Reality

bury it, to deliberately implicate someone or to exonerate people of the blame for their misdeeds.'

On 28 September 2002, The *Hitavada*, however, had the courage to hit out at Modi's detractors in a strong front-paged report by its editor Vijay Phanshikar. He wrote: 'When German supremo Adolf Hitler asked his close associate and Propaganda Minister Goebbels how he would propagate the Nazi message to unbelieving masses, Goebbels answered in effect, "Feuhrer, by telling it again and again and again and again. This way, we would be able to prove that even a lie is a truth."'

In Gujarat, too, this Goebbelsian principle was used to malign the Narendra Modi regime, to accuse Modi of political conspiracy and misuse of official machinery to protect the miscreants of the Godhra train tragedy. But the report of the Justice Nanavati-Mehta Commission absolved Gujarat Chief Minister Narendra Modi of having indulged in a criminal conspiracy of heaping violence upon his own state.

The Godhra issue, however, still did not die. It was resuscitated by The *Indian Express* whose news service editor, Shishir Gupta, moderated a discussion between Narendra Modi and half a dozen aggressive reporters, in which the Gujarat chief minister came out with flying colours. Modi has never been defeated in verbal warfare and this tête-a-tête with media representatives further proved it.

The BJP National Executive was scheduled to meet in Goa on 12 April 2002, where Narendra sprang a surprise on them. Sick and tired of the daily sniping at him by the media, with not much loud support from the executive, Narendra decided to submit his resignation. The executive was to meet the next morning, but Narendra did not want to wait for long. Soon after the formal inauguration of the national executive at 1630 hours, Narendra announced his decision to quit. He told the body: 'I would prefer to sit here as a general executive member and not as a chief minister.' The announcement came as a shock to the executive which decided to hold its meeting the same night instead of the next morning as originally planned.

A reporter from The *Indian Express* wrote a sneering report on what happened next, almost on cue. The report of 13 April 2002 said:

'The party president spoke, and how. In a spirited defence of the embattled Gujarat Chief Minister Narendra Modi, BJP President Jana Krishnamurthi said: "I strongly condemn the hue and cry of those who demanded the head of the CM. The nation needs to be saved from these forces."'

According to the report, Krishnamurthy said that the Godhra attack was the handiwork of Pakistan's ISI and 'then went on to read his version of the Riot Act to Muslims'.

The report tauntingly said that Krishnamurthy 'did not once refer to Muslims as Muslims but held out long and hard on the provoked theory without leaving any doubt that he was talking about Muslims.' No sooner had Krishnamurthy completed his presidential address, than Narendra stood up and said in his sombre, chaste Hindi:

'*Adhyakshji*, I want to speak on Gujarat. From the party's point of view, this is a grave issue. There is a need for a free and frank discussion. To enable this, I wish to place my resignation before this body. It is time we decided what direction the party and the country should take from this point onwards.'

Reporting this, *India Today* (19 April 2002) stated:

'He (Modi) didn't need to say more. With one stroke, the Gujarat chief minister had seized the initiative. He galvanized his supporters who now stood up to be counted. Food Minister Shanta Kumar, who had spoken out against Modi and the VHP's extremes, found himself being rebuked and facing a disciplinary committee. He was forced to apologize.

Even if the prime minister may have thought Modi's resignation prudent for the sake of both his personal image and the unity of the coalition, there was absolutely no way he could go against the ferocity of the pro-Modi sentiment. He tried shelving the issue for a day but even that was resisted.'

The then Union Parliamentary Affairs Minister, the late Pramod Mahajan, intervened to say that any delay would mean uncertainty and uncertainty could cause riots in Gujarat.

Of Commissions and Reality

India Today noted in its report dated 29 April 2002:

'By the time Vajpayee left for the public meeting, he had been infected by the mood. Departing from his prime ministerial grandeur, he delivered a speech that could have been a replay from his heady Jan Sangh days. "We don't need lessons in secularism from anyone," he thundered. "India was secular even before the Muslims and Christians came. There are two faces of Islam: one pious and peaceful and the other fundamentalist and militant."'

Summing up the happenings in Goa, *India Today* concluded in the issue dated 29 April 2002:

'When the members of the BJP National Executive trooped into the Marriot Hotel in Goa on 12 April, the mood was funereal. By the time they departed two days later, there was an extra bounce in their steps and a touch of triumphalism in the air. The catalyst of this remarkable transformation was the ubiquitous Narendra Modi.'

The *Indian Express* (16 April 2002) also had its say. It reported:

'Nearly four years of leading a coalition government had left the BJP somewhat a tired and fragmented organization. At a plush hotel on Miramar beach, the party reclaimed its identity and felt free to reassert it, whatever the consequences. To use old cliches, hardline *Hindutva* is back on the party's agenda, but there's a new face – Narendra Modi.'

What the secularists did not want to see happened soon after. The BJP Executive gave permission to Narendra to dissolve the state assembly and seek a fresh mandate from the people of Gujarat.

Narendra wanted to know whether the people of Gujarat backed him or wanted him to be thrown out. The secular and the English media was attacking him day and night. He had every right to test public opinion. But he had to get clearance from his party. It was not his intention to 'create high drama' in Goa, as some noted. But it was in Goa that the party national executive was meeting. And the executive alone could authorize him to seek the public mandate. For seeking that mandate, secularists charged him with wanting to play 'the Hindu card, nakedly and brutally'.

What was amusing is that the paper even charged 'supercop' K P S Gill, who had been sent to Gujarat to inquire into the situation there, with supporting 'the Modi view'. Elections were to be held in Gujarat in February 2003. Modi wanted them to be held in September 2002, barely eight months after the riots. And he was quite right in demanding this. He had been insulted and humiliated. He wanted the Gujaratis either to clear his reputation or boo him out.

Such was the viciousness with which the English media attacked Narendra that even the United States chipped in with an official – and demeaning – quote in Washington that it was keeping a 'close watch on the situation'. It should have been unhesitatingly told to keep quiet. During all the years when Martin Luther King and the blacks were humiliated in Georgia, New Delhi never made any announcement that it was keeping a 'close watch' on the state. If US Assistant Secretary of State for South Asia, Christina Rocca, a known India-hater, could term the events in India 'horrible', a relatively unknown Erkki Tuomioja, Foreign Minister of Finland, said that 'the pictures of carnage (in Gujarat) were very disturbing'. One does not know what Mr Tuomioja said when over ten thousand vehicles in France were set afire by angry Muslims in 2005. Did that not disturb him?

Significantly, The *Times of India* raised some relevant questions. The paper said that the Gujarat riots were not 'communal' riots, any more than 1984 Delhi's riots were. It maintained:

'From the time the Republic came into being 52 years ago, the political establishment has done little to nurture and promote secularism as a core value in a multi-cultural, multi-religious context. Instead, they have exploited it as a convenient political tactic to malign one another.'

Test of Faith 10

March and April 2002 were months of great turmoil in Gujarat. Though the killings and arson had been brought under control, the Union government felt that the state needed greater preparedness to check any further communal violence.

K P S Gill, well-known for leading anti-terrorist operations in Punjab, was appointed Security Advisor to the Gujarat chief minister, at the latter's own request. Being a senior police officer with enormous experience in dealing with complex law and order problems, Gill was expected to coordinate with the chief minister's office, the home department, and the state police to chalk out effective policies to combat communal strife. It was also expected that Gill would assist in the deployment of police and para-military forces wherever they were needed.

Narendra welcomed Gill's appointment. He told the media: 'The riots are over, but in a sensitive state like Gujarat, the police have to be trained to deal with such situations professionally. The NHRC had given its recommendations, one of which was better professionalism in the police. Gill is a respected officer and Gujarat is a border state. So, if someone like Gill helps me, it will be better for the state.'

As The *Times of India* reported, the first thing that Gill did on his arrival in Ahmedabad on 3 May 2002 was to meet other officials such as the Director General of Police, K Chakravarthy, along with the chief minister. The Union Minister of State for Home, I D Swamy said: 'If Gill is appointed advisor or asked to serve in any other capacity, I think it shows the sincerity of the chief minister's efforts to ensure that normalcy returns to the state. And if he wants to take any help, any suggestion, it is good.'

Narendra announced that riot victims could lodge individual FIRs naming culprits, though critics were to say that this was no concession because the police were enjoined by Section 154 of the Criminal Procedure Code (CrPC) to register forthwith a case based on any information relating to the commission of a cognizable offence.

The point was forcibly made by one critic, Manoj Mitta, writing in The *Indian Express* (16 May 2002):

'To be fair, Modi is not the first politician to have presumed the authority to override Section 154 of the CrPC. Sonia Gandhi's husband did it earlier when about 3,000 Sikhs were massacred in three days in 1984. If anything, Modi can claim to have been more generous than Rajiv Gandhi in this regard. Modi took just 70 days to let Muslims lodge FIRs. Sikhs, on the other hand, had to wait six years for the police to begin taking note of their individual cases. It was only in 1991 (incidentally the year in which Rajiv himself was killed) that Delhi Police set up a special riot cell to pursue the 1984 cases that were taken up for the first time at the stage.'

Very few commentators, incidentally, have taken note of this event in their desperate desire to paint Narendra as a demon. What Rajiv Gandhi took six years to do, Narendra took no more than seventy days, when the memories of victims were still fresh to let people register their FIRs against the killers. Would a man accused of genocide ever have done that?

It was his faith in Narendra's rectitude, no doubt, that strengthened Prime Minister Atal Bihari Vajpayee's conviction that Narendra alone could have set matters right in Gujarat. But there was a certain amount of negativity against Narendra from both the secularists and the entire Opposition that led the prime minister, at one stage, to feel that a change in the Gujarat leadership was due. He confessed as much in replying to a seventeen-hour debate on Gujarat in the Rajya Sabha where the Opposition had moved a censure motion against the government.

Addressing the Rajya Sabha on 6 May 2002, Vajpayee admitted that at one stage, he had indeed made up his mind to remove Narendra from power. However, he added, 'It was my own assessment that removal of Modi would not help and what was worse, could rather have led to more violence ... In retrospect, we feel that it was a right decision.'

The decision to retain Narendra indeed was right as future events were to prove. It was Narendra's leadership that gave the BJP a resounding victory in the polls. Narendra Modi's security advisor, K P S Gill, attested that the riots had been sponsored by the ISI. Long before the fact became known, Gill had said at a function on 28 August that he had 'information about the ISI response to the communal riots'. He then added, 'It was in the form of ordering the Kashmiri militants to sneak into the state and launch terrorist assaults, including serial blasts.'

After a month-long stint in Gujarat, Gill began to feel that despite facing the worst communal flare-up, members of the minority community would not fall prey to the nefarious elements trying to create trouble from across the border. As early as 30 May 2002, in an interview to a journalist, Sheela Bhatt, he said, 'For quite some time the ISI never used Indian Muslims. Till recently, most of the Muslims, I would say ninety-nine per cent, rejected the ISI. Only 1 per cent fell into their trap. Look at the maturity of this country. If Gujarat had happened in 1992, the whole of UP, Bihar and Rajasthan would have gone up in flames. This time it has not happened.'

In the same interview, Gill indicated that he was in favour of fresh elections. He said, 'Yes, the state can face an election. Because, if you look at the state today, the disturbed areas are very limited. The process of an election reasserts democracy. It is a corrective process. It helps change political equations.' Narendra too felt that way when he dissolved the Gujarat Assembly on 19 July 2002 and recommended early polls.

But he was to clash with Chief Election Commissioner J M Lyngdoh on this decision. Earlier in July, a series of *rath* yatras had been taken out amidst tight security arrangements. Referring to them, Gill said, 'Seventy-nine yatras were taken out in Gujarat and except for one small incident of stone-throwing in one area, all passed off peacefully.' That clearly showed that normalcy had come to stay. But the Election Commission thought otherwise. Ahead of the three-member Election Commission's visit to Gujarat, a nine-member team had visited the state for an on-the-spot assessment of the situation and had come to the conclusion that the situation was 'not conducive' for polls. According to the Election Commission, minorities constituting twelve per cent of the population, including five per cent still in relief camps, were unlikely to participate in the electoral process and, therefore, it held that elections were inadvisable in the near future.

It was possible that the Commission was thinking of what happened in Vadodara where on 1 March 2002, following the torching of the Sabarmati Express at Godhra, rioters armed with petrol bombs set fire to a bakery, known as Best Bakery, burning alive fourteen inmates, eleven of them Muslims, and three Hindus. The arson and killings were witnessed by several people, including the wife and daughter of the bakery owner who subsequently testified to the police, the NHRC and several others.

The Bakery case became a major issue and there were demands for a re-trial of the case *outside* Gujarat. But why, asked Balbir Punj, a BJP MP, did the secularists not make any suggestions to re-open the Debgarwad mass burning case of Ahmedabad where eight Hindus had been burnt alive and all the accused acquitted? Punj also raised the issue of the incineration of six women and three men – all Hindus who were locked from outside in their home on the night of 7 January 1993 in Bombay's Radhabai Chawl. Five of the inmates died on the spot; one succumbed to his injuries in hospital. Based on the statements of eyewitnesses, the Bombay police arrested seventeen persons – all Muslims. They were said to be notorious goons. The case was admitted in a Terrorist and Disruptive Activities (Prevention) Act (TADA) court where it dragged on for more than three years. In October 1996, the Additional Sessions judge of the court, S M Deshmukh, sentenced eleven of the seventeen accused to life imprisonment. A petition against this was filed in the Supreme Court in April 1998; all the eleven accused were acquitted. In their fifty-three-page verdict, Justices G N Ray and G B Patanaik severely criticized the Mumbai police for indiscriminately picking up Muslim suspects and added that eyewitnesses had exaggerated their account of the incident.

Chief Election Commissioner J M Lyngdoh was a strong-willed man and he was not in favour of early elections. He thought that the government would do better to focus on relief and rehabilitation measures than to press for elections. He had to be told politely by the BJP general secretary in charge of Gujarat, Arun Jaitley, that several rehabilitation measures were already in place. Jaitley said,

'The Election Commission should bear in mind the constitutional requirement of Article 174 which mandates that the next sitting of the Gujarat State Assembly has to be called in early October.' And to press his point further, Jaitley added, 'Ninety-eight per cent of the state is normal. Most of the victims have returned home. It would be a bad precedent to suggest that elections can be deferred. We have gone through elections in Kashmir even under the shadow of jihadi guns and we have gone through elections with a minuscule voting percentage in Assam. In comparison, it would be too far-fetched to suggest that elections cannot be held in Gujarat.'

But Lyngdoh was in no mood to listen to the voices of reason. He wanted to show that he was a secularist and on a visit to Vadodara on his inspection tour, he ticked off the collector in front of TV cameras over some misunderstanding about the proprietors of Best Bakery coming to occupy their premises. Naturally, in the eyes of the pseudo-secularists, he became a celebrity overnight.

Meanwhile, the Union government sought a direction from the Supreme Court to hold elections in Gujarat within six months and for the dissolution of the state assembly through a presidential reference. The Supreme Court said that there was nothing wrong in the Election Commission's order on holding elections sometime in November-December 2002.

But the court's final decision was announced on Monday, 28 October 2002. Following that, the Election Commission announced that elections to the Gujarat state assembly would be held on 12 December and that the last date for withdrawals would be 28 November. It was decided that counting would take place on 15 December. Since the elections were to be held in a single phase, Lyngdoh said he would need four hundred companies of para-military forces to ensure free and fair polls. As many as 35,052 polling stations, he added, would be set up for the one-day poll throughout the state.

In June 2002, Narendra had decided to take out what he called the *Gaurav* Yatra to uphold Gujarat's *gaurav* (pride). The yatra was to start on 4 September and he intended to travel throughout the state bearing the message of peace and to expose those who were trying to portray Gujaratis as 'violent, communal and insensitive to suffering'.

Narendra was to be accompanied by Rajendrasinh Rana, the State Party President. A well-equipped *rath* had been readied, complete with a public address system and a collapsible platform. The centre of attraction, of course, was to be Narendra, who had been described in an internal party document in Gujarat as *lok hriday samrat and Sardar Patel jeva lokhandi manobal dharavta* (the king of the hearts of the people and the possessor of the iron will of Sardar Patel).

The yatra was to have been flagged off by Home Minister L K Advani from the temple town of Ambaji, but things were not that easy. The Opposition feared that the proposed yatra might upset the process of return to normalcy.

On the other hand, pressure from within the party kept building up and Narendra decided that he would begin the yatra on 3 September 2002. 'I am determined to take out the yatra and tell the world the *gaurav gatha* (story of pride) of five crore people of the state. It is not the story of Godhra, Naroda Patia or Gulbarg. Gujarat is not a state of murderers and rapists as the pseudo-secularists and power-hungry Congress leaders are attempting to project,' he said. But once again, fate intervened.

Narendra was to set off on his yatra from the Bhathiji Maharaj temple at Phagvel village, when the announcement came that the Gujarat Pradesh Congress President, Shankersinh Vaghela, was planning a similar yatra from the same temple and that too on the same day.

Narendra wrote a letter dated 1 September 2002 to Vaghela stating:

> Dear Shri Shankersinhji,
>
> You know very well that BJP had announced the start of its Gujarat *Gaurav* Yatra from *pujya* (respected) Bhathiji Mandir, Phagvel, on 3 September 2002.
>
> Your Congress party had objected to the yatra. But now, just two days before, and all of a sudden, for reasons not known, you have declared to undertake a parallel programme. It is natural that this would cause worry to society's leaders, *sants* and lovers of democracy – they have expressed their concern to me.

Test of Faith

> For Gujarat's good, for society's unity, and because of our faith in Bhathiji Maharaj Mandir, we have taken a unilateral decision to clear the way for your programme.
>
> Facts very clearly show that truth is only on the BJP side, yet we have postponed our programme.
>
> Neither you nor anyone else has asked for the government's permission for your programme. If you had asked for it, it would have been given.
>
> I pray at the feet of God for the successful completion of your programme and *Pujya* Bhathiji Maharaj's blessings to give you the strength to tread in future on the path of truth and democracy.
>
> With best wishes.

Narendra's letter was clearly intended to assuage the acrimony to a great extent and to deny Vaghela an opportunity to complain of harassment. It worked. Additionally, it portrayed Narendra in a better light – as an accommodative person who harboured no ill-will towards his political opponent and only wished him well. If gods ever laugh, that day Bhathiji Maharaj must have been pleased at Narendra's subtle move.

As promised, Narendra's *Gaurav* Yatra started off with predictable fanfare. It turned out to be more of an election rally and a show of strength than just a yatra. Over and over again, Narendra urged people who came to hear him in thousands to respond to the allegations made against the people of Gujarat via the ballot. He emphasized on his pet theme – invoking the *asmita* (pride) of five crore Gujaratis whose self-respect, he claimed, had been insulted by the Congress. He did not segregate the Muslims or other minorities even once.

Sharing the platform with him were BJP General Secretary Rajnath Singh, former Gujarat Chief Minister Keshubhai Patel and state BJP President Rajinder Singh Rana. Reminding the audience of the legend of Bhathiji Maharaj, the heroic Kshatriya of Phagvel, a place about eighty kilometres from Ahmedabad, who died fighting against cow slaughter, Narendra said, 'We are ready to follow the path of Bhathiji Maharaj. Is the Congress President (Sonia Gandhi) ready to tour the state to counter my yatra? We will make necessary arrangements. We will even create a helipad for the occasion to help her go around Gujarat.'

He would refer to Sonia Gandhi as *Italy ki beti* (daughter of Italy). Dismissing her 'political victory' in getting the *Gaurav* Yatra deferred from July to September 2002, Narendra wrote to Prime Minister Vajpayee that the yatra turned out to be a boon because it rained thereafter.

The yatra received tremendous response at every halt. On the second day of the first leg of his long journey, Narendra passed through one of the worst hit districts in north Gujarat. The yatra skirted Kadi town in Mehsana district and the scheduled public meeting was cancelled as a mark of respect to the deceased BJP councillor, Kirit Patel, who had been assassinated by a gunman the previous day. Narendra and Rajendrasinh Rana visited the family of the deceased to pay their homage before resuming the yatra from Detroj.

In Vijapur town, citizens weighed Narendra against silver and a promise was made that the proceeds would go towards the promotion of girls' education in the state. Such were the large crowds that waited for the yatra patiently that it put the yatra behind schedule by four hours. The enthusiasm at Himmatnagar was immense; a huge crowd was waiting for him at the unearthly hour of 2 am.

Narendra stuck to one basic point: he would repeatedly say that the people of Gujarat would never allow the Congress to 'fulfil its dream of returning to Gandhinagar via Godhra'. And he added that it was high time to 'teach a lesson' to those who had tried to hurt the pride and self-esteem of the people of the state through 'malicious and false propaganda'.

The first of the eleven-phase *rath* yatra ended with a meeting at Chanasma, also in Mehsana district, much to the delight of the BJP which found the enthusiasm of the people contagious.

The second phase began on 14 September. The yatra was flagged off by Union Minister for Social Welfare Satnarain Jatiya from Ahmedabad district's Jhanjraka, a place revered by the Dalits. Addressing the gathering at Jhanjraka, Narendra rejected the charge that his yatra would divide society. He blamed the Congress for the division of the country and for driving a wedge between Hindus and Muslims. 'In 1857, Hindus and Muslims had put up a united front against the British, but by the time 1947 arrived, not only the society got divided, even the country got divided,' he thundered. 'The division of the country is the sin committed by the Congress. Congress was guilty of the partition of India. At that time, the BJP was not even born.'

Reacting to Congress State President Vaghela's comment that the Kargil war was the handiwork of the BJP, Narendra said, 'A person who loves his country will never talk like this'. Narendra addressed Congressmen as *naffat* (shameless). Trying to cash in on the Dalit vote bank in Saurashtra, a Congress stronghold, he described the second phase of the yatra as a Dalit yatra. 'In Parliament, the BJP has the largest number of Dalit MPs and the largest number of Dalit women MPs. And in Gujarat, too, the BJP has more Dalit MLAs as compared to Congress. This is making the Congress party nervous,' he said.

Addressing a rally at Jam-Jodhpur, on the last day of the second phase, he said the *Gaurav* Yatra was not a ploy by the BJP to retain power. Narendra accused the Congress of humiliating Sardar Vallabhbhai Patel. He also mentioned that if Sardar Patel had been the first prime minister, the Kashmir issue would have never cropped up.

During the third phase, Narendra tried to soften his remarks. Speaking at Chikhli, for example, he said: 'The BJP is not ruling in China, but the country has introduced family planning. My utterances about family planning have been given a communal colour. If something is wrong, it is wrong.'

The yatra was a difficult task to undertake. Narendra visited various parts of Gujarat in a Swaraj Mazda vehicle. There were as many as fifty stops each day and though his address at each halt was not longer than three to four minutes, the response of those who came to listen to him was terrific and rapturous.

The fourth and fifth parts of his yatra followed a familiar pattern. The yatra would start early in the morning and end late at night. Narendra hardly ate anything during the day, contenting himself with some biscuits and fruits. What surely kept up his energy was not just his commitment, but the applause of the multitudes. The sixth phase of the *Gaurav* Yatra was launched from the temple town of Shamlaji that is situated at the border that Gujarat shares with Rajasthan. Its purpose was primarily to woo the tribals to vote for the BJP. Here, he changed his approach. Talking to the largely tribal audience, he spoke of the steps his government had taken for tribal welfare and announced the setting up of the Eklavya Academy for training tribal youth in athletic and sporting events. During this, he moved mostly through the tribal-dominated areas covering twenty-two assembly segments in over just three days.

The yatra had hardly got into its stride when tragedy struck Gujarat again. On 24 September, two Pakistani Islamic terrorists stormed the Akshardham temple in Gandhinagar, killing thirty-seven persons and injuring eighty-one. For a state that was still trying to recover from the earlier communal violence, this new attack was a grim reminder that the forces of disruption were still determined to sabotage peace.

Such was the shock created by the new carnage that Prime Minister Vajpayee cut short his visit to the Maldives and flew straight to Ahmedabad. Even Deputy Prime Minister L K Advani reached the state capital within three hours of the assault. After the terrorists had been gunned down, a note from the Tehriq-e-Kasa (literally, Movement for Revenge) was found in the pocket of one of the dead terrorists which read: 'This is a gift to Modi and Advani'.

Despite the havoc that was created at the Akshardham temple, Narendra resumed his *Gaurav* Yatra on 5 October, unmindful of the Pramukh (Chief) Swamiji's request, and sharply attacked the Pakistan president. The VHP called for a national bandh, frightening the Muslims who had returned to their homes to flee to the refugee camps once again. The Congress, not to be outdone, also called for a bandh. Charges and counter-charges flew thick in the air; emotions ran high. When Prime Minister Vajpayee expressed his grief over the fact that terrorists had entered a religious place, secularists were quick to point out that during the Ahmedabad riots, an eighteenth-century tomb of a Sufi saint, Vali Gujarati, had been destroyed. Asghar Ali Engineer, a well-known columnist, lambasted Narendra while

Test of Faith

condemning the terrorist attack on Akshardham temple, claiming that 'there is a complete polarization between what is moral and what is political. Had the BJP leaders been honest and not played politics, they would have correctly understood the implications of the politics of violence and would have resolved never to resort to it,' he said magisterially.

Throughout October, tempers remained high. Addressing a public meeting at Ahmedabad on 1 October 2002, Narendra challenged Pakistan President Musharraf to send more terrorists to Gujarat claiming that this time, the people of the state were ready to take them on. Addressing the Pakistan president directly, Narendra said, 'Attack us, stop attacking innocents and send us your terrorists whom we will face bravely.'

On his use of the word '*miyan*' (Muslim gentleman) to describe Musharraf, Narendra said, 'Non-communal forces have not liked me addressing Musharraf as *Miyan* Musharraf, but I will continue to do so. Narendra said that there was no difference between Musharraf's speech and what was written in the note found in the pocket of one of the terrorists. That, according to him, indicated that the attack on the Akshardham temple was carried out on the directions given by Pakistan.

Narendra noted that since Pak-sponsored militancy was now dead in Punjab, and the elections in Jammu & Kashmir were on track, Pakistan had turned to Gujarat. Then, amidst loud applause, he added, 'The people of Gujarat are peace-loving people and they do not disturb anyone, but if one creates disturbance, then the Gujaratis do not leave them. It was Mahatma Gandhi who, after suffering insults in South Africa, decided to throw the Britishers out and his one-man force was successful. Gandhiji was also a Gujarati. We have decided to fight against terrorism and you, *Miyan* Musharraf, have dialled the wrong number by sending your terrorists to Gujarat. We will eradicate terrorism from the whole country.'

The shrillness in Narendra's speeches was matched by the assault in the English media against him.

Unofficial, self-styled 'tribunals' with vested interests mushroomed in the name of citizens who wanted peace. The market was flooded with write-ups, which in turn just created confusion. In many ways, it was a free-for-all. Individuals with some intellectual pretensions felt free to quote figures to show how Gujarat's fiscal balances were deteriorating and how the state was overspending, though little notice was taken of the fact that the tax collections in Gujarat had risen by 3.2 times in the 1990s in per capita terms (in Maharashtra and Andhra Pradesh too, it had risen by 3.2 times), regardless of the waterless Kutch and the agriculturally unproductive tribal belt. Many people deliberately forgot the fact that Gujarat ranked number two in industrial investments in the country with a seventeen per cent share, or that Gujarat's share was thirteen per cent in industrial production with forty-one ports handling the highest share for import and export of goods. Gujarat also had the highest number of airports (eleven), an excellent road network, and industrial peace with the least number of man-hours lost. Along with all this, Gujarat boasted of educational and research institutes of international standards, had the largest number of investors, thirty per cent of the country's stock market capitalization and the highest Gross Domestic Product (GDP) growth rate in the country. But none of this seemed to matter. Why was Narendra Modi not given credit for these achievements?

In the midst of all this, J M Lyngdoh announced single-phase polls to be held on 12 December 2002, even as he banned all religious yatras.

When the date for the polls was announced, it released more anti-Modi, anti-Gujarat sentiments in the English media. Thus, *Business Standard* (3 December 2002) published an article, penned by its correspondent Ajay Singh, who among other things, said that in many townships the response of residents (to Narendra's public addresses) was one of indifference.

Harihar Swarup, stated in *Business Line* (10 December 2002):

> *Certain trends stand out a few days before the Gujarat polls. The Hindutva wave, on whose crest Mr Narendra Modi hoped to achieve a landslide, appears to be losing momentum ... A recent pre-poll survey by Outlook-Core revealed that the Hindu card has not worked all that well for the BJP in Gujarat. Religious sentiments appear to be losing ground to factors such as anti-incumbency, governance*

and unemployment ... Godhra and its aftermath have unsettled the middle class, traders and the poor. The industry, too, has suffered badly and the entire economy of Gujarat has been affected. For the thousands of people who have lost their livelihood, the daily bread is more important than Mr Modi's fanatic brand of Hinduism ...

Earlier, on 22 November, Lyngdoh had certified that the police administration in Gujarat had become 'quite professional' and that he was satisfied with the arrangements made for the assembly elections to be held in December. When asked whether the chief minister and other top political brass were cooperating with the commission, Lyngdoh said that the commission was dealing with the police and not with the politicians. 'It is entirely a relation between the police and us and not the political executive,' he said loftily.

But Narendra seemed indifferent to the 'hate-Modi' campaign, even as electioneering gained momentum. Extremely conscious of the feelings of the people, the Congress, too, launched its campaign from the famous Ambaji temple, shedding in one stroke all its pretenses of secularism.

Election fights are not tea parties, as some famous leader once said, but electioneering in Gujarat in November-December 2002 violated all bounds of decency. To top it all, the English media shamelessly took sides, indulging in lies, half-truths and downright partisanship.

But Modi fought back ferociously. A classic instance is a highly emotional ninety-second video clip starring Narendra that was beamed on local cable networks and at the BJP group meetings. *Ghana chhe bhakshak, ekaj rakshak* (There are many killers, only one saviour) was spelt out on the dark screen. As if on cue, two images of Narendra appeared: one examining the bodies of the two terrorists following the Akshardham attack, and another standing at the door of the burnt Sabarmati Express.

As the date of polling drew nearer, Narendra turned more and more eloquent. A week before the elections, he told an audience that the 12 December 2002 election was 'a democratic war against terrorism' in which the voter would respond against the bullet with the ballot. 'This election is part of the international war against terrorism and I am sure the voters would defeat the designs of the terrorists. Next week's poll is a festival of democracy in which the BJP will give a democratic face to the global war against terrorism,' he said.

Looking back at those days, it is amazing to see the vilification, hatred and harshness that Narendra had to face. Never before in the history of elections since Independence would any *one* politician have faced such animosity! He was reviled, abused and condemned in no uncertain ways. It was then that Deputy Prime Minister Advani came to Narendra's defence.

In a speech that he delivered on 8 December, Advani came down heavily on the Congress campaign against Gujarat and its Chief Minister, Narendra Modi, and termed it all false propaganda. Addressing a huge election gathering in the tribal town of Pavi Jetpur, about 120 km from Vadodara, Advani said, 'Modi, who is being described as a demon by the Congress, is actually the most sincere, honest man of integrity, committed to his duty. Whatever role he has been assigned by the party, he has done with perfection and excellence.'

Even as Narendra and Congress leader Shankersinh Vaghela were battling it out at the hustings in the backdrop of one of the worst communal riots in the country, a lot of curiosity was being expressed concerning the total absence of any noteworthy Muslim campaigner from the Congress party.

Keeping in mind the fact that Muslims were considered to be the main victims of the riots, the general impression was that Congress would take advantage of that fact and send some of its Muslim members to do some active campaigning for the party. The names of Mohsina Kidwai, Salman Khurshid and Ghulam Nabi Azad were frequently mentioned. However, none of them appeared on the scene and the word was passed around that the Congress leadership felt that sending some of its Muslim members to Gujarat was likely to prove counter-productive.

But what could have been the real reason?

Salman Khurshid provided one answer. He was quoted as saying: 'Our approach has been the result of strategic fine-tuning. Modi is already on a sticky wicket. He has a lot to explain. Why give him a chance to score? We realize Modi may get a high percentage of votes where incidents (of rioting) took place, but overall, the BJP will not bag many seats. And we are cornering him on important matters like the collapse of administration and law and order, and lack of basic amenities like water.'

Khurshid did not mention Godhra. He could well have said that the Muslims were innocent and that the fire in the coaches was strictly coincidental. He could have condemned Narendra on moral grounds. But he did not do any such thing.

Interestingly, the BJP did not field a single Muslim as its candidate for the assembly elections. And the Congress which had earlier fielded over a dozen candidates in past elections fielded only five in the 2002 elections. But the party apparently had no Muslim willing to campaign for them.

Till the first week of December 2002, the prime minister had stayed away from Gujarat except during his brief visit to Akshardham following the terrorist attack on the temple. But as the electioneering came to a close, he made one more appearance, this time coming out in full support of Narendra.

Addressing his first election meeting in Vadodara on 7 December, Vajpayee asserted that there should be no dispute over religion and that the time had come to end all communal tension. 'The bitterness that we have seen during the campaign should end here. During election time, bitter comments are common. But they serve no purpose,' Vajpayee philosophized.

Not to leave anything to chance, top BJP leaders kept coming to Gujarat to fight Narendra's war, by his side. In addition to Advani and Vajpayee, Union ministers Dr Murli Manohar Joshi, Pramod Mahajan and Sushma Swaraj also visited Gujarat. Their presence was further strengthened by the arrival of then BJP President Venkaiah Naidu, Rajnath Singh and Arun Jaitley. Strangely enough, it was left to the then managing editor of NDTV, Rajdeep Sardesai, to expose the Congress hypocrisy. He was amongst the first to bring to light Shankersinh Vaghela's pretensions of secularism. Sardesai opined: 'By virtue of the fact that he has switched over to the Congress, Vaghela's past is being erased, and he is suddenly a symbol of secularism. Nor was Vaghela's defection from the BJP based on an ideological shift. The man left the BJP because he lost out in an internal power struggle.'

Sardesai, in a correct interpretation of ground realities, added: 'To that extent this election is not as clear cut a battle between secular and communal forces as one would like to believe. Instead, both parties are competing for the same Hindu constituency in Gujarat – each leader seeking to be crowned the *Hindu Hriday Samrat* (King of the hearts of the Hindus).

In its fear of offending the Hindu vote, the Congress, reported Sardesai, had even abandoned its traditional ritual of Iftaar parties (evening meals when Muslims break their fast) during Ramzaan, for fear that it would be seen in Gujarat as yet another example of minority appeasement.

As the day of the election approached, the hysterical attacks against Narendra in the English media increased. He was a good target to laugh at and to be made fun of, as Pamela Phillipose showed in a piece written for the *Sunday Express* (8 December 2002). The piece was a tongue-in-cheek speech supposed to be made by Narendra who is also known to people as Namo.

'As *amaro* Gujaratis say, it takes a diamond to cut a diamond, *hero herane kape*. People are rushing to see me, hear me, laugh with me, touch me. *Hun, him, hun ... Me*, me, me ... Only me. *Tatnaro Namo*, your Namo, is today the Amitabh Bachchan of Gujarat; make no mistake. Evergreen hero number one. The voice of the people is the voice of God, *panch kahe te parmeshwar*. You watch, God will speak in four days and will say he wants only Namo.'

It was supposed to be a very funny take-off on Narendra and, no doubt, many readers had a hearty laugh. But in the end it was Narendra, 'Namo', who had the last laugh!

The truth was that the people were indeed treating Narendra like a hero, his media detractors notwithstanding. It was he and he alone who was wanted as the main speaker.

On 5 December 2002, the *Times News Network* put out the text of an interview that Sunil Raghu conducted with Narendra, which tells us as much about the man as his mission. In the first place, Narendra declined to evaluate the last five years of the

BJP rule in Gujarat. He wanted to let a neutral body do it, and asked that the evaluation be based on some fifteen to twenty pre-decided parametres. The only thing needed, he said, was that the evaluation should not be based on hearsay and the parametres should be set without any bias. He averred that after Godhra, substantial investments had come into the state. Not long after the post-Godhra riots, festivals like Navaratri, Ganesh Utsav and Holi had taken place in a peaceful atmosphere.

Narendra said that he was not fighting the polls on the *Hindutva* plank. He wanted to fight the elections on the basis of his performance. When he was reminded about what he had said during his *Gaurav* Yatra, he insisted that the yatra focussed on countering the false propaganda against Gujarat by pseudo secularists and minority appeasers.

Narendra discounted rumours that there was any rift between him and Keshubhai. He said they were doing grave injustice to Keshubhai who had been their guide and leader all along. The interviewer then asked, 'But contrary to statements by L K Advani and Venkaiah Naidu, Keshubhai has been maintaining that you are not the BJP's chief ministerial candidate. How do you reconcile these differences?'

Narendra was not one to be caught off-guard so easily. He completely stumped his interviewer by saying that he fully agreed with what Keshubhai had been saying. He pointed out that it was the responsibility of the elected members of the new legislative assembly to elect their leader. That was the constitutional requirement. He added, 'I feel that all the national leaders should say what Advani and Venkaiah Naidu have been saying while all the state level leaders should stand by what Keshubhai has been saying.'

The interviewer then went off on a different track. He attacked: 'The economy of the state appears to be in tatters and the debt has reportedly crossed the ₹40,000 crore mark. How do you evaluate this situation?'

Narendra was equally blunt in his reply. He said, 'They are unable to tolerate that we are still the leading state in attracting investments.' Then he tried to explain the debt situation.

The Man of the Moment: Narendra Modi

As the day of reckoning neared, there was endless speculation as to who, in the end, would win – the Congress or the BJP. Two leading weeklies had carried out their own opinion polls. First came the *India Today* (25 November 2002) poll. This predicted a cakewalk for the BJP with a two-thirds majority (120 to 130 seats in a house of 182). According to *India Today*, almost half the Gujaratis (forty-eight per cent) thought that Narendra was the best chief ministerial candidate, with Vaghela trailing miserably at a twenty-nine per cent. Similarly, according to the journal, fifty-six per cent of Gujaratis felt that the Modi government's performance was good or outstanding. As many as sixty-one per cent felt that this government had handled the riots fairly and effectively.

The *Outlook* poll (9 December 2002) followed. *Outlook* had been a consistent Modi-hater and had lost no opportunity in the past to denigrate him. The poll it conducted said that far from winning, the BJP might be the loser with the Congress just pipping the BJP to the post with some 95 to 100 seats. The waiting period was full of anxiety and tension.

Meanwhile, Muslim groups issued fatwas on 10 December 2002, just two days before the elections, that the community should vote 'in large numbers' against the ruling BJP. 'The vote is our only weapon against this madness,' a former city councillor of Ahmedabad, Sayeed Sahidar Rehman, was quoted as saying.

Muslims made up only ten per cent of Gujarat's thirty-three million voters, but community leaders said they were counting on a strong turnout to swing the outcome in a close race between the BJP and the Congress. And to ensure that turnout, Muslim leaders were seen arranging buses to ferry Muslim voters from their homes to the polling booths. The big question in everybody's mind was: 'Modi *ka* magic *chalega kya*?' (Will Modi's magic work?) Narendra was constantly on the telephone, talking to party candidates, then getting in touch with the BJP high command. He looked unruffled, revealing very little. He seemed composed, even a little pensive.

Congress leaders kept spouting optimism. Thus, the state Congress Vice-President Hasmukh Patel said that the Congress party would retain its seats in central Gujarat and, maybe, even gain a few more. After Ahmedabad, the communal riots that had swept the state had been most widespread in central Gujarat, particularly in the tribal-dominated districts of Panchmahal, of which Godhra was the district headquarters, and in Dahod, Kheda and Anand.

For a while, it seemed that Congress President Sonia Gandhi's success in pulling crowds in the tribal belt and the good response to the former GPCC President Amarsinh Chowdhary's *Adivasi Yatra* would bring success to the party to some extent. But after the polling on 12 December 2002 and the announcement of the results, it was all over for the Congress and other political parties. The people of Gujarat administered a well-deserved slap to all the false propaganda of the pseudo-secularist brigade.

The Congress had based its election strategy around traditional caste loyalties. Furthermore, it was confident of winning because as many as eighty per cent of the village panchayats and most of the *taluka* panchayats, barring one district panchayat, were all under its control. Besides, it was in power in the four main cities of Gujarat as well.

Besides, the elections had to be seen in the context of some turbulent weeks. On 22 November, Narendra had to be hospitalized as a result of fatigue. At the same time, Keshubhai, to the surprise of many, projected Narendra as the chief minister. On 3 December, VHP General Secretary Dr Jaideep Patel was shot at in Naroda and had to be operated upon. Once the election results were out, all tension vanished. The BJP bagged 126 out of the 182 seats. As many as 61.52 per cent of the voters had cast their votes. There was re-polling in some constituencies but when the whole process was over, the BJP ended up with 126 seats as against the 51 won by the Congress.

Narendra himself won the Maninagar assembly seat, defeating his Congress rival Yatin Oza, by a margin of 75,331 votes. Narendra polled 1,13,587 votes while Oza got a meagre 38,256. Atal Bihari Vajpayee was jubilant and hailed the victory in Gujarat as the beginning of the party's march towards victory in other states as well. The Congress party was shocked with the BJP victory in central Gujarat which had been a traditional Congress stronghold. Here, the BJP won forty-one of the area's fifty seats; the Congress barely managed to win seven. BJP spokesman Arun Jaitley said,

The Man of the Moment: Narendra Modi

'I don't think we have benefitted because of the riots. I think the people of Gujarat strongly reacted to the negative campaign by Congress, discrediting the state.'

The Leftists, of course, were nowhere in the picture. Of the 968 candidates in the fray for the election for 182 seats, the Communist Party of India – Marxist (CPI–M), and the Communist Party of India (CPI) together had a symbolic presence in only two seats.

Later, a commentator was to say that 'never in recent history has a state assembly election in India created such a sensation as the Gujarat state election of 2002.' Narendra came in for the most vicious hate commentary from some of the pseudo-secularist commentators.

But there were others – intellectuals like Debraj Mookerjee – who saw through the rantings and ravings of the self-styled secularists. Thus, writing in The *Pioneer* (28 December 2002), Mookerjee said that the election results had irrevocably altered the contours of the secular discourse in the country and while what had happened in Gujarat after the massacre at Godhra was shameful, 'what is equally shameful is the manner in which this human tragedy was turned into the pocket borough of a select group of self-appointed seminar circuitists ... these angst ridden self-absorbed bullies, who believe only they hold the right to give shape to secular discourses in India, used (yes, used) Gujarat to add sheen to their moribund secular platform, at best edging out and at worst, alienating in the process, other secular voices.'

On 14 December 2002, a group of local and foreign businessmen from companies like Shell and United Phosphorus travelled to southern Gujarat to assess the mood just two days after the polling. They visited Vapi, Ankleshwar and Bharuch, part of the state's Golden Corridor of prosperity. Leading the business group was Sunil Parekh of the Confederation of Indian Industry (CII), who was, very frankly, expecting to find the state in an economic depression. On 18 December 2002, *Business Week Online* reported that instead, Parekh found 'a surprisingly upbeat region which was looking forward to the implementation of Modi's promise for Gujarat's development'. Actually, foreign investors like British Gas, that had invested five hundred million dollars in oil and natural gas exploration and distribution in Gujarat and neighbouring Maharashtra, stayed on despite the riots. They knew better.

Test of Faith

The secular media's mood was understandably one of frustration at Narendra's unprecedented success in the polls. *Indian Observer* noted in the 15 December 2002 edition:

'He knows the mantra – to terrorize minorities so that they should not come out to cast their votes. Landslide victory in Gujarat is his personal victory, his personal charisma, which is going to be the trendsetter in all the coming elections. Modi's mantra will be applied. It is really creditable. In spite of mass killings of the Muslims, he secured a clean two-thirds majority which puzzles every one. Even Atal Bihari Vajpayee was not expecting such impressive results.

'All exit polls had failed miserably ... Questions were being raised whether Modi will accommodate and bring minorities into the mainstream despite their not supporting him wholeheartedly ... The situation in the country will be alarming in the coming days because Modi's mantra may bring the BJP into power in various states, but the very fabric of secularism and unity will be destroyed.'

That nothing of that sort has happened till date is another story.

The *Times of India* (16 December 2002) looked at BJP's victory on almost similar lines. It commented:

'Democracy is no respecter of even the democrats' wishes. This is the sobering message of Gujarat polls where the mandate given to "Modi-ism" must be democratically acknowledged. That said, it should also be clearly seen that the results are not a vindication either of the Modi government's record in office or the BJP at the national level. Gujarat 2002 is a victory for *Hindu Hriday Samrat*, Narendra Modi's politics of polarization. This is borne out by the fact that the BJP's success was most evident in the regions worst affected by post-Godhra violence. In contrast, the Congress faced a phenomenal rout in the same region, losing as many as 25 seats ....'

The paper said that the credit for the BJP victory 'goes without doubt to Narendrabhai, who braved anti-incumbency, poor governance and challenges to his own leadership to hawk his hardline wares.'

What was lacking in all commentaries was scholarship. A presumption was made and it was then followed up with ruthless

The Man of the Moment: Narendra Modi

demagoguery, only to exasperate people more and add to existing tensions. One has to take note of a lengthy article written by the resident editor of the Ahmedabad edition of The *Indian Express*, Virendra Kumar. According to him, 'When violence raged in the state in March and April, and rampaging mobs killed hundreds of innocent people, the Congress leadership proved to be gutless' and 'even their own former MP Ehsan Jafri's desperate calls for help failed to move them.'

The common public can ask why help was not given at the time when it was needed the most. The plain answer is that anti-Muslim sentiments are deep rooted in the hearts of most Hindus in Gujarat; to suggest that those who came out in the streets in anger over the torching of the Sabarmati Express consisted only of men from the VHP or the RSS is to fool oneself. *Hindutva* is not the creation of the BJP or the RSS. It is the creation of a deep sense of guilt among Hindus engendered by the Congress and the secularists. No Congressman wants to come face to face with the truth. According to Kumar, 'Nobody in his wildest dreams could have imagined the kind of game Modi was going to play. He has played his game, won the match and won it convincingly, proving the pollsters and pandits wrong.'

To show that Narendra had ruined Gujarat, Kumar went on to say that 'Modi's victory cannot hide the facts that, in the seven years of the BJP rule, the state's economic growth has been stunted, investment is falling, the government's fiscal deficit and borrowings have been mounting and it needs overdrafts to run its affairs.'

If the editor had taken the trouble to look at the state of affairs in other states, he would have been more credible. At a time when Narendra was being damned for running up a public debt of ₹47,000 crore, Maharashtra had a public debt of about ₹68,000 to 70,000 crore. And some other states were even worse. But the 'hate-Modi' propaganda was in full swing.

At this point, it is worthwhile to recount how a senior journalist and keen observer of the Indian polity looked at Narendra's success in the assembly elections. Editorial advisor to The *Indian Express*, T J S George, wrote in his column in the 23 December 2002 edition:

> How boringly predictable have been the reactions to Narendra Modi's triumph! At one end was jubilation climaxing in a mad claim that India would be a Hindu rashtra (nation) in two years. At the other end was despair – that all was lost and ruin faced the nation ... Modi is the beneficiary of that extremist upsurge cleverly put to political use. But it is just as true that fundamentalism has always failed because it blocked progress ....

Commenting that Christian Europe too was a snake pit of bigotry until the sixteenth century, George added:

> Islam has remained stuck in an anti-modern groove because most Islamic rulers have found safety in fundamentalism and autocracy. Saudi Arabia has even been exporting the Wahabi brand of fanaticism.

Pointing out how religious fundamentalist rulers have never succeeded in destroying either Buddhism or Hinduism, George wrote:

> Hinduism prevailed – despite prolonged onslaughts by fundamentalist Islam and predatory Christianity, because, in essence, it is a conglomerate of mutually accommodating doctrines ... The Modis will pass. The power seekers will have their fifteen minutes of glory and pass. The timeless values of Sanatana Dharma will return and the meek shell [shall] inherit the earth.

In contrast to the above view is a piece by one Dr Iffat Malik quoted by *Pakistan Link* on 27 December 2002:

> Any hope that political Hinduism could be on its last legs was emphatically shattered as Narendra Modi – a super-hawk in a party of extremists – swept to a landslide victory in India's Gujarat state. The result here is an indication of how badly values have become messed up in India, and a warning of worse to come.

Dismissing *Hindutva* as 'barbarism', Dr Malik condemned Narendra as a 'very much hands-on leader in the violence.

That someone from Pakistan – a nation that has practically driven out all Hindus from the country and whose ISI has been responsible for the death of countless Indians, not to speak of the torching of the Sabarmati Express coaches – speaks about Hindu barbarism, should evoke contempt!

The Man of the Moment: Narendra Modi

The biggest compliment that Narendra received after the victory came from a columnist of The *Times of India* on 22 December 2002. Swaminathan Aiyar wrote:

> ... Despite widespread media criticism, Narendra Modi won a landslide victory in Gujarat ... I see Narendra Modi as a future Prime Minister of India ... The prospect does not fill me with joy, but analysis is not about joyfulness. Just look around for young politicians who can move the masses, who can be more than regional leaders and make a national impact. I see no new faces, in or outside the BJP to match Modi ... Narendra Modi has many decades ahead of him. After his Gujarat victory he is obviously the star vote-getter of the party, leaving far behind older aspirants like Murali Manohar Joshi. Bhairon Singh Shekhawat may have some rival claims but he is an aged gentleman who has been kicked upstairs already. Besides, Shekhawat constantly needed help from others to form coalition governments. By contrast, Modi won with a crushing two-thirds majority in Gujarat. You may hate him, but you cannot deny his vote-getting power.

As Aiyar saw it, because of the peculiar problems that Musharraf faced in Pakistan, one could expect constant new jihadi attacks on Indian temples and state institutions. That was why, he added, he viewed Modi as a future prime minister.

> Let me not exaggerate; India is a large, complex land with many social and economic problems that have nothing to do with militancy or Pakistan. Many of these other issues will dominate from time to time, which is why I do not expect the BJP to have a monopoly of power at the Centre or the states. Others will win from time to time. But unquestionably, the jihadi phenomenon has created a bright future for the BJP and for Narendra Modi.

When Modi came to Mumbai to address a meeting at Shivaji Park, the tremendous welcome that he received came as a surprise to many people who had gathered there. Shivaji Park is the bastion of the Shiv Sena, a nationalist party of the country that deeply associates itself with public sentiments and values. It was there that the Shiv Sena leader, Bal Thackeray, made his occasional appearances before huge audiences. But on 12 January 2003, Narendra drew a crowd that was bigger than any such that had gathered in the past.

Test of Faith

It was also a show to remember. As Narendra's helicopter prepared to land, the tune of *Vande Mataram*[1] rent the air. His appearance on the dais was stage managed to make him emerge from a pink-coloured lotus flower. When he addressed the audience in a few words in Marathi, he was cheered loudly.

His speech followed a familiar line. He spoke tauntingly about Congress leaders and of 'Italy *ki beti*' amidst loud cheers. He condemned '*miyan*' Musharraf as an enemy of humanity. And he lauded *Hindutva*. He said that the over ten thousand-year-old civilization of Bharat had survived only because of *Hindutva*.

This public performance won Modi plaudits from a predominantly Maharashtrian audience and boosted the image of his party. Unquestionably, he played to the gallery! One could feel his hatred of terrorism and Musharraf who, according to Narendra, was running a semi-terrorist campaign in India. He blamed Musharraf for the Ghatkopar bus blast, fake currency rackets, drug pushing and attacks against churches. 'He is responsible for the death of a small child at Akshardham. That child will become Durga *mata* and seek vengeance against him for every drop of blood shed at Akshardham,' he added. Harsh words undoubetedly but Akshardham haunted him! Judging from the reaction of the huge audience, what he said touched many hearts. What was also significant was that never in history had a Gujarat chief minister addressed an audience at Shivaji Park or received such spontaneous ovation. At that point in time, he was the 'man of the hour'. One suspects that his success lay in his sarcasm. Marking his words, 'Congressmen ask me why I refer to Musharraf as *Miyan* Musharraf. How else should I address him? As *Aadaraniya Mananiya* (Respected) Musharraf?' There was loud laughter all round.

Congress leaders, he said, were prejudiced against Sardar Patel. In all these years, not a single member of the Nehru family had so much as visited the Sardar's birthplace. But when he set out on his *Gaurav* Yatra, the Congress brought out a pamphlet with a picture of the Sardar. For fifty years, said Narendra, the Congress

---

[1] *Vande Mataram* is the national song of India, composed by Bankim Chandra Chatterjee.

The Man of the Moment: Narendra Modi

had forgotten the Sardar. But at the time of elections it had turned to him. Rajiv Gandhi, Narendra went on, was given a Bharat Ratna but it took nine years thereafter for Sardar to be awarded the honour.

Narendra asserted that he was in favour of modernization and not Westernization. He wanted to take technology to the villagers. Gujarat had become the first state to implement river grids. In five hundred days, Gujarat had laid down seven hundred kilometres of pipes that brought the waters of Narmada to Kutch and Kathiawar.

On 22 December 2002, Narendra was formally sworn in as the chief minister by Governor Sundar Singh Bhandari at the Sardar Patel Stadium, amidst unprecedented jubilation. Thousands of people converged at the stadium to witness the swearing-in and, as *BJP Today* noted, to celebrate the fact that their 'pride and self-respect have been redeemed'.

Present at the ceremony were Prime Minister Vajpayee, Deputy Prime Minister Advani, Party President Venkaiah Naidu, NDA convenor George Fernandes, Tamil Nadu Chief Minister Jayalalithaa and many other prominent party leaders.

Narendra had been sworn in as chief minister for the first time in 2001. He had had to board a running train and head a jumbo cabinet, which was already in place. But in December 2002, when he was sworn in as the chief minister for the second time, he had the support of his people. He chose very few people for the cabinet. The concept of a minimum cabinet which should not be more than fifty per cent of the total strength of the legislative assembly was not in existence then. In fact, one could say that Narendra wanted to prove that with a bare minimum of ministers, one could function efficiently and effectively – quality standing tall as against quantity!

Possibly the best presentation of the 'Modi Phenomenon' was the cover story in *India Today* (30 December 2002) written by the then Managing Editor Swapan Dasgupta. It remains unrivalled in its understanding not only of Narendra but of the BJP victory in the December assembly elections.

Test of Faith

Dasgupta began by recalling what happened at a public meeting held in Ahmedabad four days before the elections took place, and which was attended by as many as one thousand people. The audience comprised people belonging to the city's medical fraternity. Aware of the profile of his audience, Narendra took off on themes that had not found resonance at the hustings, such as education, development and industrialization. He shared that he did not get an opportunity to speak on such subjects very often and he was using this opportunity to address some particular issues, instead of talking about Musharraf. At that point, many in the audience were heard saying, 'No, no, we want to hear about Musharraf!' and that suggestion was greeted with thunderous applause. The Modi act had broken through the class barrier!

What follows is Dasgupta's comment:

> *The doctors of Ahmedabad confirmed that this was not an election about development and promises; it was a referendum dictated by raw emotion. The Chief Minister did not perform that evening, but in meeting after meeting, to urban and rural audiences, he elevated combative populism to electrifying heights. He successfully established a direct co-relation between demonology and adulation: the more he became a 'hate figure' in cosmopolitan circles, the more his popularity soared in Gujarat. By the time the magnitude of the BJP victory sank in on the morning of December 15, Modi had established himself as a cult figure with an appeal that extended well beyond Gujarat of Militant Hindu nationalism, as an icon.*

Dasgupta said that it would be facile to suggest that the Gujarat verdict was an enthusiastic endorsement of Hinduism, but he added that 'there were strong undercurrents of Hindu solidarity in the shrill expressions of anti-terrorism and sympathy for the victims of Godhra which was undeniable'. He went on to say:

> *This was only incidentally an election centred on ideology: the real issue was leadership. In his department Modi did not face any competition. Not even from the two stalwarts of his party, Prime Minister Atal Bihari Vajpayee and Deputy Prime Minister L K Advani. His main challenger, state Congress chief Shankersinh Vaghela, was reduced to the level of a caste leader and Sonia Gandhi never crossed the detachment of an outsider ... Narendra's victory*

at the polls was as much a personal triumph as it was the Gujarati way of registering their protest at the manner in which they had been vilified by the English media.

Addressing the BJP parliamentary party on 17 December 2002, Prime Minister Vajpayee had raised an important point. He said, 'We are being asked whether we will adopt the Gujarat formula elsewhere. I ask them, "Will they repeat Godhra as well?" It saddens me that not many from the Muslim community are stepping forward to say they are repentant for Godhra. Even now, no one is saying that whatever happened was wrong and that we have to live together.'

The silence, not only of many Muslims but the entire band of secularists, on the issue of Godhra, was what turned some Muslims vengeful. To many Muslims, it was as if Godhra had never happened and that the killings of Muslims in Ahmedabad in late February and March 2002 had to be avenged. The man who exploded bombs in Mumbai at the Gateway of India and at a teeming bazaar is reported to have said that he did so to avenge Gujarat.

That is what the anti-Modi, anti-Gujarat stance taken by the English media achieved. The blood of those killed in Mumbai was again on pseudo-secular hands. The pseudo-secular press misled many Muslims into thinking that not Muslims but Modi had been responsible for the riots in Gujarat.

When the Gujarat assembly met for the first time after the elections and the matter of alleged police complicity during the riots came up for discussion, Narendra took the floor and was at his sarcastic best. He wanted to know why Gujarat's critics in Parliament had been silent when fifty-eight people, including forty innocent women and children, had been burnt alive. Were the deaths of these people on 27 February 2002 different from other deaths, he wanted to know. He said:

'I do not understand why Gujarat has been made a target of criticism. From the floor of this House I wish to tell the entire nation that there have been constant efforts to blame Gujarat over various issues. It is a serious cause for concern. It was proved that Surat had become plague-free, yet it became infamous in the entire world ....'

Test of Faith

Narendra went on to say that it was immaterial who was in power in Gujarat. Gujarat was immortal; the spirit of Gujarat was immortal. Gujarat was a border state and the government had to be vigilant. It had recovered AK-56 rifles, pistols, RDX explosives, radio sets, remote control systems and a thousand cartridges from Patan in just one week. It had seized provocative literature, objectionable maps and explosives from a *maulvi* (Islamic priest) of Dabhel madrasa in Navsari district.

The government had also exposed the evil conspiracies of SIMI, an organization banned by the Government of India, and more than a hundred headstrong elements of this organization had been caught and put behind bars. Narendra said these actions had moved terrorist organizations to seek revenge. They had hatched a conspiracy to defame and demoralize the police force.

Rising to the defence of the police officers, Narendra said that he was committed to accepting all responsibility and was willing to be hanged if anyone felt that he was the culprit. He said he was committed to protecting police officers because they were making sincere efforts to bring normalcy back to the state. Narendra then said that he was not greedy for power, that he was committed, and ended up quoting a poem:

Kuch mukhdo ki narazi se

Darpan nahin dara karte hein.

(Some faces may show annoyance, but the mirrors are not scared)

Renaissance Outside the Labyrinth   11

On 1 May 2003, Gujarat celebrated its forty-third foundation day. And Narendra, as chief minister, issued a message to his fellow Gujaratis, seeking their cooperation in establishing peace, creating trust and healing the wounds inflicted during the riots. The law, he said, would take its course. His message was clear:

'We have completed forty-two years of our "development yatra". In the course of these years, many have become martyrs for Gujarat. There has been communal violence in Gujarat in recent times ... It is as if Gujarat has lost its humanity.

'It is necessary to get it back. It is vital to create an atmosphere of trust among the people. There has been a conspiracy to defame Gujarat. Nobody has cared to understand our pain. Our critics are more interested in post-mortem ... Can't they cooperate in our peace efforts? The pain is of five crore people and not of mine alone ... Don't trust rumours. If we don't trust each other, it will be difficult to live ... Some elements have targetted Gujarat for destruction. They take refuge in terrorism. But they function only in a few places. In all of Gujarat, there are just about five to ten police stations around where mischievous elements function. We should separate them, alienate them and stand up as one society. In time, the situation will change.

'I need to present another picture to people in trust ... Five crore citizens should announce to the world in full self-confidence that we are not the kind of people that you paint us to be. This is the Gujarat where, during the crisis, one crore, twenty lakh students appeared for their examinations. There was opposition to this but we crossed the hurdles in our way. We took every possible step to see that students did not suffer.

'When Hajis returned from Haj, the whole village received them with the same pomp as they would receive a Hindu returning after his pilgrimage to all the four holy places in India ... some 1,000 *tajias* were taken out to celebrate Moharrum. Holi has also been celebrated in unison. All sections of society participated in celebrating Holi in 18,000 villages ... during the crisis period we are talking about, 1,700 villages held elections, and as many as 75 per cent of the people voted. There were no untoward incidents. Gujarat can say proudly that, in the entire country, it is the only state which has elected representatives to all gram panchayats ... More than ninety-five per cent of Gujarat is quiet. Incidents of violence may have taken place only in 60 to 70 out of the 18,000 villages. Out of 143 cities, only 40 reported incidents, and that, too, in the early stages. Now, incidents are confined to some five to ten police stations in Vadodara and Ahmedabad. I request my friends not to spread misinformation. Criticize us as much as you like but help us maintain peace and quiet in the state. You have all the right to dislocate us from seats of power in a democracy, but at least for the time being, help us establish peace.'

Narendra assured the people that law breakers would be punished. Gujarat, he said, had signed up agreements to the tune of ₹5,000 crore and as far as industrial progress was concerned, Gujarat was number one in the country. He said, 'To encourage the diamond industry, we have taken a major step by eliminating sales tax. We have also removed sales tax on electricity to make it cheaper.' After paying homage to the police officials who had been killed and the hospital staff who had rendered round-the-clock service to people in times of need, he added, 'With sadness in my eyes, pain in the heart and with a sense of compassion, I pray to you with folded hands to make Gujarat great.'

The message was well received. It showed a contrite man who was determined and committed to re-establish trust amongst people – *all* the people.

For weeks following the Godhra incident, it became fashionable for the secular media to propagate that Gujarat had failed economically. The truth was far from that. By 2004, Gujarat accounted for seventeen per cent of the total industrial development in the country, twenty-one per cent of total exports, eighty per cent of diamond processing and seventeen per cent of the country's total tax revenue. According to the data published by the Centre for Monitoring Indian Economy (CMIE), Gujarat stood first in industrialization in India (January 2003) with projects worth ₹33,958 crore under implementation.

Narendra was a man in a hurry, even if his critics were not willing to give him any credit. Investments kept pouring in. He was very focussed on the development of Gujarat. He did not talk about the past, and did not make any attempts to silence his critics. His thoughts were similar to that of Arjun of the *Mahabharata* who saw only the target and nothing else.

On 19 January 2003, Narendra addressed a meeting of the CII organized by business captains in Mumbai where he outlined his economic vision for Gujarat. He laid stress on cutting red-tapism and bringing in transparency in the workings of the government. He reiterated his government's commitment towards creating a conducive economic environment to facilitate private sector initiative. He called for re-enforcement of the partnership between the public and the private sectors which alone, he felt, could help the state achieve a growth rate of more than ten per cent in future.

Narendra Modi was invited to deliver the inaugural address at the International Conference on Bio-informatics and Contract Research in New Delhi in February 2003. He called upon all present to make India the global bio-informatics headquarters by building on its success in IT and combining that with its skills in biology and chemistry. The market for bio-informatics, according to him, was expected to be around ten billion dollars. Narendra also focussed on the need to invest in five areas of biotechnology: pharmaceuticals, agricultural biotechnology, industrial enzymes and the two new areas of environment – biotechnology and marine biotechnology. In the last two, Gujarat just needed investment as it had the resources, including the largest state coastline in the country. He emphasized Gujarat's potential in contract research. The state, he said, had forty per cent of India's pharma manufacturing sector, many big hospitals and an entrepreneurial culture. All it needed was some venture financing and Narendra promised that his government would set up a venture capital fund. On 2 March 2003, he was invited to address an 'India Today Conclave' in New Delhi on how Indian states could get their act together. He pointed out the Konkan Railway project promoted by the Indian Railways and four states, namely, Maharashtra, Karnataka, Goa and Kerala, as an illustration of how states could work together in 'asset creation without delays and cost over-runs. We must apply our minds to see what organizational capacity went into the application of such a project,' he said.

He felt that the problem of People's War Group (PWG) could be solved if Andhra Pradesh, Madhya Pradesh, Chhattisgarh, Maharashtra and Bihar would get their act together.

While FICCI partnered with the Gujarat government for the 'Vibrant Gujarat Global Investors' Meet' scheduled in September on the sidelines of the Navaratri festivities, CII offered to organize a special interaction between Narendra and the European business community in collaboration with the World Economic Forum in Zurich and Geneva on 21-22 August 2003. Modi would project Gujarat internationally in terms of exports from the state and the investments that could be made there.

Modi addressed a gathering of 2,500 Gujaratis at Wembley. He received three standing ovations during his seventy-minute long address. The next day, Narendra inaugurated the Shakti Hall of *Gujarat Samachar*, a bilingual local weekly. In his speech he said, ... Journalists should not act like flies, carrying dirt from place to place and spreading diseases. Rather they should be like the honeybee which flies from one flower to another, savouring honey and, at the same time, stinging severely in adverse circumstances.'

On 21 August 2003, Narendra left London to collect the ashes of the freedom fighter and revolutionary, Shyamaji Krishna Varma, who had died in Switzerland in 1930. Talking of Varma, Narendra Modi said: 'His last wish was to have his ashes returned to India when India became independent. Sadly, this wish was not fulfilled for more than fifty years after Independence.'

Vibrant Gujarat

Global Investors' Summit 2003

The Global Investors' summit was organized at the two major commercial cities of the state – Ahmedabad and Surat, in association with the Government of India (GOI), UNIDO, FICCI and CII. There were one-on-one discussions between prospective investors, government officials and project promoters. As many as 176 project proposals were compiled and scrutinized for their viability. Internationally reputed credit rating agencies like Credit Rating Information Services of India Limited (CRISIL) and Credit Analysis and Research Limited (CARE) lent their support as financial advisors to these projects. Leading private and public sector banks like ICICI, IDBL, State Bank of India, Bank of Baroda, State Bank of Saurashtra, Corporation Bank, IDFC and NABARD extended their support for financing these projects. The Deputy Prime Minister of India, L K Advani, inaugurated the summit on 28 September 2003. Chief Minister Narendra Modi, Arun Shourie, Ram Naik, Mukesh Ambani, and A C Muthaih were among the dignitaries present. Union ministers, senior officials from state governments and the Central government, as well as experts in textiles, gems and jewellery attended the Meet. Seventy-six MoUs worth fourteen billion US dollars were signed for investment.

Global Investors' Summit 2005

The state government held a second 'Vibrant Gujarat Global Investors' Summit' in January 2005 at Science City, Ahmedabad. Inaugurated by the then Vice President of India Bhairon Singh Shekhawat, it was attended by notable industry representatives from India and overseas. As a reflection of faith in the state's potential to become a leading global destination, MoUs worth ₹870 billion were signed on the very first day.

Among the galaxy of over five thousand delegates, there were 950 NRIs and 432 foreign delegates; the remaining were the stars of corporate India – they included representatives from Reliance, ESSAR, Videocon, Larsen & Toubro, the Torrent Group and the Sanghvi Group. The summit was planned to coincide with *Uttarayan* – Gujarat's famous Kite Festival. Sectoral theme pavilions showcasing the strength of Gujarat in relevant areas were put up. The event hosted exhibitions and seminars on various focus areas – gas, petroleum, IT, biotechnology, agro-industries, energy, non-conventional energy, port and port-led industries, financial services, textiles and apparel, gems and jewellery, tourism and others.

The Gujarat government decided to induct a private company for its proposed Biotechnology Park near Baroda. Narendra proudly said, 'If IT is India today, BT is Bharat tomorrow. We are identifying focus areas within biotechnology for the state – pharmaceuticals are a natural choice ....'

The *Free Press Journal* (13 January 2005) noted that the slew of new industrial and infrastructural projects to be set up in Gujarat called for an estimated investment of ₹51,500 crore. On the concluding day of the two-day Investors' Summit, Investments worth ₹1,060 billion were signed in the form of MoUs with 226 units.

Narendra Modi told The *Pioneer*, 'The reason why Gujarat has attracted so much attention is that we have excellent roads; ours probably is the only state with the best water management scheme where every single village is connected to the network of irrigation and drinking water supplies.'

He announced his intention of setting up a 'Green Revolution Company' that would help farmers increase their productivity. Gujarat State Fertilizers and Chemicals Ltd and Gujarat Narmada Fertilizer Company Ltd were two state-run companies that had made a profit of ₹15 billion. He wanted the farmers to join hands to 'give birth to a new company called the Green Revolution Company'. Buoyed with the success of the summit, he added: 'Punjab led the country in the first green revolution. Gujarat will lead the country in bringing about the second green revolution, just as it had led in the white revolution'.

Global Investors Summit 2007

The government of Gujarat hosted the Vibrant Gujarat Global Investors' Summit 2007 at Ahmedabad. Two significant messages were sent out to prospective investors:

- In Gujarat, there is only Red Carpet and no Red Tape.
- It is where investors can sow a rupee and reap a dollar as return.

The Man of the Moment: Narendra Modi

The event, spread over four days, saw foreign delegations from the US, China, Japan, Singapore, Australia, South Korea, Italy and Israel and two hundred representatives from various countries. As many as sixty industrialists and investors had meetings with Narendra over the course of two days. Shree Balaji Sadashivan, Minister of State for Foreign Affairs of the Singapore government, was the chief guest. The chief minister opened the summit with the message that the main goal of the state was to transform the whole of Gujarat into an SEZ (Special Economic Zone), with a unique interpretation of the term SEZ – namely: Spirituality, Entrepreneurship and Zeal. The ultimate aim was to put Gujarat on an equal footing with the developed nations of the world.

The speakers at the inauguration ceremony extolled the progress made by Gujarat. Mukesh Ambani said: 'Gujarat is a land that has transformed opportunities and challenges into a powerful entrepreneurial vision.' Mr Ratan Tata stated: 'Gujarat is an ideal investment destination. One is stupid if one is not in Gujarat (as an investor).'

During the course of the summit, a total of 343 MoUs were signed and twenty announcements were made aggregating prospective investments worth ₹4,61,835 crore. On top of the investment brackets were twenty-eight MoUs for special economic zones with an investment of ₹1,70,886 crore.

Kite-Flying Carnival

Even as the concept of 'Vibrant Gujarat' was taking root, Narendra was trying to work out another extraordinary idea – developing the kite industry in the state. A state-wise survey conducted by the Gujarat Industrial and Technical Consultancy Organization (GITCO) surmised that there were about thirty thousand artisans in Ahmedabad alone who were engaged in kite-making round the year, besides another twenty thousand seasonal workers. There were around three hundred and fifty contract manufacturers and wholesalers and a thousand retailers.

The estimated market size of kites in Ahmedabad was over forty crore rupees per annum that included twelve crores from the sale of kites, eighteen crores from the sale of thread, ₹2.50 crore from *phirkees* (reels around which the flying strings are wound) sans thread and ₹40 lakh from allied consumables like gas balloons and gum tape. Narendra sensed a great business idea in the kite-flying carnival on the occasion of *Makar Sankranti* in January when he could 'invite the attention of the NRIs to the state's development'.

The idea was to roll out the red carpet for Gujarati NRIs from 12-14 January 2004, which would coincide with the kite-flying festival of *Uttarayan,* and call the event *Vishwa Gujarati Parivar Mahotsav* (Worldwide Gujarati Family Festival). The *mahotsav* would closely follow the Pravasi Bharatiya Programme that the Central government had planned to observe from 9-11 January 2004. To Narendra's benefit, 12 January coincided with the birth anniversary of Swami Vivekananda. As was expected, Narendra took full care that the programme was fully and properly implemented. The state government sent fifty thousand e-mails to Non-Resident Gujaratis (NRGs) worldwide. The entire state machinery was mobilized to ensure maximum participation of all Gujaratis, NRGs included, to make this *patang-utsav* (Kite Festival) a success.

Uttarayan is traditionally celebrated as a festival in all parts of Gujarat. Narendra took a smart step by deciding to use it for cultural integration and promotion of tourism. It brought together international and local kite fliers from eighteen countries, including the US, China, Holland, Brazil, Chile, Australia and Italy. S N Ruia, Chairman of Essar group commented: 'Festivals like this are an ideal platform to forge greater social harmony.' He summed it up in the following meaningful words: 'Terrorism divides the world; tourism unites the world.'

Setting the dates for the Kite Festival immediately after the Bharat Divas organized in Delhi by the Government of India and FICCI was to be over, was a smart idea. Kite-flying was only a one-day event but various trips were organized in and around Gujarat for the visitors to see the main tourist spots and the developmental projects undertaken by the government. This attracted Gujaratis back to their homeland and also gave other visitors the opportunity to explore the beauty of the state.

Prime Minister Atal Bihari Vajpayee inaugurated the *utsav* in the presence of over ten thousand children and college students.

He also released two books: *Vatan ni Vate* – a compendium of NRGs' contributions to their home state, and *Beyond Boundaries* by Markand Mehta, that highlights the trade links that the Gujaratis had established ever since the Harappan civilization around 2500 BC. Five prominent NRGs and three top experts were commended. They were Skye Morrison who presented her Canadian collection of stamps that had kites printed on them, Bhanubhai Shah who had been running a kite museum for forty-eight years in Ahmedabad, and eighty-year old Rasul Chacha, the oldest kite manufacturer in Gujarat. The *mahotsav* turned out to be a grand success.

Today, this festival is organized by Collectors of various districts at their respective district headquarters to promote tourism. The focus is not so much on promoting it as a business; kite manufacturers all over the state get an opportunity to earn money by making kites of striking shapes and forms.

V-Governance and Other Projects

Post the Festival in January 2004, Narendra decided to launch another ambitious project to train five lakh employees in 'V-Governance' (Vibrant Governance)! He addressed about two thousand government officers in Gandhinagar's Town Hall on how to be *karmayogis* (those dedicated to service). Narendra was constantly on the go. His primary aim was to convert all employees into *karmayogis* and he called his seven-hundred-day plan the *Karmayogi Maha Abhiyan* (Campaign to transform public servants into *karmayogis*).

Narendra's detractors would take a dig at him for coining fascinating – even if appropriate – titles for all the programmes he envisaged. As The *Times of India* noted on 18 February 2004, '... his innovative coinage of terminology to package new government schemes smartly has left his opponents gasping.' Modi gave a brand new name to the pipeline project initiated by his predecessor Keshubhai Patel and called it 'Sujalam Suphalam Yojana' (SSY) project which means 'Good, Sweet Water, Yielding Good Results'. Narendra is an expert at launching campaigns that can then recur annually or biennially. The year 2003 was declared the year for promoting the education of the girl child. The year 2004 was declared as the year of E-governance, and 2005 – the development of the Urban Sector. Tourism was the centre of attention in 2006 and 'Nirmal Gujarat' in 2007. The year 2008 was declared as the year for the Healthy Child. The purpose of these campaigns was to concentrate energy and focus on that particular area and re-orient the energy of the entire administration towards achieving the goals that had been set.

Alleviating the Water Problem

One of the major problems continuously faced by Gujarat was non-availability of water. This problem had been festering for years. Demand kept increasing and with the expanding industrialization of the state, water pollution had taken a turn for the worse. Some of the statistics were frightening. In the Saurashtra district of Gujarat, there were 7,50,000 deep tube wells drawing water from under the earth. In the Mehsana district in north Gujarat, the number was 25,000. Worst hit were the Saurashtra region and Kutch, bordering Pakistan. These areas were hit by water shortage even in years of normal rainfall. Experts feared that matters would worsen by 2025 when the state was expected to fall short by about 7,294 million cubic metres (MCM) of water.

Over the years, governments had taken various steps to alleviate the water crisis. In 2000, a law was enacted to restrict the haphazard use of sub-soil water. Forty sub-divisions were declared 'scarcity zones', where underground water was depleting fast. Excessive use of underground water had led to chronic water scarcity in over 9,000 of the 18,000 villages in the state. And that was despite the fact that more than ₹1,200 crore had been spent on tapping water resources in the previous decade.

Even if Narendra has not done anything else for Gujarat except providing its people with drinking water, he will still go on to be a part of its history as a saviour. What Narendra has done for the people has exceeded all expectations. Today, in Gujarat, water scarcity is a matter of the past. The reason for Gujarat standing out in the crowd despite all odds is Narendra's SSY project, a programme meant to provide equitable long-term water

The Man of the Moment: Narendra Modi

security in the state, especially to the ten worst affected districts: Ahmedabad, Gandhinagar, Mehsana, Patan, Banaskantha and Sabarkantha in north Gujarat, Surendranagar, Kutch, Panchmahal and Dahod.

The SSY is a multi-purpose programme that has already served many other purposes besides just providing irrigation and drinking water. It has facilitated storing rain water using various types and scales of water conservation. This is a tremendous achievement as this rain water would otherwise have simply trickled into the sea. In the first place, the state utilized the Narmada river waters for reviving various other rivers in Gujarat like the Banas, Rupen and Saraswati. By 2005, the Narmada waters had reached Kutch – a live example of a stupendous engineering feat!

Then there was the issue of check-dams and farm ponds. Between 2001 and 2005, more than 50,000 check-dams were constructed in Gujarat, ten times more than the number constructed in the previous forty years. When Narendra called upon the people of the state to construct one lakh farm ponds in a hundred days in the year 2004, few believed the target would be achieved. But, it *was* achieved, and that too because the people of Gujarat rose to accomplish the task. By 2005, there were 1.37 lakh farm ponds in the state. The water level rose to about a hundred feet in some places. In the past, the distribution of surface water in Gujarat was highly unbalanced – 74 per cent in south Gujarat, 10.6 per cent in north Gujarat, 15.8 per cent in Saurashtra and 2.2 per cent in Kutch. Narendra decided to remove this imbalance by supplying water through pipelines from the Narmada to Kutch.

This plan was executed and 1,400 kilometres of water transmission lines costing ₹1,690 crore were laid. Thanks to that effort, the water scarcity problem in more than two thousand villages, fifty two towns and three municipal corporations has been resolved for good. Narottam Patel, the Minister for Water, was quoted as saying: 'Today we are quite safe in Gujarat with regard to availability of drinking water. The water is being provided almost free.'

Many are therefore hopeful that the Kalpasar Project will solve the state's water woes. As envisaged, the Kalpasar Project will involve building a sixty-four-kilometre-long dam across the Gulf of Khambat (known in the past as the Gulf of Cambay) from Ghogha in Bhavnagar district to Hansot in Bharuch district. The dam will trap the water from twelve rivers that flow into the Gulf, including the big ones like the Narmada, Mahi, Sabarmati and Dhadar, to create a large freshwater lake. The Kalpasar reservoir will have an area of two thousand square kilometres which will be fifty times bigger than the existing Bhadar Reservoir in Rajkot. It will store more water than all the existing major, medium and minor dams in the state. Indeed, it will store three times more water than the Sardar Sarovar reservoir. More importantly, the reservoir will hardly displace any inhabitants of the region.

There are other positive facts that favour the project. It will be able to generate 5,880 mega watts (MW) of tidal power and will provide around 5.61 MCM of water annually to irrigate 1,054,500 hectares of land in southern Saurashtra. Besides, it will provide 900 MCM of water for domestic usage and another 500 MCM for the industrial development of Kutch and Saurashtra. And, if the suggestion made by Haskoning, an international company that carried out a survey of the proposed plan, is accepted, it will be possible to build a multi-lane highway and a railway line across the length of the dam, which would slash the distance between south Gujarat and Mumbai by about 225 kilometres.

By the beginning of 2004, the NDA was in great form at the Centre. The market was buoyant, the economy had registered a record 10.6 per cent growth, and politically, it was a time for stability, not to speak of peace between India and Pakistan. Elections were due in September 2004 but such was the 'feel good' factor that some within the BJP felt that it would be a smart idea to call for general elections in early March or April, even though Prime Minister Vajpayee himself opposed it.

There were some factors to cheer the BJP. One was a *Week-TNS* poll that showed that the BJP and its allies would get between 230 and 265 seats, though that was much less than what they got in 1999 (291 seats). The majority voice in the BJP held sway and the Lok Sabha was dissolved on 5 February 2004. The BJP wanted the new House to be constituted by late March but the Election Commission called for a four-phase election ending on 10 May. By the end of the second phase, the once cocky BJP stalwarts became jittery by what they could gather from exit polls. *India Today* noted in its 24 May 2004 issue:

> For the BJP, allies turned out to be the real antagonists. Tamil Nadu was the suicide point ... Karunanidhi handed over all the 39 seats to Sonia Gandhi ... Even in Uttar Pradesh, where the BJP had won 25 seats in 1999, it was able to get only ten in 2004, because of factional fights ....

In Karnataka, the BJP had done well in the assembly elections and had become the single largest party. In the Lok Sabha elections too, the BJP did well, capturing eighteen seats. In Gujarat, Narendra hoped to win all twenty-one seats, but could manage to win only fourteen. The Congress, in its best performance in fifteen years, won twelve.

The *Week* wrote on 23 May 2004:

> Party seniors, including state campaign chief Suresh Mehta, blamed the summer heat and the wedding season for the low voter turnout – the 'sole cause' for the BJP's losses ... The Congress made inroads in constituencies like Junagadh in Saurashtra, Mehsana in north Gujarat and Anand in central Gujarat. The party also reclaimed the tribal seats of Valsad, Mandvi and Chota Udaipur. Senior Congressman Siddharth Patel feels the state has voted against Modi's autocratic ways and the BJP's total neglect of farmers' issues . . .
>
> Modi will have to do a lot of explaining to the party. The price of over-confidence, arrogance and autocracy were being openly discussed among the few party workers present at the BJP state headquarters and all fingers pointed at Modi. With arch-rival Shankersinh Vaghela likely to find a place in the Union Cabinet, this could be the beginning of rough days for the Modi regime.

These words turned out to be prophetic.

Once the election results were out, so were the knives. All Narendra's detractors and opponents within the party, who had been lying low, now began to come out against him openly. Some protested against his style. *Times News Network* said: While the local RSS was not against Modi, 'there is no love lost between the CM and Sanjay Joshi, the party's organizational general secretary and RSS man.'

TNN also reported: Informed analysts estimate that as many as 85 MLAs in the BJP Legislature Party of 128 may want Modi out.'

TNN reported Vajpayee as saying: 'We are thinking afresh on the situation in Gujarat. The matter will be considered ...'

Narendra stolidly put up with all this abuse and embarked on a three-day *Gyan Ratha* Yatra (Journey of Knowledge) to enrol girls in schools.

The RSS itself seemed to have been split vertically on the Narendra Modi issue. Finally, BJP president Venkaiah Naidu who spoke to Vajpayee over the telephone clarified the issue by saying that there was no proposal to replace Modi. Even the RSS chief K Sudarshan rejected the idea that the Gujarat riots were to blame for BJP's defeat and the RSS spokesman Ram Madhav went a step further, saying that the Sangh would not accept that 'blame' for the election debacle was being put on Narendra Modi.

'In reality, the situation is serious. Modi is non-corrupt and very intelligent and that is conceded by his detractors. Whatever he picks up, he takes it to its logical end. He can impress people. But his working style, egoism, superiority complex, lack of trust in anyone around him, goes against him. He can insult and condemn anyone.'

As the plot to make Narendra the centre of all discussions gathered momentum, he despatched some of his senior colleagues to plead his case before the BJP parliamentary board meeting being held in Delhi. But by then, the belief that it was Narendra's handling of the post-Godhra riots that had been responsible for the BJP's failure in the general elections, had undergone a change. What followed was a climb-down on the part of Vajpayee. Speaking to newspersons in Kullu, Vajpayee said that the issue of Modi's removal has become 'a thing of the past'. A crisis was averted.

And a warning was sent to the dissidents by the BJP working committee to go slow or else face disciplinary action. Things changed immediately after that.

But the United Progressive Alliance (UPA) government was not going to let off Narendra easily. The Gujarat government had set up the Justice G T Nanavati and K G Shah Commission to investigate the circumstances in which the Godhra carnage had taken place. The UPA government also decided to constitute a high-powered Committee – headed by former Supreme Court Judge U C Banerjee – to probe the incident. The BJP described the government's decsion as 'unconstitutional and politically motivated'.

Going against all well-known and established facts, the Banerjee Commission found that the fire in the Sabarmati Express bogies was 'accidental'. The general public treated the Commission's findings with the derision that they deserved.

As weeks passed, the tide began to turn in favour of Narendra. On 18 September 2004, The *Statesman* gave credit to the Modi government for turning two public sector units – Gujarat Alkalies and Chemicals Ltd (GACL) and Gujarat State Fertilizers and Chemicals Ltd (GSFC) – from loss-making to profit-making companies. In the 22 September 2004 issue of The *Statesman*, Narendra was asked whether he was not concerned about his image; his reply was sharp. He said, 'Why should I be conscious about my image? The people of Gujarat have given me a job. I will work with the strength that God has given me. Image, perception – all such things – I have left for others to decide on. Let them enjoy what they are doing. Let them decide – let them come to their conclusions.'

On 4 October, the paper reported that the Gujarat State Petroleum Corporation had struck oil at a place that was barely four hundred metres away from twenty-eight wells that the Oil and Natural Gas Corporation (ONGC) had dug but found dry. This was followed by a media report that within four years, about forty thousand check-dams had been constructed in Gujarat with peoples' participation. The report said: 'By 2010, all the regions of Gujarat will become green and not even a single village will face drinking water problem.' That was high praise indeed. Then came *Navaratri*. From 14 October to 22 October, Gujarat became a colossal stage for a dance festival. It was 'Vibrant Gujarat' all over again. Money flowed in.

To ensure that the *Navaratri* festival became a mega event, Narendra got the then President A P J Abdul Kalam and Vice President Bhairon Singh Shekhawat to visit Ahmedabad. The president inaugurated the 'Destination Gujarat' function while the vice-president launched a colourful programme marking the beginning of the *Navaratri* festivities. President Abdul Kalam had words of praise for Gujarat for its initiative in taking religious and spiritual tourism from the narrow confines of the state to national and international levels. The President said that Gujarat had shown the way to the country by promoting 'festival tourism' in the form of the Vibrant Gujarat *Navaratri* Festival 2004.

To complete the circle of praise, the Commonwealth Association for Public Administration and Management (CAPAM) awarded Gujarat the gold medal for 'innovations in governance' for its post-earthquake reconstruction at a presentation ceremony held in Singapore in October.

An article in *Gujarat Times,* London (5 November 2004), said that 'Industry, effort, courage, adventure, moral courage to take initiative and plain-speaking give a special touch to his personality. He keeps his political competitors and opponents on their feet, trembling.'

Narendra would say: 'Business is in our DNA. This single characteristic supported by geographical advantages will make Gujarat a global player.'

In the last week of November 2004, Narendra set out on a journey to South-East Asia to make Gujarat the 'investment destination' for global investors.

He started with a three-day visit to Singapore on 27 November. 'Investment Avenues and Development Strategies in Gujarat', organised by the institute of South Asian Studies (ISAS), Narendra averred that Gujarat had attained credibility as having the best investment climate. He pointed out that the private sector had developed chemical ports with large refineries, gas grids and LNG terminals, while a third of Gujarat's villages were getting regular power supply. Modi was praised by ISAS chairman Gopinath Pillai who said that Gujarat had proved its credit-worthiness to Singapore and other South-East Asian countries.

From Singapore, Narendra flew to Hong Kong and Sydney to discuss their interest in food-processing, higher education and medical tourism. Narendra had a special meeting with Andrew

Feshauge, premier of New South Wales Province, where an understanding was arrived at to enhance cooperation in the field of education. The chief minister's team also visited the Melbourne port where they discussed possibilities of developing ports in the private sector and increasing foreign trade from Special Economic Zones (SEZs) through sea routes. Narendra was indefatigable. No other state chief minister in the past had made such wide business forays to invite investment.

The General in Command   12

The waves of success at the Global Investors' Summit had hardly died down when the Railway Minister Lalu Prasad Yadav released the 'so-called' Interim Report of the Justice Banerjee Committee on the Godhra train fire. It appeared to many that the release was timed to smother Narendra's success at the summit. The gist of the Banerjee Report was that the fire was 'accidental' and was not caused by any outside elements. The timing of the release of the report was not a surprise as Bihar was about to go to polls and Lalu Prasad wanted the Muslim vote desperately. The Congress, and of course, the Leftist parties, welcomed the Banerjee report with glee. Anything was welcome as long as it damned Narendra Modi.

The Election Commission was quick to understand the implications of the report and described its publication as 'unfortunate' when the assembly elections in three states were at hand.

It appealed to political parties and leaders not to use it during the election campaign. As a matter of fact, scarcely anybody in the political class took the Banerjee report seriously. Pratap Bhanu Mehta, the CEO, Centre for Policy Research, said that the time and manner in which Banerjee disclosed his findings 'have done grave harm to the cause of truth ... Playing politics with truth can be as insidious as subversion by lies. Unwittingly, perhaps, Banerjee has ensured that truth will remain hostage to politics.'

The BJP, on its own, raised some vital questions that went unanswered. The questions were addressed to Banerjee:

- Did you consider the evidence that two meetings took place on the night of 26 February 2002 at Aman Guest

House at Godhra where the conspiracy to set fire to bogey S-6 of the Sabarmati Express was hatched?

- Did you consider the evidence that 140 litres of petrol was purchased from a nearby petrol pump on that night and kept at Aman Guest House?
- Did you consider the evidence that one of the conspirators, Salim Badam, was verifying the movement of the Sabarmati Express at 1.30 am from the Godhra railway station? Since the train was running four hours late, the conspirators re-assembled at Aman Guest House at 6 am.
- Did you consider the evidence that the conspirators entered bogey number S-7 and cut open the vestibule cord between bogies S-6 and S-7, after which the entire quantity of petrol was poured into bogey S-6?
- Do you realize that the 'Accident Theory' propounded by you is not an original thought but was propounded by the accused in the case and repeated by Lalu Prasad Yadav, Railway Minister, while announcing your appointment?
- Why was the Chief Justice of India not consulted in the appointment of a retired judge? You were the choice of the railway minister!

Understandably, secular forces raised their own questions in defence of Banerjee and efforts were made by interested parties to raise a revolt against Narendra from within his own party, as had been done on earlier occasions as well. The point made was that what some of the BJP MLAs were against was 'the style of functioning and policies of Narendra Modi'. Vithal Pandya, father of the slain former Gujarat minister Haren Pandya, even went to the extent of charging Narendra with being 'the author and architect of the Godhra carnage'.

The dissident leaders led by former Gujarat Chief Minister Keshubhai Patel called on BJP President L K Advani only to be told firmly and categorically that there would be 'no leadership change' in the Gujarat government. That, at least, temporarily, ended another dissident revolt against Narendra.

The viciousness that the English media in India showed towards Narendra was not without its inevitable consequences.

Representatives of the foreign press in Delhi invariably take their cue of what is happening in India from the country's English media. Their views are all too frequently shaped by what is reported and commented upon in the English press. Vir Sanghvi, then Editor of the *Hindustan Times*, described Narendra as 'a mass murderer' in the 19 March 2005 issue of the newspaper. No wonder, then, that Narendra was being demonized in the United States!

Fundamentalist Christian missionary organizations in the US, too, had a grouse against Narendra. Their evangelical activities among the tribal people were being carefully watched, much to their discomfort. Some fundamentalist Indian Christians were noticeably active in Washington in marshalling hatred against Narendra. Others to carry out an anti-Modi campaign were the Washington-based Institute on Religion and Public Policy and the Islamic Society of North America.

It so happened that Narendra was to pay a five-day visit to the United States in March to attend the 2005 Annual Convention and Trade Show of the Asian-American Hotel Owners Association in Fort Lauderdale, Florida. For days prior to the visit, rumours were floating around that the US government might deny him a visa. And this was at a time when the US Secretary of State, Condoleezza Rice, was visiting Delhi. On Wednesday, 16 March 2005, Rice was having a one-to-one meeting with L K Advani, leader of the Opposition in Parliament, when the latter brought up the issue of a likely denial of visa to Narendra.

Advani told Rice that he had received reports that a section in the US was opposed to Narendra's visit and urged her to dissuade policy-making authorities in the government from being influenced by such protests. Interestingly enough, Modi had visited the US twice after the February 2002 riots. He already had a tourist-business visa, but this time, he had applied for a diplomatic visa that had been duly endorsed by the Home Ministry and the Ministry of External Affairs (MEA). Rice gave no firm assurance to Advani and her response, to say the least, was evasive.

But on the morning of 18 March, Narendra received a letter from the Minister of Consular Affairs and Consul General in the US embassy, William M Bartlett, notifying him that his passport

The Man of the Moment: Narendra Modi

and cancelled visa were being returned to him. The US embassy spokesperson said that Mr Modi 'was denied the diplomatic visa under Section 214 (b) of the Immigration and Nationality Act because he was not coming to the US for "the purpose that qualified for a diplomatic visa ... His (Modi's) tourist/business visa was revoked under Section 212 (a) 2 (g) of the Act which makes any government official who was responsible for or directly carried out at any time, particularly severe violations of religious freedom, ineligible for visa,"' said the spokesperson.

Within hours of the revocation of Narendra's visa, the External Affairs ministry summoned US Deputy Chief of Mission Robert Blake and conveyed to him the Union government's protest. MEA spokesperson Navtej Sarna said that the US action was 'uncalled for and displayed lack of courtesy and sensitivity towards a constitutionally elected chief minister of a state of India.' But the government did not take any tit-for-tat action. The protest, in the circumstances, seemed routine, lacking any real fervour.

The United States got away with it.

Among those who joined the anti-Narendra campaign from Gujarat itself were advocate Girish Patel, Hanif Lakdawala and J S Bandukwala. They had extended support to a group known as the 'Coalition Against Genocide', which had launched a campaign in the United States by flooding US government officials, senators and others with hundreds of letters and e-mails on why Narendra should be kept out.

The refusal of the US to issue a visa to Narendra triggered a huge controversy with opinions being expressed on both sides of the issue. The anti-Modi politicians in Gujarat, of course, were delirious with joy, claiming that the denial of a US visa to Narendra was correct. Logic deserted them in their visceral hatred of Narendra and patriotic sentiments were wholly alien to their thinking.

But in the Rajya Sabha, Prime Minister Manmohan Singh said that the American goverment had been 'clearly informed' of India's stand. He said, 'We do not believe that it is appropriate to use allegations or anything less than the due legal process to make a subjective judgement to question a constitutional authority in India.'

As usual, the English media had a grand time attacking Narendra. 'Gujaratis see Modi as a liability,' reported The *Times of India*. The *Business Standard* summed up the situation saying that 'a large section of the intelligentsia feels Modi has been treated "the way he should have been treated".' But there were other papers that were by no means Narendra's admirers, who nonetheless took an objective view of the US action. The *Telegraph*, for instance, said on 20 March 2005 that while the US action 'might warm the cockles of secular hearts, the matter needs to be looked at without ideological blinkers and without condoning Mr Modi's responsibility for the killing of Muslims in Gujarat ... The US government chose to ignore the verdict of Indian democracy.'

The *Telegraph* opined that under Bush's leadership, US intelligence agencies had produced false evidence about the existence of weapons of mass destruction in Iraq and unleashed an unprovoked war on that country. It questioned, 'What does this make Mr Bush? Some would suggest that he should be charged with crimes against humanity. Yet he is elected president of the people of the US and this status has to be respected despite moral and ideological opposition to his policies and actions ... Nobody demands that the US Government should respect Mr Modi as a person. The elected office Mr Modi holds is worthy of respect. Is that too much to expect from holier-than-thou Uncle Sam?' The paper also reminded everyone that presidents like John F Kennedy and Lyndon B Johnson, despite their killings of thousands of Vietnamese, were allowed to travel because of the official position they had acquired through a democratic process.

On 20 March 2005, The *Statesman* commented, 'Modi has reason to feel done in.' It pointed out that Saudi Arabia, 'a staunch ally of America', does not provide legal protection for freedom of religion and such protection does not exist in practice. It went on to say that Islam is the official religion and the law requires that all citizens be Muslims. The government prohibits the public practice of non-Muslim religions ...'

In its issue dated 21 March 2005, The *Pioneer* said that the US 'pontificates, but thinks it needn't practice what it preaches. Hyperpowerdom breeds arrogance (and double standards) ... America doesn't want to host a popularly elected leader and constitutional post-holder in the world's largest democracy ... When America rapped Saddam or the Taliban or Osama, people asked: Who created them? ... 1968's My Lai massacre in Vietnam makes Iraq's Abu Ghraib shine – and the Gujarat riots pale – by comparison ... Yet the US's record isn't Mr Modi's best defence. It is that his own country's judicial processes have not indicted him.'

The *Free Press Journal* (21 March 2005) told off the US by averring that 'domestic politics need not become a matter for non-Indians to exploit ... But the larger point that seems to have been missed in the shrill noises over Modi's alleged complicity in the riots is whether or not independent sovereign nations would allow the US to behave as the super-cop of the world'. On the morning of 21 March 2005, Narendra addressed members of the Asian-American Hotel Owners Association assembled at Madison Square Garden in New York city via video – an address that was not prohibited by law. Narendra appealed to NRIs and non-resident Gujaratis to ensure that decisions about their beloved country are not taken on the basis of contentions of a handful 'of vested interests or motivated groups'. He termed those listening to him as the carriers and protectors of Indian pride. Narendra spoke for about a hundred minutes to loud applause. He appealed to the NRIs to make India an 'investment locale and global hot spot' and sell the concept of a 'robust and developed Gujarat'.

If the US government did not grant Narendra a visa, Britain was not willing to follow Washington's ignoble example though it had its own reservations. A nation guilty of the Jallianwala Bagh massacre could hardly have behaved in any other way. Narendra was scheduled to go to Britain on a thirty-six-hour visit to attend a 'Gujarat Day' concert at London's Royal Albert Hall on 26 March 2005, and the British High Commission in Delhi routinely agreed to Narendra's right to be in the British capital. The High Commission's spokesman Jeff Wilson said, 'He (Narendra) had an existing visa and we saw no reason to deny him the right to travel.'

However, things took a different turn. In the first place, intelligence agencies reportedly sent word to the government that the Dawood Ibrahim gang and certain jihadi groups were planning to eliminate Narendra if he went to London. Narendra did not take that seriously even when three Union government functionaries,

The General in Command

including Home Minister Shivraj Patil, telephoned Narendra to cancel his visit. Prime Minister Manmohan Singh also advised Narendra not to go. Narendra is reported to have said, 'If you are advising me not to go, I won't go.' That ended the matter.

Narendra put behind him the visa mess and went back to what he was good at – working for the common man!

Set to launch *Krishi Mahotsav* 2005 on 11 May, Narendra attended four rallies the week before to inform farmers about modern technology and new methods of cultivation. Additionally, the idea was to set off 229 *kisan raths* to cover every village across the state.

Gujarat has about thirty-five to thirty-seven lakh farmers with land holdings, although the number of *kisan* cards given out did not exceed seventeen lakh. The state government planned to study one lakh hectares of land under drip irrigation, build at least one small bund in each of the 18,000 villages, construct 4,000 village ponds, and form at least 1,400 self-help groups.

The *Krishi Mahotsav* was a grand show. It went on for a month, from 10 May to 11 June. First, the department of agriculture facilitated a series of meetings at the Junagadh Agricultural University. During a discussion on the programme, which was attended by the chief minister, other ministers and department secretaries, a decision was taken: the focus of the *Mahotsav* would be the poor farmers. In the first preparatory phase, routes for the *kisan raths* were developed; teams were formed for the daily execution of activities within the villages, and training was given to officers and functionaries, so that they could implement the programme efficiently. The second phase focussed on holding *Gram Sabhas* for generating awareness among the village communities about the event. About thirty-six activities were formulated. The third phase began with the chief minister flagging off the *kisan rath* from Kalawad, Jamnagar district, amidst a massive gathering of farmers.

What was the *kisan rath* like? It had about six hundred square feet of exhibition space for posters, panels, audio-visual material and demonstration of modern implements. At every stage, it was accompanied by agricultural scientists and departmental experts who explained to the farmers which crops could be grown, the use of fertilizers, pest management and soil management. Senior members and district officials interacted with the farmers on various levels and discussed agricultural problems that the latter faced. A manual on agricultural practices was distributed to the villagers.

The focus was on doubling agricultural income and the entire yatra covered all the 18,600 villages impressively. Approximately one lakh government employees, from the secretary to the *talati* (sub-district level revenue official) level, worked together in harmony throughout the one month of the *rath* yatra, and as many as eighteen government departments joined hands for the synergistic implementation and coordination of activities. The Agriculture and Cooperation Department was responsibe for the whole *Mahotsav*.

While launching the programme at Navsari and addressing a large *shivir* (camp) of farmers, Narendra said:

'The state government is fully committed to improving the economic standards of all poor and tribal farmers. Under the 'Wadi Yojana' (a programme for development of fruit and flower farms) in Kaparda, a remote tribal block of Valsad district, the tribal farmers have produced four crore kilograms of cashew nuts. Such experiments will be replicated. I want to invite you all to join in these efforts. This is not a political programme but a constructive effort.'

Gujarat certainly was abuzz with activity. Even as the *Krishi Mahotsav* got underway, information was available that the Kutch *kesar* mangoes had replaced the Pakistan variety called *chorso* in the UK market. Around 250 tonnes of *kesar* mangoes had been exported to the UK, Taiwan and Dubai in 2004, bringing in ₹1.5 crore worth of foreign exchange. According to S B Moratia, Deputy Director of District Horticulture in Kutch, the production of *kesar* mangoes had gone up to 30-35,000 tonnes, which was about 10-15,000 tonnes more than what it had been in 2004.

There were other pleasant stories to relate. An overall upswing in business activity, coupled with Ahmedabad being granted a mega city status, had helped the hotel industry to grow faster. New hotels came up in Ahmedabad, Gandhinagar, Surat and other cities. Import of energy-related products like crude oil, coal and natural gas fired import activity in Gujarat ports that handled 97.12 million tonnes of goods in 2004-05. And taking into consideration the time of five years from 2000 to 2005, Gujarat was reported to have attracted ₹94,000 crore of investment as on 31 March 2005, beating Andhra Pradesh by ₹3,000 crore. This was actually the figure placed before the Lok Sabha by Union Minister of State for Industry and Commerce Kamal Nath. A day after the UPA government acknowledged Gujarat's achievement, the state Cabinet met to congratulate Narendra for bringing laurels to the state.

On seeing the impact of *Krishi Mahotsav* 2005, Narendra institutionalized it as an annual event. Again, a month-long *Krishi Mahotsav* was organized in 2006 to inform and educate people about the latest developments in agriculture by bringing all the stakeholders together to usher in the second green revolution in Gujarat.

Even as life was settling down, Gujarat witnessed another shock in the form of floods. An earthquake had shaken the state to its very roots; the riots had torn to pieces the communities that had lived together for years. The floods hit Gujarat as another natural calamity. The pharmaceutical industry seemed to be the worst affected, especially in Kheda and Baroda districts. Floods affected the tourism industry too, and there was as much as a fifty per cent drop in business. In just one week, the industry incurred losses worth hundreds of crores. In Ahmedabad, telephone lines went dead. And once again, the government went into action mode. Unfortunately, however, the floods only served to evoke more political wrangling between the BJP and the Congress.

On 11 July 2005, The *Asian Age* reported:

> *It seems Gujarat politicians have not learnt anything from the London bomb blasts where the Opposition stood behind the government in the hour of crisis. The ruling BJP and the Opposition Congress in the state have made a mockery of the sufferings of people by playing politics.*

Instead of cooperating with the BJP, the Congress tried to use the 'floods' to run Narendra down.

The government declared 2,056 villages in eighty *talukas* of fourteen districts as flood-hit. It was estimated that 4,500 industrial units had suffered to the tune of ₹113 crore. A special meeting of the State Level Bankers' Committee (SLBC) was held in Ahmedabad which committed to financially rehabilitating flood-hit industries, traders and farmers. That was the spirit of Gujarat in action.

The Gujarat government decided to use the 'floods' for constructive purposes. It planned to revive rivers that had dried long ago by starting work on 490 big and medium-sized check-dams alongside the rivers. Some twenty-five rivers had been dry for ages, but now the government, along with private parties like the Saurashtra Jaldhara Trust, constructed fifty-one check-dams in Bhavnagar, Amreli and Junagadh alone. As Narottam Patel, the Minister of Water Resources, recalled, 'As many as 175 big check-dams have been constructed in Saurashtra region alone. The results are there for all to see. About 35 million cubic metres of water has been tracked for revival of these check-dams.' The *Asian Age* reported on 25 July 2005: 'Big and medium-sized check-dams have also been constructed or are under construction across the Khari in Mehsana and Patan, Mesvo, Majam, Vatrak, Mohar, Varanasi, Dhamni, Jarmar, Lavri, Vetri, Sabannati, Hathmati, Luni, Kun, Mesti, Sipu, Rupen, Pushpavati, Saraswati, Banas and Balaram rivers.'

The floods occurred at a time when the state had barely recovered from a train disaster. The Sabarmati Express had rammed into a stationary goods train at Samalaya railway station on 21 April 2005 killing fifteen passengers and injuring ninety. The remarkable thing was that within minutes of the mishap, the residents of Samalaya village had rushed to the spot – the time was around 3.10 am and it was still dark – and extricated forty-five passengers from the debris using the light of their tractor headlamps. The villagers were also quick to inform the district collector and the commandant of the Vadodara Army station.

This time Railway Minister Lalu Prasad Yadav decided to visit the scene of disaster to show his concern. The man who had sought to malign Narendra over the Gujarat riots that followed the Godhra carnage was unwanted in the state, and as his car drove to Samalaya, it was stoned. Lalu Prasad once again sought to blame Narendra for arousing public anger. Instead of expressing sympathy for those killed and wounded, he charged the Sangh Parivar with attempts to 'eliminate' him, provoking the BJP parliamentary party spokesman V K Malhotra to say, 'Lalu is not bothered about the railway ministry. He is trying to cover it up by making wild and baseless allegations.' Instead of bearing responsibility for the train mishap, Lalu was demanding the dismissal of Gujarat's chief minister. But Narendra had other things to do – visiting the injured in the hospital, consoling relatives of the dead and appreciating the work of the Godhra and Vadodara district collectors and police officers for their prompt action. Among those who rushed to the scene of the accident were the RSS volunteers. No Congress workers or volunteers were seen at the scene of the disaster.

Ice cubes were reportedly pelted at Lalu's car when he went to the hospital and it turned out that those who indulged in this show of anger were relatives of the dead and wounded. But Lalu used this incident to demand Narendra's dismissal.

Modi's aim was to undertake comprehensive and integrated development of Gujarat, building upon the strengths and overcoming the weaknesses. Along with industrial growth and economic development, the focus was also on rural development, improvement in education, education of the girl child, social justice, agricultural development, science and technology and disaster management.

The unique 'Jyotigram Scheme', launched by Narendra, has successfully introduced round-the-clock, three-phase electricity to all eighteen thousand villages. The multi-faceted Jyotigram Scheme, in addition to providing twenty-four hours' non fluctuating power supply, also ensures metred supply, elimination of power theft, reduction in transmission losses, collection of bills and more importantly, people's participation. Due to availability of uninterrupted power, cottage and agro industries are developing in the Jyotigram villages, providing employment and preventing migration to urban areas. The 'Jyoti Gramodyog Vikas Yojana' promotes village industry in rural areas. Financial assistance, including subsidy under bankable schemes, is provided to rural artisans, entrepreneurs and self-help groups who want to set up new projects with investment ranging between five and twenty five lakh rupees.

The Man of the Moment: Narendra Modi

The attention and priority that Narendra gives to education as compared to any other former chief minister of the state is also noteworthy. His realization that no amount of economic, industrial or commercial resurgence can be sustained on a long-term basis without the foundation of proper academic and professional education, has made him re-work the whole system of education in Gujarat. Successive annual campaigns for enrolment of all children in schools, with a special focus on enrolment of the girl child, have brought lakhs of children back to school. Special incentive schemes such as 'Vidyalakshmi Bond' have been introduced to encourage education of the girl child by giving Narmada Bonds worth ₹1,000 to girls for their education. The dropout rate has reduced drastically due to the special drive through which the progress has been monitored on a continuous basis. In the year 2000-01, the dropout rate was 20.81 per cent; it came down to 3 per cent in 2005-06. The government has spent as much as ₹17,56,946 to promote the education of the girl-child.

Narendra's concern for the education of the girl-child is reflected in the fact that he has created a fund called *'Kanya Kelavani Nidhi'* (Fund for Education of the Girl-Child), exclusively for this purpose. As per the norms, gifts received by the chief minister are to be deposited in the *toshakhana* (treasury). They are then auctioned and the proceeds are deposited in the state's treasury. However, earlier this was more on paper than in practice. In the forty-one years of the state's history, thirteen chief ministers had deposited a meager ₹4.55 lakh in the *toshakhana*. As against this, Narendra regularly deposits the gifts received by him in the state treasury. The proceeds are diverted to *Kanya Kelavani Nidhi* for the education of girls. Seeing the dedication of the leader, many now felicitate him with cheques worth lakhs of rupees for the fund. The *Nidhi*, which started in 2003-04, is worth more than seventeen crore rupees after a period of five years.

Without much hype, Narendra saw to it that the socio-economic development of the most backward classes was given priority. Thus, fifteen per cent reservation has been provided for admissions in government schools and hostels. Treading the path laid down by a former maharaja of Baroda who financed Dr B R Ambedkar's studies abroad, Narendra set up a loan scholarship for students from the most backward classes to help them study in foreign countries. Brilliant students belonging to the scheduled castes are given a loan of up to five lakh rupees. As many as forty-six students have received the loan scholarships so far, amounting to ₹230 lakh.

Special attention is given to science and technology. For instance, the emerging field of biotechnology is promoted by the Gujarat State Biotechnology Mission and the Gujarat Council of Biotechnology. At Savali Baroda, a biotechnology park is coming up that covers an area of about seven hundred acres. Similarly, plans are under way for an Agro Biotech Park and Marine Biotech Park. All these show the dynamism with which the government of Gujarat works.

The *gram sabhas*, which were held as a matter of formality to fulfill the mandatory requirement under the Panchayat Act, were slowly dying. Village development was paid only lip service as a subject for many years, but Narendra has taken many concrete steps to make the villages real centres of harmony, peace, growth and development. Panchayat elections, which are meant to be contested on a non-party basis, had become a source of rivalry, feuds and revenge and hence, were an obstruction in the growth of villages over a period of years. The 'Samras Yojana' (Harmony Scheme) was launched at the village level to end petty rivalries by encouraging unanimous election of the Panchayat members. Each village, which became a Samras village, was given a grant of one lakh rupees towards development schemes in the village. A village where there was no feud or rivalry, and was free from any police or court case, was treated as a *Teerth Gram* (village for pilgrimage) and provided with an additional incentive of one lakh rupees for development. Thousands of villages have become Samras villages; hundreds of villages have become *Teerth Grams* and have been given cash incentives. Mahatma Gandhi's dream of an ideal village is being realized based on a vision of integrated development through the Gokulgram, E-gram, Vishvagram, Jyotigram, Samrasgram, and Teerth Gram schemes.

Modi has ensured community participation in every aspect of administration, whether it is a *Gram Sabha* meeting, earthquake reconstruction and construction of check-dams or enrolment of school children. No wonder the communities have voted Narendra as the Number One chief minister of the country. His ultimate aim is to link the villages with the rest of the world through IT by providing connectivity to each village and converting all of them into *Vishwagrams* (world-villages). The Jyotigram scheme has made it possible to have computers in villages and upgrade villages into e-*grams*. As a result of this, the uninterrupted power supply has generated many employment opportunities in the villages. The documents related to the land are computerized and are thus easily accessible. Governmental resolutions and forms are available online.

Gujarat, which was leading in economic and industrial growth, was ranked low in many indices pertaining to health. However, Narendra quickly realized that health is one of the major sectors that needs focus for sustained development of the state and immediately took corrective measures. Clean air, clean water and clean food have become the mantra in Gujarat. The introduction of Compressed Natural Gas (CNG), provision of piped water supply, the SSY and prevention of adulteration of edible oil are some of the concrete measures that have been undertaken to improve health in Gujarat. Common affluent treatment plants have been set up at several places to check industrial liquid effluent pollution. The Narmada waters were brought to dry and arid areas where underground water had become unpotable, in a planned manner.

Food quality is being improved by fortifying the portions of vitamin A, iron and folic acid in wheat flour and edible oil to be distributed to the public at large. Further, vitamin and folic acid fortification is also being carried out through the Integrated Child Development Services (ICDS) and 'Mid-Day Meal' schemes provided to expectant mothers, adolescent girls and infants. Gujarat is now focussing on preventive and public health in a big way. One example is the way in which the health machinery functioned and prevented the outbreak of epidemics in the aftermath of the unprecedented rainfall and floods in July 2005 and August 2006. Rural health infrastructure has been strengthened; child and mother care, delivery, post-delivery follow-up, school health check-ups and regular immunization programmes are being implemented as priority programmes. Creation of Block Health Offices, Private-Public Partnerships,

Public-Citizen Partnerships, and steps for integrating IT with health care indicate the efforts of the government to add health to wealth. Gujarat is rated first among the major states of India in health care services in terms of availability, utility and patient's satisfaction as per World Bank's report (June 2002). In 2003-04, against a target of four hundred cataract operations per lakh population, the government conducted 862 operations per lakh.

In order to save mothers and their children, a new and innovative 'Chiranjivi Yojana' (Long Life Scheme) has been launched to involve private gynaecologists in the remote rural areas to facilitate safe deliveries to BPL (Below Poverty Line) women. Under the scheme, women who are below the poverty line in the identified backward areas of the state can avail the services of accredited private gynaecologists free of cost for ensuring safe delivery of babies. It is not surprising that this scheme received the Asian Innovation Award at Singapore in 2006.

Narendra's government celebrated 2005 as the year for urban development, focussing on providing safe drinking water, strengthening urban governance and management, upgrading urban roads, and implementing solid waste management programmes, amongst others. Construction of houses for EWS (Economically Weaker Sections) and constructing pay-and use toilets have been greatly appreciated by all. Solid waste management programmes have encouraged private enterprises to collect garbage from door to door. Construction of parks and gardens has developed the 'healthy lungs' of the cities. The government initiated several reforms in the urban sector in 2005. These included repealing the Urban Land Ceiling Act, rationalizing stamp duties, reforming rent control laws and area-based property tax, introducing a double entry accounting system, and making amendments in the Bombay Provincial Municipal Corporation Act, 1949, and the Gujarat Municipalities Act.

Above all, Modi's motto was to encourage public participation to ensure a sense of ownership among the citizens, leading to better urban governance. He believes that all-round development of a state cannot be achieved without developing human resources. Good governance depends on skilled, competent and motivated employees. The five-lakh government employees of Gujarat were always looked upon as a financial charge on the exchequer, but Narendra looks upon them as a human resource that can and must play an active role in the development of the state.

For the first time, a State Training Policy was announced to train civil servants with clearly spelt-out objectives, strategy, content and modalities of training. In-service training has been given as much importance as induction training. A committee under the chief secretary has been set up to review, monitor and coordinate the implementation of the training policy. The Sardar Patel Institute of Public Administration (SPIPA) was given autonomy in October 2004 to enable it to become an institute of excellence. The Gujarat Institute of Disaster Management (GIDM) was established in 2004 to train all stakeholders in various aspects of disaster management. Also, centres of excellence were established for biotechnology at Anand, post-harvest technology at Navsari, oil and water management in Junagadh and castor research at Sardar Krishi Nagar.

One of the earliest tasks Narendra took on was to change the work culture of the government. In one of the initial *chintan shibirs* (brain-storming sessions) headed by the chief minister himself, it was decided that making mistakes with good intentions would be condoned. This provided a much-needed fillip to officers to take quicker decisions. Bureaucrats started taking up projects that interested them. Projects taken up by officers beyond the call of their duty were termed *Swantah Sukhay* (Welfare of All) projects. They were people-oriented projects undertaken with public participation and under the concerned officer's leadership without any government budget. Visualizing government employees as *karmayogis*, Modi wanted government employees to be agents of change. However, Narendra also understood that this transformation could not happen through a government resolution. He conceptualized the *Karmayogi* Scheme with a focus on long-term gains, giving due attention to awareness creation, motivation and imparting skills. The training of more than 3.5 lakh employees belonging to Class I, II, III and IV categories in the short span of less than a year is truly incredible.

In the scheme of things which existed before the implementation of the *Karmyogi* Scheme, many government employees entered the government and retired without undergoing even a single training programme for self-development, motivation or skill-building. The training programmes were looked upon as paid holidays. The training did not merely aim to increase the productivity of the employees, but also at self-motivation and change of mindset, ultimately leading them towards self-actualization, which is the real purpose of human resource development. Even the employees nearing retirement were included in the training programme.

Citizen Facilitation Centres have been set up in every district, along with a single window system, which enables foreign investors to submit documents at a single location. Information technology, computers and upgraded facilities are used to meet the demands of citizens. The commitment on the part of the collectorate to deliver a particular set of services to the citizens within twenty-four hours led to the concept of 'one-day governance' which is an innovation in e-governance.

Narendra has been constantly innovating with new methods and techniques for improving the efficiency and productivity of various sectors. One such innovative step has been the decision to involve the private sector for the development of huge wastelands. Another innovative step is the celebration of traditional festivals and converting them into events of major tourist attraction.

In spite of having a large number of heritage monuments, beautiful temples, and a rich cultural heritage, Gujarat's tourism industry was virtually non existent. Narendra provided an action plan tapping Gujarat's tourism potential. Today, Gujarat is a state that attracts tourists not only for religious trips, but also for the state's culture. Travellers come to Gujarat to find spiritual peace, and medical tourism makes it a hot destination too.

In the entire country, rural connectivity is the best in Gujarat. Out of a total of 18,028 villages, 98.53 per cent of the villages (17,763 out of 18,028) are connected by pucca roads. To connect these areas to the urban areas, 96.98 per cent of the state highways are asphalt roads. Handling of public grievances is a major job for any state administration. Narendra focussed on the origin of the different kinds of grievances and devised a multi-pronged strategy using both traditional ways of redressal like *gram sabhas* as well as technology-based innovative solutions like one-day governance and State Wide Attention of Grievances by Application of Technology (SWAGAT). In the initial months of taking over as the chief minister, Narendra emphasized that *gram sabhas* should be the appropriate popular forum to tackle day-to-day grievances and developmental issues of the villagers. Towards this end, he ordered that every three months, a full-fledged *gram sabha* should be organized wherein all the villagers, especially from the backward sections, must participate; these *gram sabhas* are also attended by senior district-level officers so that they can respond to and redress the issues.

Computerized grievance redressal centres were set up and activated at the level of *talukas* too. At the district level, computerized civic centres were set up. This has turned out to be a pleasant experience for the citizens as they deposit their applications in the morning and get the required transactions by afternoon. The centres have proved to be exemplary models of 'One-Day Governance' and many of them have been awarded for their work and effective governance. However, the most innovative, effective and interesting programme of grievance redressal is SWAGAT. Gujarat's strength is the Gujarat government's huge Wide Area Network (GSWAN) which connects government offices upto the *taluka* level. Making use of this strength, Narendra has introduced a novel programme where he himself interacts with the aggrieved citizens.

On the fourth Thursday of every month, applicants are invited to the state headquarters at the Chief Minister's Office (CMO) in the morning. Their grievances are registered and instantly transmitted online to the concerned authorities at the secretariat, as well as the district level, whereupon the authorities feed in their replies. In the afternoon, the chief minister personally listens to the applicants one by one. The grievances as well as replies of the concerned authorities are available on his screen online. Narendra interacts with the concerned authorities at the district level in the presence of the applicant through video conferencing. At the time of the interaction, the applicants are free to interact with or interrupt the authorities. Since the chief minister interacts personally, the administration is on its toes. This has proved to be a very effective system of grievance redressal. It has been recognized by the Commonwealth Telecommunication

The General in Command

Organization and Manchester University as a global case study in e-transparency, openness and accountability. At the district level too, the district authorities hear the public grievances on the same day and the same programme has been extended upto the *taluka* level too.

An effective computerized system has also been set up to address grievances received through the peoples' representatives, that is, the MLAs and MPs. Urgent references are taken up for immediate action and instructions are conveyed to the concerned authorities on telephone or by fax. Depending upon the issue, concerned authorities are also called in person to the CMO. The status of the disposal and pending cases is monitored on a fortnightly basis by the senior bureaucrats of the CMO. The concerned officers of various departments are also called periodically for review and are given instructions for speedy and effective disposal of grievances.

A high target of 10.2 per cent was set for Gujarat in the Tenth Five-Year Plan (2002–07). In the first four years – (2002–06) – the economy achieved an impressive growth of 9.7 per cent. The agriculture sector registered an average growth of 15.53 per cent. This was nearly four times higher than the state target of 4.03 per cent in the first four years set by the Planning Commission. Due to innovative initiatives like the *Krishi Mahotsav*, Soil to Satellite and Lab to Land, the gross value of output from the agricultural sector increased from ₹13,129 crore in 2001-02 to ₹30,795 crore in 2005-06.

The industrial sector registered an average growth of 9.92 per cent in the first four years. The manufacturing sector added ₹58,308 crore in 2005-06, which was second after Maharashtra The communication sector progressed significantly with an average growth of 20 per cent from 2003–07, trade and the hotel sector registered an impressive performance of 10 per cent in the same period of time, while banking registered an average growth of 9 per cent.

Narendra also brought about a miraculous turnaround in public sector units owned by the Gujarat government which had been running in losses for a long time. He proved that if there was a will to work and if the right people were given the right kind of work, public sector units could perform better than private sector enterprises. One such classic example was the performance of the Gujarat Electricity Board (GEB). The case of GEB can become a case study for many other state electricity boards to follow. Some of the major steps undertaken for bringing about these changes in the GEB were:

1. The vertically integrated utility, the erstwhile GEB, was split into seven companies – one each for generation and transmission, four distribution companies; the seventh company was Gujarat Urja Vikas Nigam Limited (GUVNL) – the holding company. The cash collections went from ₹765 crore per month in 2003-04 to ₹1,028 crore for the first half of the financial year 2006-07. Re-negotiation of the Power Purchase Agreement (PPA) led to savings of ₹550 crore towards fixed costs. Timely payment of power purchase dues earned a rebate worth ₹150 crore during the financial years 2006–09. Power purchase costs showed a steady decline from ₹2.29 per unit in the financial year 2003-04 to ₹1.99 per unit in 2005-06.

2. Improvements in coal linkages, use of washed coal and imported coal, negotiation of Low Supply Heavy Stock (LSHS) price with the Indian Oil Corporation (IOC) led to savings of ₹559 crore in fuel costs. Various financial institutions were approached for restructuring of the loans. With restructuring of ₹4,130 crore of loans, the sector achieved savings of about ₹351 crore. The interest cost was reduced from 10.67 per cent in 2002-03 to 8.60 per cent in 2005-06. A stringent Anti Theft Bill was passed to check power theft. Vigilance activities led to detection of theft and malpractices leading to savings of ₹547 crore. The above activities along with metre replacements, metre box provisions, sealing of connections and bifurcation of feeders resulted in consistent reduction in losses from 30.9 per cent in 2003-04 to 26.9 per cent in 2005-06.

3. The Jyotigram Yojana involved a total outlay of ₹1,150 crore, funded entirely by the Gujarat government, for erection of more than fifty-three kilometres of lines and eleven thousand transformers across a total of 18,065 villages.

The scheme led to savings of ₹500 crore from April 2005 to March 2006. Due to the reforms undertaken in the power sector, and also due to the economic and administrative measures undertaken, the state power sector, that suffered losses of over ₹1,900 crore in 2003-04, and ₹927 crore in 2004-05, registered profit before tax of approximately ₹180 crore in the financial year 2005-06 (Provisional).

4. Gujarat was ranked the second best State Electricity Board (SEB) in the ratings conducted by the Ministry of Power for the second year running in 2005 and was awarded for its 'outstanding' performance Turnarounds also occurred in the Gujarat State Fertilizer Company Ltd (GSFC) and Gujarat Alkalis and Chemicals Ltd (GACL). GSFC, which had incurred a massive loss of ₹391 crore in the year 2002-03, was turned around in 2003-04, posting a profit of ₹174 crore, thanks to the vision and direction of Modi, who gave a free hand to the techno-bureaucrats in the day-to-day operations along with the required support. In 2004-05, the public sector undertaking posted a net profit. Yet another example was that of GACL which was put on track with profits rising from ₹28.04 crore in 2002-03 to ₹63.15 crore in 2003-04, and then further to ₹144.28 crore in 2004-05.

The story of transformation of the Gujarat State Petroleum Corporation Limited (GSPCL) from a small public sector enterprise owned by the Gujarat government to a giant oil and gas company under the able leadership of Narendra Modi deserves to be mentioned. Under his mentorship, various path-breaking developments in the oil and gas sector have taken place in Gujarat, as a result of which, Gujarat has emerged as the petro-capital of India. These include the increased activities and the largest ever discoveries, acquisition of acreage in the upstream sector, LNG terminals, largest gas grid network, along with others. Today, Gujarat has emerged as a smart energy strategist state that excels in a wide gamut of activities associated with hydrocarbons.

Discovery of India's biggest gas reserve of more than 20 TCF at the Krishna-Godavari basin (KG-OSN-2001/3) in 2005-06, discovery of superior quality of oil and gas reserves from the KG-17 well (KG basin) in 2006, discovery of crude oil in the Ahmedabad block

The Man of the Moment: Narendra Modi

having a potential of sixty million barrels of oil-in-place in 2004-05, discovery of oil and gas from the Sanand-East exploration block in June 2006, discovery of crude oil, gas and condensate from Tarapur wells in 2005-06 were some of the milestones reached by GSPC. In addition, the 2,500 kilometre-long high gas pipeline network was developed in Gujarat as a part of the state-wide gas grid to connect all district headquarters. Gas distribution network was established for industrial, commercial and household consumption through the GSPC Gas Company Ltd to enable a concerted focus on gas distribution in twenty cities in the state.

GSPC also developed a Compressed Natural Gas (CNG) infrastructure to promote clean pollution-free auto fuel for the automobile sector across the state, and an eco-friendly gas-based power plant at Mora (Surat) in Gujarat, generating low cost electricity.

The Gujarat Energy Research and Management Institute, a world-class institute for training energy professionals, was set up in Gujarat by GSPC. It continues to expand its E&P business beyond Indian shores, with the biggest names in the global hydrocarbon business as partners. It has also received a large number of invitations from various state governments to help them replicate the natural gas transmission and distribution model in their respective areas. GSPC is a shining star of the hydrocarbon industry now and its never-ending journey will see Gujarat stay way ahead, as the 'Petro-capital of India' and the 'Industrial Power House', thus fulfilling Narendra's dream.

Narendra Modi knew that the strides made in economic and industrial development could be sustained without bringing about revolutionary changes in higher and technical education. While he focussed on improvement in primary education and the education of the girl child, he simultaneously focussed on achieving excellence in higher and technical education by providing autonomy through legislation. During 2005–09, the state created five technical universities, four agricultural universities, one Sanskrit university and one state university. Qualified self-financed technical institutions were given university status to facilitate the Public Private Partnership (PPP) in achieving excellence.

Though Gujarat tops the list of industrially developed states in India, technically qualified manpower in Gujarat was grossly inadequate. There were only five thousand seats in undergraduate technical courses when Narendra Modi took over as the chief minister. By 2009, due to various steps undertaken by the government, the number of seats in undergraduate technical courses increased to 15,000 and the technical manpower available increased three-fold from 20,000 in 2001 to 60,000 in 2006.

All this was achievable by creating centres for excellence through new legislation concerning technical universities such as Nirma University, Dhirubhai Ambani Institute of Information and Communication Technology, Sharamsinh Desai University, Ganpat Vidyanagar University, CEPT University and Sanskrit University.

Keeping in mind the inadequate infrastructure and the remoteness of Kutch, the government created Shri Shyamji Krishna Verma Kutch University. The government laid down the benchmarking of accreditation to the technical universities as well as to all institutes providing higher education. This benchmarking created an environment that led to more institutes seeking the same by improving their quality. They aspired to become independent deemed universities or state universities. Creation of a law university in Gujarat was a sure step towards fortifying the judicial system and its knowledge and within three years, it became a popular destination for students from all over the country.

To suit the needs of emerging industries, a number of new subjects were introduced in higher and technical institutes. Biotechnology, biomedicine, nanotechnology, automobile engineering, aeronautical engineering, marine engineering, oceanography, and many more were added to undergraduate courses. Plans were drawn up to establish a university for petroleum and related subjects. Modi was also keen to set up an Indian Institute of Technology (IIT) campus in Gujarat to introduce courses like marine engineering, oceanography and aero-mechanic science, which are highly relevant to Gujarat.

The View Beyond the Prism   13

By 2009, definite opinions had been formed about Narendra Modi. If he was disliked, abused and reviled by a certain section of the media, there were many others who had known him from close quarters and held him in great regard. In an effort to understand the man, we, the authors, interviewed over sixty people from many walks of life at this juncture and while some considered him to be aloof or haughty – even brusque – there were others who spoke of him in the most affectionate and endearing terms.

Ramanbhai Shah, an old RSS hand and a *swayamsevak* for more than sixty-six years, had known Narendra for over three decades and had been in close touch with him all along. Narendra, on his part, was a very close member of Ramanbhai's family. The first thing that Ramanbhai mentioned when he talked about Narendra was the fact that 'his memory is unmatched'.

Narendra had met Ramanbhai's grandson Chintan when he was a mere lad. Years passed by and they did not get an opportunity to see each other. A few years earlier, Chintan had taken up a job in a construction company that had been given the contract to build Samskardham, the school started by Narendra. During a discussion between the company's executives and Narendra, the latter recognized him immediately and said, 'Chintan beta! How come you are here?' Chintan was amazed and impressed to see that Narendra had remembered him by name even after so many years. Ramanbhai said, 'We always knew that Narendrabhai would reach great heights one day. We have been witness to his progress from a *swayamsevak* to a *pracharak* to the chief minister.'

According to Ramanbhai, Narendra was an outstanding speaker, was an extremely sensitive and affectionate person when it came

The View Beyond the Prism

to family and relationships, and one who maintained good relations with most of the families he knew. When Ramanbhai's family celebrated his seventy-fifth birthday, they had invited Narendra. Ramanbhai recalled, 'We phoned him. He came from Delhi without making any fuss and stayed on from 8.00 am to 4.00 pm. He was very natural and casual with every member of the family, mixed well and was frank.'

The well-known poet Suresh Dalai was full of admiration for Narendra. Dalai said, 'When NM meets you, he is completely with you. He is relaxed because he is in tune with himself. His *astitva* (existence) depends on his ability to transform words into action. He speaks from his heart and therefore, there is conviction in whatever he says.

Dalai recalled a time when he and Gopal Dave, the owner of Image Publications, had called on Keshubhai, the then Chief Minister. They were waiting outside Keshubhai's office when Narendra, who had just come in, spotted them. Recognizing Suresh Dalai and learning that the two were waiting to see the chief minister, Narendra had said, 'A poet should never be made to wait outside,' and saw to it that they were immediately taken to see Keshubhai.

Ashok Bhatt, Narendra's long-time colleague, had held various portfolios in his ministry at different times. According to Bhatt, Narendra never lost his cool even when the media's onslaught against him was 'heavy'. He told his interviewer, 'After Godhra, he used to meet Muslim leaders frequently and he also formed an all-party committee under the governor's chairmanship. The committee had Congress workers like Amarsinh Chaudhary, Siddharth Patel, Majoor Mahajan Sangh's Amathaabhai and a representative of the Vepari Mahajan Mandal. This committee was meant to formulate policies to tackle the aftermath.'

Bhatt said that even in turbulent times, Narendrabhai had emerged as 'a clear and strong decision-maker'. When refugee camps were set up, each camp was assigned to one Indian Administrative Service (IAS) officer and his team. Health and hygiene were paid special attention.

Vijay Rupani had been in charge of electioneering activities when Narendra contested elections from Rajkot. This is how

The Man of the Moment: Narendra Modi

he summed up Narendra: 'Narendrabhai has no ego. He has always fought for a cause. He believes everything should be well managed. He is highly literate and has great curiosity to read, to know. He likes to be with knowledgeable people. He meets all who come to see him, sometimes till as late as 1.00 am. He knows how to assess people and can find the right man for the right job. Narendrabhai knew Vaghela's greed for power and had said so to many. Ultimately he [was] proved right. He is never afraid of getting into a controversy. He takes it in his stride. After Godhra, he had a terrible time but he faced it ...'

Gunvant Shah, a leading thinker and one of the most widely read writers in Gujarati, had written a discerning analysis of Narendra's personality in the Gujarati journal *Abhiyaan* on 8 March 2003. He had written: 'Remembering the first anniversary of the "Godhra episode" makes one's heart beat faster. Something happened whereby Godhra turned to be a synonym for "thought" ... What is the essence of the thought called Godhra? The essence is neither *Hindutva* nor hatred for Muslims. If it is to be said in one sentence, it is: "Now on, in this country, synthetic secularism will not work".

'Although my personal encounter with Mr Narendra Modi is almost nil, I can definitely say that he is made of strong mettle, because he has gone through the hardest of tests for purification ... Narendra Modi remained firm in a situation where any other person would have broken down. After Godhra came Naroda; after Naroda, what? The third unfortunate occurrence was that the media disgraced Gujarat before the world. The *dusht* (spiteful) secularists connected with the English newspapers and electronic media started singing one raga. Shall we call that raga a hatred tune or *dhikkar* (disdain) raga?'

At the time of conducting the interviews, we, the authors, strongly sensed that many Hindus were feeling as if they were outsiders in their own country. This feeling in their minds and hearts, and the balm that Narendra Modi had applied to make them feel at home again, had made him the 'Hindu Samrat (Hindu Emperor) in their eyes. Hindus, by nature, are neither cruel, nor bitter as history has revealed time and again. They were not at all anxious to harass Muslims. They were, however, justifiably disgusted with the one-sided talk of secularists. In Narendra, they had found a leader who was their 'own'. This leader had a strong will power and great clarity of thought. From the storm had emerged a leader who could give voice to their intense, suppressed anger and feelings. The response given to every word uttered by Narendra Modi during the *Gaurav* Yatra was the collective reaction of Hindus. Narendra Modi's mettle worked wonders during that period. He took full advantage of this whirlwind because he was a politician, not a mahatma.

Dr Kalindi Randeri met nineteen of Narendra's school friends in a group and had a lively exchange of views with them. Interestingly, no one harboured any negative thoughts about their school-mate who had become Gujarat's First Citizen. All of them expressed their pride at the fact that their old friend had become the chief minister. In fact, they had all been invited with their families to Narendra's residence for dinner where they had a great time talking about old times. 'He hasn't forgotten us,' one of them remarked.

There were others who were interviewed separately. Mukundraoji Bhankar, media in-charge of the Gujarat RSS, had lived and worked with Narendra at different times and held his colleague in high regard. Of his distinguished friend, Bhankar said, 'Narendra has a knack for organizing all kinds of programmes. He can talk to anyone on the subject of their interest. He is great at creating slogans and works well in times of crisis.'

Jasoodkhan Pathan and Ganibhai Mansoori had been Narendra's school-mates and had lived in Vadnagar in the adjoining *mohalla* (neighbourhood). According to them, religion had never been a factor in their relationship with Narendra. They had met daily, interacted with each other and never experienced social discrimination in their everyday activities. They had celebrated all the festivals together.

Narendra's dynamic personality allowed him to make friends easily and he did not forget anyone, thanks to his sharp memory. Not all people interviewed were able to give a first-hand account of their feelings about the man, but many sent in their thoughts in writing.

Harshad Shah of Bardoli, an RSS worker who had known Narendra since 1975, wrote that Narendra was 'an unusual worker' who was quick at solving problems and had 'instant empathy' with those he met. In Shah's words, 'He (Narendra) did not become a leader out of the blue.' Ramesh Mehta, also from the RSS, and his wife Dr Kirtida Mehta, wrote glowingly of Narendra, commenting on how he had endeared himself to their entire family for more than twenty-five years. According to Kirtida, Narendra is 'spontaneous, affectionate, warm and quick to establish rapport' with anyone he comes across.

Tarak Mehta, a popular Gujarati humourist, recalled Narendra's sense of humour when he had been invited to a book release function. Seated on the dais were well-known Gujarati humourists and literary figures. But it was Narendra who had kept the entire audience in splits with his jokes, pithy satire and endless wordplay. Tarak Mehta wrote: 'He was the best among all!'

Kishor Makwana described Narendra as a litterateur. As Makwana saw it, Narendra was an acknowledged writer – learned, knowledgeable and sensitive. The RSS sang many of the songs written by him but without crediting them to him, as was their wont. Besides, Narendra had written many articles on *Hindutva*, personalities, culture, society, religion and politics. The fact that Narendra had written short stories as well as a short novel – unusual for a man so fully engaged in political activities – was also revealed.

During the day, Narendra was actively involved with the RSS. For some time, he had written a column in the *Sadhana* magazine under the pen name Aniket. He had also written songs on an occasion to felicitate the RSS *swayamsevaks* over the age of seventy-five.

When Narendra took up chief ministership, there were many who were concerned about his lack of experience in administration. But those who were either sceptical or critical ate their words fairly quickly and by 2009, they had only words of praise for him and his ways of working.

Once, during an unstructured discussion, a group of officers working with him said that success had come back to Gujarat due to Narendra's approach towards the various problems. He first saw the problem in its entirety. He spent a long time in understanding and studying the problem from all possible angles, because he felt

The View Beyond the Prism

that a problem well understood was half solved. He then thought of a solution. He did not take ad hoc steps or look for a short cut or cosmetic changes. He pondered over permanent and long-term solutions with a futuristic vision and transformation from the roots. He was open to ideas and was a good listener. After that, he worked out a road map with clear targets and milestones, objectives and monitorable indicators. It was only then that he charted the implementation mechanism. He had the inherent ability to choose the right process, the right agency and the right persons for a particular task. Last, but not the least, he had the capacity to monitor, and follow up. Even though he was not a management graduate, his wisdom and innovations surpassed what was taught in management schools.

As a strategist, he could envisage and implement projects at a fast pace, which had a positive bearing across the state. At times, he appeared impatient to see the results but that was understandable. If he did not function that way, Gujarat would not have seen the successful interlinking of a dozen rivers while the rest of the country was still debating about the ways to do it. Similarly, in just three years, a 300-kilometre-long canal had been built, new transmission lines of 56,599 kilometres had been laid down and 12,621 transformers had been installed.

Narendra was described as a master at visualizing and implementing large multi-million projects as well as incorporating smaller solutions and local technologies. One such example was 'Bori Bands' (putting sand and stones in empty gunny bags and checking the water flow through such bags) and farm ponds. He encouraged and respected the experiments and experience of local farmers, accepted suggestions from government employees, and kept in mind the ideas and opinions given by the common man through e-mails and letters.

A lot of questions were raised to understand what Narendra actually was, and what made him tick. Prashant Dayal and Radha Sharma, writing in The *Times of India* on 31 December 2007, tried to provide an answer. According to them, no one really knew 'the real Modi'. The fifty-seven-year-old BJP leader from Gujarat had preferred to remain solitary all his life. Only a handful of people were apparently welcome to his residence; he seldom entertained guests. There were no trappings of power at his residence – Bungalow No. 26 in Ministerial Enclave. His entire household staff comprised three people – a cook and two peons to run errands. If the cook went on leave, one of the peons prepared his meals.

An early riser, Narendra would get up at 5.00 am, finish his morning ablutions, and then surf the net for news. The State Information Department delivered all the local newspapers at his doorstep. Rarely had anyone seen his family members at his residence. His mother, then ninety-five, who had lost her hearing, lived with her eldest son Som in the Ranip area of Ahmedabad. Prahlad, who came next after Narendra, was fifty-five years old and ran a fair price shop in the state capital; the youngest brother Pankaj, aged fifty, worked as a clerk in the Information Department in Gandhinagar. Few people had heard of them and fewer still would recognize them as the chief minister's blood brothers. They were never seen with him and he probably never called on them either.

Once, Modi was asked what *Hindutva* meant to him. His answer was straight and to the point. He said:

'I believe that *Hindutva* is a way of life. It has survived all kinds of assaults. In the past ten thousand years, so many *vicharadharas* (ideologies) have suffered in some way or the other. Not Hinduism. Hinduism stays with the times. It keeps up with the times. It is relevant to our times. *Hindutva* teaches restraint, advises individuals not to be a burden on society, and suggests responsibility. *Hindutva* is over ten thousand years old; Christianity some two thousand years old, and Islam about 1,400 years old. Christianity and Islam are religions. *Hindutva* is a way of life. It is incomparable and scientific. In ancient Sanskrit it is known as *sanatana dharma* or the eternal way of life. It is not rigid. It is liberal, able to adjust.'

Once, a correspondent of the *Time* magazine came to stay with him for three days. He was stunned by the amount of work Narendra put in, day after day. The correspondent could not resist and asked Narendra from where he got all his energy. Narendra's answer was: 'Mine is total commitment. The God sitting over there makes me do everything.'

Modi followed a particular way of life. During *Navaratri* (twice a year), for nine full days, he had only water to drink – no milk, no tea, no juice, no salt, no sugar, no fruits – only water. He did puja for two hours. In addition, he did *pranayama* yoga and meditation. He worshipped the goddess Ambaji Shakti. The test of his faith and endurance came when he had to begin the Somnath Yatra with L K Advani. It was *Navaratri*. Narendra was in charge of all arrangements. Mrs Advani came to know about Narendra's self-imposed discipline of taking nothing but water during the period. With tears in her eyes, she asked Narendra: 'What are you doing?' He told her: 'This is my life. Leave it to me.'

During *Chaturmas,* from July to November, he had only one meal a day. He began his day with *samarpana* (dedication) and *sankalp* (resolve). This gave him direction and a sense of conscious fulfilment of life. It is widely known that when the BJP decided to take the *Ekta* Yatra from Kanyakumari to Kashmir, the responsibility to organize it was given to Narendra. As expected, he did it so effectively and efficiently that it was a big success.

That Narendra was completely fearless was once again evident when he went to Srinagar. Terrorists had sent out threats and the whole nation was tense. Narendra was advised to wear a bullet-proof jacket as he had been receiving threats everyday. But he refused to do so. When asked why he was so fearless, he said he did not know. He had always been like that.

There is an interesting anecdote about the *Ekta* Yatra and the credit for it goes to Narendra. He is a storehouse of the most extraordinary and original ideas. At a planning meeting, he suggested to the stalwarts that on 26 January, when the Indian flag was hoisted at Srinagar, the impact of it should be felt at all the levels of the party. He suggested that each unit of the party be asked to collect people, draw a map of India, mark out Srinagar, and plant the tricolour there at the same moment when the flag was actually hoisted there. That was a terrific idea and made a great impact.

Narendra also had the ability to laugh at himself – a rare virtue among politicians. He was asked whether he had any bad habits. 'Yes,' he said, smiling. 'I don't smoke, I don't drink. According to societal norms I have no bad habits. But at a personal level my bad habits are: I sleep very little, I should sleep more. They say lack of sleep creates stress. I don't know. I am very fond of clothes, of new electronic gadgets. These are all bad habits!' When asked how he saw himself, this is what he had to say:

'One, I think a man should have a lot of confidence in himself. If there is no self-confidence, you cannot achieve anything; you will be dependent on others. That may be okay for a while, but not for long. Have confidence in yourself, I tell everyone. If I don't have confidence in the car in which I sit, how will I reach Mumbai? I should have confidence in the vehicle God has given me. If there is any weakness, it should be corrected. That is my first principle. This body is my vehicle, this thinking is my vehicle. Then I must have full confidence in it. This is my first view of life.

'My second belief is: Every person has some ability, strength. Our efforts should be to use these abilities. I do not belong to that category of philosophy that says: "O sinners, submit yourself to me!" My belief is that God resides in every human being and there is something good in everyone. We should have the insight to discover that strength. This helps a lot in attaining success.

'My third belief is: There is that concept of a person endowed with thirty-two virtues. All the mythological books I read during my childhood talked about making a sacrifice of that man as if he was of no further use. We should use everybody for the welfare of society, depending on their abilities. I still believe society accepts our mistakes, but not our dishonesty. Society does not expect total perfection in man. People would say of one: "Poor fellow, he had such high ideals but could not implement them." That is accepted as only natural. What society expects in one is transparency and openness. People tell me I am straightforward – I speak plainly. Frankly, whatever I say is out of conviction. Strictly speaking, I do not want to criticize anyone. But if I think something is bad, I must say it is bad. If ever I am in the wrong, and this is pointed out to me even after six days, I will correct myself. This is how I think about life. I am a man with the notion of: One Life, One Mission. One should spend life with one aim in mind. One mission. Whatever happens, let it be. I consider power as an instrument.'

And throughout his life so far, Narendra has functioned as an instrument of God, as he conceives God meant him to.

Narendra Modi joined the Vadnagar branch of the RSS as a balswayamsevak *or child volunteer. (Inset: A rare photo of Modi as a child)*

The only advice Modi's mother had for her newly appointed CM son was never to take bribes.

As an underground worker during the Emergency, Modi had to don several disguises. He even grew a beard and looked like a proper Sikh with a turban.

A disciplined soldier of the RSS

Modi's various yatras have added to his popularity. Seen here with Rajnath Singh and Arun Jaitley.

Modi was mentored by L K Advani to become National Secretary of the BJP in 1995.

In 1999, the then PM Vajpayee appointed Modi as party spokesperson and nominated him to be the CM in 2001.

When Modi became National Secretary of the BJP, Jammu and Kashmir came under his organizational purview. During the Kargil war, he worked there 'like a colleague' with army volunteers.

At the Vibrant Gujarat Investors' Summit in 2003, Mukesh Ambani was a key dignitary. He said: 'Gujarat is a land that has transformed opportunities and challenges into a powerful entrepreneurial vision.'

Ratan Tata on moving the Nano project to Gujarat from West Bengal: 'Gujarat is an ideal investment destination. One is stupid if one is not in Gujarat (as an investor).'

At a Gujarati function held at Ramlila Maidan at Malad, Mumbai, in 2006, Modi was weighed against 100 kg of silver. It was later auctioned for ₹26 lakh and the money was donated to Modi's Kanya Kelavani Nidhi (Girls' Education Fund).

Namo's winning combination for India's development:
IT (Indian Talent) + IT (Information Technology) = IT (India Tomorrow)

आँधियों से जाके कह दो,

ज़रा औकात में रहे ,

हम परों से नहीं,

होंसलों से उड़ा करते हैं !

Narendra Modi – poet, philosopher, thinker

One of Modi's biggest challenges today is to win the confidence of Muslims, not just in Gujarat but all over India.

Modi dons different hats to suit varying occasions ...

The traditional Gujarati turban

A proud Gujarati!

At the Kite Festival in the presence of foreign investors

Governance with a vision

'Capping' it – Sangh style!

Evolution of Narendra Modi ...

Starting out in the world of politics

Style statement of a confident Modi!

From gulli-danda to golf!

With Anil Ambani: The corporate look!

Modi's worldview: He aims to put India on par with the best in international development.

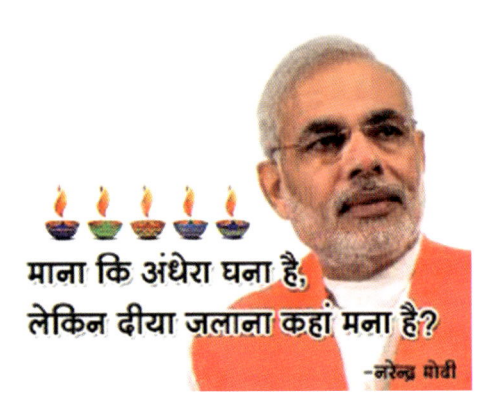

माना कि अंधेरा घना है,
लेकिन दीया जलाना कहां मना है?
—नरेन्द्र मोदी

Even if the darkness is deep, it is not forbidden to light a lamp: Narendra Modi

Modi has been greatly inspired by the poet Subramaniya Bharathi and the philosopher Swami Vivekananda.

At the Sadbhavana Meet in 2012, Modi is flanked by L K Advani on his left and Surjeet Singh Badal on his right.

Body language ...

'Don't fool with me' – Is that what Modi is saying?!

On a winning streak!

Taking the RSS vow with Keshubhai Patel

Narendra Modi selected Amitabh Bachchan to be the brand ambassador to promote Gujarat tourism.

No Full Stop; Not Yet 14

By August 2007, there were rumblings in the Gujarat BJP against the leadership of Narendra Modi and dissidents within the party had begun to raise their heads. They were picking up courage to openly defy Narendra Modi and party stalwart L K Advani. The party high command had no option other than to take action, which it did, by suspending five party MLAs for indulging in anti-party activities. The section that was unrelenting in its opposition belonged to the Leuva Patel caste to which former Chief Minister, Keshubhai Patel, belonged. But Keshubhai himself was practising restraint. As The *Free Press Journal* noted on 9 August 2007:

> Evidently he has skeletons in his cupboard which Modi is aware of ... There can be little doubt that Modi is no pushover. His personal integrity and what he has done for the state's development stand out strongly in his favour. He has imparted a new impetus to the economy ... Corruption, which was endemic during the days of his predecessor Keshubhai, has to some extent been controlled ... The electoral record of his party under his chief ministership has been quite exemplary ... While chief ministers in the past have been known to dole out favours through grant of offices like chairmanship of corporations, Modi has largely eschewed this practice. Modi would not be Modi if he sheds his toughness.

Nevertheless, the paper warned that no leader could survive without a measure of tact and humility and it was time for Narendra to introspect.

Whether Narendra introspected is not the question, but Keshubhai seemed determined to damn his successor to Gujarat's chief ministerial *gaddi* (seat). In an interview, Keshubhai lashed out at Narendra, calling him a dictator. As a political commentator noted, 'No Congress leader had ever attacked Narendra so viciously' as Keshubhai did. The Congress party was apparently content to watch from the sidelines.

The Man of the Moment: Narendra Modi

In The *Hindu* dated 5 October 2007, Vidya Subramaniam stated that the mood in the tribal areas that witnessed some of the worst anti-Muslim violence in 2002 was difficult to assess. A visit to the Tribal Academy in Tejgadh followed by informal stops in the surrounding villages made her feel that a measure of support for the *kamal ka phool* (the lotus – symbol of the BJP) seemed evident. However, some tribals had also told her that they had been used by Narendra against Muslims during the riots and then sent to jail for it. But Narendra was apparently unfazed. 'Unsurprisingly,' she wrote, 'Mr Modi treated the rebels with contempt.' 'As I returned to Ahmedabad,' she concluded, 'the negatives seem to outweigh the positives for Mr Modi in an election which the Gujarati intellectual class – barring a minuscule section – said the chief minister could find tough but which he would win anyway.'

Subramaniam was not entirely negative herself. In a subsequent article, she took note of the string of *mahila sammelans* (women's gatherings) that Modi addressed and presided over the handing over of ownership rights of forest lands to thirty tribals – 'a gesture calculated to draw attention to the Congress' prevarication on notifying the rules of the Forest Rights Act'. Would the strategy pay off, wondered Subramaniam. As she saw it, Narendra knew that 'the raw, surging passion that won him two-thirds majority in 2002 has long cooled off' and the Congress resurgence in the 2004 Lok Sabha elections had proved this. Finally she said, 'Mr Modi is an indefatigable campaigner. The Congress is as usual a divided house. The Congress leadership has refused to project Shankarsinh Vaghela, the one man capable of taking on Mr Modi, for fear of alienating other chief ministerial candidates. The Congress is also mixed up with the BJP dissidents, which has robbed it of its individual identity. So, on one side, there is Mr Modi. And, on the other, there is the Congress without a programme and without a leader.'

This was a very close description of the events as they actually panned out.

With barely two months to go for the elections, pressure was mounting on Narendra. First, Siddharth Parmar, a Dalit leader from Rajkot and a BJP legislator, resigned claiming that other rebels would follow suit. At least one did. It was Ramilabehn Desai, a

No Full Stop; Not Yet

senior leader who had already been suspended from the party for her stand against Narendra. Suresh Mehta, who had not resigned till then, made it plain that he would not support Narendra in the election campaign. A strong face of the party in Vadodara, Nalin Bhatt, had joined the BSP. 'Rebellion has raised its head in the BJP like never before and anti-Modi noises are getting louder by the day,' reported The *Hitavada* on 8 October 2007. But the BJP top brass was with Narendra. At a high-profile meeting held in Delhi in early October to release a report on Gujarat's economy, L K Advani and the former Vice-President Bhairon Singh Shekhawat pointed out that such an economic miracle would not have been possible in any other state. To stress the point as it were, the former Disinvestment Minister Arun Shourie went to the extent of saying that 'Modi is Prime Ministerial material'.

'Gujarat and Narendra Modi have become synonymous with performance and for getting things done,' Shourie said, giving a clean chit to the controversial chief minister. Echoing Shourie's sentiments, Advani said that Modi was a hero who had tirelessly and sincerely worked for the progress of the state despite having been vilified by his opponents. While the mood of the rest of the country was that of cynicism, Gujarat had done quite the opposite, Advani said. Modi himself said that progress in Gujarat lay in the fact that 'the state administration has made it possible through its philosophy of "minimum government and maximum governance" and by creating an enabling environment for industry ... Gujarat has improved its social indicators and position on the Human Development Index (HDI).'

His detractors may have walked out on him, but when examined closely, Narendra had little to worry about. True, his detractors carried some influence but in a very limited way. Keshubhai lacked the guile to turn the tables on Narendra. Kashiram had some influence in the Surat region, but not anywhere else. The Congress was quite aware of some of the BJP dissidents' shortcomings. It was aware that the Muslims had scarce respect for Goverdhan Zadaphia who was suspected of being involved in the post-Godhra riots.

Narendra knew how to face the media onslaught against him. Knowing fully well that the *Hindustan Times* was one of his worst critics, he nevertheless attended the Hindustan Times Leadership Seminar organized in Delhi in October. He told the summit that both Mahatma Gandhi and his idea of *Rama Rajya* (governance under which people are very happy) were relevant to him. He said that he believed in *Gram Swarajya* (Village Self-rule), according to which village-level representatives should be appointed unanimously, as elections led to violence and bad blood. He said that shortly after he had become the chief minister of Gujarat, as many as eleven thousand villages were due for elections. He had announced a scheme wherein any village that unanimously chose its leader would be given a development fund of one lakh rupees. 'Forty-five per cent of the villages chose their leaders unanimously,' he said with pride.

He defended *Hindutva* by saying that it was 'an all-encompassing philosophy' that accepted the fact that there were different ways of approaching the truth. He was proud of the fact that India had found a place in the official book of Israel as being the only country where Jews had not been persecuted. When the Parsis had landed on the shores of Gujarat, he went on to say, the Indian king had agreed to their condition that no non-Iranian would be allowed within fifty metres of their sacred fire. *Hindutva* was opposed to the 'holier than thou' approach. And when asked if the Muslim minority community in Gujarat felt secure, he remarked, 'When will people get rid of this negativism and see the whole truth? If 18,000 villages are getting electricity 24 hours a day, you can't split it in 90 per cent and 10 per cent. Similarly, the waters of the Narmada are brought for the entire Sabarmati and not for parts of it.' This indicated that Modi's development model did not discriminate between Hindus and Muslims and silenced his critics.

On 10 October 2007, the Election Commission announced the schedules for two-phased elections in Gujarat on 11 and 16 December. Announcing the schedule, Chief Election Commissioner (CEC) N Gopalaswami said that the model code of conduct would come into force immediately and it would be applicable to all candidates, political parties, the state governments concerned and the Union government. The 2007 elections in Gujarat were the second one to be held after the post-

No Full Stop; Not Yet

Godhra violence and the CEC assured that the people belonging to the minority communities, who are still living in camps, would be able to exercise their franchise without any fear.

Understandably, the Election Commission went into high gear. It set up a three-man committee to screen all electronic material before it could be put to use by political parties or their candidates. Those involved were informed that all electronic material, including CDs and DVDs that constituted electoral propaganda would have to be cleared by the committee before being put to use. It later came to be known that the commission also ordered video-graphing of all political meetings that could have a direct or indirect bearing on the ensuing polls.

Narendra had been smart. He had had DVDs prepared highlighting the development activities of the state for public propagation. An Internet protocol-based network had already begun showcasing development works being carried out in Gujarat. The *Hindu* reported on 13 October 2007: 'Mr Modi is now talking of a "vibrant Gujarat" with the focus firmly on infrastructure and investment ... The strong man demands that he be judged only on the basis of his performance in the last five years and his promises for the next five.'

Having said that, the newspaper could not help saying slyly, 'Yet there is no mistaking that beneath the slogans stressing development is a reliance on the *Hindutva* card'.

The election scenario was electrified overnight by an event that shook the media world. Narendra had agreed to be interviewed by Karan Thapar on CNN-IBN but decided to walk out after four-and-a-half minutes of being interviewed. The talk went as follows:

Karan Thapar: Mr Narendra Modi, let's start by talking about you. In the six years that you have been the CM of Gujarat, the Rajiv Gandhi Foundation has declared Gujarat to be the best-administered state. *India Today*, on two separate occasions, declared that you are the most efficient chief minister. And despite that, people still call you to your face, a mass murderer and they accuse you of being prejudiced against Muslims. Do you have an image problem?

Narendra Modi: I think it's not proper to say that there are 'people'. There are two or three persons who talk in this terminology and I always say: 'God bless them'.

Karan Thapar: You are saying this is the conspiracy of two or three persons only?

Narendra Modi: I have not said so.

Karan Thapar: But you are saying it, only two or three people.

Narendra Modi: This is the information I have. It's the people's voice.

Karan Thapar: Can I point out to you that in September 2003, the Supreme Court said that they had lost faith in the Gujarat government? In April 2004, the Chief Justice of the Supreme Court said that you were like a modern-day Nero who looked the other side when helpless children and innocent women were being burnt. The Supreme Court seems to have a problem with you.

Narendra Modi: I have a small request to make. Please go through the Supreme Court judgement. If there is anything in writing, I'll be happy to know everything.

Karan Thapar: There was nothing in writing. You are right. It was an observation.

Narendra Modi: If it is in the judgement, then I'll be happy to give you the answer.

Karan Thapar: But do you mean a criticism by the Chief Justice in court doesn't matter?

Narendra Modi: It's a simple request. Please go through the court judgement. Hand out the sentence you are quoting and let the people know it.

Karan Thapar: Okay. In August 2004, the Supreme Court re-opened some 2,100 cases out of a total of around 4,600 – almost forty per cent, and they did so because they believed that justice hadn't happened in Gujarat.

Narendra Modi: I'll be happy. Ultimately the court of law will take the judgement.

No Full Stop; Not Yet

Karan Thapar: But isn't this the reason that despite the fact that *India Today* called you the best chief minister, and the Rajiv Gandhi Foundation says Gujarat is the best-administered state, tens of millions say Modi is prejudiced against the Muslims. This is why I ask you: do you have an image problem?

Narendra Modi: Actually I have not spent a single minute on my image. And that can be the reason. I am busy with my work. I am committed to Gujarat. I am dedicated to Gujarat. I never talk about my image, never spend a single minute for my image and confusions may be there.

Quietly, and without any fuss, Narendra terminated the interview. It was pointless to begin with. Instead of trying to raise serious issues, Thapar was personalizing the talk. It ended abruptly. An excellent opportunity to understand events and their significance was thus lost. When, in the third week of October 2007, some television channels started telecasting the *Tehelka* tapes in which certain extremists confessed to having organized the post-Godhra riots, there were many who believed that this could damage Narendra's reputation and undermine the BJP's prospects in the December elections to the state assembly.

The undercover operations for which *Tehelka* is notorious showed Hindu extremists in poor light. They also revealed to what length rebel BJP members could go to damage Narendra's reputation. In a way, the *Tehelka* operations did not reveal anything new. As The *Free Press Journal* noted in its issue dated 27 October 2007, 'Most of the confessions emanate from acting ministers and politicians who have now fallen out with the Modi Government.' Thus, among the main protagonists of the tapes was Babu Bajrangi who was once close to Modi but by 2007, had had a falling out with him. He was out for revenge. Though much was made about the tapes, the fact remained that they had revealed nothing new and many of the so-called confessions had already been made before the Nanavati Commission. To this day, no one knows who financed *Tehelka*. The timing of televising the tapes just before the state elections led many to think that there was politics behind it all. Indeed, Congress spokesperson Jayanti Natarajan left no one in doubt that the party would be using the tapes to the hilt. She even demanded Modi's resignation for his alleged active role in the 2002 riots.

The Man of the Moment: Narendra Modi

The truth seems to be that with elections round the corner, the Congress was eager to make Narendra Modi the main issue. The belief was that if somehow he could be effectively defamed, the election rug could be pulled from under his feet. The *Free Press Journal* saw through the game clearly. It said on 29 October 2007:

> Look at the Tehelka sting operation. Was it not timed to ignite the communal fires on the eve of the elections and thus milk the resulting divide for electoral gains for the Congress party? Of course, the idiotic foot-soldiers of Hindutva were caught on the camera, talking loosely, boasting emptily before someone who had deceived them into believing that he himself was one of them. You can play the confidence trick on any fool and thus con him into saying what you had set out to hear.

The hope, especially in Congress circles, was that the people of Gujarat would be so shocked after watching the tapes that they would throw out the ruling party. At that point, there were many who sincerely believed that the Congress party was behind *Tehelka*. Narendra refused to react to the sting operations, insisting that the people of Gujarat were the ultimate judges of all his actions. When in an exclusive interview to The *Indian Express*, he was charged as being perceived to be too close to business houses, he replied by saying that he met the business leaders 'openly' to attract investment in Gujarat. 'I do not meet anyone behind closed doors which was a weakness of the politicians in the past,' he added.

But the defection of some BJP leaders to the Congress had emboldened the latter to believe that this could be in its interests. Thus the Congress general secretary in charge of Gujarat, B K Hariprasad told the press that what the Congress was fighting in Gujarat was not Narendra but the 'terror' he and his associates had 'unleashed'. 'We have to regain the state,' Hariprasad said. He was unusually acerbic in his attacks on Narendra though, and was pulled up by the Election Commission for that. But the defections from the BJP gave Congress some false hopes for which it was to pay later. As he told the media, the political situation in Gujarat was 'good' for the Congress. The Congress party felt it held all the cards. And it had the full support of some eminent columnists, some of whom openly demanded that Narendra Modi should not be 'left alone', meaning that he should be arrested. The

No Full Stop; Not Yet

demand had originated from Lalu Prasad Yadav against whom incidentally, there had been many charges of corruption!

By the beginning of November 2007, electioneering started in right earnest. Everybody from parties and politicians to the media jumped into the fray. The fight did not turn out to be BJP vs Congress, but the media and the Congress vs Narendra Modi. Kuldip Nayar wrote in The *Tribune* on 2 November that the people of Gujarat were being tested and that 'they should not allow Modi to convert his communal approach into an issue of Gujarati self-respect'.

Writing in The *Free Press Journal* on 19 November 2007, R K Misra stated, 'For all those entering the poll fray in Gujarat from the main opposition, the Congress to BJP rebels, the NCP, BSP and the like, the election battle is essentially a straight fight between Narendra Modi and the rest. The votes will be cast either for Modi or against him. There is no third choice and there is no third factor.'

The fact was that Narendra Modi dominated the scene, not necessarily deliberately, but because of what he, and not the BJP, stood for. 'There is not an iota of doubt as the state inches towards elections that Modi has, as per his own calculations, long outgrown Gujarat,' wrote Misra. He also gave credit to Narendra for his 'modern-day, tech-savvy and development-oriented profile, tempered with lurking hardline *Hindutva* for a backdrop'. He added that 'the methodical manner in which the dissidents are going about creating a haze of dust, as they operate into a plan may be a matter of concern for Modi, but is not beyond his combating powers.' As far as they were concerned, the rebel strategy was clear. Keshubhai Patel and the former Union Textile Minister Kashiram Rana were not to leave the BJP but the former Chief Minister Suresh Mehta and suspended rebel Zadaphia were to resign, though not to join the Congress. They were to take charge of the Sardar Patel Utkarsh Samiti (a body floated by Gujarat BJP rebels led by Keshubhai Patel and Suresh Mehta) to coordinate the effort to defeat the BJP in Gujarat.

Efforts were made to separate Modi from the BJP and, as Misra put it, 'the man is the party in Gujarat'. He averred that the party, by itself, had long ceased to exist.

The Man of the Moment: Narendra Modi

Had Narendra Modi alienated the party? It did not seem so. Indeed, as many as eighty-seven BJP leaders were scheduled to kick-start the BJP campaign, addressing around 180 meetings across the state on a single day on 27 November 2007, a day after the last date for withdrawal of nominations for eighty-seven seats for the first phase of election on 11 December. With its *'Jitega* Gujarat' (Gujarat will win) slogan, the saffron party chanted the Narendra Modi mantra and highlighted him as the *vikas purush* (the man to bring about progress) and natural leader of the state. Some of the BJP's topmost leaders, including L K Advani, Rajnath Singh, Murli Manohar Joshi, Venkaiah Naidu, Jaswant Singh, Yashwant Sinha, Sushma Swaraj and Arun Jaitley, were there. Would BJP dump its *Hindutva* slogan during the election campaign? When asked the same, BJP's Vice-President Mukhtar Abbas Naqvi said that the party had never raised *Hindutva* in an election campaign and was not going to do so either.

The campaign started in its entirety on 27 November 2007 with the BJP promising accelerated development in Gujarat and blasting the Congress-led UPA government at the Centre for its injustice to Gujarat. Narendra himself was all fire and brimstone as he tore into the UPA government for a long trail of injustices to the state. 'The map of India on the two rupee coin has [been] removed after Sonia Gandhi's government came to power at the Centre. Why?' he asked. That was a good start. Meanwhile, the Congress itself pitched Union Minister of State for Petroleum, Dinsha Patel, to contest against Modi in the Maninagar constituency. An MP from Nadiad, Dinsha Patel, the Congress hoped, would play the Patel card well. That hardly mattered to Narendra. Before submitting his nomination papers, he had stated in his affidavit that he was a resident of Ranip in Ahmedabad; he had no farm or commercial land; owned a house in Sector-I area of Gandhinagar that he had bought for about ₹1.30 lakh years ago and whose current market price was ₹30 lakh. Narendra stated that he did not own a vehicle but had ₹8 lakh in bank deposits and his savings account had an amount of ₹55,000. He also declared that he possessed ₹11,200 in cash and had three gold rings worth ₹50,000. He had National Saving Certificates worth ₹3.39 lakh.

Despite open rebellion by a group of BJP MLAs against Narendra Modi, the central leadership of the party was quite hopeful that he

No Full Stop; Not Yet

would sail through the elections safely. The Congress, it seemed, was somewhat reluctant to make the Godhra riots a campaign issue lest it polarized the voters on religious lines. But apparently, the Congress felt that any direct appeal to the Muslim vote might thereby antagonize the Hindu voter. As far as the Congress was concerned, talk of secularism was out. That point was well made by Harish Khare in The *Hindu* on 6 December 2007. 'Above all,' he wrote, '2007 represents an opportunity to rescue Gujarat from the professional secularist-fundamentalist, unreasonable and unaccommodating in the defence of "secularism". These last five years, because of their unreasonable and unaccommodating defence of "secularism", many of these professional secularists have ended up validating the Modi appeal in Gujarat. As it is, the reputations and pretensions of so many secular voices in the country have, of late, come into question. Gujarat can do without these screaming professional crusaders and there is no need for the non-Modi forces to be dictated by these self-appointed custodians of the secular creed.'

But suddenly, Narendra allowed himself to be the target of 'secularist' forces when, in an election speech, he was incorrectly reported to have justified Sohrabuddin's killing in a fake encounter. That was the kind of issue the Congress was eagerly looking for to hit at Narendra. A confirmed anti-Modi activist, Teesta Setalvad, filed a formal complaint with the EC urging it to take action against him for fomenting hatred and violence against Muslims. But Modi, too, had his weapon. Releasing the Congress party manifesto, the party's General Secretary Digviyay Singh had called for a crackdown on Muslim terrorism as much as Hindu terrorism. Modi picked that up at a meeting he addressed, accusing the Congress of defaming Hindus by calling them 'terrorists'. He asked the large gathering if they were Hindus. 'Yes,' came the response. 'Are you terrorists?' Modi asked. The reply was loud and clear 'No'.

If Modi had infuriated his opponents on the Sohrabuddin issue, Congress President Sonia Gandhi infuriated Modi and the BJP with a puerile comment in one of her election speeches. She described Narendra as *'maut ke saudagar'* (merchant of death). That was to cost the Congress dearly! Understandably, the Congress stood by Sonia Gandhi's statement which must, in the first place, have been written for her by professional speech-writers. At the same time, an effort was made by a senior Congress leader, Kapil Sibal, to be partly apologetic by saying that Sonia Gandhi had not specifically named Modi or any BJP individual as a 'merchant of death'. But that did not make any difference.

Modi himself charged Sonia Gandhi with 'insulting' Gujarat when she spoke of *'maut ke saudagar'* and said that the real merchant of death was the Congress which was 'protecting terrorists like Afzal Guru'. At the same time, the BJP hit back at the Congress by demanding action by the Election Commission against Sonia Gandhi for her comments on Modi. L K Advani called a press conference at which he defended Modi saying that his remarks on Sohrabuddin had been in response to Sonia Gandhi's comments and should be seen in that context. Advani said, 'I would like to know whether Gandhi has been issued any notice so far. The EC should not have double standards. Gandhi demonizing a democratically elected chief minister as a "merchant of death" is a provocation of the gravest kind. It was a personalized attack and betrays a perverse mind.'

The Election Commission did pursue the matter against Sonia Gandhi, though she was let off later with a mild rebuke. Narendra himself answered the charges against him in a letter addressed to the EC. He wrote:

I am in receipt of your notice dated 6th December, 2007, wherein on the basis of the media reports and a complaint dated 5th December 2007 by Teesta Setalvad, I am alleged to have made an open exhortation to violence and misuse of religion for political ends. The Election Commission has further stated that linking the name of Sohrabuddin to terrorism in my speech amounts to indulging in [an] activity which may aggravate existing differences, creating mutual hatred and causing tension between different communities. I deny this charge in its entirety.

1. The Commission has acted on the basis of a complaint which alleges that my stand is contrary to what the State of Gujarat has stated in its affidavit before the Supreme Court. The basis of the complaint appears to be a report dated 5th December 2007 of The *Times of India* by one Shri

Prashant Dayal. The relevant extract in The *Times of India* reads as under:

'**Modi:** You tell what should be done to Sohrabuddin

People at the rally: Kill him, kill him.

Modi: Well, that is what I did. And I did what was necessary.'

The last sentence of the report of The *Times of India* has generated controversy in the whole nation. Television channels and newspapers have made comments to the effect that I have stated that 'Sohrabuddin got what he deserved' or that 'it is a professional statement by me', or that 'Modi has justified a murder'. All other newspaper cuttings which the Commission has taken into account are dated 6th December 2007 which do not report my speech delivered on 4th December 2007, but are comments inspired by false imputation in The *Times of India*. This last sentence is not reflected in the CD as having been used by me.

2. The *Statesman* dated 6th December 2007 quoted me as having said: 'He (Sohrabuddin) has got what he deserved'. The *Hindustan Times* of 6th December 2007 quoted me as saying: 'Well then, that's it.' I had on 6th December 2007, immediately after receiving the Election Commission's notice, requested that I may be supplied a copy of the CD of the speech and also various inputs which have influenced the issuance of the notice. I have since received the copy of the CD on the evening of 7th December 2007 at 5.45 pm. I find [that] none of the above statements are contained in my speech as recorded in the CD. The EC notice is issued on the basis of unverified and false media reports.

3. As I am also involved in a campaign, I am sending this as a preliminary reply, which I am sure would satisfy the Election Commission with regard to the contents of my speech. Before I answer specifics raised in the notice of the complaint, I wish to state that India is governed by rule of law and the Constitution. I am entitled to my right of free speech. Free and fair election involves a debate on

the political issues in the marketplace of politics. When statements are made by political opponents, others are entitled to reply to them. The tone and content of the statement must necessarily adhere to the model code of conduct. I wish to categorically state that I regard the Election Commission as a constitutional authority under an obligation to ensure free and fair elections which will defend my right of free speech against those who have started a hate campaign against me.

4. On 1st December 2007, AICC President Mrs Sonia Gandhi visited Gujarat and referred to me by suggesting those who are ruling Gujarat are 'liars, dishonest and merchants of fear and death *(maut ke saudagar)*. On 3 December 2007, AICC General Secretary visited Gujarat and referred to it as a state which has unleashed 'Hindu terrorism'. The newspapers reported these statements extensively. Separate complaints with regard to the code of conduct were sent to the Election Commission. I am sure the Election Commission would at least now proceed to take action on those reports.

5. One of the critical issues in our country is the problem of terrorism. India has lost the lives of almost 90,000 innocent citizens and security personnel in the last 17 years, to terror. In the last four years, 5,619 innocents have been killed by the terrorists. The Government of Gujarat has a strong policy against terrorism. I believe that the UPA and Congress party are indulging in vote bank politics and have sent soft signals on terrorism. My party and I have repeatedly made these charges against the Congress party. In Gujarat, only one life has been lost in the last four years through terror. This is the result of our strong policy against terrorism. The nation and the people of Gujarat are entitled to witness a fair debate on terrorism. If any of the viewpoints is censored or not permitted, it will be interference in the right of free speech. Our Constitution and the Election Commission's obligation to conduct free and fair elections will not extend to preventing me from expressing my strong views against terrorism.

6. My speech, therefore, has to be read entirely in this context. It was a political response to Mrs Sonia Gandhi referring to me as those who rule Gujarat as *maut ke saudagar*. Surely, it cannot be [a] policy of the Election Commission first to ignore the violation of the code of conduct in her statement and then censure my political response to that statement. I have gone through my speech on the CD supplied. It is merely a response to Mrs Sonia Gandhi calling me *maut ke saudagar*.

7. This part of my speech was entirely against terrorism. I criticized the Congress President for calling me a *maut ke saudagar*. I responded that the *maut ke saudagar* are all those who attacked the Parliament. It is the Congress Party which is delaying the execution of the guilty. I have made a reference to the Sohrabuddin case and mentioned the allegations against him. I have accused the Congress of suggesting that I have engineered a fake encounter. I said that I am open for any action on this count. At no point in time have I either justified the specific encounter of Sohrabuddin case, nor have I used the specific inculpate sentences used in The *Times of India* report. It is clear that my comment is a part of my speech where, on several occasions, I have put questions to the audience which the audience has answered. It is my political response to Smt Gandhi's allegation that I am *maut ke saudagar*. I have replied back alleging that the Congress party is helping those who have spread terrorism in the country ... My criticism in the media was concocted and engineered by this 'Hate Modi' campaign. Nowhere in my speech have I explicitly referred to the religion of any person. I have spoken against terrorism. It is not my speech but the complaint which assumes terrorism is linked to a religion.

8. Am I to be prevented from giving my point that terrorism will not be allowed on the soil of Gujarat or that the Congress is soft on the terrorists and thereby helping *maut ke saudagars*? If the Election Commission imposes any such regulation, it would offend our constitutional values and my right of free speech. At no state have I controverted the

affidavit filed by the Gujarat government in the Supreme Court of India. I have already clarified my position that I do not support fake encounters. Encounters can occur but there should be no fake encounters. I have nowhere tried to prejudice any pending litigation. I am fully committed to the enforcement of the Model Code of Conduct [as specified] by the Election Commission and shall comply with it. I believe that the Election Commission should not be misled by motivated media reports which are based on falsehood.

I therefore request the Election Commission to withdraw this notice.

As usual, the English media was at Narendra Modi's throat. The *Deccan Herald* said in its 8 December 2007 issue that the Election Commission had done well to haul up Modi for his 'incendiary remarks', even while condemning Congress for not offering the electorate 'an alternate vision. The 'Congress has emerged as Hindutva's B-Team in Gujarat,' stated the paper. The *Times of India* loftily said on 7 December 2007 that 'Modi's may be a conscious attempt to whip up emotions and polarize society ahead of the assembly elections.'

Then there were reports that Modi was failing to draw crowds. Writing in The *Free Press Journal* on 7 December 2007, R K Misra said that Sonia Gandhi was proving to be 'a crowd puller' while Narendra Modi was 'failing to match paces'. Vidya Subramaniam penned her views in The *Hindu* saying that Sonia Gandhi had 'a mesmeric hold' on Gujarati audiences. At Idar, when Sonia Gandhi arrived, she wrote, 'the ground was filled to overflowing' and Adivasis and Dalits, 'who had voted for the BJP in 2002 but who now seemed to want to return to the party they had deserted', were a part of the audience. The impression was that Modi was slowly but surely losing. The point was indirectly made by The *Free Press Journal* on 6 December 2007. Inter alia it said:

'In the Lok Sabha elections of 2004, the Congress party's vote share increased from 39.28 per cent to 43.86 per cent and the BJP lost 2.49 per cent of the vote share. As a result, the BJP lost its majority in thirty-eight assembly segments. Pollsters say that if the 2004 Gujarat election mood is repeated in 2007, the BJP will get eighty-nine seats and the Congress party will get ninety-one seats.'

No Full Stop; Not Yet

Then there was the possibility of harm being done by BJP rebels, some of whom like Keshubhai Patel, could make it very hard for Narendra in certain constituencies. Junagadh, with a Muslim population of thirty-five thousand, was being eyed both by the Samajwadi Party and the RSP. Some people felt that Keshubhai's diatribe against him was bound to have an impact, and the guess was that the BJP may 'just scrape through'. Importantly, the point was made that the BJP may fare poorly in Saurashtra where the government's attempt to bring down widespread electricity theft had annoyed the farmers. While the step was good on face value, the farmers were not very happy.

But Narendra seemed unperturbed, at least in public. His popularity had reached such heights that Modi-masks were selling in thousands and fans were wearing them with evident delight. Media reports suggested that the BJP's election symbol – the lotus – was taking a second place to Narendra Modi's masks that were becoming popular with every candidate's entourage.

It is not that the entire media was anti-Narendra Modi. Some intellectuals could see beyond the hate campaign run by the secularists. The *Times of India*, for example, ran a column on 9 December 2007 by Swaminathan Anklesaria Aiyar that showed a better understanding of Narendra Modi and his mission. Among other things, Aiyar said:

> *Sonia Gandhi calling the BJP 'merchants of death' is working entirely to Modi's advantage ... After the mass killings of Muslims in Gujarat in 2002, Modi is reviled by secularists. But he is also a good administrator and a relatively clean politician ... People outraged by Modi's remarks on Sohrabuddin are calling for legal action. But it is far from clear that he has actually transgressed the law ... Modi appeals to the Hindu vote by saying that Islamic terrorists have killed 5,617 Indians in the last three years, but only one has died in Gujarat, showing how well the BJP protects Hindus ... He is factually on firm ground in saying that political parties who have resorted to extra-judicial killings galore in other states are hypocrites in trying to portray Gujarat as a den of sin.*
>
> *'In Kashmir, Indian troops and police have committed atrocities galore. Most parties (and most Indians) regret this but see it as an inescapable side-effect of the battle against militants. However, the*

very parties and persons complicit in atrocities in Kashmir claim to be outraged by atrocities in Gujarat. Modi is quick to exploit the double standard.

If the reader takes into account the views of Swapan Dasgupta, who has a following all over the country, aired in The *Times of India* on 16 December 2007, the reader would notice the following:

> In Gujarat, Modi is not just a politician; he is a combination of folk hero and superstar. Many of his election rallies are akin to rock concerts marked by spectacular exhibitions of mass frenzy ... Narendra Modi is the creation of an India that is fed up with sloth, inefficiency and the missed opportunities of the past fifty years. This is an India that found its voice after socialism was junked in 1991 and has steadily grown in confidence with every percentage rise in the growth rate. Gujarat is one of the principal citadels of this explosion of suppressed energy ... With an image of being uncompromisingly tough, ruthlessly driven, politically innovative, fanatically honest and culturally rooted, Modi has evolved into the leader of new Gujarat ... For the moment, Modi is a regional leader. But the phenomenon on which his politics is grafted is pan-Indian. Whatever the Gujarat verdict, India is going to be pre-occupied with Modi for a long time. He is a voice of the future ....

The fate of both the BJP and Narendra Modi was a topic of intensive study in the media, for what the latter had achieved, no one else, in all the parties put together, had even come close to; he had stood for a certain set of values. Neither the Congress, nor the BJP rebels, nor all the miscellaneous parties hungering for publicity – nobody seemed to stand for anything worthwhile. But Narendra Modi had a vision.

Swapan Dasgupta, who was covering the election campaign, wrote:

> The point to note is that Modi has a larger-than-life presence throughout Gujarat. Those who admire him do so with a passion that has hitherto been reserved for pop stars and religious gurus ... Today, Modi is India's foremost political Hindu. If Modi repeats his 2002 victory, there is little doubt that opinion polls will record a sharp increase in the numbers of those who see him as the Prime Minister India should have ... Modi's sense of regional pride mingles happily with robust Indian nationalism. He complements it with a wholehearted endorsement of globalization which he views as a phenomenal

> *opportunity and not a threat ... Modi's appeal in Gujarat cuts across regions, gender, castes and generations. He is seen as a leader who has overcome fear and is not afraid of doing what he thinks is right, even if it involves treading on the toes of his own party ... Modi is not just another politician: he is a phenomenon ....*

Narendra, incidentally, did not campaign in his own constituency where Congress had fielded Union Minister of State for Petroleum Dinsha Patel in a bid to harvest the 95,000 Patel votes, some 12,000 Muslim votes, in addition to an equivalent number of Dalit and about 16,000 Marathi-speaking people's votes, even when the party was fully aware that it was going to be a 'David versus Goliath battle', as a Congress leader put it. Patel was to lose heavily!

The first phase of the voting was hardly over when fears began to arise among Narendra Modi's opponents. Their desperation was to be seen in the kind of advertisements that began to appear in the media. On the eve of the crucial second phase, advertisements carrying semi-naked pictures of women dancing during the previous year's Vibrant Gujarat Summit began appearing in some local dailies reportedly sponsored by the Sardar Seva Utkarsh Samiti. That was in poor taste and only encouraged even fence-sitters to vote for Modi. There were strong indications following the first phase that Modi was faring well. The second and final phase of voting ended on 16 December and predictions started pouring in. In all, there were elections to 182 seats and the magic figure for getting back into power was 91+1 or 92.

The NDTV exit poll projected that the BJP would win between 90 and 110 seats. It had won 127 seats in 2002. The Congress share was put at somewhere between 70 and 95 with other parties obtaining three to five seats. The CNN-IBN-CSDS (Centre for the Study of Developing Societies) exit poll gave BJP 92-100 seats, with Congress notching somewhere between 77 and 85. Others were given 3 to 7 seats.

The exit poll of Star News-Nielsen saw the BJP getting 103 seats and losing about 24 seats, mostly in central and northern Gujarat. In the 2002 elections in the same regions, the BJP had swept 73 of the 95 seats at stake. The Congress was expected to get 76 seats, a gain of 25. Zee News and C-Voter projected the BJP getting 93-104 seats, followed by the Congress at 75-87 seats. It gave a vote share of about forty-eight per cent to the BJP and forty-five per cent to the Congress.

All of them were to be proved grievously wrong!

When the final results were published, exit-pollsters, BJP-hating pseudo-secularists, and Congressmen in general bit the dust. 'UNSTOPPABLE' was the front page headline in The *Indian Express* on 24 December 2007. Another edition put it more clearly when it screamed: 'MODI, MODI AND NOW MEGA MODI'. The Mumbai-based *DNA* understood the shock that Congressmen felt when its leading heading said: 'MODI'S VICTORY JOLTS DELHI.' Nagpur-based The *Hitavada* titled its report with a headline which said: 'MODI DOES A HAT-TRICK IN GUJARAT.'

Narendra won for the third time running against all the Hate-Modi, Hate-BJP propaganda run by all opposition parties, including the Congress. He won 117 seats which The *Hitavada* described as 'just a flea bite less than its last high of 127 seats in 2002.' All the so-called experts proved to be miserably wrong.

Actually, in all the regions, barring central Gujarat, Narendra emerged triumphant. Following the announcement of the results, 'the first knives were being brought out in the Congress'. The BJP had wrested twenty-six seats from the Congress in the Saurashtra/Kutch and south Gujarat regions where it was expected to do badly.

The *Tribune*, which had a reputation of being anti-Modi, described the BJP victory as 'LOTUS BLOOMS IN GUJARAT'. In its editorial dated 24 December 2007, the paper said:

> Had the BJP lost the Gujarat elections, the entire blame would have gone to Mr Narendra Modi and his Moditva. Now that he has won in a big way, he will also have to be given the credit of victory even by his critics ... Mr Modi has also in the process trounced Congress and scored a personal point or two against Mrs Sonia Gandhi who had herself focussed on Mr Modi ... The Congress has conceded defeat, but if it actually thinks that it lost only because Chief Minister Modi harped on Hindutva and other such divisive issues, it will be missing the wood for the trees. There were other arrows in Modi's quiver which helped him pierce the target and even the Congress did not make Hindutva a big issue. There was considerable development work which stood him in good stead ...

No Full Stop; Not Yet

The *Hindu*, in its full-length editorial on 24 December 2007, made the point that in the wake of the election results, the UPA would dare to go for mid-term elections. It noted that for the fourth time running, the BJP had vanquished its adversary in Gujarat, 'comprehensively beating it in every department – popular appeal, propaganda, strategy and tactics – and establishing its supremacy in three of the four regions of the State'.

Narendra himself won by about 87,000 votes from the Maninagar constituency in Ahmedabad, defeating the Congress candidate and Union Minister of State Dinsha Patel. The Gujarat BJP came up with interesting messages pertaining to their victory in Gujarat which then, in a way, became the way to taunt the Congress party. One such message read: *'Aaj Gujarat kal Delhi hamara hai.'* There were others like: *'Gali gali me naara hai, aaj Gujarat kal Delhi hamara hai'*, and *'Jo Hindu hit ki baat karega wohi desh par raj karega'*.

Intellectuals and secularists started seeing new light on the national horizon. Those who had gone all out to attack Modi prior to the elections stayed back to give new meaning to his victory. Following the results of the elections, *DNA* published a meaningful study by two political commentators, Chandrika Parmar and Shiv Visvanathan. Some of their findings reflect how minds could change:

> Narendra Modi has created history. Defying the incumbency factor, he has wooed, won and virtually constructed a new definition of Gujarat. He has out-thought and outplayed his critics ... Modi was playing authoritative chess, showing that even his pawns could outplay the dissident bishops. It is not that Modi represented truth or peace or goodness; it is just that he was a better politician, who understood the symbolic domain.

> Modi's genius lay in showing that an anglicized media and politics were barking up the wrong political tree. Rahul Gandhi's speeches were an exercise in Anglo-Saxon Hindi ... Modi could construct a cognitive map of Gujarat which was exciting and new. He was tired of the ritualistic contentions, the ideological formula of RSS, BJP and VHP, and tired of the spoils system that paid obeisance to caste and traditional constituencies.

Very few in the media gave credit to Modi's fantastic electioneering efforts. During the entire pre-voting period, he had addressed 155

The Man of the Moment: Narendra Modi

assembly constituencies, including eighty-seven constituencies that went to polls in the first phase. According to one estimate, he must have addressed over three crore people out of a total population of 5.5 crore. To fishermen, he spoke about his Sagar Khedu Scheme, to the tribals he described his Van Bandhu plan, and the subject of his talk to women was *Mahila Sammelan*. The Sagar Khedu project involving eleven thousand crore rupees was meant for the welfare of the population inhabiting the 1,500 kilometre-long coastline stretching from Kutch to Vapi. The Van Bandhu project, worth fifteen thousand crore, was aimed at the tribals who inhabited the entire flank of the state and Ambaji bordering Rajasthan, to Dohad near Madhya Pradesh and Dangs near Maharashtra. Understandably, the inclination of the tribals towards the Congress was only thirty-eight per cent while it was forty-five per cent towards the BJP.

Tribal and Muslim votes, thought to be safe Congress assets, were channelled in large numbers to other parties, independent candidates, and even to the BJP. In fact, 23.6 per cent of Muslims seemed to have voted for the BJP. The Muslim turnout was relatively low, being just about 51.7 per cent of the total Muslim voters.

Among the seven BJP rebels who fought the elections on a Congress ticket, only one candidate, Bavku Unghad, won from Babra in Amreli district. Prominent among the Congress candidates who lost at the hustings were its State Women's Wing chief and former minister, Chandrika Chudasama, from Mangrol. In Kutch, out of the six seats, the Congress could win only one – Rapar. In the 2002 polls, Congress had bagged four of the six seats. The two BJP rebel MLAs, Narendrasingh Jadeja and Gopal Dhuva, who contested from Abdasa and Mundhra, lost to the BJP. In contrast, the two Congress rebel MLAs, Nimaben Acharya and Padubha Manek were elected from Anjar and Dwarka constituencies. This merely showed the popularity of the BJP. Significantly, Mayawati's BSP and Uma Bharati's BJSP failed to make any impact on the Gujarati electorate. There were many who believed that Mayawati might steal the Dalit vote from the BJP and the Congress. But it was the BJP that won eleven out of the thirteen seats reserved for the scheduled castes. Narendra had taken some risks. One major change he had made was dropping forty-seven sitting MLAs and bringing in new faces. That was an enormous risk! While thirty-three candidates won, fourteen lost.

The party had been watching the antics of its rebels and had maintained quiet, but once the elections were over and before the results were announced, it cracked the whip against the dissidents. Keshubhai Patel and former Union Textile Minister, Kanshi Ram Rana, were served with show-cause notices while Vallabhbhai Kathiria and Somabhai Patel were suspended from the party for 'indiscipline' and 'anti-party activities'. Keshubhai had not campaigned for Modi but then, neither had he campaigned for the Congress.

What was remarkable was the courage shown by Modi to take on the Bharatiya Kisan Sangh (BKS). According to The *Indian Express* dated 24 December 2007, Modi's government had cracked down on more than 1.22 lakh farmers for power thefts! It was reported that about 3,200 farmers had been 'handcuffed and jailed too', and BKS president Praful Senjalia had threatened that farmers would vote to 'throw Modi out'. According to the *Express,* a month before the elections were announced, the BKS had even launched a powerful movement against Narendra in Saurashtra, organizing rallies and campaigning in favour of the BJP rebels and Congress candidates. That Narendra Modi had dared to establish a law even if it hurt the farmers showed his spirit of fairness.

Narendra's victory 'is people's rebuff to the Congress' attempts to communalize polity,' said Sukhbir Singh Badal, Working President of the Shiromani Akali Dal. Kapil Sibal belatedly admitted that his party's confidence had been 'misplaced' but had the grace to say that Narendra's success was 'a remarkable achievement'. The CPIs National Secretary, D Raja, said that it was not enough for the Congress to just realize secularism, but it must also rethink its policies. High praise came from All India Anna Dravida Munnetra Kazhagam (AIADMK) chief, J Jayalalitha. Not unsurprisingly, she said that she had 'no doubt that under Modi's leadership, Gujarat would rise to greater heights of all-round progress and development.' It was only much later that Modi called on her and was treated to a rich repast, leaving observers with little doubt that a BJP-AIADMK alliance was in the offing.

Only the Congress remained stunned. It was sure that its so-called secularism would get the votes and Sonia Gandhi's charisma would win Gujarati hearts. That did not work. Bharat Solanki, President of the Gujarat Pradesh Congress Committee (GPCC), sounded heart-broken when he said, 'For once, the party was united in its efforts to defeat. But even that was not enough. Obviously there was something seriously wrong.'

Business leaders, it seemed, were the most pleased with Modi's victory. Thus, J O Patel, Managing Director of the Ajanta Group that had invested five hundred crore rupees in Kutch to manufacture ceramic tiles, told the media that 'easy clearance for industrial projects made life easier for business houses and also made Gujarat an attractive destination for global investment'. As Patel saw it, allowing corporate houses to set up projects even before the paperwork was cleared had worked wonders. He was right. In the year 2006-07, Gujarat attracted 17.8 billion dollars in investment when the RBI had put the total amount invested in India that year to be sixty-nine billion dollars. And Gujarat's GDP grew at thirteen per cent compared with nine per cent in India as a whole. As the most industrialized state in India, Gujarat accounted for twenty per cent of the country's industrial output, twenty-five per cent of its textile production, forty per cent of its pharmaceutical production, forty-seven per cent of its petrochemical production, and twenty-one per cent of its exports – a remarkable achievement by any stretch of imagination.

For all that, Narendra had his determined detractors. The *Deccan Herald* noted in its editorial section dated 24 December 2007 that his brand of politics 'is a threat not only to India's religious minorities but also to the country's secular democracy.' Running down his achievements, the paper said that his victory 'is, however, not so much the result of any of his achievements as it is of the failure of the Congress to put up an uncompromising fight against his brand of politics.' Amulya Ganguli, a well-known commentator, insisted that his image continued to be that of a hard-line anti-Muslim leader and that factor would continue to haunt him despite his victory.

No Full Stop; Not Yet

Compare that inane statement with what Shishir Gupta wrote in The *Indian Express* on 25 December 2007:

> Modi had legitimate reasons for showcasing his government's firm commitment towards internal security issues in post-2002 riots Gujarat. ... not one major terrorist incident has taken place in Gujarat in the past five years of BJP rule. The State Government was able to harmonize internal conflict with economic and industrial reform. ... Today, Indian entrepreneurs and people at large do not need government support in the form of licenses or quotas. They just want the government to provide a terror-free or violence-free environment, so that they can get on with the job. Like it or lump it, Modi was perceived by the majority of Gujaratis to have provided just such as environment. ...

Narendra Modi was humble in his victory. The results seemed to have softened him. He put in a call to an ailing Atal Bihari Vajpayee. At a meeting of the BJP legislative party, he issued a call for reconciliation, going out of the way to scotch speculation that he was planning to challenge the existing situation. 'Those who say Modi is bigger than the party don't know the history of the BJP and the Jan Sangh. A son cannot be bigger than his mother,' he declared his voice choking with emotion.

Narendra also displayed magnanimity. He asked for the pardon of the main rebel Keshubhai Patel who had been slapped with a show-cause notice. In his half-hour-long speech at the Gandhinagar Town Hall, Narendra kept fighting back his tears. He said that if he looked tall, 'it is because I stand on the shoulders of lakhs of *vicharnishta karyakartas* (ideological workers) who are my true army.' He said that if they were invisible to others, it was because the media did not have cameras 'with good enough resolution to spot them'. He further said that his victory was about responsibility, not power.

He spoke about his proposal to the Centre to create a separate 'Intelligence Cadre' and a university for developing talent needed for the internal security of the country. Some Gujarati newspapers that were critical of him seemed to change their mindset overnight. They highlighted Modi's message when the vote-counting had begun; it said: 'I am a CM and will always remain CM, for the CM means Common Man!'

The Man of the Moment: Narendra Modi

Interestingly, Narendra's victory gave a jolt to Congress supporters, especially in the media. *The Tribune* noted that Sonia Gandhi's 'charisma did not seem to be working either in Punjab, Bihar, Jharkhand, Uttarakhand or Uttar Pradesh. 'The leader has also to translate his or her appeal into vote-gathering capability,' it said. Writing in *DNA* on 26 December 2007, Rajiv Desai said that Modi's success was a vote against the elitism of the Congress. He wrote that 'trouble is [that] socialism became an excuse for the license-permit raj; secularism mutated into pandering to a Muslim vote bank; non-alignment became an anti-American ideology and democracy became a family business. Gujaratis would have none of it; they first turned to Jayprakash Narayan; now they were willing to take their chances with Modi.'

Prem Shankar Jha, writing in the 28 December 2007 issue of the *Hindustan Times*, pointed out that while Modi's campaign 'was never devoid of communal tones, he did not win this election on its basis.' If Modi beat the anti-incumbency factor, he said, it was because 'the last five years have brought the fastest growth that Gujarat has ever experienced ... The sooner Congress apologists stop putting the blame for their defeat on Modi's communal platform and admit that it is high growth and an efficient, relatively corruption-free administration that has brought him back to power, the more the nation will gain from what otherwise would have been a regrettable victory,' Jha stressed. As Jha saw it, 'Modi's victory will reinforce the belief ... that the electorate has changed and now wants results.

A day after his stunning victory and hours after he was elected as chief minister designate by his party, Narendra Modi gave a free-wheeling interview to The *Times of India* which was published on 26 December 2007. He was at his best at answering provocative questions. Thus, when he was asked whether he had felt vulnerable at any point during the campaigning when the odds seemed to be stacked against him, he said, 'Not for a moment'. He said he missed the excitement of elections because of the weak condition of the Congress party. The adrenaline was just not flowing. The local team of the Congress was a complete disappointment to him. When confronted with the accusation that he had run a communal campaign, he struck back hard. 'Appoint a panel of three eminent and independent persons and

No Full Stop; Not Yet

let them read all my speeches,' Modi said, adding, 'I am ready to submit CDs of all my speeches to them. I declare I will concede defeat, if they find that I have made a single communal speech.' Talking against terrorism, he said, was not communalism. 'How can it be when no development is possible without guaranteeing safety.' He reminded his questioner that he had rarely, if ever, retaliated against the provocations that had been hurled against him incessantly. He said that the Congress had lost its chance much before the elections. It should have played an aggressive opponent from the beginning and occupied the entire opposition space. When asked whether he was angry with the media, he sounded conciliatory. 'Not with the media in general, certainly not,' he replied, adding, 'I also feel that the media can be a partner in the development process.'

Those who accused Narendra got their comeuppance in a sharp column written by Swapan Dasgupta in The *Times of India* dated 30 December 2007. Dasgupta laughed at the ability of the editorial class 'to shift track shamelessly'. Till election results were announced, said Dasgupta, Modi had been portrayed as the Indian equivalent of Satan. After they were out, Modi was being projected as a future prime ministerial candidate who would nevertheless fail because 'Gujarat isn't India!' Dasgupta defended Modi by saying that he didn't have 'connections' in the right places, he was a workaholic who slept only four hours and was crazy enough not to have taken even a day's holiday in six years. 'It is this aloofness and refusal to be co-opted by the beautiful people that make him a delicious target of those who think they are born to rule ... He has unsettled the Establishment because he is undaunted by hypocritical political correctness and persists in calling a spade a spade ... The Gujarat model is not in conflict with the Bharat model. What has clicked in Gujarat is a leadership style built on innovation, dedication and a resolute defiance of a compromised establishment,' he concluded.

It was The *Hindu* that described Modi's victory as a 'BJP Rising' on 27 December 2007. This was after the BJP had also won the elections in Himachal Pradesh and Punjab. The *Hindu* said: 'Three years ago the BJP was a demoralized loser ... Today with three successive Assembly election wins, the BJP has not just wiped off the ignominy of the 2004 defeats. It seems to have stolen a march over its rival with a maximum of 18 months left for the 15th general elections.' The paper said that for the Congress to regain its ground it needs 'far more than Ms Gandhi's helmswomanship. It needs a reformed party organization, a new unity of purpose and above all, a fighting spirit that distinguishes it from the BJP and a socio-economic programme that is responsive to mass deprivation and livelihood issues.'

Praise for Narendra came from an unexpected quarter in January 2008 – *Freedom First*, which was founded by Minoo Masani. An article in it by Amit Dholakia, a well-known scholar, gave him credit for 'standing up to the unsympathetic predictions of a cluster of psephologists and vilification by much of the national media ... Modi won in the fairest of all Indian elections so far and in the face of the most unfavourable circumstances ... not only did Modi's juggernaut finally crush all adversities, but actually increased the BJP's lead over the Congress party ....'

Dholakia made the point that for the most part, the elections in Gujarat had not been ideological. 'Only the gullible observers and the ideologues blinded by prejudices would like to see Gujarat's electoral contest exclusively as one between secularism and communalism or between fascism and democracy. Is it not now high time our political punditry re-orients itself to perceive India's variegated and complex political forces in their unique and special context rather than labouring hard to impose cherished formulae and western frameworks to explain away their workings?' Dholakia asked.

What contributed to Modi's success? Dholakia had the answer ready. He said:

'Modi set the agenda ... He came to symbolize many elements that Gujarat's voters could identify with – bold and decisive leadership unaffected by the barrage of criticism from many sides, balance between regionalism and nationalism, can-do masculinity, capacity to challenge the Centre's fiats, high personal integrity and credibility ... His charisma has even compelled the BJP to orient itself ideologically and organizationally ...'

But the strongest support came from another unbelievable source – The *Times of India*, with a column by Swaminathan Anklesaria

No Full Stop; Not Yet

Aiyar in the issue dated 6 January 2008. Aiyar came down heavily on the Congress. He referred to the killing of innocent Sikhs in Delhi in 1884 following the assassination of Indira Gandhi. He then added:

'According to data tabled in Parliament, the 2002 toll in Gujarat was 790 dead Muslims, 254 dead Hindus and 223 people missing. Far more were killed in Delhi in 1984. Many critics call Modi a fascist who carried out pogroms. They do not apply the same label to the Congress. Yet, the 1984 data are more suggestive of a pogrom than the 2002 data. The Hindu causalities in 2002 were a quarter of the total, suggesting two-way violence (even though Muslims suffered far more). But no Hindus died in Delhi, so it looks much more like a pogrom ... In 1984, there was no police firing at all on Hindu mobs ... On virtually every parametre you can measure, 1984 was worse than 2002. No, Gujaratis are not a bunch of communal fascists. They are no different from the Delhiwallah who killed far more people in 1984 ....'

This was definitely not an analysis that our secularists would have liked to hear. In the end, one might as well ask – why was Narendra Modi popular when the English-language media and the television channels were constantly targetting him?

There were some definite answers. One was the astounding work he had done for the economic and social benefit of the people, and not just for the industrialists and investors. As such, Gujarat has always been a progressive state but what made Narendra different from the others? In the past, some leaders had power and some had passion. But Narendra had both. Where he had will power on the one hand, he had the ability to carry out what he planned on the other. He was a visionary with an eye for details. His biggest strength was his capacity to reach out and connect with the hearts of the people. He was able to develop an emotional cord with the common man. His fan following ranged from the urban intelligentsia to the rural masses, among the old and the young, men and women, within Gujarat and outside and even beyond the boundaries of the nation.

Narendra's method of governance was based upon performance and not appeasement. Looking back, one could not help but be truly amazed at the sheer industry of the man. No single chief minister had been known to put in the kind of hard work that Modi had put in over the months and years.

An RBI report brought out soon after the election said that under Narendra Modi, Gujarat had become the favourite destination for investments in the country in 2007. It ranked first on the list, with proposed investments of ₹73,170 crore in eighty projects, accounting for 25.8 per cent of the total. The State's Planned Expenditure had grown at an annual rate of 32.25 per cent between 2002 and 2007 and its non-planned expenditure had dropped by 8.98 per cent.

The annual growth in revenue expenditure over the said period was 4.75 per cent while revenue receipts had grown by 3.66 per cent. This clearly showed that the state had not indulged in financial profligacy. Modi had cut energy subsidies from ₹3,536 crore in 2001-02 to ₹1,747 crore in 2006-07. The state had moved from a revenue deficit of ₹4,037 in 2004-05 to a revenue surplus of ₹1,803 crore in 2006-07.

There were other surprises. Modi's government saw an increase in the level of average employment and reduction in migration from rural areas by thirty-three per cent. Even more importantly, an innovative experiment of evening courts disposed of over fifty thousand cases between 14 November 2006 and 31 March 2007. Data provided by the state government suggested that the Kanya Kelavani Yojana, which focussed on literacy of the girl child, had seen a net enrolment ratio of the state go up to ninety-seven per cent and the drop-out rate, a fall from thirty per cent to three per cent in five years! And almost a lakh of rural-poor expecting mothers had deliveries done by private gynaecologists, all paid for by the state. The state was riot-free, curfew-free and terror-free. More than 1,40,000 check-dams and village ponds across the state had solved the drinking water and irrigation problems in the state that was perennially drought-prone. Value of farm-output grew by four hundred per cent.

But hardly any newspaper or TV channel gave publicity to these facts. Even the GEB turned the corner and reported a profit of ₹219 crore in 2006-07. '*Jeetega* Gujarat' (Gujarat will win) had been Modi's battle cry. It registered in the minds of the people.

No Full Stop; Not Yet

The *Indian Express* published an abridged version of a discussion with Narendra Modi on 26 October 2008 which showed clearly who had won the battle. The questions were sharp but the replies were sharper.

Q: How far do you hold yourself responsible for killing the spirit of secularism in the country after the 2002 riots?

A: This is not a question but an accusation. And the accusation is absolutely baseless. We have a vibrant media, an active judiciary and global human rights working in the country. If there was even the slightest truth, the government in Delhi is such that it will prevent me from returning to Ahmedabad from Delhi right now, if it finds a pretext. So, if you have any evidence that Modi has done something wrong, please bring it forward. Secularism in India was not invented by the Constitution. It is our age-old tradition.

He was asked why a Muslim should vote for him. Narendra hit back. He said, 'It is this country's curse that everything is weighed in votes. The only yardstick should be welfare of the poor. I'll give you the example – I have been successful in ensuring 100 per cent enrolment in schools – of both boys and girls. And when I say 100 per cent, I mean 100 per cent. I don't see people as Hindu or Muslim as you do.'

The dialogue went on in the same aggressive way.

Q: Ashis Nandy had charged the Gujarat government with harassment over an article he wrote.

A: One citizen filed a writ against Nandy for insulting the Gujarat people. How does my government prevent a citizen from filing a writ in court? If my police had gone after Nandy, you could blame me. Nandy went to the media and claimed that the Gujarat Government was hounding him. I remained silent because it's not in my nature to get into such quarrels.

Q: Sonia Gandhi has apologized to the Sikh community for the 1984 riots. Have you ever considered apologizing to the Muslim community for your failure as a Chief Minister during the 2002 riots?

A: I have said this repeatedly: I seek punishment, not forgiveness. If I have done something wrong, punish me.

The Man of the Moment: Narendra Modi

Q: The NHRC has indicted your Government for the 2002 violence. What is your opinion of the NHRC as an institution?

A: Institutions need to be honoured and strengthened and clashes between them and the government should be prevented. But there is no adverse remark against me so far. All the NHRC's directive has been complied with. This is just political sloganeering. I have always said, let the inquiry commission come out with its report and let the Supreme Court decide.

Q: After the 2002 riots, there has been considerable insecurity among the Muslims of Gujarat; how will you allay this sense of insecurity?

A: I am sending every child to school; I'm providing health care to every citizen. I'm giving everyone a share of the fruits of development. The Sachar Committee report, you'll be surprised to learn, says that Muslims in Gujarat are better educated than Hindus. I always address my people as my five-and-a-half crore Gujarat brothers – the entire population of the state.

Q: Do you admit that your government failed to contain the situation in 2002?

A: A commission is looking into the charges of who failed and on which fronts. The media trial is over, the sloganeering is over. I always said that the commission of inquiry will bring out the truth.

Q: Many people have questioned the Nanavati Commission's report because it was set up by the Gujarat government, which is itself accused of wrong doing in 2002.

A: The Constitution gives every state government the right to appoint a judicial commission of inquiry and to decide who'll head that commission. My government did not appoint the members of the commission. I wrote to the Supreme Court and the High Court for a sitting judge to head a commission of inquiry into the 2002 riots. My request was turned down citing the workload of sitting judges. I then wrote asking for a retired judge to head the commission. I have the letter from the Chief Justice of India suggesting Nanavati's name – the same Nanavati whose report on the anti-Sikh violence in 1984 has been applauded by the Congress.

No Full Stop; Not Yet

The answers to two questions must truly have foxed the interviewers. One of them asked whether Narendra Modi is 'a disciplined democrat or a lenient dictator'. He replied with a straight face, 'The fact that you are able to ask me this question and that I am answering it in your office should be proof enough of my being a democrat.' The other question was just as badly dismissed. 'Did Sonia Gandhi's description of you as "a merchant of death" have an impact on the Gujarat elections?' Modi answered, 'I don't think there's a leader of such stature in the country whose one statement can alter election's fortunes.'

How did Narendra Modi bag the Nano deal immediately after Ratan Tata announced that he was withdrawing his project from West Bengal? To start with, Ratan Tata was an open admirer of Narendra Modi and the entrepreneurship of Gujaratis. Ratan, as a Gujarati-speaking Parsi, was comfortable with Gujarat's leaders and the people at large, and had no difficulty in understanding their ethos and thinking. Indeed, in 2007, he had stated at the annual Vibrant Gujarat Summit that one would be 'stupid' if one was not (an investor) in Gujarat. At that time, Narendra had reportedly told him in half-jest that Nano would be welcome in Gujarat if the Tatas faced any problems in Singur. Perhaps at that time, Narendra did feel that heavy industry and communist West Bengal would not go together. The only Tata investment in Gujarat then was Tata Chemicals. It would have been a glorious feather in his cap if the Tatas transferred the Nano project to his state. It wasn't that other states were indifferent to Nano. There were contenders like Andhra Pradesh, Karnataka, Maharashtra, Uttaranchal and Tamil Nadu, all anxious to bag the deal. But it was Gujarat that got it. The story, as was revealed by Narendra himself, is that when Ratan Tata finally announced that he was quitting West Bengal, he sent Tata a text message saying just one word: '*Swagatam*'! (Welcome). It must have amused Ratan Tata. Narendra had studiously stayed away from putting pressure on the Tatas when Singur was exploding with anger. He knew that pressurizing Ratan was a foolish thing to do, considering the latter's love for Gujarat. He waited for the right time. When the right time came, his message, wrapped up in one word, said it all.

Ratan Tata happily took up the offer. What clinched the deal was the seriousness with which the Gujarat government moved. The

Managing Director of Tata Motors, Ravi Kant, said that it took the state just ten days to tie up all the loose ends to make the land at Sanand, not far from Ahmedabad city itself, ready for possession, with all papers cleared. The evening before the signing of the deal, Tata gave the go-ahead. What was even more fascinating was the fact that even before Ratan Tata arrived in Ahmedabad, the state government had approved the terms of the deal and everything was in its proper place. What is interesting to note is – though it may have been a mere coincidence – that Ratan chose to sign the MoU on the seventh anniversary of Modi's assumption of office. On 9 October 2008, The *Free Press Journal* noted that 'Evidently, Ratan wanted to pay tribute to the spirit of Gujarat under Modi.'

The 1,100 acre land at Sanand was sold to the Tatas at a nominal price of a thousand rupees per square metre on a staggered payment basis. The payment of VAT was reportedly deferred over five to seven years and according to media reports, the Gujarat Industrial Development Corporation committed to developing infrastructure worth a hundred crore rupees including roads, power, drainage and water. What was truly amazing – and this speaks for Narendra's push and daring – was the swiftness with which everything was coordinated and completed. As the *Free Press Journal* mentioned in the issue dated 9 October 2008: 'Gujarat and Modi have proved that they are second to none in terms of management of the economy ....' For a man of Modi's calibre, no challenge was daunting. One advantage of situation that the Nano project has in Gujarat is that fifty per cent of the ancillaries that would support the Nano project were in any case to be manufactured in the Kutch region and would now be easily transported. The National Highway is in close proximity and Modi must have thought about all those details as well. An airport has been planned close to Sanand which is just twenty-five kilometres from Ahmedabad on the way to Jamnagar. And importantly, Gujarat's well-developed ports would prove to be a boon for shipping consignments of the small car to Africa, Europe and the United States. Tata expects to produce 2.5 lakh units per year and the amount of money saved in transportation because of the suitable geographic location will now surely be a bonus.

The 16 November 2008 edition of *Business Today* showered high praise on Narendra whom Ratan Tata called 'The Good M' after

No Full Stop; Not Yet

finalizing the Nano deal. Tata had reason to be an admirer of Narendra. A recent study by the RBI showed that Gujarat state had received investment proposals of ₹62,442 crore, 22 per cent of the total investment in the country up to March 2008.

When Narendra Modi took over the government in 2001, Gujarat had a revenue deficit of ₹6,700 crore. Today it has a revenue surplus of ₹2,500 crore. There was a time when he was severely criticized by Thermax chairperson Anu Aga for the way he handled the post-Godhra riots. Now the same company is investing ₹450 crore in its new venture at Vadodara. That speaks clearly about the ways of working of the government.

Meanwhile, something quite inexplicable happened. Narendra Modi wrote an open letter in the *Ananda Bazar Patrika* – a departure from conventional political niceties – to his counterpart in Kolkata, Mamata Banerjee. He penned his innermost thoughts on why Gujarat had succeeded where West Bengal had faltered, thereby risking being accused of gratuitous triumphalism and gloating over the discomfort of fellow Indians. Surprisingly, his diagnosis was greeted with a measure of reflection by Bengalis on all sides of the political divide. Commenting on that, Swapan Dasgupta, writing in the magazine *Eternal India*, in November 2008 said that 'there are many who attribute Gujarat's resurgence to the personality of Modi. His frenzied pace of work, his attention to detail, his impatience with power brokers, his fanatical sense of personal integrity and his intellectual openness have built him a large fan club. Barring the unforeseen, he is on course to be a future prime minister of India. No wonder that those who denied him visa and continue to boycott him diplomatically are looking for ways to extricate themselves from a corner they have painted themselves into.'

Incidentally, Narendra Modi's government had talked about 'Nano' on 19 April 2008 by making an announcement that the 'Gujarat Government is building a Nano City and the Gujarat International Financial Tax City (GIFT) at Gandhinagar.'

The proposed GIFT would be built by the company that created Shanghai in China. The necessary formalities have been completed.

The hundred-storeyed Nano City will have ultra-modern facilities from human resource development to process houses.

SECTION II

FROM GOVERNMENT TO GOVERNANCE

Open letter to Narendra Modi from Prof. B M Hegde

One of the best letters of congratulations, an open one despatched to Narendra Modi following his election victory in 2012 was from someone he had once met briefly. The man was Prof. B M Hegde, Vice Chancellor of Manipal University and a cardiac surgeon.

> *Congratulations! You have succeeded in achieving the impossible. May God be with you in your future endeavours. You are a great statesman, not just because you won the recent elections against Himalayan odds, defeating the nefarious Herculean designs of your detractors in your own party and, of course, your venomous opponents, aided and abetted by the crafty media. You are a statesman because you showed rare courage in forgiving your arch opponents. As a victor, you have been more than kind to the vanquished. Your visit to Keshubhai Patel's residence immediately after winning shows you as a great humanitarian. You have shown the way for a new political humanism in India. Let the world know that forgiving one's tormentors needs greater courage than being a suicide bomber. The latter does not have to face the consequences of his/her action while the former has to face the music later.*

Prof. Hegde pointed out that Modi's opponents had tried to paint him as a cruel dictator who despised a particular community. Happily, no one had been able to point a finger at Modi as a corrupt politician. Hegde said that respect for Modi had gone up in the common man's mind. Continuing, he said:

> *Let me add that you have been a unique administrator in that you are the only one in the country to think of the genuine health needs of the population; you started to fortify the wheat and rice provided to*

> *pregnant women ... Modern science has shown that if the pregnant mother is malnourished, the foetus in the womb does not develop its organs fully....*

Explaining the requirements of pregnant woman, Prof. Hegde made a series of suggestions for developing an adequate health agenda by the Gujarat Government. He also congratulated Modi for the economic empowerment of village women by supporting small-scale industries.

And, on a personal note, Prof. Hegde added:

> *I had the good fortune of meeting you once in the past for a prolonged period of nine hours at a stretch. You were returning after your London trip some years ago and I happened to be on the same plane. I was kindly upgraded by the commander of the plane and so, happened to sit in the first class along with you. We were the only two passengers there. It was my pleasant surprise when, after about an hour into the flight, you walked over to me and sat by my side, a gesture that shocked me. I had expected Chief Ministers to be demigods or, at least, that is how many of our state CMs behave. You struck up a pleasant conversation and I could realize that you had the good of the people at heart. Your behaviour towards the various in-flight crew members gave me an indication that you are a good man. I always judge people by the way they behave with their subordinates as the yardstick of goodness.*

Pointing out that, in fact, Gujarat is the only state where nutrition of the children is almost as good as in many developed Western countries, Prof. Hegde concluded by saying, that 'the oppressed, suppressed and the denied section of the population ... needs your sympathy.' Noting that Modi was providing it, Prof. Hegde added: 'For all this, God will certainly bless you. May Gujarat, may India, be a better place to live in with leaders like you emerging everywhere ... Once again, let me congratulate you on your success.'

Focus on Governance

No one can deny that during Narendra Modi's years of chief ministership, Gujarat has not succumbed to whatever natural or man-made disasters that have hit the state and its people. In spite of enormous set-backs, there has been commendable multi-pronged development.

Earthquake and Rehabilitation

Gujarat nurses some unforgettable wounds. On the tenth anniversary of the 2001 earthquake, *One India News* (26 January 2011) reported:

Gujarat is on a high with development and infrastructure on in full swing. But Gujarat also nurses a secret sadness today as the whole of India celebrates Republic Day. It marks the tenth anniversary of the 2001 earthquake that killed around 30,000 people.

Bhuj has however witnessed rapid development in these ten years. New buildings, shopping malls, apartments have been constructed in the city. Hospitals and schools have been developed and new roads constructed in the region. Expressing their appreciation of the development activities, the locals here (in Bhuj) said that they were planning to migrate when the mishap occurred as most of them lost their relatives in the natural calamity.

One India News quoted a local, Tarun Mehta, as saying that when the earthquake took place, everybody thought that nothing would be reconstructed and that it would be wise to migrate. But seeing the rapid development taking place, Mehta felt that if he migrated, the loss would be his. Additionally, the newspaper stated:

The Gujarat Government introduced various schemes and compensation programmes for the victims and their families. Those who had lost their houses in the city and whose apartments were also destroyed were provided with three sites in Bhuj by the government. They were given plots in three locations of 100 sq metres each; also ₹1.5 lakh as per the area so that they could build their own houses ....

Emily Buchanan and Bhaskar Solanki of the BBC had this to report on 30 January 2011:

Ten years on from the huge earthquake that razed swathes of India's western state of Gujarat, BBC finds the place transformed from a pile of rubble in a neglected backwater into an economic power house. How?

Kutch is a remote region in the arid borderlands of North West India. For centuries life was brutally tough – rains often failed, there were few jobs and the enterprising would migrate.

Then, in January 2001 a magnitude 7 earthquake stuck, devastating a huge area, flattening cities including the district capital Bhuj, and wrecking over 8,000 villages. Twenty thousand people were killed and more than a million others made homeless.

> *Those who witnessed the devastation at the time must have thought this would set back the development by decades ... Contrary to what many feared, aid and government grants were put to use. In the first two years after the quake, nearly all the damaged villages were rebuilt. Mithapashvira, near Bhuj, is a small village that was completely destroyed. It was rebuilt with donations from the UK. Families showed us the ruins of their old, dark, two-room houses and then took us to the new village. Houses there were light and airy, with four rooms, running water and a toilet. The village also had a medical centre, a temple and communal areas it hadn't enjoyed before.*

Navin Prasad of Sewa International, a non-governmental organization said:

We have taken people out of the Middle Ages and into the modern world ... Since the earthquake, over 1,10,000 new jobs have been created in Kutch and there are thought to be hundreds of thousands more on the way ... The region is now a cornerstone of the Indian economy – a fact almost unthinkable ten years ago.

Three years earlier, Uday Mahurkar, writing in *India Today* (4 April 2008) had mentioned in a similar vein:

As one crosses the Surajbari bridge, a gateway to Kutch from Gujarat, the skyline comes as a surprise to anyone who is familiar with the area. Instead of a sparsely populated arid landscape, it now boasts of a series of modern factories churning out the best known brands in the country.

This was once the world's largest marshy desert cut off from the rest of the country. But the killer quake of January 2001 that turned parts of Kutch into ruins changed all that. Help poured in from all parts of the world and the five-year excise and sales exemption lured the best industries to Kutch.

The resilience of the locals and the private-public partnership model of development and rehabilitation helped in rapid resurrection of the area. The new Kutch is to be seen to be believed, with a massive economic boom and changed lifestyle of the people of the district.

The change is most visible in Adani Port at Mundhra, a private sector enterprise. Besides the port, the Adani group is setting up a multi-sector SEZ – a 4,000 MW power plant investing around ₹25,000 crore while the Tatas are also setting up a 4,000 MW power plant.

The Adanis have already set up a private airstrip here. In four years, Kutch district will be the largest manufacturer of cement in the country. In power generation, it will occupy the Number One spot generating 7,000 MW. "Kutch has emerged as the biggest manufacturers of saw pipes in Asia, thanks to a series of manufacturing units that have come up in the past five years," says Rasik Mamtora of the Federation of Kutch Industries Association.

Perhaps these reports do not tell the full story of industrial and economic development, but they are reflective of the general situation in Kutch, made possible by a concerned chief minister.

Strides in Agriculture

Gujarat has done phenomenally well in the field of agriculture too. That point was well made by Swaminathan S Anklesaria Aiyar in the *Economic Times* (22 July 2009).

Aiyar made the point that when Narendra Modi won the 2007 election, the media focussed on Hindu-Muslim issues. Some journalists highlighted the rapid industrial development that had made Gujarat India's fastest growing state but Aiyar admitted that he had drawn attention only to Gujarat's successful port-led development. Actually according to an International Food Policy Research Institute (IFPRI) paper, titled 'Agricultural Performance in Gujarat since 2000', written jointly by Ashok Gulati, Tushaar Shah and Ganga Sreedhar, Gujarat's agricultural performance was by far the best in India.

Between 2001 and 2007-2008, agricultural value grew at a phenomenal 9.6 per cent per year (despite a major drought in 2002). That was more than double of India's agricultural growth rate and much faster than Punjab's farm growth rate in the heyday of the Green Revolution. When Modi took over the chief ministership in 2001, the total production of cotton was 23 lakh bales. In 2012, the number had reached 1.23 crore!

During his chief ministership, Modi also tackled animal husbandry. It is believed that the government eradicated 112 common cattle diseases. Gujarat was the only state in the world where cattle cataract operations were conducted and dental check-ups were done. And jokingly, but accurately, Modi added, 'Due to this, I guarantee that if you have tea in Singapore, it will contain milk from Gujarat!'

He further added:

'We were not known for our agricultural sector. But now I guarantee that if you visit Europe, you will find *bhindi* (lady's fingers) which are grown in Bardoli and you will also find in Afghanistan tomatoes that have come from Gujarat ....'

Since the bulk of Gujarat's population is still rural, this mega boom in agriculture must have created millions of satisfied voters. Hence, it must have played a major role in Modi's 2007 victory. What is interesting is that – and as Aiyar observed: 'Not a single media analyst mentioned it.'

Aiyar noted that Gujarat is drought prone, with 70 per cent of its area classified as semi-arid and arid. Although journalists focussed on the Sardar Sarovar Project, its canal network was hopelessly incomplete and around 2007, it irrigated only 0.1 million hectares. No less than 82 per cent of irrigation in the state came from tube wells that depleted the ground water. By the mid-1990s, ground water extraction exceeded natural recharge in 31 *talukas* and 90 per cent of the safe extraction yielded in another 12 *talukas*. The situation was grim.

And then came Narendra Modi. According to the IFPRI study, 10,700 check dams were built by the year 2000; they helped to irrigate 32,000 drought-prone hectares. Under Modi, the number of dams rose ten times. Better water availability helped raise livestock population and consequently milk production.

Drip irrigation was promoted, subsidies and loans were offered to farmers, and procedures were simplified. According to Aiyar, as many as one lakh acres were under drip irrigation. This is how Aiyar saw the situation:

Gujarat has one of the best rural road networks in India, with 98.7 per cent villages being covered by pucca roads. Modi's Jyotigram Scheme for power has provided regular, high-quality electricity to villages, greatly helping farming. The Jyotigram Scheme provides separate electric feeders for domestic use and pump sets. This allows the state to supply round-the-clock domestic supply, while limiting agricultural supply which is continuous and of constant voltage, to eight hours a day.

This has facilitated a switch to high-value crops like mangoes, bananas and wheat that need assured water. Constant voltage has protected farmers from damage to pump-sets – a problem that was earlier caused by fluctuating voltage. The irrigated area has expanded at the rate of 4.4 per cent. The fastest growth in crops has been in wheat, followed by cotton and fruits and vegetables.

Aiyar noted that private seed companies had brought in new technology for several crops, ranging from *bajra* to castor, but above all to Bt cotton. Thirty seed companies were producing 20 varieties of Bt cotton. Vimal Dairy and Vadilal Industries had entered the dairy sector and palm oil, respectively. He also noted that food retail chains like Food Bazaar, Reliance Fresh and Spencer had sprung up in Gujarat cities, and were sourcing produce from farmers directly. Agrocel had taken on organic farming. Atreyas Agro and Godrej Agrovel had planned contract cultivation of *jatropha* (purging nut) and palm oil, respectively.

Aiyar summed up his views as follows:

Modi's electoral success points to a new way of winning rural votes. Others should sit up and take notice, and ask: How did Gujarat become a farming paradise?

One answer was provided by a report (www.netafimindia.com/howdid-gujarat.htm) that is reproduced here in full.

The onset of summer in the Saurashtra region in Gujarat can be a frightening prospect. The rocky terrain of low hills and the semi-arid plains begin to radiate immense heat. Rivers and wells dry up in tandem. Water shortage looms large and the memory of the severe drought of 1999-2000 returns to haunt. God bless the man who tries to indulge in cultivation of crops in these parts.

But that's exactly what hundreds of farmers do several times a year in the heart of this unfriendly terrain. Wheat, cotton, bananas, papayas, sugarcane, tomatoes and a variety of other crops sprout all over, erasing forever the cliché of Saurashtra being a parched expanse.

Today, one can spot crops that were not grown in these parts just four or five years ago. In Adtala village, farmer Vallabhbhai Patel, who was previously cultivating cotton, grows papaya. With a limited supply of water, he was able to get plentiful of yield. In Sarangpur, also in Saurashtra, Swami Arunibhagat is surely a blessed man. A leader of the liberal religious group, Swaminarayan Movement, he has converted 175 acres of dry land into a lush haven for sugarcane, tomatoes and genetically modified cotton. He has achieved record yields that have attracted farmers from more fertile lands to come and learn how he did it. It almost looks like a miracle wrought by Lord *Hanuman* of the famous temple in Sarangpur. The Swamiji is not alone. The entire region of Saurashtra, along with neighbouring Kutch, a half-desert, half-salty marsh region, has become the engine of a farming revolution in Gujarat, propelling the state into one of the fastest growing agricultural economies in the country. Gujarat's agriculture has grown by 9.6 per cent per annum in the last decade or so, surpassing the national growth rate of 2.9 per cent, thus boosting rural incomes.

The report gave credit to the government for amending the laws governing the marketing of agricultural produce. Contract farming was permitted. The state allowed companies to buy crops from farmers a year in advance. This helped the farmer to hedge against price upheavals and be guaranteed a similar price.

Farm Water Management

Commenting on farm water management, the report opined that the change in Gujarat had come about due to the conservation of the most crucial resource for farming – water. The state had adopted a combination of rainwater harvesting – trapping water that would otherwise drain away – and micro irrigation that supplied each drop of water more efficiently and directly to the plant.

Added the report:

Between 2001 and 2006, Chief Minister Narendra Modi ordered the building of check-dams wherever possible. His slogan was that rainwater in the fields should remain there and the water in rivulets should remain there too. There was little sense in letting all this water drain into the sea. The strategy worked. And farmers began to see a rise in water tables year after year. Modi also streamlined the supply of electricity to water pumps .... During his second year in power, Modi ordered the uninterrupted supply of quality power to farms for at least four hours a day but only at night. That ensured that farmers could use the pumps only for a limited time and had to make the most of it during the day.

Micro irrigation is spreading fast across Gujarat ....

Actually, water harvesting had become a social movement as early as 1988 when the farmers of Dhoraji, a small township of Saurashtra, started filling up their wells with flood water passing near their farms. A three-year drought had showed them the way to collect rainwater and, to their surprise, they found that floodwater filled in the wells, raised the water level and farmers could reap the *kharif* crop. This simple and handy solution attracted the attention of the Saurashtra Lok Manch Trust, an NGO working on water harvesting. The NGO studied the system and prepared literature to educate the farmers on well recharging. This was how the water conservation movement was originally launched in Gujarat. Besides encouraging the movement, the state government itself did a commendable job by constructing more than two lakh check-dams, *boribunds* (cement sacks placed strategically to prevent the water from flowing away) and farm ponds.

Krishi Mahotsav

The *Krishi Mahotsav* is the first-of-its-kind initiative that was started by the Gujarat government and has led to tremendous growth in the state's agricultural sector. It began in 2005 under the direction of Chief Minister Narendra Modi. The idea was to organize *krishi raths* (chariots that were equipped with audio-visual materials and other tools to educate the farmers about latest agricultural techniques) and take multi-disciplinary teams of scientists, horticulturists and agriculturists to the villages to train and educate farmers in scientific farming. The aim was to disseminate newer technologies in agriculture, animal husbandry, dairy and other allied fields. Fundamentally, the *Krishi Mahotsav* served as a catalyst in transforming agricultural and rural development through technology, innovation and implementation.

The *Mahotsav* had started with modest hopes. But by the time the seventh *Mahotsav* was inaugurated in 2011, the state had achieved phenomenal success. It had brought 13 lakh hectares of additional land under farming. The *Mahotsav* was to be seen to be believed. According to one estimate, almost one lakh government officials, employees and agricultural scientists were engaged in covering all the 18,000 villages in 225 *talukas* in the state. Something unheard of before! Chief Minister Modi was fully involved in the work himself. He set up a first-of-its-kind animal hostel at Akodara equipped with modern gadgets to handle all sorts of needs of farmers. Addressing a farmers' meet on 7 May 2011, Modi said that due to efficient water management, nearly 13 lakh hectares of barren land had been made fit for farming. With the completion of the Narmada Canal Project and the Sujalam Sufalam Project, he said he hoped to increase farmland by 20 lakh hectares. He further said that the government's top priority was availability of drinking water and water for innovative methods like sprinkler and drip irrigation that not only curtailed wastage of water but also reduced soil erosion. He pointed out that Gujarat was the only state in India that had given unique soil health cards to farmers to plan ahead as to which crops they should grow under which soil conditions. Modi further said that MOUs for projects worth ₹37,000 crore for agricultural value-addition had been signed during the Vibrant Gujarat Global Investors' Summit.

The eighth *Krishi Mahotsav* was held in June 2012 and lasted, as usual, for one complete month. Modi interacted with farmers across the state via video conferences and announced assistance worth ₹720 crore to around 15.17 lakh farmers. Modi lauded the efforts of government officials and agro-scientists who visited 225 *talukas* and 4,397 village clusters – something of a record. During the fest, around 3.5 lakh soil specimens were tested in labs and 2.75 lakh soil health cards were issued to farmers. On 17 May 2012, Modi inaugurated a mega *Krishi Mahotsav* of seven districts of south Gujarat at the tribal-dominated Nana Phonda village of Valsad district. No wonder tribals voted in large numbers for BJP during the December state elections! At the same time, he also inaugurated an impressive exhibition containing over sixty stalls, depicting new methods of farming and value-addition technology in agriculture.

Of course, there have been critics with their complaints. Thus, Arvind Nair, writing in The *Indian Express* (3 November 2012) made the point that the *Krishi Mahotsav* seems to have done little in influencing farmers to adopt new practices on their farms. He quotes a study conducted by researchers from the IWMT-Tata Programme at Anand, Gujarat Institute of Development Research (Ahmedabad) and Sardar Patel University, Vallabh Vidyanagar, as saying that while the *Krishi Mahotsav* was high on awareness, it was low on adoption. According to the study, the rate of adoption of new ideas and practices from the *Krishi Mahotsav* was between 2 to 11 per cent.

One of the researchers, Tushaar Shah was quoted in the study: 'We are not disappointed with the results. The awareness impact is the key and it takes time for implementation. The study found that almost 70 per cent of sample farmers were aware of the *Mahotsav* and 65 per cent thought it to be a "good" programme.'

B K Kikani, former Vice Chancellor of Junagadh Agricultural University, said, 'I feel that the *Krishi Mahotsav* has helped in cutting the cost of cultivation by 50 per cent and has pushed crop production upward by two to three fold in the Saurashtra region. There is a lot of awareness among farmers regarding agricultural practices. On account of this increased awareness, we are also seeing a rise in the number of students who want to join agricultural universities.'

It now transpires that in addition to agricultural produce, a certain segment of farmers have also gone into milk production. Milk production in Gujarat increased by 68 per cent between1992-2012 and the share of cooperative dairies increased from 46 litres to 100 litres per day during the same period. In value terms, the increase was from ₹2,400 crore to ₹12,250 crore.

According to Modi, the number of primary milk cooperative societies in this period increased from 10,000 to 16,000, memberships from 22 lakhs to 32 lakhs, and the number of milk societies run by women from 800 to 2,250. The government spent ₹185 crore to strengthen the dairy sector, giving equal importance to animal husbandry as well as tree plantation alongside traditional farming, in order to improve the overall economy. The government had set a target of doubling the income of 5 lakh small and marginal cattle owners in tribal regions only to end up exceeding the target by one lakh!

Rural Development

Modi's vision and leadership made it possible for Gujarat to not only attract industries and investment but also to improve the quality of life in rural areas. It may be argued that the root of Gujarat's approach towards rural development can be traced back to Modi's early years. As a *pracharak* and party worker, Modi had travelled through the length and breadth of the country. He had stayed with local workers, shared meals with them unpretentiously and learnt a great deal about rural problems first hand.

In the past, panchayat elections often used to be acrimonious and the bitterness created as a result of inter-personal rivalries created impediments in the development of the village. In order to prevent such hindrances, the Modi Government launched the Samaras Gram Yojana. Under this initiative, villages that selected a sarpanch by consensus received monetary benefits. This was a smart way of solving conflicts. Almost 3,700 villages in the state are now 'Samaras' villages and have received some ₹2,306.4 lakh from the government.

It is a known fact that houses in rural India often lack toilets, leading to uncomfortable situations for the residents who often have to defecate openly in the fields. This is especially embarrassing for women. Empathizing with them, the Modi government launched the 'Nirmal Gram Yojana'(Clean Villages Scheme). According to government records, in the decade 2002-2012, over four lakh toilets were set up in Gujarat and currently it is recorded that there are over 4,000 'Nirmal' villages in the state, as compared to only four a decade ago.

Understanding the importance of a clean and green environment for the well-rounded development of the state, the government launched schemes to promote cleanliness in the villages. Under the 'Swachch Gram Swastha Yojana (Clean and Healthy Villages Scheme), sanitation and hygiene were highlighted and monetary incentives were offered to villages that undertook cleanliness drives. Under the 'Panchvati Yojana', the advantage of tree plantation was explained to the people and fallow lands were identified for tree plantation drives. These schemes not only made the villages more scenic but also helped to improve rural health.

To address the housing problem in rural areas, especially among artisans and landless labourers, the government of Gujarat launched the 'Sardar Patel Awaas Yojana'. Under this scheme, the government provided free plots of land to BPL (Below Poverty Line) cardholders.

It is interesting to note that technology has been given its place in the administration of rural areas. Thus, the claim is made that under the 'E-GRAM Vishwa Gram Yojana', computers with broadband Internet connections have been installed in all gram panchayats across the state. These centres provide a number of services to the people such as issuing birth/death certificates, proof of income, caste certificates and residence proof.

The Gujarat government launched the 'Gram Swagat Programme' to provide aggrieved citizens in villages with the facility of lodging complaints at the E-Gram centres. If the government found that the claims were acceptable, these complaints were taken up by the *taluka mamlatdar* (government executive working at the sub-district level) and solved in a time-bound fashion.

In addition to these, schemes like the 'Garib Kalyan Mela' and *Krishi Mahotsav* have been instrumental in the overall development of rural areas. The Garib Kalyan Mela, a ground breaking programme of the Modi Government, made it easier for people to receive entitlements from the government. It is claimed that the government organized 1,000 Garib Kalyan Melas resulting in 85 lakh people receiving benefits worth ₹12,500 crore from the state government.

The 'E-Mamta', a mobile-phone-based technology innovation was conceptualized and first implemented by the Gujarat Government in May 2010 and claims have again been made that it has 'borne much fruit'. Under this scheme, rural health workers, trained by the National Rural Health Mission (NRHM) go from door to door, collecting information on pregnant women as well as infants. This information is then transmitted through mobile phones to the State Rural Health Mission (SRHM), the government body that collates the data into a centralized repository. The data is then used to alert rural health workers – through SMSs – to make sure that they reach out to pregnant women and mothers of infant children regarding immunization dates or medicines to be administered. The programme understandably improved maternal health and childcare in the state and reduced maternal deaths from 702 to 589 in one year and infant deaths from 7,263 to 4,732 in the same year.

Panchayati Raj

On 30 September 2012, Chief Minister Modi addressed a Panchayati Raj Convention, as part of a programme to celebrate fifty years of Panchayati Raj. To start with, he announced a nine-time increase in the special allowance of gram panchayat mantris (village panchayat ministers) from ₹100 to ₹900 per month, ₹100 per month as cash allowance for maintaining accounts, and a conveyance allowance applicable to government *talalti mantris* (ministers of sub-districts).

The valedictory address he delivered indicates the progress that the state has made. He cited the example that the working of the panchayat *mantris* had visibly improved the cleanliness of the villages. He described 6 lakh pairs of hands of the employees as the strength of the Gujarat government. He exhorted the Panchayat *mantris* to take up the cause of water management in each village the way the legendary Lakha Vanjhara had single-handedly built 100 *vavs* (step-wells) in the state. He said that creating new districts and *talukas*, introducing the concept of *Aapno Taluko – Vibrant Taluko* (Our district – Vibrant district) and doubling the number of *prants* (sub-districts) from 55 to 110 for decentralization of administration, had activated the neglected *anganwadis* (Centre-sponsored child care centres) and *sakhi mandals* (women's self-help groups) to generate a new wave of energy down to the village level.

He stressed the importance of technology and said that it was indispensable for contemporary human life. The government, he reminded his audience, had launched the Empower Project to make the *talati mantris* computer savvy. He cited different computer-based development programmes and schemes of the Gujarat Government such as broad-band connectivity, 'E-*Seva*' and accessing information through the Internet at village panchayats.

At an earlier meeting, Modi had announced a programme that he stated was 'close to his heart', namely, honouring all the elected representatives who had served in various panchayat bodies since the creation of Gujarat in 1960. As he put it: 'To honour these powerhouses of experience and wisdom after many years has been a matter of great joy to me. In the last fifty years, the number of elected representatives has crossed the one lakh mark and it is our privilege that we have got a chance to remember their invaluable contribution in the annals of history.'

Samras Grams

Mention has been made of Samras Grams earlier on but it is to the credit of the Modi Government that there are 250 Mahila Samras Grams where the keys to development are completely in the hands of women!

To enhance the spirit of *sadbhavana* (harmony) in the villages of Gujarat, the state government came up with the Tirth Gram Yojana in 2004-2005. A village that is free of any social disturbance for a period of five years is a Tirth Gram entitled to receive ₹2 lakh. By 2012, the state boasted of 1,075 Tirth Grams.

The success of these experiments encouraged the Government of Gujarat to set up a 'Pani Samiti' (Water Organizations) in every village, to be completely operated by the *Gram Sabhas*. It was a revelation to see that samitis of between ten to fifteen members projected women in the majority. Each samiti was handed over funds ranging from seven to eight lakh rupees to facilitate water and sanitation needs.

These are grass-root changes that Chief Minister Modi envisioned in which the state could authorize its panchayats to play the role of catalysts. From the time Modi became chief minister in 2001, right up to 2012, the government's budget for Panchayati Raj-related initiatives has been around ₹5490.57 crore which is mammoth and 615 per cent times the budget spent between 1991and 2001. Sometime in July 2012, the government even raised the limit for 14,000 *Gram* panchayats to undertake development work without tenders for amounts ranging from ₹2 lakh to ₹5 lakh. The result has been there for all to see. Between 2002 and 2012, the government has added housing for 12 lakh people, while, in the preceding forty years, houses were built for just 10 lakh people.

E-Gram Vishwa Gram Yojana

In order to ensure that villages of Gujarat do not remain isolated and cut off from the rest of the world, the government has launched the E-Gram Vishwa Gram Yojana. Gujarat is the only state where all panchayats are connected with broadband. This has helped in providing essential services at the doorstep for people in villages. By providing information and accessibility, it has helped people as an instrument of empowerment. Taking this further, in July 2012, the government launched 'eMPOWER' which seeks to impart basic IT skills to the people almost free of cost. eMPOWER will surely go a long way in bridging the digital divide among people, enabling the poorest of the poor to stand on their own feet through the use of technology.

Focus on Governance

It should be clear from all this that the success of the Panchayati Raj mode of governance across the state is due to the tireless efforts and dedication of thousands of unsung heroes who are working day and night to ensure that the villages of Gujarat become places of progress. What is noteworthy about this initiative is the fact that more than four-fifths of those felicitated by the government have been members of non-BJP parties. What this clearly shows is that it is the welfare of Gujarat and not petty politics that is the dominant mindset of the government.

WOMEN, TRIBAL WELFARE AND SKILL DEVELOPMENT 16

Women's Welfare Programme

The Modi government has been getting increasingly concerned with social issues. The disproportionate child sex ratio was alarming. Female infanticide and foeticide had brought the sex ratio in Gujarat from 994 per thousand in 1991 to a dismal 920 in 2001. It was a depressing 874 females per 1000 males in the age group 0-5. A multi-pronged strategy was called for to stem the rot.

So, the government launched a blitzkrieg in the media to eradicate the social evil. Private doctors were asked to file declarations, committing themselves never to perform sex-selective abortions. Health department officials were asked to implement the Pre-Natal Diagnostic Techniques (Regulation and Prevention of Misuse) Act 1994 effectively. All scan centres and hospitals, genetic counselling centres, genetic clinics and genetic laboratories were registered. Hospitals and nursing homes were especially asked to maintain records of the number of births and gender of new borns.

The Minister for Women and Child Welfare and Education, Anandibehn Mafatbhai Patel, was only too aware that official records had been silent on the prevalence of infanticide and foeticide. She told the media, 'But the government has evolved a foolproof deterrent mechanism to ban clandestine abortions.'

What had come as a shock to the Modi government was a survey in Godhra district that had revealed that in that district alone, about one lakh girls under 14 as also pre-natal women were suffering from acute malnutrition. Based on this finding, the government started supplying six kg of rice to their families and saw to it that a monthly weight chart was monitored, reviewed and assessed in December 2003.

Another detailed survey by the government in three districts, including Ahmedabad, had thrown up the statistic that nearly 70 per cent of adolescent girls were anaemic. They were provided with the required medication. The state had 80,000 self-help groups and ₹40 crore was deposited in banks as their savings.

In 2004-05, Gujarat reported only 54 per cent cases of institutionalized delivery. This naturally used to result in high infant mortality rate. Infants would die soon after being born, often risking the life of the mother too. Modi's efforts to help took the figure of institutionalized deliveries to as high as 90 per cent in 2011. His Chiranjeevi Scheme did the magic. Under that scheme, the government signed MoUs with gynaecologists. The entire expense of the delivery of Below Poverty Line (BPL) women was thus borne by the state government. Additionally, financial assistance of ₹1,000 was given to the pregnant mother for her stay in the hospital and to-and-fro trips.

Seven years later, the Modi government was all ready to look after women's needs in a big way. The occasion lent itself during a two-day celebration on International Women's Day. On 6 March 2010, Modi was invited to address a *Virat Mahila Sammelan* (Mega Women's Convention) that was attended by thousands of women from Vadodara, Dahod, Godhra, Bharuch, Narmada and Anand. It was there that Modi appealed to the younger generation of the state to contribute as many as 100 hours during the year-long celebration of *Swarnim* Gujarat (Golden Gujarat). Modi suggested that of those 100 hours, young people could play a positive role in any field in which they were interested.

Aiming to encourage women in sport activities, scholarships worth ₹3,20,800 were given to 109 sports-women of central Gujarat, while 126 women benefitted with ₹21,08,000 cash assistance under the 'Mata Yashoda Award Scheme'. At least 1,280 girls were given savings certificates worth ₹8 lakh under the 'Balika Samruddhi Yojana, while ₹3.5 lakh were given from the Mata Yashoda Award Gaurav Fund to seven women. Modi further dedicated five *anganwadi* mobile vans purchased at a cost of ₹12,35,636 for the *anganwadis* of Chota Udepur, Dahod, Narmada, Bharuch and Panchmahal. As many as 245 trained widows were given Widow Aid kits worth ₹12.25 lakh for self-employment. For the first time in the country, *anganwadi* workers were given cookers, gas connections and burners.

Modi once said: 'Woman is an incarnation of *Shakti* – the goddess of power. If she is bestowed with education, Gujarat's strength will double. Let the campaign of *Kanya Kelavani* (education of girls) be spread in every home. Let the lamp of educating daughters be lit up in every heart. Then only will the vision of *'Jay Jay Garvi Gujarat'* (victory for proud Gujarat) be realized.

Modi had schemes and plans to improve the lot of woman in every sphere. As was mentioned earlier in a different context, Modi had arranged to provide free services to ante-natal mothers on the ninth day of each month. This was called the 'Matru Vandana Scheme'. Under the scheme, as many as a thousand gynaecologists provided free services as *matru vandana* doctors.

Not forgotten were the sex workers in the state; the idea was to see that sex workers gave up prostitution and sought to live a life of dignity. A scheme was introduced by the Gujarat Women & Child Development Department through which sex workers would be given vocational training in tailoring, handicrafts, toy-making, embroidery, kite-making and even running beauty parlours.

But one of Modi's most telling concerns for the welfare of women came through in an address he delivered before the Kadva Patidar Samaj in Jamnagar district on 9 February 2012. A large audience listened to him with rapt attention. He spoke highly of the Patidar community saying, 'Those who want to see progress and development in India should study the success story of the Patidar community of Gujarat.' The Patidar community, he said, has not 'come forward because of somebody's obligation but has come up by its own efforts and very hard labour.' However, he also wished to share a bitter truth. He said: 'In the entire state of Gujarat, Unjha, the abode of Maa Umiya, is the source of inspiration for all of us. The Umiya Dam is the centre of our inspiration. But one thing pinches me. If anywhere in the whole of Gujarat, there are less girl children born than male children, it is in Unjha *taluqa*, the abode of Maa Umiya.'

He pointed out that it was not a natural phenomena that only sons have been born and not daughters. He averred: 'The fact is, we are on the path of sin. Let's take an oath at this holy place that from now onwards, we will not commit the sin of killing daughters in their mothers' wombs.'

Modi told his audience that pregnant mothers should get nutritious food because 'if the mother is healthy, the child in her womb will be born healthy too. There won't be any disability or mental retardation. If there is a natural atmosphere to fight against malnutrition in society and if the children are healthy, the future of Gujarat will also be healthy.'

Matri Shakti

Addressing a well attended state-level women's convention on 31 March 2012, Modi attributed Gujarat's all-round development to the participation and contribution of women in various fields. He said that Gujarat was blessed by the motherly figure, *Matri Shakti* (Mother Goddess) and this served as a talisman to ensure its continuous progress.

On the occasion, Modi presented the Mata Yashoda Awards worth ₹3.81 crore to 2,254 outstanding *anganwadi* workers, cash awards worth ₹61.04 lakh to 1,390 sportswomen who had excelled in various national and state-level events, and cash awards of ₹1.04 crore to 3,339 meritorious girl students from the government's fund for girls' education called *Kanya Kelavani Nidhi*.

Elaborating on motherly prowess, Modi said *anganwadi* workers, though hailing from economically poor families, performed a yeoman's job of nurturing future citizens and instilling higher moral values among children in their formative years. Furthermore, he said, the government had allocated ₹400 crore during the new financial year's budget to construct newly designed 12,000 *Nandan Ghars* across the state, each equipped with a cooking gas connection, instead of the earlier practice of using fuel-wood ovens.

Female Education

One of Modi's largest concerns is for female education. At every public meeting he attended, he would invariably get a gift that he promptly dispatched to the government treasury, to be sold in due course. That fetched an amount of ₹287.37 lakh over the course of five years and was added to the capital of the *Kanya Kelavani Nidhi*. Significantly, only a meagre amount of ₹4.55 lakh had been put into the fund in a span of 41 years under the tutelage of his 13 predecessors.

Modi's concern for female education came to be so much appreciated that as the years passed, organizations that normally gave him a gift as a token of respect started donating cheques in the name of *Kanya Kelavani Nidhi*. This financial support resulted in the dropout rate of the girl-child dwindling from 20.81 in 2000- 20001 to 3.68 in 2006-2007. The *Kanya Kelvani Nidhi* has understandably now become a movement in Gujarat.

Mission Mangalam

Modi often remarked that there was plenty of talent available in India, which had still not been exploited. What was needed was a programme for skill development. Only with that could India beat China. The Gujarat government began by setting up an organization called 'Mission Mangalam'. A campaign for women's self-help groups was initiated. This led to the establishment of nearly 2.5 lakh women's self-help groups in Gujarat within two and a half years. The government gave them some working capital to start with and arranged for loans from banks. Said Modi: 'These Sakhi Mandals work under the Mission Mangalam scheme and generate business worth nearly ₹1,600 crore.'

Modi said that some time during the first quarter of 2012, the Government of India had given an assurance that it would provide Gujarat 90 per cent usage of satellites. That, he said, never came about. Gujarat was the only state demanding 36 MHz capacity. The idea was to carry out activities like providing tele-medicine, long distance education and in particular long-distance education for the children living in the remote *Vanabandhu* (friends belonging to the forest) areas.

Healthcare

One thing can be accepted: with all the growth indicators pointing in the right direction, Gujarat is all set to grow multifold. It is known for a fact that both the private and the public sectors are striving side by side to drive the progress wheel. Where corporates like Zydus, Sterling, Shalby, Apollo, Narayan Hrudayalaya and many more are in the expansion stage, the Department of Health and Family Welfare have many projects in the pipeline for the benefit of the citizens.

During a public meeting, Chief Minister Modi said that Gujarat, with all its inclusive, sustainable growth, is rapidly emerging as a globally preferred place to live in and to do business.

If government statements are to be believed – and there is no reason why they shouldn't – the state's healthcare sector is witnessing an exponential growth: the number of hospitals and healthcare institutes is growing rapidly; emergency medical services have been facilitated with the help of 108 ambulance services; medical tourism shows substantial increase, successful public private partnership models are on the rise and better medical education is being provided.

Whatever the critics may say, this progress has been a result of the concerted and cooperative efforts made by the government and the private sector in the form of corporate hospital groups, research organizations, pharmacies, medical device manufacturing companies and other healthcare delivery systems that promote alternative medicines. Dr Ashutosh Raghuvanshi, Managing Director, Vice Chairman and Group Chief Executive Officer of Narayan Hrudayalaya Hospitals, has been quoted as saying that this success can be attributed to three important components that the state has focussed on: technology advancement, quality-oriented healthcare service and government initiative taken to increase accessibility.

It is interesting to note that Gujarat has 13 medical colleges, 1,072 Primary Healthcare Centres (PHCs), 7,274 sub-centres, 273 Community Health Centres (CHCs) and 85 mobile healthcare units. The share of primary care in the total healthcare market of Gujarat is around 80 per cent, secondary and tertiary care account for 17 per cent and 4 per cent, respectively. The doctor-to-patient ratio is 1:10 and nurse-to-patient ratio is 1:5. Shahid Parvez, Deputy General Manager, Health Care Services, Apollo Hospitals International, is quoted as saying, 'Gujarat has made 58 per cent increase in its health budget with more than 6 per cent of the total state budget being allocated to the health sector. In recent years, the health sector has become one of the biggest employment generators after tourism.'

Cities such as Ahmedabad, Baroda, Rajkot and Surat are leading the progress path for the healthcare sector in the state. It is claimed that Ahmedabad alone has more than 1,000 small and big diversified hospitals providing health treatment with the latest technologies and machines available in the market. According to the Healthcare Practice Division of Frost & Sullivan, South Asia and Middle East, the other major private players in Gujarat's healthcare sector are the Shalby Hospitals, SAI Hospital, Medisurge Hospital and the Krishna Heart Institute. Sterling Addlife India is the largest chain of corporate hospitals in the state. It owns and manages five centres across the state.

All this is not to say that the credit for the expansion of healthcare goes solely to Narendra Modi. Such an assertion would be incorrect. But, what makes the state a prime investment area is the availability of better infrastructural facilities. Over the years, the available medical infrastructure and easily accessible healthcare facilities have attracted attention. For instance, the 'Janani Shishu Suraksha Karyakram' (JSSK), (Programme for the Safety of Newborn Children) implemented in 2011, offers free and cashless maternity services as well as care for newborns in all government healthcare institutions. It includes diet, no out-of-pocket expenditure on drugs, disposable equipment, diagnostics, blood transfusion as well as referral transport and drop back facility.

The focus is on quality. The government has introduced Total Quality Management (TQM) in its key medical institutions. The system covers the state's medical college hospital, paraplegia hospital, district hospitals and community health centres. The aim and objective, as stated by the Health Department, is 'to enhance the patient's quality of life by providing specialized medical treatment and preventive healthcare.'

Among the other steps taken by the government are the medical emergency call centres where citizens of Gujarat would be able to call up 104 and get treatment/medicine for general health problems, and the 'Samay Daan Scheme' (donation of time), an interesting concept to encourage social responsibility amongst the youth towards the society.

The Gujarat government also claims that it has effectively controlled communicable diseases like HIV/AIDS, TB, leprosy and malaria with meticulous implementation of national health programmes like the Rural National Tuberculosis Control Programme (RNTCP), National Leprosy Eradication Programme (NLEP), National Vector-Borne Diseases Control Programme (NVBDCP), Gujarat State AIDS Control Society (GSACS), and National Blindness Control Programme (NBCP). The state's success in controlling sickle-cell anaemia was acknowledged when it received the prestigious Prime Minister's Excellence Award for administration in public health programmes.

It is interesting to note that a recent study conducted by the GVK-Emergency Management and Research Institute (GVK-EMRI) 108 service (telephone number for free emergency services) reveals that the majority of patients in the state preferred to avail cost-effective healthcare facilities offered at subsidized rates.

Tribal Development

The State of Gujarat comprises 43 *talukas* in 12 scheduled tribe-dominant districts with a population of around 75 lakh. The challenge for the government was to find ways and means to improve the quality of life of these people.

The Constitution of India itself had the welfare of tribals in mind and advocated a policy of positive discrimination and affirmative action. This led to the setting up of a Tribal Sub-Plan (TSP) Strategy since the fifth Five-Year Plan. Consequently, Gujarat earmarked 15.85 per cent of its 2008-09 budget for the development of tribal areas.

Earlier, in 2007-08, the government had made a financial provision of ₹2,350 crore with the major objective of doubling the income of the tribal districts. The aim was to improve the capabilities of tribal communities in accordance with their cultural values.

The majority of scheduled tribes were engaged in agricultural activities for their livelihood and the goal of the Chief Minister's Ten Point Programme known as the 'Vanbandhu Kalyan Yojana' (welfare scheme for forest dwellers), with a capital outlay of ₹15,000 crore, was to provide the people with opportunities in dairy, agriculture, horticulture, floriculture and food processing under the guidance of Agro Service Centres.

Equipped with qualified and efficient personnel, D-SAG (Development Support Agency of Gujarat) spearheaded many of the Vanbandhu Kalyan Yojana's core activities: modernization of agriculture, skill development and education.

A major problem facing the tribal belt was lack of reliable water supply throughout the year. Even though it received the highest amount of rainfall in a year, the terrain was not helpful in saving water, not even underground. Rivers got swollen during the monsoon time only to dry up during the summer.

The 2001 census showed that about 50 per cent of rural tribal households relied on hand pumps, while only 4 per cent had tap connections within their houses. The members of as many as 70 per cent of households had to walk a distance of around 500 metres to collect water.

The concept of providing piped water was more challenging because of the manner in which tribal settlements were structured. A cluster of houses could rarely be found. Most houses were 500 to 700 metres apart from each other. In order to tackle this situation, the government came up with an array of plans and implemented them successfully. Around 1,47,000 hand pumps were installed in the 12 tribal-dominated districts, with the highest number being in Dahod, followed by Valsad. The government saw to it that there was at least one pump for every 50 tribal citizens. At spots where the habitation had a low and scattered population, the government introduced a more advanced UNICEF-approved India Mark II level hand pump, which revolutionized water supply and storage in the tribal belt. With the capacity to discharge water up to 6 metres above the ground level, it has facilitated water storage in tanks. This hand pump has the ability to fill up an 800 litre tank in around one hour!

Earlier, hand pumps were plagued with the problem of sick bore wells. There were bore wells that went dry and hence had to be recharged. In order to resolve this issue, the government invested heavily in bore well-recharging techniques. By 2012, some 5,500 sick bore wells were recharged.

The approach towards the idea of providing sustainable water supply was built on downright pragmatism and innovation. The government involved its main stakeholders, that is, the tribal communities in the decision-making process. The celebrated Pani Samitis were formed as bodies of the gram panchayats to look after the planning and implementation of the village water supply system. Out of the 5,164 tribal villages, Pani Samitis were formed in 5,012.

How were these pumps to be operated? Electricity was not available. Arrangements were therefore made by the government to install 290 solar pumps, which, besides being environment friendly, were cost effective and reliable. As of 2012, over 17,000 villages are being taken care of by Pani Samitis. The enormity of the government action can be gauged with over 1.5 lakh check-dams, 2.5 lakh farm ponds and 1.25 lakh boribunds in operation in the state, including of course, in the tribal belt. At present, the state can boast of providing 'direct-to-home' water supply to over 41 per cent tribal families, as compared to 4 per cent a decade ago!

The government did something more than merely supply water to tribal homes. It invested ₹710 crore for building up to 32,000 sq km of roads and bridges in the tribal areas. To support easy travel, approximately 17,000 km-long roads were built, linking 99 per cent of all villages.

Education is a major foundation on which sustained development rests. The government set up 452 *ashram shalas* (schools) and 97 secondary *ashram shalas* in the tribal belt. The media has quoted an experienced tribal archery coach as saying: 'Had it not been for my *shala*, I couldn't possibly have become what I am now.' And how right he was! In all, the government has also started 28 technical institutes for higher education, and the successful Eklavya Model Residential School has been replicated at 55 different places. At present, the government spends ₹42,000 per student per annum.

The Man of the Moment: Narendra Modi

At the same time, an ambitious project was initiated to cater to the higher aspirations of tribal students. Under this project, five agriculture polytechnics, three engineering colleges and a physiotherapy college were set up in tribal districts.

With the desire to strengthen the body as much as the mind, the 'Doodh Sanjivani Yojana' (Life Reviving Milk Scheme) was implemented in 252 primary schools, belonging to seven tribal *talukas*. About 200 ml of fortified and flavoured double-toned pasteurised milk was distributed to students under this project, and brand new uniforms were provided to over 9,83,000 students at a cost of ₹20 crore. Each *taluka* in Gujarat has an Industrial Training Institute (ITI) and in 2012, the state saw the formation of 33 new ITIs. Besides this, the state has also proposed to start 30 new Kaushalya Vardhan Kendras (KVKs) (Skill Development Centres) in tribal *talukas* to impart skills based on WISH (Women-oriented, Industry-related, Soft skills and Hardcore traditional courses). More significantly, the government has come up with an interesting scheme, which provides interest assistance of six per cent on loans up to ₹50 lakh to MBBS doctors belonging to the scheduled tribes.

Health initiatives for tribals have been of various kinds. Health has invariably been a problem among tribals. First detected in 1994, leptospirosis, a disease that spreads from animals to humans and needs to be identified quickly, had risen considerably to become a big threat and cases had been detected during the monsoons in places like Surat, Valsad, Navsari and Vapi. Accredited social health activists were trained to identify early symptoms and local diagnostic centres were set up in the affected districts. An advanced testing laboratory was also set up in the Government Medical College in Surat to confirm diagnosis and the Health Department had over 2.5 lakh pamphlets distributed all over the state. TV and radio advertisements were aired to create awareness. All this helped. From 621 cases detected in 2007, the number went down to 89 in 2012, which was quite an achievement.

Another major initiative, the Sickle-cell Anaemia Project, was declared the winner of the Prime Minister's Civil Service Award in 2011. Sickle-cell anaemia, a hereditary disease, is predominantly found among India's tribal population. According to one of the hypotheses, it is a natural mutation in the haemoglobin molecule to protect red blood cells (RBCs) from malarial parasites. Consequently, the sickle-cell gene is mainly found amongst tribal groups who originated from malaria-endemic forest areas.

The programme was launched in the first week of August 2012 and within the first month itself, a total of 1,46,315 tribal people were screened. Post the screening, each individual was presented with a colour-coded card. A white card indicated absence of the sickle cell; a half yellow card suggested the possibility of the trait, but an entirely yellow card confirmed the presence of the disease. After distributing the cards, adolescents were advised to avoid marriages between two yellow card holders. In all, 2,11,211 sickle-cell trait gene carriers were provided counselling about their status.

Not to be forgotten are ambulance services provided to the tribal people. Thanks to these, the needs of an astounding 4 lakh pregnancy cases were satisfactorily met. And to think that just a year earlier, prior to the expansion of the service, a bare 36 cases would have been taken care of!

Tribals have also benefitted from other social welfare schemes in the state such as the National Old Age Pension Scheme, National Family Benefit Scheme, Personal Accident Insurance, Social Security Scheme and Gujarat Disability Pension Scheme. Additionally, the Gujarat Scheduled Castes and Scheduled Tribes Development Finance Corporation has been providing economic assistance to SC/ST families living below the poverty line by way of arranging institutional credit under the Margin Money Loan Programme (MMLP) for various income generating schemes.

Tribal Contribution

So little is known about the contribution made by tribals in the fight for Indian independence that Modi felt compelled to refer to it on 30 July 2012 on the occasion of the 63rd *Van Mahotsav* held in Mangadh, the birthplace of Shri Govind Guru, who Modi described as 'an unsung hero of India's freedom struggle'.

Shri Govind Guru was a social reformer who showed great courage to spread awareness of the country's need to fight

The Man of the Moment: Narendra Modi

for independence. The British were uncomfortable at this development. According to Modi, a conspiracy was hatched to kill Shri Govind Guru and people were hired for the job. When the *Adivasis* came to know of the conspiracy, they decided to protect their Guru.

Said Modi, addressing, a largely *Adivasi* audience:

'The British were equipped with cannons and barrels of guns; fierce fighting started and one after another, my *Adivasi* brothers sacrificed their lives to save Shri Govind Guru. Dead bodies could be seen everywhere. The number of people who died fighting were double the number of people who were massacred at Jallianwala Bagh by the Britishers. The sacrifice made by my *Adivasi* brothers has been forgotten.

People like Birsa Munda and more than 1,500 *Adivasi* youth led by Shri Govind Guru laid down their lives without any hesitation, only to make India free from the clutches of the British empire, but, unfortunately, no one remembers the sacrifice made by them.'

Modi also referred to the services rendered by Shyamji Krishna Verma, a son of Kutch, who actively participated in the freedom struggle against the British and died in 1930 in Switzerland. Modi had brought back the freedom fighter's ashes in 2003 and saw to it that a memorial was built in Mandavi, in Kutch, which is now visited by thousands of students. Said Modi: 'Martyrdom cannot be ignored and left to go waste.'

Modi expressed his happiness that *Adivasis* were benefitting from the development plans his government had introduced in tribal districts. Time was when tribals had no jobs and merely worked as labour. 'Today,' said Modi, 'I am proud to say that every *taluka* of Panchmahal district is home to many *Adivasi* road contractors.'

In the Dang district, there were no schemes for *Adivasi* welfare. But Modi's government took up milk production as a way out of poverty and provided cattle to *Adivasi* families. 'Now,' said Modi, '*Adivasis* of Dang district have become self-sufficient.'

There is something else that the Modi government has been working on: creating forests on lands that were once desert areas. The *Van Mahotsav* at Mangadh was being celebrated in a *van* (forest). The idea was to press home the necessity to grow forests wherever possible. Thus, a Magalia Van was created near Abaci Hill and a Thirtankhara Van was created on desert land where the 24th Jain *thirtankara* had attained enlightenment. A similar *van* was created at Somnath called Harihar Van, and another at Shamalaji to be known as Shamal Van.

Inculcation of Work Culture

Modi has always believed that technology alone can foster e-Governance and that good governance in turn can only happen through an efficient, pro-active and citizen-friendly system. That is why the government of Gujarat initiated a massive training programme to re-orient over 5,00,000 state government employees and to strengthen the administrative machinery. The *Karmayogi Maha Abbhiyan* (literally meaning a mega campaign for transforming employees into dedicated workers), an initiative unique to Gujarat is all about harnessing the strength of government employees and sensitizing them towards their accountability as public servants. Self-motivation, communication skills, empathetic response, proactive attitude, cost consciousness, team work – no government employee ever in the past had any formal training in these essential values of work. It is only in Gujarat that an effort has been launched to train, on a continuous basis, its *karmacharis* (employees) in order to transform them into *karamyogis* committed to work.

The *Karmayogi Maha Abhiyan* consists of *Chitan Shibirs* (reflection workshops for profound thinking) as well as V-Governance. *Chitan Shibhirs* are annual retreats for the ministers and senior government officials for brain-storming, progress review, goal-setting and developing a collective vision.

Skill Development

But, what Modi sought was skill development. That was one sure way of making progress. Whether it was in the field of agriculture, engineering or enterprise, unchallengeable skill was a must for making steady progress. Over a period of time, Gujarat had established itself as second to none in India, especially in the manufacturing sector. Gujarat's share in national production was high in many fields like the manufacture of power-driven pumps (74 per cent), air and gas compressors (57 per cent), soda ash (94 per cent), liquid chlorine (70 per cent), drugs and pharmaceuticals (45 per cent) and phosphatic fertilizers (66 per cent). In every department, skills had to be constantly upgraded.

Even as the nation was celebrating Swami Vivekananda's sesquicentennial birth anniversary on 16 January 2012, Modi called for an upgrading of skills, coining a new success sutra: SKILL + WILL + ZEAL = WIN!

Inaugurating a three-day techno-management carnival called NU TECH -12 organized by the Institute of Technology at Nirma University, Modi said that with India having the largest number of youth in the world, it was not enough to make them just degree holders; it was important to get them to upgrade their skills to solve various problems of society.

Modi cited the example of Gujarat's Forensic Science University which was helping farmers in testing the purity and quality of seeds, fertilizers and insecticides. Modi said that for students of engineering and technology, the mantra should be: 'Science is universal but Technology is for local.' If things went wrong, it was important for local technologists themselves to set things right rather than wait for an outsider, whether from India or the rest of the world, for help. Technologists in Gujarat had to be competitive.

The idea received unexpected support from Maruti Suzuki India when it decided to set up a skill-developing centre in Gujarat where it was investing ₹4,000 crore to set up a manufacturing facility. The plan was conveyed to Modi himself, by the Chairman of the company's parent, Suzuki Motor Corporation when the latter called on the Chief Minister. Modi was informed that Maruti Suzuki India (MSI) was planning to set up a Skill Development Centre in Gujarat and 500 people would be initially dispatched to Japan for training, so that they could get accustomed to the Japanese culture of working.

Modi's insistence on skill development was based on two hypotheses: One, it was necessary to keep up with the times and two, it helped to create employment.

Gujarat had, in fact, already taken note of these stands and had taken several strides in the field of vocational training through the setting up of Industrial Training Institutes (ITIs) to meet the rising aspirations of Gujarati youths. By providing vocational training, these ITIs redefined the progress of the state and encouraged continued development of skills. Additionally, fundamental parametres of development such as physical quotient and spiritual quotient were also stressed.

As Modi realized, in India, vocational education was often looked down upon and a graduation degree was invariably the preferred option. That, in turn, led to a 'catch-22 situation' where, on one hand, scores of unemployed graduates sought work and, on the other, there was a huge shortage of skilled labour. Keeping this in mind, the ITIs in Gujarat were revamped and the infrastructure modernized with a corporate touch. As an ITI Principal, R J Kaila put it: 'Earlier, students were not ready to study at ITIs and considered vocational training as the last option, but now the trend is changing and students are considering it as an attractive option.'

Meanwhile, a positive and significant trend has become increasingly noticeable: there is a large percentage of women – about 70 per cent among the trainees. This clearly showcases Gujarat's success in the field of women's empowerment! In addition to providing campus interviews and job placement facilities, the state started demand-driven courses like call-centre training, hotel management and motor driving. Statistics testify the success achieved. In 2001, the state offered a total of 81,925 seats for ITIs. This has witnessed a mighty jump and in 2011, government and self-dependent ITIs offered 1,24,098 seats; skill-development centres offered two lakh seats, and 174 vocational training providers offered 31,000 seats. As many as 67,245 women were trained in 2011 as compared to 3,390 in 2001. Additionally, 44,300 candidates from the weaker sections were trained in 2011-12, which was 418 per cent higher than the 2001 figure.

It was noted that young workers were utilizing their courses as add-ons to improve their skills and qualifications, enabling them to seek better job opportunities with more responsibilities and better salaries.

Apart from applying for jobs in the private and public sectors, ITI-qualified youth can set up their own motor, generator, transformer and winding garage shops, depending upon the trade they choose. The Army, Navy, Air Force and para-military forces like the BSF also provided job opportunities for ITI-qualified candidates.

In the recent 2012-13 budget of the Government of Gujarat, Finance Minister Vajubhai Vala made substantial provisions for the vocational sector. Under this, the Labour and Employment Department came up with a scheme for imparting training to 4.5 lakh youth. Further provisions to the tune of ₹130 crore were made to establish 10 new ITIs, construct 50 new buildings for ITIs and upgrade 27 of them. Additionally, the Modi government will provide ₹11.60 crore to increase the present capacity by 12,780 seats in the already functioning ITIs. This is Modi's contribution to fulfilling the aims and objectives of the young to make a better living. As he explained in his address to the Industry Responsive Skill Convention held in Ahmedabad on 20 September 2012: 'I see India's youth as one of the biggest strengths and most valuable resources. I strongly believe that if India is able to invigorate its talent pool, its youth in one decade will be the engine of growth not just for India but for the world.'

At another meeting, Modi illustrated his view on skills by relating an anecdote.

I would like to share with you a story of a man I know who repairs watches. One day, he received a watch for repair in which he noticed a manufacturing defect. He then wrote a letter to the watch-manufacturing company based in Switzerland, pointing out a defect and the company not only appreciated the points raised by this man but also had to withdraw the watches from the market.

Asked Modi: 'What does the example of this man show? It clearly shows that innovation knows no boundaries; that every individual possesses the power to innovate. With perfection in work and work culture, the best of innovation can take place. But a major component of attaining this perfection is acquiring the relevant skills in whatever we seek to do.'

As Modi saw it, the twenty-first century rests on three major pillars: IT (Information Technology), BT (Biotechnology) and ET (Environmental Technology). Though all the three technologies are important, it was Modi's view that special attention needs to be paid to ET- Environmental Technology. As he put it: 'Our ITIs can stimulate stellar research in tapping energy from natural resources such as the wind, water and the sun. In fact, I have even urged solar companies to initiate awards, which could serve as incentives to stimulate innovation. Such steps can truly benefit all of us.'

Addressing a business meeting in Ahmedabad on 29 October 2012, Modi spoke about the importance of skill development and the steps taken by the Gujarat government to promote skill development in the state. He pointed out that the UPA government had started a pilot project of providing broadband connectivity to 3,000 villages. In the past three years, Gujarat had done the same thing in 18,000 villages. Was that not 'pilot' enough, he asked?

In 2003, Modi had formulated an Industrial Policy, the basic approach of which was to comprehensively address the requirements of new entrepreneurs, right across the value chain from initial information needs to marketing the products, by creating the most conducive environment for the business to flourish. Making available skilled professionals to do their job was part of the support the government gave to entrepreneurs.

NOVEL DEVELOPMENTS

Apart from the schemes and programmes introduced by Narendra Modi in the fields of education, healthcare, tribal welfare and women's empowerment, he also introduced a slew of unique schemes in other areas, some of which have been detailed below.

Panchamrut Yojana

Promoting the use of solar energy for producing power was no big deal for Narendra Modi considering the context in which it was conceived. From the time he became the chief minister, Modi conceptualized many grand plans that he categorized as the 'Panchamrut Yojana'.[1]

The Panchamrut Yojana consisted of the following:

1. **Gyan Shakti:** Emphasizing and using the power of knowledge
    - Emphasis on educational infrastructure, training of teachers and computerization of schools
    - Introducing new courses to meet the demands of time
    - Emphasis on total enrolment and maximum retention of children in schools
    - Campaigns in the villages with the mission of universal education
    - Creating special funds for education of the girl-child

---

[1] *Panchamrut* is a drink made with five items namely milk, curd, ghee, honey and basil leaves that is distributed after a worship session as *prasad*. Here, it is used in a symbolic manner to denote the integration of five forces that have driven the growth of Gujarat.

Novel Developments

- Setting up 11 new universities, 400 new colleges with 1.25 lakh new teachers, 38,000 new school rooms and doubling the seats for technical courses
- Campaigning for a reduction in the drop-out rates at all primary levels
- Promoting the teaching of English among youth

2. **Urja Shakti:** Making energy the power of the state
   - Turning the loss-making State Electricity Board into a profit-making, professionally managed company
   - Venturing into large-scale exploration of oil and gas
   - Setting up of a 2,200 km long state-wide gas grid
   - Securing huge deposits of oil and gas in Gujarat and abroad
   - Electrifying all villages
   - Turning Gujarat into a gas-based economy
   - Making Gujarat the petro capital of India

3. **Jal Shakti:** Harnessing and management of water
   - Emphasis on harnessing of rain water and scientific management of water
   - Introduction of micro-irrigation techniques
   - Linking villages with a state wide water grid
   - Interlinking of 21 rivers of the state
   - Near completion of the Sardar Sarovar Project with benefits of water and electricity reaching 500 km away from the dam
   - Creating of 2.25 lakh new water bodies by construction of check-dams and farm dams

4. **Jan Shakti:** Empowering the people
   - Involving people in the process of development
   - Making the Gram Sabha an effective forum for harmony, progress and grievance redressal
   - Encouraging free elections in Panchayat Raj

- Organizing women's self-help groups for economic activities and resolution of conflicts through *Nari Adalats*
5. **Raksha Shakti:** Enhancing Security: Physical, Social and Economic
    - Developing the mitigation capacity for natural and man-made disasters
    - Making Gujarat polio free, leprosy free and reducing the incidence of HIV/AIDS
    - Reducing infant and mother mortality through innovative schemes
    - Creating a Seismology Research Institute

Intensely concerned with the timely delivery of justice with the belief that justice delayed is justice denied – from November 2006, the Gujarat Government introduced 'evening courts'. The response, to say the least, was overwhelming. Using the existing infrastructure, 67 evening courts were made operational and by 2012, some 1,16,000 cases were disposed of. The evening courts provided one advantage to citizens: they did not have to waste their working hours to seek justice.

Power and Energy

At a function held in Mumbai on 6 March 2012, Narendra Modi received *Business India*'s 'Businessman of the Year Award,' and was introduced as 'the longest running Chief Minister'.

Speaking straight from his heart, Modi began by saying that when he had been given the responsibility of Gujarat State for the first time, the state showed a financial deficit of ₹6,700 crore. 'Today,' he said, 'we show a surplus.' He continued:

When I started my career as the Chief Minister of Gujarat, people used to request for power supply just for dinner purposes, which showed that Gujarat was short of power supply. From there we started our journey in the power sector and now, we are the only state in the country where three-phase uninterrupted power is being supplied. Now we don't know the meaning of load shedding. In the rest of the country, if power supply is received, it becomes news. While in Gujarat news is created when there are power cuts. We had a deficit of 2,000 MW but with our innovations, the situation has changed. In our country, all state-owned electricity companies are in huge debt. When I became Gujarat's CM, our power companies were incurring ₹2,600 crore losses per year. I added ₹900 crore to the losses by giving discounts to schools and farmers, and the total deficit reached ₹3,500 crore. We are now reaping a profit of ₹700 crore. During the last ten years, we have doubled the power production and it is great to know that we haven't increased the tariff by a single rupee. We could do this by taking precautions and stopping leakages.'

He continued:

'We initiated solar energy power production. Gujarat was the first state in the country that introduced the solar policy, and then the Central Government followed. When we started the policy, we quoted a rate of ₹12, while the Central government quoted ₹19 and it was mandatory that suppliers go to them. But it went the other way round and they came to us at lower rates, and now Gujarat is the world leader in the field of solar energy production.

Solar Power

Early in January 2009, the Gujarat Government took a bold initiative and announced a Solar Power Policy; the foundation stone for the first Solar Park was laid on 20 December 2010.

By that date, Gujarat had already set up a structure to make use of wind power with an installed capacity of 2,255 MW for producing 4,500 million units of electricity. The innovative idea of the Gujarat Solar Park at Charanka aimed to produce 24,000 million medium units of electricity. If the same amount were to be produced using coal, it would require a mammoth 12,000 million kilograms of coal which, in turn, would mean a drain of ₹90,000 million in foreign exchange. Embracing solar power, in these circumstances, was truly a win-win situation.

The Solar Park set up at Charanka is the largest in Asia, spread over 5,000 acres and offers a state-of-the-art infrastructure, adequate utilization of wasteland and high solar radiation. The project was completed within a year by 28 January 2012. It is

India's first canal-top solar power project capable of producing 1 MW electricity. Importantly, it has helped save 1 crore litres of water per kilometre annually by preventing its evaporation.

Presiding over the inauguration of the completed park on 27 April 2012, Modi said that while the success of the Park and the commitment it has received from the investors and generation companies was very motivating, his own aim was to produce solar power on roof tops and in farmers' fields. As he put it: 'It is not enough to produce renewable energy. It is also important to produce it in a decentralized way.' He added, 'Through the PPP model, Gujarat has floated the Gandhinagar Photovoltaic Roof Top Programme. Now, residences will have the opportunity of producing solar electricity on their roof tops and will even generate additional income from it.'

When asked if a lot of research had been required to make the project viable, Modi responded: 'When there is such large-scale development, how can research and capacity-building be left behind? While we want to make Gujarat a solar hub, we also want our youth to conduct pioneering research and provide an effective energy solution for future generations. In 2008, PDPU (Pandit Dindayal Petroleum University) launched the School of Solar Energy, the first of its kind. We are actively supporting GERMI (Gujarat Energy Research and Management Institute) research and other innovations in the field of solar energy. Six solar photovoltaic ITI laboratories have been established and students are already signing up to learn.'

Kalpasar Project

There is one project, however, that has not taken off – but that is hardly Modi's fault. It is the Kalpasar Project.

The Project was originally conceived in 1975, when Modi was nowhere on the scene. It was identified as a promising site for tidal power generation by the UNDP expert, Eric Wilson. In 1988-89, a reconnaissance report was prepared for the dam across the Gulf of Khambhat. The report had then concluded that assuming sound foundation conditions, the closure of the Gulf was technically feasible. Years passed; ministers came and went.

In January 2002, it was reported that construction of the project would begin in 2011. A state government release said that the ₹55,000 crore (11.7 billion dollar) project would be completed by 2020 and would have a fresh water reservoir with a gross storage of 16,791 million cubic metres of water, and a 35-km long dam across the Gulf of Khambhat, connecting Ghogha in Bhavnagar with Hansot in Bharuch district. It was to have a tidal wave power generation house with an installed capacity of 5,880 MW.

The National Institute of Ocean Technology was to begin the work on fixing the dam alignment and mapping the ocean floor. Then doubts surfaced. One doubt was that at least 10 port sites in the Gulf of Khambhat, most of them functioning, would be adversely affected if the Kalpasar Project was initiated. The reason stated was that when a large barrier connecting Ghogha and Hansot was built, it could give rise to high tide variations, affecting shipping and port-related activities. Another doubt expressed was that the dam could lead to earthquakes in the state. Scientists were quoted as saying that large water reservoirs could induce earthquakes measuring more than 6 on the Richter scale. The 2001 earthquake that damaged scores of buildings in Ahmedabad measured 7.9 on the Richter scale. The thought was frightening.

Former Gujarat Chief Minister, Keshubhai Patel, criticized Modi over the latter's 'failure' in launching the Kalpasar Project. But, Modi who had faced the terrible earthquake of 2001, had to think of the future as well. Damage could not be considered in the name of development!

Port Development

Before discussing Gujarat's port development, it is important to understand that the strategic location of Gujarat – that of opening into the Arabian Sea – was historically important for trade and commerce with ancient countries like Sumer, Phoenicia, Rome, Egypt, East Africa, Malaya, Sumatra and China. Ancient Gujarat, with its many ports, marked one of the most glorious chapters in India's trade history. Lothal was an important maritime trade centre and had the oldest dockyard in the world. Padri, a site in the Gulf of Khambhat, also had a strong maritime presence. It is believed that Harappans of Padri had mastered the technique of deep sea fishing, travelling the ocean in huge boats. Kuntasi, locally known as 'Bibino Timbo', a port situated at the creek mouth during the Harappan period, was a centre for acquiring and processing raw materials for manufacturing articles for export. Other ports were Dholavira, Bet Dwarka, Malva, Vallabhi, Bhagatrav, Khambat, Mandavi and Surat. The most popular and well known was Surat, which the British used as an entry port during the days of the East Indian Company. Today, Gujarat has 41 ports out of which four, including the Mundra port (which is the largest private port in India), are operated by the private sector.

The Gujarat Maritime Board (GMR) was first created in 1982 under the Gujarat Maritime Board Act 1981. Its functions included management, control and administration of the minor ports of Gujarat. Over the next two decades and a half of operation, GMR planned the integrated development of new ports, also taking the lead in developing privatized port services, and facilitating private and captive jetties. The State's Port Policy Statement of December 1995 spelled out an explicit strategy of port-led development, including the creation of 10 completely new world-class ports in which private sector participation played a dominant role.

According to Pankaj Kumar, Vice Chairman and CEO of the Gujarat Maritime Board, the Board did not meet with success overnight. It had to struggle to find its feet and get its act together. Major privatization occurred only after 1991-92, when the state government decided to develop Pipavav as a joint sector port with private participation. The Build-Own-Operate-Transfer (BOOT) policy and Ship Building Policy were also announced. According to the CEO, Gujarat's success in port development would not have been possible but for the far-sighted policies announced by the state from time to time. Since 2001, when Modi came to power, GMB ports have more than doubled their capacity from 135 million tonnes in 2001 to 284 million tonnes in 2011. GMB ports now handle approximately 26 per cent of the national cargo and 72 per cent of cargo handled by ports under state governments of India. In 2010-11, traffic at ports under the control of the state government showed an impressive growth rate of 12.24 per cent.

According to a media source, things changed with the Modi government in operation. The government apparently realized

Novel Developments

that modern ports could be major attractions for companies to set up plants in Gujarat. Modi has been reported as saying, 'Our progress and development is not just limited to ports. Our vision is for port-led development with port-based Special Economic Zones (SEZs), warehouses, cold storage networks, railroad connectivity and related infrastructure facilities being established.' Cited was a decision taken by Maruti Suzuki to open a ₹4,000 crore facility in Gujarat in the Mehsana district.

Reportedly, out of the many options that were provided to the company, it chose the one in Mehsana due to its proximity to the Mundhra port. According to the report, the Special Economic Zone at Dahej was recently rated among the world's top 25 Economic Zones. In its second year of operation, it had reported record exports of more than ₹800 crore.

An objective report in The *Times of India* (9 January 2011) by Srivatsa Krishna provides a glimpse of at least how one newspaper looked at Gujarat's progress. Said the report:

> Gujarat no longer competes with the rest of India, but with China instead. The rate of growth of the state's GDP from 2002 till date has been, on average, 12.8 per cent. That is above the Indian average of 7.7 per cent or even Gujarat's own past performance of 3.25 per cent per annum in real terms from 1997 to 2002, as per data from the Central Statistical Organization. One of the quietest yet proudest achievements for Gujarat in the last decade has been the astonishing 9 per cent rate of growth of agriculture per annum, which is three times the national average.
>
> A recent World Bank study on Gujarat's highways reveals that its superlative performance can be benchmarked by global standards.
>
> 'Cato Institute', the high priest of political liberalism, has done a detailed study on port-based development, which says that in 2007, Gujarat's ports handled 176.6 million tonnes of cargo, making it India's best handler of traffic.

According to the report, Gujarat's economic progress has been 'a quiet yet puissant tale'. Said the reporter:

> A couple of years ago, I had the opportunity to lead a global investment delegation to the state. Two facts hit one right between the eyes. One, the average Gujarati is eager to do 'dhandha' (colloquial name for

'business') and we were, in fact, met by sarpanches, often in trendy, torn designer jeans, with maps and data, and enthusiastic to attract investment. Two, the quality of roads even in small towns like Dahej, beat even the legendary US I-94 hands down.'

The reporter, however, added that not everything was perfect. Data from the Centre for Monitoring Indian Economy showed that Gujarat had dropped, on an average, about 26 per cent of its signed Memoranda of Understanding (MoU) over the past seven years. On the other hand, it had managed to garner promised investments running into several billion dollars.

Continuing, the report stated:

The state's per capita electricity consumption is almost twice India's average of 704.2 kWh (2007-08). An impressive 99.7 per cent of its villages have electricity (compared to the national average of 84.4 per cent) according to the Central Electricity Authority. The Jyotigram Power Project is an intelligent rationing of power that bifurcates electricity supply with parallel lines and feeders for agricultural and non-agricultural use. The state has also invested about ₹1,000 crore in a parallel power grid and laid 56,000 km of high transmission lines and 22,000 km of low transmission lines.

What else? Ahmedabad's BRTS, the ambitious rapid transport system that's being developed by the Gujarat Infrastructure Development Board, is being replicated in other states. Last year's UN Public Service Award went to Gujarat for improving transparency, accountability and responsiveness in public service, perhaps on the grounds that there is no 'Adarsh'[2] to sully its image so far. And the state has perhaps the smallest cabinet in all of India – just 15 Ministers, which may indicate that there is good governance in practice rather than mere theory.

The Modi government was aware of problems that people in the coastal region faced. And it tried to meet them through the Sagarkhedu Sarvangin Vikas Yojana. The unique twelve-point flagship programme amounting to ₹11,000 crore for a

---

2 The multi-crore *'Adarsh'* housing society scam rocked the government of Maharashtra during 2010-11 with at least two chief ministers (Ashok Chavan and Vilasrao Deshmukh) and several senior bureaucrats coming under the scanner of investigating agencies.

five-year plan focussed attention in an integrated manner on the development issues of people living in coastal districts of the state. The programme was an answer to those critics of the state, who kept saying that the government only focussed on privatization and ignored the poor and the downtrodden.

A steady increase was noted in the number of tourists visiting Gujarat, which had a 'trickle down' effect in increasing the earnings of the poor. The *Khushboo Gujarat ki* (Fragrance of Gujarat) campaign that featured Amitabh Bachchan as the brand ambassador of the state, has turned out to be a 'mega success' if officials are to be believed. Indeed, according to officials, the state had presented a proposal for coastal tourism, and the Planning Commission had granted ₹1,200 crore for the project under which ten beaches will be developed. An official has been quoted as saying, 'It is not a fluke that Gujarat leads the way in so many arenas. While so many states have flourishing shipyards, why is Gujarat the first state in the country to come up with a Ship-Building Policy? While almost all states along the Arabian Sea, Indian Ocean and the Bay of Bengal have ports, is Gujarat the only state that has managed to link industrial growth and port development? We must realize that there is something the Gujarat government and its Shri Narendra Modi are doing correctly; there is something different about Gujarat.'

Moreover, the state was winning all sorts of awards. In October 2007, the Gujarat Maritime Board (GMB) won the 'Excellence Award' in the International Maritime Expo – INMEX 2007; the Indian Maritime News Maker of the year 2008-09 Award was given by the Maritime Gateway of India; the Award for Best Initiative taken by a state in Maritime Industry was given at the World Expo 2010 in March 2010, and the Port Authority Maritime Board of the Year Award was given in 2011 by the Maritime and Logistics Award organization (MALA).

The question, as always, was how to make Gujarat an international cargo hub. The matter was discussed at a brainstorming session attended by business honchos and top government officials in June 2010, in Ahmedabad. Officials were clear in their minds that with 42 ports handling 33.7 per cent of India's cargo, it was not that easy to meet international standards. The subject of discussion was

'Port-led Development in Gujarat', in the particular context of the completion of the Delhi-Mumbai Industrial Corridor (DMIC). The idea was to meet the challenges as well as the opportunities that would be brought to the state with the country's longest coastline.

Some achievements in port development

Long before Modi came on the scene, the GMB had already set up the following:

- India's first private port at Pipvav in 1996
- India's deepest draft port at Mundra in 1998
- Largest Single Point Moorings (SPMs) for POL export at Sikka in 1999
- The country's first dedicated chemical terminal at Dahej in 2001

With the taking over of power by Modi, the following were set up by GMB:

- The first private rail link in the country at Mundra in 2003
- India's first double stack container train at Pipavav in 2006
- India's largest coal terminal for an Ultra Mega Power Plant (UMPP) in 2010 in Mundra
- The country's most advanced Vessel Traffic Management System (VTMS) in 2010

Tourism

Gujarat also concentrated on the service and tourism sectors. There was little in Gujarat that had earlier attracted tourists, apart from the Gir forest, perhaps, and, of course, the Somnath and Dwarka temples. But starting 2001, Modi's government launched an aggressive campaign. The result: Tourism in Gujarat grew by 40 per cent in just three years, through a massive blitzkrieg of advertising. There was so much to see in Gujarat that many people had not even been aware of.

Modi was quick to realize that there were various kinds of tourist attractions that could be exploited to great advantage. To begin

Novel Developments

with, Gujarat could exploit its beaches. The state has a 1,600 km long coastline that could lure tourists by the thousands. But the infrastructure was poor. The government decided to put a beach development plan on a fast track. The government set aside prime land, complete with survey numbers and ownership details, overlooking 16 beaches to attract resort projects. Tenders were floated for development of infrastructure. Of the beaches identified, two were in Kutch, four in south Gujarat and ten in Saurashtra. The government announced that a master plan had been prepared, that it already had in hand 80 proposals, many of them signed at the recent 'Vibrant Gujarat' meet. The proposals were for building resorts along the beaches, worth ₹18,000 crore.

Another area of tourist attraction was development of water sports. As Vipul Mittra, put it: 'Gujarat has huge untapped potential in adventure tourism comprising water, aero and land activities like para-gliding, para-jumping and hot-air ballooning. On 26 May 2011, on the occasion of laying the foundation of a ₹50 crore Integrated Tourism Development Mega Circuit, Union Minister of Tourism Subodh Kant Sahay said that the centre was willing to make Gujarat the brand ambassador for tourism development. He said, 'We cannot ignore Gujarat. It has contributed to a great extent in the country's growth. I wish the state takes a lead in utilizing its resources in promoting tourism and becomes the brand ambassador for development of tourism in the country. The tourist circuit at Kabir Vad should be replicated in other spots.' The Centre, he promised, would provide financial aid of ₹150 crore for the development of the Integrated Tourism Development Mega Circuit.

Surprisingly, an unexpected form of tourism also emerged. It was seen that a large section of NRIs estimated between 20 to 25 million, visited India regularly – a large percentage of them being Gujaratis. In 2009 alone, as many as 4.50 lakh tourists visited Gujarat to avail medical care. Ahmedabad had become one of the most sought after medical tourism destinations in India. A top official was quoted as saying: 'Gujarat is an ideal location for promoting health tourism in a big way because of its unique position of having a large Gujarati population settled outside Gujarat and India. Gujarat has service providers who offer state-of-the-art treatment facilities, robust planning for integrated health care and companion care facilities, as well as world class support services and connectivity. Medical tourism contributes to a total of 25-30 per cent of the total health care market in Gujarat.

Yet another kind of tourism – spiritual tourism or religious tourism – started to attract a large number of tourists almost overnight! It so happened that in 2009, the Gujarat Archaeological Department discovered remains of Buddhists monasteries in Vadnagar which happens to be the home town of Modi. Apparently, Hieun Tsang, the famous Chinese Buddhist pilgrim and scholar, had visited Vadnagar in AD 640.

The idea of archaeological excavation in Vadnagar was mooted by Modi who, even in his youth, had always wondered about Buddhist influence in Gujarat. The Archaeological Department was to find other Buddhist sites at Vallabhi, Devi Mori (Sabarkantha) and Junagadh, thanks to Modi's interest.

In 2010, an International Buddhist Heritage Seminar was held in Vadodara, at which the Dalai Lama was present. During the seminar, Modi announced the construction of a Buddhist temple in Gujarat. 'This,' he said, 'will not just be a place of worship or a revenue generation exercise to attract tourists, but will also be developed as a centre for research on Buddhist philosophy.' The discovery of Buddhist caves in Khambalida, Talaja and Dunger further stirred him to develop a tourist circuit at par with international standards.

Apart from Buddhism, another potential winner emerged in the form of the 'Rama Trail'. During his 14-year exile from Ayodhya, Sri Rama, accompanied by Sita and Lakshman, had passed through the Dang district in Gujarat. The 'Rama Trail' became a big hit with Hindu tourists, resulting in a quantum jump of 30 per cent in tourist arrivals from 2009 to 2011.

Under Modi's guidance, the novel efforts of promoting tourism in Gujarat began to yield quantitative yields. In addition to the natural wonders of the Gir forest with its lions, and the attraction of Kutch, Mandvi and Saputara; attention was being drawn to places of antiquity like Lothal and Dholaviria; medieval marvels like Somnath and Modhera, not to mention Sri Krishna's own Dwarka. Modi's dream of making Gujarat a tourist paradise was being fulfilled! The promotion of events like the Kite Festival, Rann Utsav, Navratri Festival and the Tarnetar Fair only added to the attractions of Gujarat.

Sabarmati River Front Project

There was something else that caught the eye of many tourists – the cleaning up of the Sabarmati River on whose bank Gandhi had set up his ashram years earlier.

As Modi began to hear of the deterioration of the condition of the Sabarmati, his government came up with a unique plan. The Sabarmati River Front Development Corporation was established for the development of an 11-km stretch on both sides of the river that runs through the city of Ahmedabad. All the drainage outlets were diverted to clean and purify the flow of water. To maintain the river's water level, water was diverted from the river Narmada through the main canal of the Sardar Sarovar Project to Sabarmati. Today, the Sabarmati is a sight to see. A young engineering graduate, Abhishek M Chaudhari who visited Gujarat as a part of *Prakash* yatra, an initiative of the Mumbai-based Rambhau Mhalgi Prabodhini, wrote about the project:

> *Sardar Sarovar is a huge project for diverting water from the river Narmada in southern Gujarat to central-northern-western Gujarat through canals. The main canal is 456 km long. Other canals of approximately 1,900 km in length will then take this water to several parts of the state. Moreover, canals will also discharge water into the rivers Sabarmati and Mahi. This project was praised as one of eight incredible projects in the world in 1994. The project is dually useful as it supplies water and produces energy. The plan is to supply 28 MAF (million acres feet) water and to produce 1,450 MW energy. This will bring 18 lakh hectares of the land of Gujarat under irrigation, and at least 9,000 villages and 131 towns will receive water supply. Thirty thousand hectares of land will be protected from floods and there will be 10 lakh employment opportunities.*

Chaudhari was one of fourteen young professionals who had participated in *Prakash* yatra and they were given an opportunity to meet Modi and interview him. The meeting was fixed in Gandhinagar Circuit House. Modi arrived punctually at 11 am. Later, Chaudhari was to write:

The Man of the Moment: Narendra Modi

He waved at us and asked: 'Are you enlightened through this tour? After the introduction session, he was willing to hear the ideas of young Indian minds. Each of us spoke about what we saw, experienced, felt in the last three days. He listened to us silently, with his face full of enthusiasm. He carefully took notes of our suggestions. When he started speaking, he had taken threads from our talk. He spoke passionately, his words coming straight from his heart. It was his vigour, patriotism and experience supplementing his words. He modestly admitted that the development of Gujarat has just started (this was written on October 18, 2012) and it had to go a long way. We were surprised: if this was the beginning for him, what exactly was the 'end'?

Bus Rapid Transport System (BRTS)

The Bus Rapid Transport System (BRTS), named *Janmarg*, has set an example before the nation. It has transformed the urban transportation system of Ahmedabad. The population of Ahmedabad is 5.5 million. People generally commuted by autorikshaws, municipal buses and private cars. A faster, reliable, comfortable and eco-friendly public transport system was the cry of the day, especially in view of the fact that the city's population was swelling rapidly.

BRTS started in August 2009. It covers 45 km at present and is being expanded to increase the coverage to 135 km. The number of passengers per day has gone up from 18,000 to 1,30,000. Its salient features are a closed BRTS system with medium bus stations, specially designed buses with right hand side doors and bus floor and bus station platform of matching heights. The planning is done so carefully that pedestrians too find it easy to travel on this route. It is noticed that it has reduced air pollution considerably. Several users of two wheelers have switched over to the BRTS buses.

BRTS has won several awards including the National Award for 'Best Mass Transit Rapid System Project – 2009' from the Government of India and the 'Sustainable Transport Award – 2010', at Washington DC, US.

Economic and Industrial Growth 18

Part of Swapan Dasgupta's column written in The *Telegraph* (6 July 2012) had much to say about Modi and his critics. As he put it, the mere mention of Narendra Modi evoked controversy. To his admirers, the Chief Minister of Gujarat was the type of no-nonsense leader that India needed at this juncture – decisive, single-mildly purposeful, hugely popular in his state and with an uncontested reputation for honesty and personal integrity. He was sworn in as the leader of Gujarat and had steered the state in the direction of efficient growth. To his detractors, Modi's style of leadership was authoritarian, divisive and unsuited to a complex and diverse country like India. For them, the development of Gujarat owed nothing to Modi. The chief minister was merely riding piggyback on a pre-existing high growth rate that owed everything to location and the entrepreneurship of the Gujaratis. They averred that Modi or no Modi – Gujarat would have developed anyway.

However, wrote Dasgupta:

The quantum of development in Gujarat can be measured by statistics. Using statistics culled from the Planning Commission, Bibek Debroy has shown that Gujarat's average growth has risen since the 1990s but unevenly. The average growth was 6.1 per cent during the 7th Plan (1985-1990), 12.9 per cent during the 8th Plan (1992-1997), 2.8 per cent during the 9th Plan (1997-2002), 10.9 per cent during the 10th Plan (2002-2007), and an estimated 11.2 per cent during the 11th Plan (2007-2012). What is more, the growth rate has been consistent across sectors. Despite four years of drought, agriculture grew on an average by 10.7 per cent in the period 2001-2002 to 2010-2011. Although jumping to instant political conclusion would be rash, statistical evidence would bear out the belief that sustained double-digit growth has coincided with Modi's tenure as Chief Minister.

Dasgupta said that apart from Karnataka, that equalled Gujarat's 11.2 per cent growth during the 11th Plan, none of the big states of India had equalled Gujarat's sustained growth over the past decade. Modi's critics, he continued, had pointed out that Gujarat's growth rate had been overtaken by Bihar (which began from a zero base), Delhi and Pondicherry. 'But that is like saying as some politicians do that India's faltering six per cent growth is better than the United States' projected two per cent growth,' Dasgupta added. To make his point clearer he went on to say:

The question therefore arises: Is economic growth of the kind Gujarat has witnessed over the past decade completely unrelated to politics and governance, as Modi's critics have maintained? If true, Modi, it would appear, has steered political economy in an entirely new direction by insulating economic activity from the dirty business of politics. Aspiring for this autonomy has long been the cherished dream of the Indian corporate sector. Are Modi's critics crediting him for this unintended achievement?

Then Dasgupta made his most telling comment. He wrote:

In the past decade, Gujarat has focussed on the upgrading of infrastructure, particularly roads and ports. In addition, the government has taken proactive steps to attract enterprise by laying down attractive facilities and terms. This may explain why Tata Motors abandoned the troubled Singur in West Bengal and moved to Gujarat. And it was the Tata decision that had a multiplier effect and contributed to the creation of a new automobile manufacturing hub in Gujarat. Yet, none of this would have happened had the state not established a record of low corruption, quick decision-making, and nurtured a civic culture that cherished entrepreneurship. True, Modi played to the pre-existing strengths of Gujarat. But had the Chief Minster been venal, unresponsive and a mindless populist – as he so easily could have been – would India be still talking of the Gujarat miracle?

Industrial Growth

In the months after the Godhra riots, some of corporate India's biggest names publicly voiced their anger at him, beside their concerns. Deepak Parekh, non-Executive Chairman of HDFC, said that India had lost its face as a secular country and he was ashamed of what had happened in Gujarat.

Cyrus Guzdar, the CMD of the shipping concern AFL, compared the violence against Muslims in Gujarat to 'a genocide'. Two of Bengaluru's biggest IT chieftains, Narayan Murthy of Infosys and Azim Premji of Wipro, issued strong public condemnations. Rahul Bajaj declared 2002 as a 'lost year' for Gujarat. He told Modi: 'We would like to know what you believe in – what you stand for. We want to know you better. We are prepared to work with a government of all hues but we also have own views on what is good for society and what works for it.'

Such were the feelings of leading industrialists towards Modi. Under such circumstances, how could one ever hope to see Gujarat develop into the highly industrialized state it was to become within a decade?

As early as 2003, Gujarat ranked first in both crude oil (18 per cent) and natural gas (10 per cent) onshore production in India. Also, Gujarat was third in value of mineral production with a 9 per cent share. As many as 26 out of 32 minerals identified in the state were being mined even at that time. With 4 per cent of the country's population, Gujarat accounted for 9 per cent of its energy consumption, thus showing relatively high level of industrial development.

Modi came to office in 2001. In the following eight years, from 2002 to 2011, NSDP (Net State Domestic Product) grew at a 10.5 per cent annual rate in Gujarat, with Maharashtra running second with 10.1 per cent. Prior to 2002, Gujarat's annual rate had been 5.9 per cent, second after Haryana's 6.3 per cent. How did this happen? According to Modi, who revealed in his address to the fifth Vibrant Gujarat Global Investors Summit, his government had taken the following steps to start with:

We tripled the number of seats in our technical and management colleges. We entered into agreements with several renowned universities in the country and abroad. We made substantial progress in oil and gas exploration. We laid down a 2,200-km long gas grid to fuel the industries and households. We made hundreds and thousands of water-harvesting structures, successfully inaugurated the working of one of the world's largest dams, the longest canal system and a state-wide water grid. We added substantial megawatts to our electricity generation (and) with careful and aggressive execution, we have broken away from the traditional pattern of governance of a developing country where the pace of progress was slow. We have redefined the approach and the level of thinking in infrastructure ....

Modi also said that his government was not only upgrading Gujarat's ports to make them world class but was also adopting a holistic coastal development approach, including the development of new coastal cities with global standards. As he put it: 'This is the reason our contribution to industrial output has been around 16 per cent consistently for a decade. This is the reason that we contribute to 22 per cent of India's exports.'

Modi also informed his audience that due to Gujarat's limestone reserves, the state was emerging as the largest cement producer in the country. It had already begun to emerge as a big steel and pipe producer. He added, 'And the best infrastructure strength that we have is our 1,600-km long coastline dotted with world class ports.'

As if that was not enough, Modi continued to impress his audience with other facts. He averred:

We are constantly expanding the horizon of our physical, social and industrial infrastructure, our governance, our policies and processes. On the industrial infrastructure front, we have moved from our traditional industrial clusters to industrial estates, and advanced further to establish 60 SEZs which is the largest number in the country. We are further moving towards setting up truly world class and huge Special Investment Regions, which we call SIRs. We have planned for 12 SIRs, which will be global hubs of economic activity...

The Vibrant Gujarat Summit 2003 was organized from 28 September to 2 October 2003, barely two years after Modi became chief minister. At that summit, as many as 76 MoUs for 80 projects were signed for ₹66,068 crore. That itself was something of an achievement.

This success was to be followed by many more, as the following figures show:

- 2005 Global Investors' Summit: 226 MoUs worth 20 billion dollars were signed.
- 2007 Global Investors' Summit: 675 MoUs worth 152 billion dollars were signed.
- 2009 Global Investors' Summit: 8,662 MoUs worth 241 billion dollars were signed.
- 2011 Global Investors' Summit: 7,936 MoUs worth 462 billion dollars were signed.

In his address at the 2011 summit held in Delhi, Modi made a meaningful presentation of the situation in India. To quote him:

India is on the path to becoming an economic power in the world. India has emerged .... We call ourselves to be the 'Growth Engine of India'. It is not a mere slogan. It has substance. India is now recognized as a robust economy mainly because of the rising exports, better infrastructure, better human capital and better market capitalization. Gujarat was among the very first states to take steps in the direction of liberalizing the economy and dismantling the barriers.

He told his earnest audience that Gujarat's growth rate had been in double digits for the entire decade. Gujarat, he said, was a monopoly producer and supplier of several goods, including polished diamonds. As he put it:

We have some of the world's largest manufacturing and processing facilities (like Reliance in petroleum refining). We house some of the leading global industries (like General Motors and Bombardier). However, our real strength lies in our medium and small industries. We house 43 per cent of micro, small and medium enterprises of India. We house 39 per cent of the total medium industries of India. With the addition of the Nano car, we have emerged as an automobile hub. We are already a global player in the steel, pipe and pharmaceutical industries. Now we are emerging as a global player in the cement industry too. Our strength in the oil and gas industry is now recognized globally.

Modi said that Gujarat had not only offered solutions to many of India's historic problems but had also provided answers to many debates in global economics. He pointed out that the whole world had been struggling with the dichotomy of the 'Big versus Small', but Gujarat 'is an amazing model of the effective co-existence of big and small, robust and inclusive, fast and sustainable'. He claimed that Gujarat had done wonderfully well on both the macro and micro indicators. 'Our double digit growth rate of GDP has actually translated into a high growth in the per capita income of the people which is at 13.8 per cent. Not only have the multinationals and big companies done well, but a large number of medium, small, rural and domestic ventures have also prospered.'

To push his point further, Modi said that Gujarat's multi-faceted growth and excellence in various sectors had not only been recognized in India, but in the entire world. He said, 'Our efforts in good governance have been applauded the world over. We have received around 200 national and international awards in the last eight years. This year itself, my office has received the United Nations Public Service Award for improving the "effectiveness, efficiency and quality of public services". We are getting such awards on a weekly basis.'

Aware that he was almost addressing an international audience, Modi said, 'Our job in the government is to create the right kind of environment for you to come and enjoy your creativity. Gujarat is known for its handholding approach for the investors. Gujarat is known for better management of its public finance, so there is enough money for the right purposes and inefficiencies are not transferred to you.'

In actual words, what Modi was trying to do was to address the unspoken doubts of foreign investors, and his concluding remarks made that clear. He said:

We have replaced several existing operations in the economy with more efficient and environment friendly systems. Through a state-wide gas grid, we have changed the nature of economy to a gas-based economy. We have introduced CNG on our transportation systems. Many of our government offices, including my own office, are TSA certified .... We are aggressively tapping renewable energy resources, particularly in solar and wind ....'

Vision for Gujarat : Address to NRIs – 2012

Narendra Modi addressed NRIs across twelve cities in the United States on 20 May, 2012. It was a long speech and Modi spoke about his vision for Gujarat.

He reminded the Gujarat NRIs about the role played by such distinguished Gujaratis as Mahatma Gandhi, Sardar Vallabhbhai Patel and Shyamji Krishna Varma. He congratulated the Gujaratis for always being open minded and willing to get along with others, which was why they were liked. He told his wide audience that in the past ten years, his government had not raised taxes in any field, not even by one paisa. It had only cut down expenses and brought in efficiency into the administration. That was how, he said, his government had a revenue surplus. Ten years ago, in the field of agriculture, the income was ₹14,700 crore. Presently he said, it had reached ₹98,000 crore. The surplus money went into developing village prosperity. He said:

I want you to remember that before 2001, agricultural land was 108 lakh hectares. Today, I say with pride that we have converted 37 lakh hectares of land into agricultural land and now have 145 lakh hectares of land for agriculture.

Earlier, he said, *vanbandhu* farmers in Gujarat used to possess a small piece of land each and earn about ₹10,000 to ₹15,000 a year from it. At present, tribal farmers in Surat, Valsad and Dang districts were growing cashew nuts, competing with nuts produced in Goa. 'In horticulture,' he maintained, 'earlier we were at 61 lakh megatons and now we have reached the production level of 181 lakh megatons.' It turned out that what Modi had in mind was to show how vastly Gujarat had changed since he had taken over the reins of government. Global production of bananas was 16.93 tonnes per hectare. Gujarat produced 54.76 tonnes within the same area. The same could be said about the production of onions. Gujarat had established a record production of 87 tonnes of potatoes per hectare, a world record hard for anyone to break.

Modi spoke about the ceramic industry, which was competing with China and was capturing the global market. Besides all the above, Gujarat had also become the automobile hub. As he put it: 'There is no vehicle in the world of which even a small part is not being produced on the land of Gujarat. Indeed, there is not a single vehicle in the world which does not use parts manufactured by labourers of Gujarat.'

Modi proudly revealed: 'Gujarat is the only state where 18,000 villages have broadband connectivity. Sitting in the US, if you want an account of your land all through the year, you can do this online.'

There were other things that Modi said that Gujarati NRIs should be proud of. He spoke about ambulance services. 'Living in India, you would know how difficult it is to call an ambulance in times of emergency. You would not know in how much time the ambulance would reach the spot. Today we have the 108 service and it is a blessing for the people. We have got the opportunity to save thousands of lives. I can say this with pride that in the US, a hundred dollars are spent for this service for one patient, while in Gujarat, only 50 cent is spent for the same.'

Then Modi spoke about the Chiranjeevi Scheme, under which poor women were brought to the maternity ward for delivery on time. He said: 'There was a time when no more than 40 per cent of the deliveries used to take place in the hospital. Today, I can say proudly that about 98 per cent of deliveries take place in the hospital, under the supervision of a knowledgeable person, no matter how poor the mother is.'

He then spoke about toilets and the lack of them. 'Earlier in our villages, there were no toilets available. For the past 10, years we have been putting in efforts into building toilets. In Gujarat, out of 56 lakh households, 46 lakh didn't have toilets. I can say that today, we have built toilets in 44 lakh households and, in the coming days, will complete the work in the remaining 2 lakh households.'

How was the education of poor children being taken care of? Modi had a quick answer. He said there was a time when the drop-out rate of school-going children was embarrassing. Then he added: 'Today there is no child that we haven't succeeded in sending to school. We have achieved 100 per cent enrolment.' When asked how that had been achieved, Modi replied: 'We have appointed

1 lakh teachers. We have built more than 50,000 school rooms, so that poor children should get education'.

The same was applicable to other spheres of education too. There were no more than 500 medical seats available at one time in Gujarat. Modi had succeeded in providing approximately 6,000 seats. In the engineering field, the quota of only 6,000 seats had risen to almost 42,000 seats.

Modi was happy to share more examples of the good work being done by his government. At hand, for example, was a project to make Dholera bigger than Shanghai and more modern. There was another plan to provide medical aid to the extent of ₹2 lakh per person to senior citizens hailing from poor families. Modi added: 'Our 'Garib Kalyan Mela' (Welfare Fair for the Poor) has become famous in India as a model for its delivery system.

But more thrilling was a programme under which the Gujarat Government had provided employment to 65,000 youth. Averred Modi: 'Perhaps it is a record in India to provide jobs to 65,000 in a week's time.' He quoted the Indian Government as saying that in the last five years, out of all the jobs provided to the youth in India, 78 per cent jobs had been provided by the Gujarat government. Said Modi: 'I am proud of this. And, despite such large-scale industrial development, there have been no strikes or labour unrests in the state.' He ended his famous speech on an emotional high. He said:

'We are progressing on the path of development with zero man-day's loss. Gujarat is a peaceful place and pursues goodwill and development. Gujarat is working hard to change India's destiny and eradicate poverty from the country. For this, we are making all the efforts and contributions we can. People from almost every state are coming to Gujarat to either settle, or invest money, or engage in labour work or, last but not the least, earn money and send it back to their homes. We have taken Gujarat to such heights and we are proud of it. We have worked more than what is expected of us. Gujarat has worked for the welfare of the entire country. Indians living across the globe will look up to Gujarat with respect and Gujaratis living outside India can be proud that we have made such an effort.'

A State Modi-fied

Modi's contribution to the development of practically every field of human activity has been understandably recognized not only by the people of the state, but by outsiders too. It was Ratan Tata who, as early as January 2007, said: 'One is stupid if one does not invest in Gujarat today.'

But Ratan Tata is not the only one to be so full of praise for Gujarat's chief minister. There have been others like Mukesh Ambani, Kumaramangalam Birla, Anil Ambani and Shashi Ruia who, on their own, have extolled Modi's dynamism. Modi had initiated the concept of Vibrant Gujarat as early as 2003. Industrialists who attended the 'Vibrant Gujarat' annual gatherings found that Modi had managed to create an investor-friendly atmosphere, largely free of red-tapism, cumbersome procedures and the need for palm-greasing. As B D Goenka, Chairman of the Wellspun Group, which has the world's third largest towel manufacturing unit in Kutch, put it: 'Once you decide to put up a unit in Gujarat, you get land, water and power within three months. That is commendable.' Ratan Tata had commented, 'The pragmatism and charisma characterized by Modi's leadership has touched all of us.'

Mukesh Ambani who announced investment worth ₹67,000 crore in the state has been quoted as saying: 'Modi has shown amazing clarity of purpose and determination. He has given Gujarat a new-found confidence.' Mukesh also said: 'Gujarat is one of the few revenue-positive states in the country which has crossed new frontiers in revenue management.' While Kumaramangalam Birla described Modi as Gujarat's CEO, FICCI Chairman H Khorakiwala described Gujarat under Modi as 'the emerging industrial powerhouse with phenomenal growth and a model of good governance.' Perhaps Anil Ambani summed it up correctly with his comment: 'Gujarat's is a great story and all good stories need a good actor. Gujarat's story has largely revolved around Narendra Modi's dynamic leadership.'

Rumours had been spread that all the talks of MoUs were farcical, considering that only a portion of what had been promised, was actually invested. These rumours were strongly refuted by the then State Chief Secretary Sudhir Mankad. According to him, 76 MoUs worth ₹66,000 crore were signed at the 2003 summit, out of which 29 projects worth ₹22,000 crore had already gone into production, and 21 projects worth ₹39,000 crore were at the stage of implementation. The 2005 summit had seen 227 MoUs worth ₹1.06 lakh crore being signed, out of which projects worth ₹2,300 crore were at the production stage and 85 projects worth ₹65,000 crore were at the implementation stage. At the 2007 Vibrant Gujarat business summit, MoUs worth ₹4.60 lakh crore were signed, of which the proposed investment spread into numerous sectors such as ports, power, textiles, agro-processing, bio-technology and tourism with a potential to create six lakh jobs.

In the Fast Lane

Perhaps Gujarat's new growth story has had the best coverage in an article of about 5,000 words written by Sohini Das, Rustam Vora and Vinay Umarji in the *Business Standard*. The question the three journalists posed was: 'What makes Gujarat an attractive business destination?' They provided their own answer: 'The reasons are well known: good infrastructure, availability of power, readily available land, port connectivity and a pro-industry government.' They gave numerous examples to show how industry has been happily thriving in Gujarat. They added that as Gujarat was taking the fast lane in positioning itself as India's manufacturing capital – not just in the auto industry, but also in global healthcare – companies were lining up to invest there. They quoted Mr M Athar, Infrastructure Consultant, Pricewaterhouse Cooper (PwC) as saying: 'The state has been able to develop an industry-friendly image over the last decade, not just in India but abroad. The international community now understands what Gujarat has to offer. Government delegations visiting parts of the globe to promote the state during the Vibrant Gujarat Global Investors Summit have helped to create a brand for the state.'

One insider has been quoted as saying: 'Corporates have easy access to government officials, right from the ground level to the top-most bureaucrats. There have been instances when a particular company requiring coordination from six to seven government departments has been able to meet representatives from all under one roof, as a pro-active state machinery would promptly organize such meetings to expedite the process.'

The Man of the Moment: Narendra Modi

It was no surprise then that India's largest passenger car manufacturer Maruti Suzuki India, global automakers Ford and PSA Peugeot Citroen, US-based pharmaceuticals giant Abbot, Israel's Teva, FMCG behemoths Amway and Colgate, as well as Nestle – all chose Gujarat, being touted as the most business-savvy state in the country, for setting up their manufacturing plants.

Based on studied opinion, perhaps it would not be out of place to predict that Gujarat will catapult itself to the big league of car manufacturing hubs by 2015-16. The expectation is that by then, in addition to what Tata Motors (250,000 cars per annum), General Motors (110,000 units per annum) and Ford India (240,000 cars per annum) are already manufacturing, there will be others in the competition to raise the total production of cars to an unbelievable 10,15,000 units per annum!

Nowhere else in the world has such a phenomenon occurred! But in Gujarat, Modi has made it happen. Not just in the field of automobiles, but in other fields like pharmaceuticals and even denim manufacturing, where Lalbhai is known to have introduced India's first international apparel brand.

Beyond the Shores of Gujarat

It is perhaps accurate to say that no chief minister has ever travelled so much and so purposefully as has Narendra Modi. The countries that he has visited include Mauritius, Jamaica, Guyana, Uganda and Kenya, Trinidad and Tobago, Switzerland, Britain, Malaysia, Singapore, Hong Kong, Thailand, Australia and New Zealand, Taiwan and China, Japan and Russia. A mention has already been made earlier that it all started in November 2004 when Narendra Modi set out on a journey to the East to make Gujarat the 'investment destination' for global investors. It started with a three-day visit to Singapore and from there, he flew to Hong Kong and further on to Sydney, Australia. Modi continued with this initiative and by 2012, he visited many other countries to build mutually beneficial relations and goodwill.

Due to a [false!] understanding of the riots that followed the merciless killing of over fifty innocent women and children in a railway coach in the Sabarmati Express at Godhra station by a Muslim crowd in 2002, the US had denied Modi a visa. Following the American example, Britain had done the same. However, in 2012, the denial was withdrawn by the British government. For Modi, his most important visits were to Russia, Japan and China, and to an extent, to Israel.

Some European countries too were opposed to granting Modi a visa on the ground that Gujarat had made conversions illegal by getting an amendment passed to the existing Gujarat Freedom of Religion Act.

But the fact of the matter is that the Anti-Conversion Act passed earlier did not have clarity on what forced conversion meant and to whom it should be applied. The amendment passed in

September 2006 made everything clear. It also limited Modi's travel in Europe.

Visit to Israel

For a long time, India had kept distance from Israel for political reasons and it was only in January 1992 that India formally established relations with the Jewish state, allegedly because of 'common strategic interests and security threats'.

India is the largest customer of Israeli military equipment and Israel is considered the second largest military partner of India after Russia. In 2000, Jaswant Singh became the first Indian Foreign Minister to visit Israel and in 2003, Ariel Sharon became the first Israeli Prime Minister to visit India. He was welcomed by the BJP-led National Democratic Alliance (NDA) and the then Prime Minister Atal Bihari Vajpayee voiced confidence that Sharon's visit could pave the way for further consolidation of bilateral ties between India and Israel. Modi's visit to Israel then became almost inevitable.

The visit led to cooperation in many fields including water management. Thus, on 7 December 2011, the General Manager of Israel's Water and Sewage Authority, Prof Uri Shani called on Modi. A long discussion followed on setting up projects relating to water conservation. There was much to learn from Israel's experience in drip irrigation, recycling, purifying sewage water and water desalination.

At a national convention in September 2012, Modi announced that talks were going on with Israel to set up an agricultural educational institute in collaboration with its universities to offer postgraduate and PhD programmes. The two-day convention was organized by the Industrial Extension Bureau and Gujarat Agro Industries Corporation Ltd with Israel as a partner country. On 15 April 2012, Modi formally inaugurated Israel's Netafin Irrigation firm's second plant at Savli in central Gujarat. The first plant had been set up in the same place in 2001.

Modi recalled that during his visit to Israel, he had been impressed by the country's success in the field of water management through a scientific method to overcome the shortage of water for agricultural purposes in semi-arid land. He revealed that his government was planning to bring 10 lakh hectares of agricultural land under micro-irrigation by 2013.

The convention's importance was evident from the fact that present at it were Netafin Board CEO Igal Isenberg, Chairman Rudolf Weber and Israel's deputy envoy to India, Yahel Vilan. The occasion was utilized by Modi to present eight progressive farmers of Gujarat with Netafin Krishi Ratna Awards. The awards went to Pravin Gajera of Junagadh for cotton manufacturing, Girish Patel of Sabarkantha for potato farming, Chandrakant Patel of Anand for the growth of bananas, Vanraj Singh Bandola of Bharuch for sugarcane production, Vijay Patel of Gandhinagar for growing roses, Gopal Patel of Vadodara for high-tech farming and Jitish Patel of Sabarkantha and Karsan Rathwa of Vadodara for precision-farming.

Modi and Britain

Modi first visited Britain in August 2003 but his visit was marred by strong protests and a call for his arrest. The British newspaper The *Guardian* carried a screaming headline questioning Modi's visit. An accompanying editorial expressed apprehensions that Modi was positioning himself to become the Prime Minister of India, 'if ever he makes it.' Added the editorial: 'India's tradition of secular democracy which has been under threat for some time will have been replaced by something much darker.' An accompanying profile reminded the reader that Modi was likened by many of his enemies to Hitler, Milosevic and Pol Pot. Hatred of Modi was all embracing, with the British media conveniently forgetting what their own military had done in Jallianwallah Bagh in 1919.

Modi's visit was intended to promote his vision of 'Vibrant Gujarat' and at his first public engagement – a meeting with 'Friends of Gujarat' – he was booed by protestors, many of whom were local Muslim activists. Waving placards describing Modi as 'murderer' and 'butcher', the demonstrators demanded his immediate arrest. The British Government was hesitant, not knowing exactly how to handle the visitor; it appeased Muslim anger by not granting Modi a single appointment with any government official. But that did not bother the Gujarat Chief Minister. At a dinner organized by FICCI on 20 August 2003 that was attended by some British businessmen and some from the industrial community, Modi stated that those investing in Gujarat in infrastructure, energy and technology projects would benefit greatly because of the state's professional ethos. And to make matters even more encouraging, he averred that India would be a leading industrial power in the 21st century and Gujarat would be the Number One industrial state in the country. But the atmosphere was anything but friendly.

The concerted effort to stymie Modi was supported by the Monitoring Group, Awaz South Asia Watch, the Council of Indian Muslims for Secular Democracy, Muslim Parliament, Southall Black Sisters, South Asia Solidarity Group and the Campaign Against Criminalizing Communities.

In 2009, Modi was invited to address India Summit 2009 organized by Dow Jones Financial News in London. This only served to infuriate the Chairman of Council of Indian Muslims, Mohammad Munaf Zeena who wrote to the British Home Secretary Ms Jacqui Smith that no visa should be given to Modi, considering that his presence in the country posed a danger to inter-communal relations. Zeena emphasized that United Kingdom was obligated under international law to ensure that a person against whom there was evidence of committing international crimes was subjected to tracing, arrest and trial, particularly if he was found on UK soil. So vicious was the attack against Modi that the Dow Jones Consumer Media Group decided it was wiser to cancel the proposed event.

Even as the election campaign was in full momentum, something remarkable and unexpected took place that took both friends and foes of Modi by surprise.

Britain decided to re-engage itself with Gujarat. On 22 October 2012, the British High Commissioner to India met Modi. Later, he was quoted as saying that Britain's decision to establish links with Gujarat should not be seen as an endorsement of Modi but as an 'engagement' with Gujarat. Delivering a lecture in Delhi on: 'The UK and India: Myths, Reality and Prospects', the High Commissioner, Mr James Bevan, cited his country's decision to re-engage with Gujarat and ease the travel advisory on Jammu and Kashmir to show that his country would like to have a robust partnership with India.

The lecture, delivered on 7 December 2012, made it clear that Britain felt that it could not ignore Gujarat if it wanted to build a stronger relationship with India. Adding that Britain was not seeking an exclusive partnership with India, Bevan said that both countries had 'many friends and partners' around the world, but his country did believe that there was a 'unique fit' between itself and India that meant they could aspire to do much together in the coming years. Our belief that India will matter more and more in future and that all of India matters, also played a part in our recent decision to change our policy on Gujarat. Since the 2002 riots, the British government has had no high level contact with the Government of Gujarat. But, if you want to build a stronger relationship with India, as we do, you can't ignore Gujarat. And if you want to deal with any Indian state, you need to deal with the government of that state,' Bevan said.

Economically, Britain was going through a downturn. It must have been watching Modi carefully as he went abroad and garnered support even from countries like China and Japan. London must, therefore, have re-examined its approach to Gujarat and Modi. Only a few months ago, Britain had lost an 11 billion dollar contract to sell 126 fighter jets to India, to the Europeans. That must have hurt. As one cynical observer commented, 'The British decision to end its decade-long boycott of Narendra Modi speaks volumes of how human rights are so easily sacrificed at the altar of commerce.' Being traders at heart, the British did not wish to see other Western and Eastern countries prosper while it stuck to supposed 'Human Rights'.

Besides, was the conduct of some Western countries in Asia and Africa not questionable too? Was their record on the Human Rights issue favourable? Additionally, as Sreeram Chaulia, Professor and Dean at the Jindal School of International Affairs noted in The *Times of India* (14 October 2012), 'One crucial force in Modi's conversion from international pariah into an acceptable gatekeeper of a thriving Indian state was the intense lobbying machine of the Gujarati non-resident Indians (NRIs).'

Gujarat and Russia

Within a month of assuming office in October 2001, Modi was invited to be part of an Indian delegation to Russia, led by the then Prime Minister Atal Bihari Vajpayee.

Modi had had eyes on Russia even prior to that. He was practically the first chief minister of any Indian state to grasp the potential of an agreement signed during Vladimir Putin's visit to Delhi in October 2000. He was especially interested in Astrakhan, a small province of the Russian state with which he signed a protocol of cooperation. That was followed by a delegation from Astrakhan that visited Gujarat in 2003.

There was a special reason for Modi's interest in Astrakhan. Some two centuries ago, enterprising traders from Gujarat had established a major commercial presence in the Astrakhan region – Russia's gateway to the Caspian –with its vast oil wealth and stocks of sturgeon. Not only did they establish their trading presence but many of the Gujarati merchants who went to that state stayed put, married local women and made it their home! Modi thought it was worthwhile to renew an old relationship.

Modi visited Astrakhan again when he went to Russia along with a 16-member business delegation in July 2006. He signed another protocol of cooperation with the Astrakhan province Governor Alexander Zhilkin that was to end in November 2011.

According to the protocol, Gujarat and Astrakhan were to cooperate in five key areas: hydrocarbon research and development, ship-building and ship-breaking, revising the trade route called the North-South International Cargo Container Transport Corridor between Okha port in Gujarat and Olya port in Astrakhan through the Iranian rail-sea-road network, distance learning in university education, and a tourism package incorporating Astrakhan's participation in the *Navratri* and Vibrant Gujarat festivals.

The delegation from Gujarat discussed with its Astrakhan counterpart the issue of using the corridor as the shortest land route between India and Russia and East Europe as well.

In November 2011, a nine-member delegation from Astrakhan led by Konstantin Markelov, Vice Governor of the state, came on a four-day visit to Gujarat. The delegation met Minister of State for Industries, Power and Energy, Saurabh Patel, as also A K Joti, Chief Secretary of Gujarat Government. After his meeting with the Astrakhan delegation, Patel said that during his discussion, many points on increasing tie-ups between Gujarat and Astrakhan came up, with the focus being on oil exploration activities in Astrakhan, ship building, agriculture and education.

Modi visited Russia again in October 2009 and used that occasion to invite the Russian telecom giant SIS TEMA to set up a Sim card and microchip manufacturing unit in Gujarat.

During his three-day visit, Modi addressed the 4th International Energy Week Conference in Moscow. Recalling that during 1964-67, Russia had conducted extensive exploration for oil in the Bay of Khambhat, Modi invited Russian oil and gas companies to invest in Gujarat once again. He told the delegates at the conference that in 2001, Gujarat had evolved a strategy for exploration in hydrocarbons. As a result, he said, Gujarat had become the petro-capital of India within a decade.

To emphasize Gujarat's standing, Modi further told the assembled delegates that his state had entered into tie-ups for technical cooperation with the world's best gas, petroleum and energy companies. Later, Modi held one-to-one meetings with CEOs and senior executives of leading oil and gas companies during which their officials apparently showed considerable interest in forging partnerships with Gujarat-based companies.

Interestingly, Modi also made a power point presentation titled 'Advantage Gujarat' in Russian, which was greatly appreciated. Chief Secretary Joti later told the media: 'A leading energy company Gazprom has shown willingness to partner with the Gujarat government-owned GSPC in joint exploration and production of oil and gas in India.'

Visits to China

Modi had made more than one visit to China in the past but his visit to the state in November 2011 really made history.

The Man of the Moment: Narendra Modi

Reference was made to it by Venky Vembu writing for The *Economist* (14 September 2011). If one asked any BJP leader about whom the party might project as its Prime Ministerial candidate, he said, one would likely be subjected to 'incoherent waffling that indicates great uncertainty'. As he saw it, media analysts given to reading the party leaves generally focussed disproportionately on Arun Jaitley and Sushma Swaraj as being the moderate faces of the party with the best chances of carrying the party forward. If Narendra Modi's name came up as a potential candidate, according to the writer, it was 'only in hushed and defensive tones,' since even the BJP reasoned that it was still paying the political price of the 2002 riots.

However, he thought, in faraway China, where electoral politics was practised as raucously as in India, Communist Party leaders and policy makers might have read their own tea leaves and come to two conclusions on the Indian polity. To quote him:

> *The first, given the changing political dynamics in India, the BJP stands a reasonable chance of coming to power in 2014. Second, in the event of the BJP coming to power, Narendra Modi's chance of becoming Prime Minister is considered better than headlines indicate.*

As he saw the situation, Chinese policymakers, pragmatic and far-sighted, may also have been betting that – as had happened under A B Vajpayee's Prime Ministership – Sino-Indian relations may actually go beyond the day-to-day paranoid scare-mongering that characterized bilateral relations currently. As Vembu surmised, it was perhaps in that context that they found Narendra Modi a man that China could do business with.

Noted was the fact that in mid-August 2011, Chinese Ambassador to India, Zhang Yen, had reached out to Modi and expressed China's interest in working together with Gujarat to sharpen the latter's industrial and manufacturing edge, which had driven it to the top of the charts of Indian states ranked on industrialization. Zhang had also invited Modi to visit China, an invitation that the Gujarat Chief Minister had accepted.

As Vembu put it:

> *The Chinese invitation to Modi is an astute political move and sends a very strong political signal, particularly in the context of the fact*

> that Modi was in 2005 controversially denied a visa to travel to the US for his role in the 2002 riots on the strength of lobbying by Human Rights activists in the US. By rolling out the red carpet for Modi, in contrast to the US visa snub, Chinese officials are making a calculated investment in the future, which they know will be well received by a leader who prides himself as an embodiment of Gujarati 'asmita' (self-respect).

He added:

And unlike US diplomats who said they were sending Modi 'a clear message regarding the US government's concerns for the state of human rights and religious freedom in Gujarat, the Chinese are open to doing business with him without offering lectures on human rights. Some of this springs from China's place in the world. As a country that is at the receiving end of a lot of unwelcome advice from the US and others about its human rights record, China makes a virtue of its 'non-interference' in the internal affairs of other countries.

On occasion, of course, this has manifested in China's mollycoddling of dictators around the world – from North Korea to Myanmar, Sudan and Zimbabwe. But since no major world power can today claim the moral high ground on that count, China has robustly pressed ahead with its single-minded pursuit of its strategic interests, unmindful of criticism.

China certainly treated Modi with great respect. As Zee News reported (9 November 2001), the Chinese Government accorded a 'red carpet welcome' to Modi on his five-day official visit to the country. Reported Zee News: 'Indications have come from Beijing that the Chinese Government is viewing Modi as India's future Prime Minister, despite his image as a hardline *Hindutva* leader. What seems to have helped the Chinese form an opinion is the projection of Modi as the future leader of India by several top Indian industrialists.' Zee News further stated, 'The positive US congressional report about the state of governance in Modi's Gujarat and its assertion that the state has become a key driver of India's growth also played a role.'

Actually, Modi is not the first Indian Chief Minister of any Indian state to visit China. He is the third, after Karnataka's former

The Man of the Moment: Narendra Modi

Chief Minister B S Yeddyurappa and Madhya Pradesh's Shivraj Singh Chouhan.

The *Times of India's* tabloid edition published a short piece comparing Narendra Modi with the last ruler of the Jin dynasty of China, known as Modi of Jin. Emperor Modi of Jin reportedly ruled for less than a day before being killed by Mongolians and was the shortest serving monarch in Chinese history.

The first important event Modi attended was a meeting organized by the Embassy of India along with the China Chamber of Commerce for Import and Export of Machinery and Electronic Products (CCEME). Addressing the meeting, Modi made a strong pitch for Chinese investments, asserting that his state, which he called the 'growth engine' of India, offered the best infrastructure that, in turn, predicted excellent returns for foreign investments.

'China and its people have a special place in my heart and I admire their hard-working, disciplined and resilient nature, and above all, their sense of history. Our cultural bonds are very strong and deep rooted. Over the years, our relations have further strengthened. We are committed to making them still better, fruitful and productive,' said Modi.

'I have seen,' Modi continued, 'growing interest among Chinese companies to work in Gujarat. We wholeheartedly welcome them. My personal visit is to reinforce that process.' Modi said he had plans to open a Mandarin school to promote learning of the Chinese language in Gujarat. As he put it: 'To give a big boost to the economic interaction, we must emphasize on cultural exchange. You may be happy to know that Gujarat has already emerged as a great tourist destination in the Asian region.'

About 80 Chinese companies took part in the meeting titled 'Business and Investment Opportunities in the State of Gujarat'. Coinciding with Modi's visit, official figures released said that Chinese investments abroad had gone up by 67.8 billion dollars in 2011, registering a 21.7 per cent increase compared to 2009. Li Jiping, Vice President of China Development Bank, was quoted as saying that China currently was the 5th largest foreign investor in the world.

Meeting with CPC Politburo Members

On 9 November 2011, Modi was received at the Great Hall of China in Beijing by His Excellency Mr Wang Gang. (To be received at the Great Hall, incidentally, is considered a great honour.) Present at the meeting was the Indian Ambassador, Dr Jaishankar, and, of course, senior officials of the Communist Party of China (CPC).

Addressing the distinguished audience, Modi said that he was delighted to be in Beijing and it was always a great pleasure to visit China. He thanked the CPC for extending an invitation to him and his colleagues to visit China and said that over the years, he had witnessed 'the expanding ties between the two great countries. I thank the people of China and CPC for their warmth, hospitality and excellent arrangements' he said.

He went on to say that India and China, two young Asian countries, were home to 2.5 billion of the world's humanity. Both, he said, were ancient civilizations. Their history was replete with the experiences of statesmen, scholars, historians, monks, pilgrims, traders and travellers of each country visiting the other. The exchanges of great ideas by these men and women during their visits had not only enriched their societies, but had benefitted the whole of mankind. Those exchanges had been a source of strength to Sino-Indian relations. It was therefore befitting, said Modi, that the year 2011 was declared as the Year of India-China Exchange.

Modi pointed out that both India and China were pulling out the world's economy from recession. Both were engaged in the task of socio-economic transformation and betterment of their people's lives. Indeed, he continued, the Peoples' Republic of China had shown to the world how the building process of a country could be fast-tracked.

In the same manner, said Modi, India was also on the path of faster inclusive growth with a model of sustainable development. 'We have a lot to learn from each other's experiences,' he opined. Claiming that within India, Gujarat represented a model of faster, modernized and organized growth, Modi said his state was considered to be the 'Growth Engine of India', something like 'Gungdong' of China. Gujarat's population of 60 million constituted only 5 per cent of India's population but contributed to 16 per cent of India's industrial output and 22 per cent of its exports.

Continuing, Modi said that for the past one decade, Gujarat had witnessed double-digit growth and the state was recognized as the 'prime manufacturing hub of India'. He added: Our state provides a highly conducive environment for foreign professionals and investments. With this strength, we are aiming at becoming a global hub of economic activities.' He pointed out that just three days prior to his visit, an MoU had been signed with TBEA (Thermal Balloon Endometrical Ablation) to develop a Green Energy Park in Gujarat with an investment of 400 million dollars. That was an example of how Gujarat offered excellent opportunities for doing business.

Then he made a personal request. He wanted to make a representation pertaining to 22 Indian nationals languishing in Chinese jails since 2010. He said they all belonged to Gujarat. 'May I request you to kindly take up this issue with the concerned authorities for an early solution to the matter? This will go a long way in creating a more favourable atmosphere for China in India,' he added. The Chinese Government released the Gujarati prisoners who had been held for smuggling.

But economic and industrial development was not the sole subject that Modi involved himself in during his visit to China. To start with, he had his visiting card made in red, with the text in Mandarin. His video presentation of Gujarat was also in Chinese. So impressed were the Chinese that one of them – according to media reports – was heard saying that Modi could be the Deng Xiaoping of China! In his discussion with Wang, Modi did not hesitate to point out the disquiet in India at the Chinese activities in Pakistan-occupied Kashmir, telling Wang that the perception in India was that Pakistan was using China against India. Modi warned his hosts that playing to the tune of Islamabad would damage all ties with India, including the lucrative business deals that Chinese companies in infrastructure, telecom and energy were seeking to conclude. Modi also brought to the attention of Wang that the Governor of Xinjiang had committed an impropriety by saying that 'in our country, show our maps, not yours', with reference to the diplomatic *faux pas* made by him when his maps showed the Indian state of Arunachal Pradesh and the territory of Aksai Chin as part of China. According to a diplomat who was present on such occasions, Modi's hosts were polite in their silence over such unusually frank criticism. However, the diplomat later remarked: 'What seems clear is that his Chinese hosts have seen in Modi a possible future where India becomes the equal of China, and not a resentful pygmy always griping about Big Brother.'

There were other things that Modi did during his 5-day visit. For example, he visited Yangshan, a deep-water port near Shanghai and decided that the Dholera Special Investment Region (SIR) in Gujarat would be patterned on the Shanghai model.

In Shanghai itself he met close to a dozen Chinese industry leaders and some Indian families settled in the city. On 12 November, he and his delegation went to Yingxiu city of Sichuan province and obtained an overview of low-cost, earthquake-resistant housing projects. Additionally, he had a delegation-level meeting with the Mayor of Beijing, Guo Jinlong, and invited him and his key officials to visit Gujarat and its cities. He also had an interesting interaction with Indian students in China.

Some specific projects and proposals were also discussed with the appropriate agencies, such as flight connectivity between Chengdu and Bengaluru via Ahmedabad, potential and scope for building a high-speed train, value addition in agro-forestry and mass housing.

Also discussed was the scope for linking the Shanghai Institute for Contemporary Development Studies for International Enterprises with a university in Gujarat. China agreed to send a 20-member Sporting Goods Federation Team to Gujarat to give its expert advice on the manufacture of sports equipment. A senior official was quoted as saying: 'On the whole, Modi's visit was an unprecedented success.'

On the fifth and final day of his visit to China, Modi addressed over 200 leading industrialists of China's Sichuan province. On that day, the India-China Economic & Cultural Council (ICEC) and the Panzhichua Guanghua Group (PGG) signed an MoU to develop trade ties between Gujarat and Sichuan.

Addressing the Gujarat-Sichuan Business Forum, organized by India's Consul General in China and the provincial Government, Modi called upon Chinese industrialists to invest in Gujarat, saying that it was the best destination for industrial investments. The ICEC corroborated that it was the best destination for industrial investments. The ICEC announced that it would open an office in Chengdu, which would work for promoting trade, investment and cultural exchange between Gujarat and Sichuan.

Modi addressed a business meet in Chengdu, at which the Consul General of India, Mr Pandey, was present.

Pointing out that he was on the last leg of his 5-day stay in China, Modi said he experienced 'the warmth and hospitality of the Chinese government and its people'. He said, 'The cycle of history has destined China and India to play a major role in the economics and politics of the world. Our real strength is in our people, particularly the younger generation. Though ancient civilizations, we are both young nations. With the strength of our people, India and China are both ascending to their well-deserved glory.'

He said:

'We are monopoly producers and suppliers for several goods in the country. In many others, we are the leading suppliers. Several products of Gujarat, including polished diamonds and towels are flooding the world markets. We have some of the world's largest manufacturing and processing facilities like Reliance Petroleum Refining. We house some of the leading global industries like General Motors and Bombardier. With the recent addition of several world-class car manufacturers, we have emerged as a leading automobile hub. We are already a global player in the steel, pipe and pharmaceutical industries. Now we are emerging as a global player in the cement industry also.'

As Modi put it, in the age of globalization, it was no longer the raw materials that attracted people and projects. The more important factors were transaction costs, which depended upon the environment of business, the ease of business and the spirit of business. In addition, the quality of governance, including the stability of governments and transparency in their policies, mattered a lot. 'I am proud to say that Gujarat offers you the best on these fronts. But we want to do still better. And we also know that with our strong fundamentals, we can do much better,' Modi said.

He added:

'Gujarat is an amazing model of the effective co-existence of the big and the small; robust and inclusive; fast and yet sustainable. It has done wonderfully well at both the macro and micro indicators. Not only have the multinationals and big companies done well, but a large number of medium, small, rural and domestic ventures have also prospered ... Gujarat's multifaceted growth and excellence in various sectors have been recognized not only in the country but in the entire world. Our efforts in good governance have been applauded the world over. We have received over 200 national and international awards in the last ten years. They are in recognition of excellence in various fields.'

Modi in Japan

As far as India was concerned, Japan was the farthest country in the east and not many state visitors, especially state chief ministers, made it to Tokyo during their respective terms in office.

But 2007 turned out to be different. Many chief ministers, including Modi, were invitees and Modi used that opportunity to keep his eyes and ears open. For example, when he was at Tokyo Big Sight (the city's largest convention centre), he spent a good part of his time studying its design. When he visited the oldest temple in Tokyo, he wanted a map of the entire area, so that he could develop Bhadrakali and Bhadra in Gujarat along similar lines. When he addressed the Indian community in both Tokyo and Kobe, the point he made was that whatever he found the best anywhere in the world, he would like to see it duplicated in Gujarat. His aim was excellence. When he was given a special tour of the Shinkansen bullet train (an honour normally reserved only for railway ministers), he was intrigued and curious about building such high speed rails and tunnels in that terrain.

Modi's visit was followed up by a visit to Gujarat by close to 120 Japanese investors on 18 January 2012. While they were expecting him to hard sell the state, they were in deep surprise when he addressed them as valued guests and family members! He showcased to them how Gujarat was handling the two essentials of industry – water and power – and his presentation left them elated.

On 22 March 2012, he received the Japanese Ambassador to India, His Excellency Saiki, along with the heads of two large Japanese and one Singaporean company. The day was World Water Day and Modi had chosen that day to announce the Dahej Desalination Plant that would be planned and set up by a global consortium of Hitachi, Itochu and Hyflux. Listening to him, the Japanese business heads were impressed with Modi's understanding of technical details.

Inevitably, Modi was officially invited to re-visit Japan, which he did – this time with a 25-member delegation. His visit was a 4-day one, beginning on 23 July 2012. On the very first day, Modi addressed an Investment Seminar held by the Japan External Trade Organization (JETRO). Thanking the Japanese Government for its pro-active engagement and cooperation with the state of Gujarat, Modi particularly thanked JETRO for having made his visit possible.

Pointing out that Gujarat had completed the first phase of development in terms of providing basic amenities like water, electricity, road connectivity and civil services, Modi told his audience that his state was in the second phase of development, with emphasis being given to the development of excellent ports at suitable maritime locations.

Modi informed the gathering that Gujarat had the least unemployment in India. There was complete cooperation between the industry and the workforce. There was no loss in man-days. A successful attempt was being made to create an engineering and technical force. The intake capacity of engineering and other training institutes had increased five-fold in ten years.

Modi affirmed that after 2007 (and his first visit to Japan), mutual exchanges between Japan and Gujarat had become a regular affair. It almost appeared, he said, that Gujarat had become the second home of the Japanese people! (This comment brought forth smiles from the otherwise reserved Japanese!) Modi reminded his audience of top executives that Japan and India had deep cultural and historic bonds, with Buddhism being a binding force between them. Referring to how Swami Vivekananda and Rabindranath Tagore had helped to reinforce a mutual understanding between India and Japan in the past, Modi said both countries also had a common administrative culture. Both believed in a liberal society and democratic governance.

He said:

'I have been saying that the present century belongs to Asia. Japan has shown what can be achieved by dedication, precision and hard work. I have always admired Japan for its perseverance and industriousness. For Asia to be the global hub of the 21st century, Japan and India are both going to play major roles. If the strength of the intelligent process of Japan can be matched with the strength of the intelligent and young people of India, we can do wonders.'

Modi also said that if Japan had the strength of experience, Gujarat had the power of enterprise. Japan had technology and Gujarat had the talent to absorb it. Japan possessed the keenness of discipline; Gujarat had the zeal for perfection. 'If the two sides can meet, we can create not only a great future for ourselves, but for the whole world community. Our strengths are complimentary.'

Later Modi met press reporters from ANI News, Reuters and other newspapers, and YouTube. In the course of that meeting, he made the following points:

- Criticism is the beauty of democracy. We must respect critics. If there is no criticism, democracy cannot work. I always appreciate criticism.
- But we must understand the difference between criticism and allegations. Criticism is most welcome. We need a vibrant and critical media.
- Japan and India share the same values; we must strengthen them.
- People across India are discussing the Gujarat growth story.
- My primary responsibility is to Gujarat; people have an expectation and I am bound to deliver that.
- Gujarat is a policy-driven state; we don't run the government on an ad-hoc basis. We think long term.

Political stability and a stable policy environment add to the confidence of investors, businesses and students.
- There is a sense of ownership and pride in Gujarat; everyone feels part of the success story.
- How can you come to the conclusion that I am against any religion? Do you have any single sentence that I have uttered against any group, religion or religious book?
- I belong to a culture where the whole world is one family. How can we hate any community or individual?
- I belong to Bharat where we have the great tradition of respecting multiple schools of thought.
- In 2012, Gujarat goes to election. My priority is to win the Gujarat election. I am hopeful the people of Gujarat will elect us again.
- I am confident that the BJP-led NDA will come to power. The country remembers the rule of the NDA under Atal Bihari Vajpayee. Inflation was under control, infrastructure growth was fast. People remember the speed with which roads were built.
- People are no longer interested in 'promises'; they now need performance. This is the contribution of the Gujarat story.

In addition to attending the JETRO seminar, Modi had a hectic day calling on many people of eminence. He met Yukio Edano, the Minister for Trade and Industry. During the interaction, Modi presented Mr Edano with a copy of his book *Convenient Action*. Modi also met former Prime Minister of Japan Shinzo Abe. He had met Mr Abe during his 2007 visit. Another dignitary he called on was Mr Koichiro Gemba, Japan's Minister for Foreign Affairs. He also met Yuichiro Hata, Minister for Land, Infrastructure, Transport and Tourism.

On the second day of his visit, Modi interacted with members of the India Centre Foundation in Tokyo which had been set up in 1996. In his short speech, he said that what he most admired about the Japanese people was their eye for detail before taking any decision. It was after gauging every likely impact that the

Japanese took a decision. He invited all the members present for the 2013 Vibrant Gujarat Summit in which he expected 100 nations to participate.

The first Indian Chief Minister to be invited to Japan, Modi captured the hearts of his listeners. Japan's largest-selling business daily set the tone of the visit. In a 742-word article, it described Modi's visit as 'path-breaking and unprecedented'. Describing Modi as one of the strongest contenders to be the Prime Minister in 2014, the article dwelt on Modi's ability to propel his state as 'investor-friendly' in an otherwise 'investor unfriendly India'. The paper said that Japan had given Modi a 'Cabinet-rank welcome' reserved for cabinet ministers only.

Work kept Modi meaningfully busy throughout his stay in Japan. On his fourth day, for example, he travelled by a bullet train from Hamamatsu to Nagoya, and from there he took another train to Osaka to attend a round-table conference organized by the Mizuho Corporation Bank. After that, he left by road to Kobe to attend a reception given by the Indian community. He told the conference that he was immensely lucky to have been able to attend 44 functions in five provinces, meet seven ministers and over 2,000 key personnel during his four-day stay in their country.

In the two-hour conference organized by the Mizuho Corporation Bank, Modi held one-to-one meetings with some of Japan's top industrial and banking executives. Modi told them about Gujarat's new vibrant textile policy and of the Textile Park Policy which was based on five 'Fs' – Farm, Fibre, Fabric, Fashion and Foreign.

He also met a delegation of Japan's renowned carmaker, Toyota. Toyota's Adviser, Dato Akira Okabe and General Manager Makota Sasagura gave Modi details of the company's operational plant in India and its future expansion plans.

The list of top people that Modi met is mind boggling. It included ministers, vice ministers, ex-prime ministers, parliamentarians, governors of provinces, chairmen of various bodies, members of the chambers of commerce and industry, diplomats and a whole lot of others. According to official sources, Modi met more than 2,000 companies varying from medium to Fortune 500 companies. Again, according to official sources, 'at every place and forum and at every meeting and reception, the response was unimaginable,' showing 'the keenness of Japan to understand Gujarat as a formidable location to grow in and a lucrative location to live in'. Reportedly, representatives of industries including JETRO, JICA, JBIC, Keidanren and four province-based Chambers of Commerce expressed 'unequivocal confidence and interest to work in and with Gujarat'.

Later, Maheshwar Sahu, Principal Secretary, Government of Gujarat, was quoted as saying that the government planned to build a 600-hectare township near the proposed Maruti Suzuki India Ltd's manufacturing factory in Hansalpur, near Mehsana, at the cost of ₹80 lakh to ₹1 crore per hectare. The expectation in Gujarat's official circles was that even though there were 29 Japanese companies already functioning in the state, the number could double within two years' time. Importantly, Maruti Suzuki was expected to set up a plant to manufacture 250,000 units per annum by 2015-16. But sceptics have been heard wondering how long all this will last, considering that in no time, the world may get depleted of iron ore. As some saw the situation, nobody – neither Modi nor his Japanese supporters – seemed to have ever given any thought to this. Production was the only consideration on their minds. Even as matters stood, iron ore was getting depleted in India itself, thanks to millions of tons of ore being exported, among other places, to China. Nobody, it seems, ever raised this question when long discussions were taking place on issues such as availability of land, water and electricity.

Global Maritime Security

Even as Modi was discussing issues concerning international links with Gujarat, he was deeply aware of maritime security. Gujarat carried almost 35 per cent of India's sea cargo and had a national port and the first two world-class private ports in the country, making the state the 'principal maritime state in India'. Modi told a Global Maritime Security Anti-Piracy Conference held in Gandhinagar on 26 November 2011, that Gujarat was blessed with the longest coastline in India, about 1,600 km long. It was, Modi said, 'the nearest maritime gateway from India to the Middle East'.

The international conference was attended by a 'galaxy of experts' who were only too well aware that the vast size and 'largely unregulated nature of the waterways' had made the maritime environment 'an attractive theatre for transnational violence'. Modi noted that 'both piracy and sea-borne terrorism have become more common in the last few decades.' He added that piracy and terrorism had increased due to global proliferation of small arms.

Taking the point further, he pointed out that several terrorist groups had developed significant capability to conduct attacks at sea and had kept pace with modern navigation and communication technologies, not to speak of developing innovative ways to challenge the security and maritime forces. Modi warned that these groups 'may soon exploit the freight trading system to trigger a global economic crisis', and may also use the container supply chain to transport weapons of mass destruction.

He said: 'The rise and decline of piracy is linked, among other factors, to the development of political structures on land. There is a nexus between organized piracy, criminal networks and governance on land. Though the maritime supply chain is the most economical, at the same time it is quite vulnerable. Securing safe supply chains, therefore, presents an enormous challenge to the globalized world.'

He reiterated that the success in exploring the immense maritime potential would depend upon national commitment and responses. But, he added, this could not happen to an optimal extent 'without international commitment and unanimity for safety and security'. Therefore, he said, 'for this purpose, a sound international legal framework and a comprehensive policy regime are essential. The legal framework necessarily has to balance the needs, concerns and interests of all stakeholder countries, whether coastal or landlocked.'

Modi was keen to impress why India was so anxious to fight piracy and other criminal networks. He told his listeners that not only did India hold a central position in the Indian Ocean System, it also had an extensive range of interests in the coastal and maritime activities in Asia-Pacific. These interests involved smooth and freer navigation, protection of strategic and security interests, and free mobility of its fishing boats and naval ships. He shared that India was also producing millions of tons of crude from its sea-bound oil fields.

In his view, the real answer to maritime safety involved three more aspects. The first one was 'people's development'; the second was their skills and the third, technology. 'We have to work on the people first. We have to enhance the economic well-being of the coastal population,' he added.

Asserting that Gujarat was serious about tackling the problem and not just indulging in talk, Modi said that to strengthen its security apparatus along its coastline, Gujarat had decided to create a maritime commando unit, recruit 600 personnel for it, in addition to setting up a dozen coastal police stations. In conclusion he said: 'We in Gujarat are quite committed. A significant step has been taken to set up a state-of-the-art Vessel Traffic and Management System (VTMS) in the Gulf of Khambhat. The radar-based system will track the movement of each vessel on the high seas along Gujarat's coasts. This will not only ensure safe navigation of hazardous cargo, but also help in detecting any untoward activity or intrusions in Gujarat's waters. The system was put into operation in the Gulf of Khambhat in August 2010. A similar system is under implementation at the Gulf of Kutch.'

The address was well received. Appreciated was the fact that Gujarat meant business and in its own way, was contributing to maritime security in international waters.

Spreading Sadbhavana

On 12 September 2011, the Supreme Court delivered an important judgement regarding the 2002 communal riots in Gujarat. It must have come as a shock to Modi-haters as it gave a clean chit to him.

For the past ten years, Modi and his Government had been subject to denigration by a host of people who called themselves secularists. It had become fashionable to defame both Modi and his government. The focus seemed to be on condemning Modi without acknowledging any of the positive developments that had taken place in Gujarat since that time. The Supreme Court judgement – unprejudiced and apolitical as it was – was the ultimate endorsement of Modi's efforts to quell the damage wrought by the riots. It told those defaming Modi where they had been wrong. After 2002, Gujarat had not spared any effort to march towards peace, harmony and progress, even amidst false propaganda, lies, conspiracies and allegations. 'Six crore Gujaratis' had not remained merely a phrase: they had become the mantra of unity and human endeavour. Gujarat had experienced an unparalleled phase of peace. Modi was anxious to strengthen it and to carry it forward to greater heights. In a statement he had said:

> There is a famous saying: 'Hate is never conquered by hate.' The real strength of our country is its unity and harmony. Unity in diversity is the defining feature of India. It is our responsibility to strengthen unity in our social life. We have got an excellent opportunity to proceed with a positive attitude. Hence, let us come together and contribute to enhancing the dignity of Gujarat. I humbly submit before you that, as part of this responsibility to strengthen social harmony and brotherhood, I am thinking of starting a movement of *Sadbhavana*. As a part of this *Sadbhavana* Mission, I have resolved to fast for three days from Saturday, 17 September 2011. My fast will conclude on 19 September. I deeply believe that this fast will further strengthen Gujarat's environment of peace, unity and harmony.

Modi said that the Mission was completely dedicated to the society and to the nation, to take Gujarat to new heights of development.

Sadbhavana Mission

On 17 September 2011, when Modi began his fast, numerous BJP leaders like L K Advani, Arun Jaitley and Sushma Swaraj were present on the occasion. Regular Modi-haters like Mallika Sarabhai who, along with some 25 activists, had to be detained as they protested against the fast. While starting his fast, Modi expressed the hope that it would contribute towards 'peace and communal harmony' and also bring to an end what he called 'vote bank politics'. He clarified that the fast was not against anybody. 'We want to take this spirit to each and every village, each and every house. I don't want to speak about anybody. Gujarat wants to move forward. We want to be in the service of India,' he said.

Addressing a gathering at the Gujarat University Convention Centre, the venue of the fast, Modi said: 'We want to move forward and *Sadbhavana* will be our strength. Development is our only motto. We will be a model for the world on how development can be achieved. Unity, peace and harmony have a major role to play in our success, our development. Because we have trod this path and I wanted this message to reach out to people, this fast was the best means to do so.' The fast itself, he said, was 'the need of the hour. If I fast, my words would carry more weight and I will be able to reach out to more people.' That, he added, was the only objective behind the fast and there was no grudge against anybody, as he put it: 'Over the last ten years, we have been vilified. I have faced every attack so that you (people) do not feel the pain. I want to ensure that Gujarat never slips below the parametres of humanity. May God give me strength not to have any bitterness or vengeance ever for any one.'

Several people from across the state came to the fast venue to support Modi's mission. Many carried banners proclaiming their support. On the final day, Sushma Swaraj praised Modi for having undertaken a peace mission. She said: 'When we hear praises of Gujarat in NTC meetings or in other countries, our heads stand up in pride. When I went to Israel to study drip irrigation, I was

Spreading Sadbhavana

told to go back to Gujarat to do so.' She added: 'No development policy in Gujarat is made with the aim of serving a Hindu or a Muslim. When 108 Ambulance gets an emergency call, it does not ask whether the caller is a Muslim or a Hindu.' Sushma Swaraj said she was a 'big fan' of Modi's one quality – to carry on irrespective of criticism. She said: 'Modi does not govern from AC rooms but he is out there amongst his people in the sun and dust.'

The fast ended on 19 September 2011, but the *Sadbhavana* Mission had just begun. The fast made many important people sit up and take notice of it. Addressing the friends who had gathered around him and hundreds sitting in front, Modi explained why he had undertaken the fast. He had seen the suffering of people and he wanted to do something about it. Above *rajneeti* (politics), there was something called *rashtraneeti* (governance). 'This fast, this mission,' maintained Modi, 'is inspired by *rashtraneeti* and not *rajneeti*'.

Modi said the 'root cause of all problems' in India stemmed from the fact that Indians had stopped dreaming big. If there were no dreams, Modi wondered, what was there to achieve? It was easy to run a government routinely. But the first thing was to integrate Gujarat's six crore Gujaratis. He had attempted that. Modi recounted how a few years earlier when he was being questioned by the Justice Sachar Committee, he had been asked what he was doing for the minorities in the state. He had shocked the Committee by saying that his government was not working for the minorities. But then he said, it was not working for the majority either! What his government was setting out to do was to look out for the welfare of all six crore Gujaratis! The well-being of all, development of all, was his government's motto.

Modi maintained that his government had attempted to completely overhaul the agricultural, educational and other sectors. In a major report, the World Bank had called for not only India but the entire world to look upon Gujarat as a model state. 'Had we only thought in narrow political terms, none of this would have happened,' recalled Modi.

Modi claimed that he had introduced 'participative governance'. Even the Planning Commission wanted to know how that had been put into action. It was that which had won the people's trust, said Modi. 'Our motto of *"sabka sath, sabka vikas"* (The support of

The Man of the Moment: Narendra Modi

everyone leads to progress for everyone) is not mere sloganeering but what we have practised religiously for ten years. This is what the *Sadbhavana* Mission is all about.' Modi stated confidently that this belief was uniting people. He also proclaimed that he sought to be a 'game-changer' and he wanted everyone in Gujarat's 18,000 villages to be game-changers. Then he made a big announcement. He said that at the end of his fast, he would start going to each district in the state where he planned to sit among the people, listen to them and boost their energy.

Modi carried out his intention diligently. The people were thrilled. Modi had strong views. Wherever he spoke, he emphasized that his aim was to sound the death knell of vote bank politics, which, he said, would break the nation. 'If we have to save the nation, the nation has to be united,' he argued. In a speech he delivered during his visit to a district on 4 January 2012, Modi was totally frank. He said that when he called for 100 per cent of all girls to attend school, he meant 'all'. There was no question of discrimination. He was also opposed to reservations on the basis of religion. Participation was by all. Development was for all. To show that he was sincere about what he preached, he had started schools with science stream in every district, increasing the availability of seats from 13,000 to 90,000!

A fortnight later, Modi addressed a meeting in Godhra – and he spoke in Hindi. The *Indian Express* (20 January 2012) reported that the Muslim presence was 'low', though a couple of priests from Muslim communities like the Ghachis and Bohars were sitting on the stage beside Modi. Even before he could address the audience, a social activist, Shabnam Hashmi, and five others had to be detained by the police and a former BJP leader, Nalin Bhatt too, as he planned to take out a rally in Godhra against Modi.

Interestingly, even as everyone was being seated, the Chief Postmaster of Vadodara region, Lt Col K S Chouhan walked up to the stage and presented him with a cover on the facsimile of which was the emblem of the *Sadbhavana* Mission. In his speech that followed, Modi held up the 'souvenir' brought out by the Central Government department and said: 'The Indian postal department has released a cover on *Sadbhavana* Mission. I don't know what fate awaits these officers!'

Modi spoke extensively at the meeting, covering many subjects like vote bank politics, water supply to people, the political culture of divide and rule, conflicts between castes, killing and shedding blood, class animosity and maintenance of peace. He gave instances of communalism and what that did to society. Godhra was one example. Modi cited the example of how in 1985, there had been a curfew in Godhra for 300 days, even though it was enforced only at night. But riots were the order of the day then. (The point to be noted is that Modi was nowhere on the political scene then!)

Modi ended his *Sadbhavana* Mission – and a series of fasts – in February 2012 at the temple town of Ambaji. In his usual address to a gathering, Modi reminded it that he had started his *Sadbhavana* Mission fasts after touching the feet of his mother in 2011. He was now ending them at the feet of the divine mother, Ambaji. He recounted how thousands of people had come to hear him. Some had walked as much as 25 to 30 km! In Mangarh, his tribal brothers had trekked for five days! Many people, he said, had voluntarily arranged special feasts for approximately 45 lakh children during his *Sadbhavana* Mission period. People had given him donations worth more than ₹4 crore for 'girl child education' and approximately 17,000 *prabhat feris* (early morning processions) had been undertaken in villages to spread the message of *Sadbhavana*.

In the past, said Modi, political instability had become a normal phenomenon. In Gujarat too, chief ministers did not last for more than two to two and a half years. 'But today, even in my eleventh year, I am bestowed with your love.' Then he went on: 'This political stability, stable policies, pace of development, new marks of progress – these are the things that compel the world to accept the excellence of Gujarat. We want to take it further. Let us make our villages and *talukas* free from even the slightest differences and disputes. 'Development,' said Modi, 'is the solution to all our problems, cure for all disease and has the ability to face all crises.' And to make that possible, he added emotionally, he was offering ₹1,700 crore at the feet of the soil of Banaskantha for widening roads, taking on canal works to make drinking water available to the people, building gas pipelines, hospitals, and other facilities.

Vivekananda Yuva Vikas Yatra

State elections were due and with the upcoming polls in mind, Modi decided that he would kick start his Vivekananda *Yuva Vikas* Yatra beginning 11 September 2011 and it would end in a month's time. During that one month, he hoped to travel 625 km in the state.

The *Sadbhavana* Yatra had ended on 12 February and had made a tremendous impact. Modi felt that a yatra named after Swami Vivekananda would also draw wide interest. The date 11 September was significant. It was on that day in 1893 that Vivekananda had given his celebrated speech at the Chicago Parliament of World Religious, addressing his audience as 'Sisters and Brothers of America', and causing 7,000 people to stand up and give him a 5-minute long ovation, the like of which had never been seen before at that platform.

In its frustration to face the fact that Modi's popularity was increasing by leaps and bounds, the Congress party's General Secretary, Digvijay Singh, suggested that the yatra should be named after Hitler. In the past too, Digvijay Singh had made some objectionable statements but Modi had ignored them. Ahead of the Gujarat polls, the Congress had already planned four major yatras in Gujarat, whereas the Vivekananda Yatra was Modi's first planned yatra. It started from Becharaji temple town of north Gujarat in the presence of former BJP President Rajnath Singh and Rajya Sabha Opposition leader Arun Jaitley. As the proposed yatra was to celebrate Vivekananda's 150th birth anniversary, the BJP proposed to take out 150 small yatras in the state to cover all *taluka* centres and villages. The BJP's hi-tech chariot was used in the yatra. Like Digvijay Singh, another politician who disparaged Modi's yatra was former Gujarat Chief Minister Keshubhai Patel who tagged Modi as a 'crime manager' in his blog. Modi was used to this kind of hate-mongering. As he began his yatra, Modi said: 'Let us remember 9/11 as the day of universal peace and brotherhood and work towards furthering Swami Vivekananda's dream of a strong and glorious India.'

Modi's yatra entered Kadi in Mehsana district on the evening of 11 September to a warm welcome from the people, for which he

Spreading Sadbhavana

expressed his deep gratitude. Taking note of the abuse heaped upon him by the Congress, Modi commented (tongue-in-cheek) that the Congress had opened a factory for manufacturing lies, but that had not disturbed the vision of the people. While Gujarat was celebrating a 'Decade of Development', Congress was celebrating a 'Decade of Lies'! He expressed his faith that 'today or tomorrow, the dream of Swami Vivekananda to see India at the pedestal of world leadership would come true.' He iterated that he shared the Swami's immense faith in youth.

Modi affirmed that the only way to go ahead was development, but ironically, the country was in the hands of people from whom there was no hope. Referring to the spurt of Congress advertisements, Modi wondered metaphorically how a car without an engine or a driver could think of showing any *disha* (direction). The *disha* of the Congress, he maintained, was that of communal and caste politics, corruption and dynastic politics. He remarked that no one had ever heard of coal being stolen but the Centre had not even spared that and looted the nation to the tune of ₹2 lakh crore.

Referring to the injustice meted out to Gujarat, Modi said that while his state gave ₹60,000 crore to Delhi, in turn the state got only ₹6,000 crore back. September 17 happened to be Modi's birthday and he was then in Rajkot where he got a right royal welcome, surmounted with good wishes. At a gathering, he felicitated Olympic medal winner Gagan Narang and cricketers Ravindra Jadeja and Cheteshwar Pujara. Many youngsters received sports kits. Modi announced the setting up of a sports university and a sports school in every district.

Interestingly, Modi asked his well-wishers to read out the letters of appreciation he had received from two legal luminaries, Jusitce Krishna Iyer and former head of CVC (Central Vigilance Commission), N Vittal. Justice Iyer had written two letters to Modi. The first one said:

Dear Narendra Modi,

I have received your letter. I hold you as a great man, a creative administrator and a humanist wonder. ... How I wish Indian political leadership had the same inventive or, at least, innovative march with one vision: to wipe every tear from every eye. Our poverty in the field of energy is a thing of the past, provided solar power and wind power are utilized. I pray for your leadership for Indian welfare. May that day dawn and Gandhiji stand fulfilled in his vision. Dear Modi, politics apart, I will be with you for the happiness of the little Indian.

The second letter was even more flattering. Said Justice Iyer:

Dear Narendra Modi,

After glancing through the material you had sent through courier, I hold you as a part of the Indian history in its modern development odyssey. You are a super patriot and your stature is beyond any particular party. Do continue the national mission you have undertaken. Indian history of the 20th century will not be complete without an excellent reference to the majestic contribution you have made in the field of Indian Energy Unlimited.

Shri N Vittal, former head of the CVC wrote:

Respected and Dear Chief Minister Hon Shri Narendra Modi, I enclose herewith my latest book *Ending Corruption: How to Clean Up India* published by Penguin Books, India. You have set before our nation an excellent example of what can be achieved if absolute political integrity and commitment to good governance are combined in a leader. You have also shown how openness to new ideas and political courage to take even unpopular but sound decisions in the interest of development and good governance can work wonders.

Warm regards.

Some of the best audiences Modi interacted with during his Vivekananda Yatra were at Surat and Vadodara. At Surat, Modi said that when the entire country was immersed in disappointment, Gujarat with its youth power, would offer a ray of hope. He recalled what Vivekananda had said in 1897, namely, the people should forget all their deities for the next fifty years and worship only Mother India. Precisely 50 years later, said Modi, India had won her independence. The important issue was creation of jobs. Of all the jobs created in India, said Modi, 72 per cent had been created in Gujarat. Moreover, Gujarat had decided to be the guarantor for youths wishing to start their own business. In fact, in the past decade, the state government had recruited 3.5 lakh people. The age bar for government jobs had also been raised from 25 to 28 and from 28 to 30, and the government was going to build modern hostels in 62 urban centres at a cost of ₹100 crore.

When Modi made the announcement about helping youth with loans to start their business, he received a thunderous applause in Vadodara. He challenged the central government further by saying that if the Centre provided jobs for one crore youth, he would generate an equal number in Gujarat. He came down heavily on the Congress saying that it had been spreading lies and defaming Gujarat. If he had maintained silence, he said, it was because he knew that the people had immense faith in him. He reminded his audience that there used to be a time when curfew, violence, caste clashes were common occurrences in Gujarat, resulting in loss of lives. He pointedly said that such things had disappeared from Gujarat for the past ten years. Instead of blood, water was flowing in the fields now and greenery was visible in the hearts of the people too, he added.

Modi's Vivekananda Yatra concluded on 11 October 2012 at Pavgadh. He had, by then, addressed 182 assembly constituencies.

The *Sadbhavana* Yatra had ended on 12 February 2012 and Modi had undertaken his Vivekananda *Yuva Vikas* Yatra seven months later on 11 September. In between, several developments of some significance had taken place.

Former BJP stalwart Keshubhai Patel was going hammer and tongs against Modi. It was Modi who had succeeded him as chief minister and what is more, had outdone him in administration. Keshubhai just couldn't forget that. Addressing a meeting of his fellow castemen, Keshubhai said that the Patidars (Patels) were living under 'the shadow of fear.' Speaking on 13 May, Keshubhai said: 'Gujarat is ruled by *pindaris*[1] and thugs and people live under fear, including

---

[1] *Pindaris* were gangs of plunderers that emerged in the 18th Century with the breaking up of the Mughal Empire in the erstwhile Maratha region. They received protection from various Maratha chiefs and were rather violent in their plundering trips. History has a record of the *pindaris* plundering Gujarat in 1808-09.

IAS and IPS officers.' He was referring to Modi when he also said, 'Those who live in the hearts of the people don't need to force-ferry crowd to their public meeting ... Power is being used for personal publicity.' An article in *Outlook* magazine noted Keshubhai's anger and said a rising rebellion amongst the Patel community could skewer Modi's political fortunes. It didn't happen, of course, but there were genuine fears among Modi's followers.

Modi and the Media

It is doubtful whether any other political leader in the post-Independence era has been more hated, vilified, damned and detested than Narendra Modi. He has been condemned as a communalist, fascist, dictator, the one who initiated a pogrom against innocent Muslims without having the decency to apologize, and a demagogue.

Special Investigation Team

There have been enough Modi-haters in the field, wishing to hurt Modi as much as they possibly could.

A petition was filed before the Supreme Court seeking to direct the Nanavati Commission, probing the 2002 post-Godhra riots in Gujarat, to summon Chief Minister Narendra Modi for his alleged role in the riots. On 26 March 2012, the Supreme Court refused to entertain the petition.

The fact was that the Supreme Court had appointed a Special Investigation Team (SIT) to look into all the charges made against Modi. The SIT, headed by no less than a former CBI Director, R K Raghavan, did a thorough job by examining all possible evidence against Modi, listening to a large number of people who claimed to be direct or indirect witnesses, and finally came to the conclusion that there was no evidence of Modi's involvement in the killing of the former Congress MP, Ehsaan Jafri. The anti-Modi elements had invested a lot in the trumped-up complaint filed by Ehsaan's widow, Zakia Jafri, even though it ought to have been dismissed outright for she had changed her version several times.

The dismissal of the *amicus curiae* petition was fully covered by The *Hindu* on 10 May 2012. What had the SIT said? To quote The *Hindu* (10 May 2012):

Giving point-by-point answers to all observations made by the amicus curiae, after investigating the charges, the SIT said: 'The offences under the aforesaid sections of law are not against Mr Modi ...' The SIT dismissed as 'false and fabricated documents', two 'fax messages' claimed to have been sent by the suspended IPS Officer Sanjiv Bhatt .... The SIT found that no such messages ever existed and that these were concocted by Mr Bhatt at a much later stage and the signatures of his superior officers were forged. Neither those claimed to be recipients nor the senders remembered anything about receiving or sending any such message. Office records did not show the existence of any such message ....

The SIT report pointed out that Mr Bhatt himself did not mention about the existence of these messages in any of the affidavits or statements he filed before numerous authorities all these years ....

The SIT report, giving details of the roles played by different police officers and how they attempted to handle the situation, said there was no indication that the police were given any instructions from the higher-ups not to act or leave the affected areas to the mercy of the riotous mobs ...

The report said the allegations of Mr Modi making provocative statements over the media could not be substantiated ....

The allegation of his having told Zee TV in an interview that the Gulberg Society massacre was the result of the provocative firing from inside by Ehsaan Jafri, could not be established as the channel, despite several reminders, did not produce the CD of the recording.

The second instance of The Times of India *quoting him on Newton's theory of action and reaction to justify the riots as a reaction to the Godhra train carnage, was also found baseless ... the newspaper was forced to carry the denial, though deliberately in an obscure corner, the SIT said.*

Many media members dismissed the judgement somewhat cursorily.

Article in *TIME* magazine

Media interest in Narendra Modi has not been confined to India. The international media too has published interviews with him. An article published in *Time* magazine (26 March 2012) analysed in some detail his life and thoughts and Modi made it to the cover – a unique honour! The article was authored by Jyoti Thottam.

It would appear that Thottam had very little idea of India's history and the see-saw of relationships between Hindus and Muslims through the centuries. She did, however, have many interesting things to say about Modi. To cite some instances:

> Unlike many Indian politicians though, Modi doesn't put his faith on display. There are no religious icons in his office; the only adornments are two statues of his hero – the philosopher Swami Vivekananda. Everything about Modi and his surroundings is carefully manicured and controlled. He gives the impression of an autodidact who has methodically plotted his journey ... succeeding without family connections or fancy education, and his appeal is obvious in a nation of strivers.

> India has seen other leaders overcome scandal or bloodshed but none has been recast as completely as Modi. His background makes him the most polarizing figure in the country... He has never shown any remorse for the anti-Muslim carnage, instead praising Hindus for their 'restraint under grave provocation ...' But the growth and consolidation of his power has not been based on religion and ideology alone. Instead, Modi has set about revamping the state's economy by attracting high-value manufacturing companies, whose bosses are now among his staunchest backers ....

> While Muslims are worse off than Hindus by nearly every measure from health to income, their status in Gujarat is no worse than in other states and by some criteria, is better ....

> Many Indians recoil at any mention of a man whose name is indelibly linked to Gujarat's brutality of 2002; choosing him as India's leader would seem a rejection of the country's tradition of political secularism ... but when others think of someone who can bring India out of the mire of chronic corruption and inefficiency – of a firm nononsense leader who will set the nation on a course of development that might finally put it on par with China – they think of Modi .... Modi is so sure of himself that he is now openly courting Muslims who have long voted for Congress by default .... The party's (BJP) success in getting about 140 Muslim candidates elected to local office has persuaded at least some Muslim voters to forget about the past for the sake of economic betterment .... Muslims, says social scientist

The Man of the Moment: Narendra Modi

> Suhrud, are hedging their bets and saying: 'If Congress cannot guarantee us a thing, these people can guarantee us something – why not accept it?' Trying to get Gujarat's Muslims to vote for him is an audacious ploy, shoring up not only Modi's position within the state but also his national ambitions. If he succeeds, India may never be the same.

By and large, the article has been fair and Thottam gives Modi credit where credit is due. She says:

> What's certain is that during his ten years in power in Gujarat, the state has become the most industrialized and business-friendly territory, having largely escaped the land conflicts and petty corruption that often paralyze growth elsewhere in the nation. Gujarat's 85 billion dollar economy may not be the largest in India, but it has prospered without the benefit of natural resources, fertile farmland, a big population centre like Mumbai or a lucrative high-tech hub like Bangalore. Gujarat's success, even Modi's detractors acknowledge, is a result of good planning ...

The article was much discussed in political circles and even his vilest critics had to acknowledge that Thottam's analysis was sound.

Thottam, however, thought that Modi had insulted Muslims when he rejected the shawls and caps they offered him as gifts. To Modi, it rightly represented communalism and he could not possibly have accepted the skull cap however well meant the Muslims were who offered one to him. Thottam, however, is all praise for Modi for not succumbing to nepotism and dynastic politics, with family members staying away from him in an act of discipline. Equally impressed is Thottam with Modi's lifestyle: a man who sleeps only 3½ hours every night, wakes up at 5 am and does 90 minutes of yoga, and has never taken even a 15-minute vacation in the last 10 years.

According to Thottam, Modi, 61, is perhaps the only contender with the right track record and name recognition to challenge Rahul Gandhi.

That is questionably an absurd value judgement to make. Rahul is still a political novice in comparison to Modi. In a recent opinion poll by the magazine *India Today*, 24 per cent of those surveyed thought Modi should be the next Prime Minister; Rahul Gandhi polled only 17 per cent.

Hang Me If I Am Guilty – The Interview with *NAI DUNIYA*

But what created ripples, especially in Uttar Pradesh, was an interview Modi gave to Shahid Siddiqui, Editor and Publisher of the Urdu weekly *Nai Duniya*. Siddiqui supposedly was a member of the Samajwadi Party, but, in earlier times, had also had stints in the Congress and Bahujan Samaj Party. The interview he published so enraged the Samajwadi Party that there was a lot of talk of expelling him from the party.

The interview was published as a cover story under the headline: '*Hang me if I am guilty!*' The English translation was published in The *Telegraph* on 28 July 2012 and, of course, only then did the English-speaking intelligentsia of India come to know about it.

The interview

Shahid Siddiqui: Muslims have got a share in OBC reservations but not their full rights 20 years after the Mandal Commission's recommendations were accepted. Say there are 500 applicants for ten vacancies. Fifty per cent of the applicants are Muslim but people belonging to Hindu backward communities get all the jobs. This is why the Sachar Committee had recommended separate reservations for minorities.

Modi: After much deliberation, India's law makers (framers of the Constitution) had decided that there should not be any religion-based reservation; otherwise it will be dangerous. At that time, there was no RSS or Bajrang Dal.

SS: Muslim leaders including Maulana (Abul Kalam) Azad had opposed reservation based on religion. But we should learn from our experience. We have made enough amendments to the Constitution and if we give reservations to Muslims after 64 years to help them step out of backwardness, then do you have a problem?

Modi: No, no. There cannot be any change to the fundamental structure of our Constitution, but I want to say something else. The percentage of Muslims in government jobs in the states that you call secular and prosperous is only 2 to 4 per cent. Muslims are 9 per cent of Gujarat's population, but their share in jobs is 12 to 13 per cent. In Bengal, there are 25 per cent Muslims, but only 2 per cent of them are in jobs.

SS: In Gujarat, Muslims were far ahead and not because of your contribution. Muslims were ahead in education and business.

Modi: Let's accept what you are saying. In the past 20 years, the BJP has headed the government in Gujarat. If we were destroying them, would they have been ahead in education and business? The Sachar Committee survey was conducted when I was Chief Minister. Of the total recruitment of six lakh in government jobs, the recruitment of three lakh took place during my tenure.

SS: Were there 10 – 20 per cent Muslims among the recruits during your tenure?

Modi: I have not counted. It is not my philosophy to count on the basis of Hindu-Muslim. If you trust the Sachar Committee report, why don't you believe its report on Gujarat?

SS: If we talk about the Gujarat riots, tell me what happened then. Why were the bodies of those who got burnt in the train in Godhra brought back to Ahmedabad? Did you not understand its repercussions?

Modi: I have answered this question in detail to the Special Investigation Team (SIT) and the Supreme Court. No matter whose body it is, it needs to be returned to the family. It was not right for everyone to go to Godhra where there was tension. There was tension in Godhra and that's why it was important to remove the charred bodies from there.

SS: You could have silently brought the bodies to a hospital and handed them over to their families. Why were the bodies taken out in a procession?

Modi: There was no place in Godhra to keep so many bodies and that's why they needed to be removed from there. It was an administrative decision to remove the bodies in the darkness of the night to reduce tension. The bodies could have been brought to the Civil Hospital in Ahmedabad, but it is a crowded place. It was a good decision on the part of the administration to take the bodies to the Sola Civil Hospital. During those days, Sola was on the outskirts of Ahmedabad and was not as populated as it is now. No procession was brought out from Sola and the bodies were handed over to the families silently.

SS: Riots broke out in Gujarat; people were killed and houses set on fire. You were the chief minister of Gujarat and you knew what was happening there in Ahmedabad. What steps did you take to stop the killings?

Modi: First, we appealed to people to remain calm and maintain peace. I made the appeal from Godhra itself. After that, I appealed from Ahmedabad on radio and TV. I asked the administration to deploy the entire police force. There had never been a riot this big in the country before and it was the first riot in the age of 24 × 7 media. Earlier, the government had the time to organize its machinery as news would break out only in the following day's newspapers. Now, the administration has to compete with the speed of TV channels as they telecast the news of any incident within a few minutes. From Ahmedabad, I can speak to someone in Baroda over the phone in a few minutes, but it would take a minimum of two hours for police personnel to reach there. The police cannot compete with the speed of TV news.

Second, I would not like to compare it with other riots in the country to make my point. A riot is a riot. In the 1984 riots, there wasn't even one shot fired from police guns, no lathi charge. There was a lathi charge only at one place where Indira Gandhi's body was kept. A huge crowd had assembled there and they (the police) lathi-charged it to control the crowds but they were not deployed to control the riots. But in Gujarat, curfew was imposed on 27 February; steps were taken and people were lathi-charged and the police had to open fire.

SS: Your party colleagues and your officials say you told the people to vent their anger in the first 48 hours. Even Haren Pandya (the then Gujarat Home Minister) and Sanjiv Bhatt (the

IPS Officer) who has filed an affidavit in the Supreme Court made this allegation against you. What do you have to say on this?

Modi: You have to trust somebody. If you don't trust me, you have to trust the Supreme Court. The Supreme Court asked for an investigation to be conducted. We should trust that. The Godhra incident took place on 27 February, the riots broke out the next day and I called the Army on 1 March. Some people in the media say I did not call the army for three days but they forget that there are 28 days in February.

SS: It seemed that the riots were pre-planned. Houses and shops belonging to Muslims were identified and set on fire as though the whole thing was pre-planned.

Modi: It's all a lie, a propaganda. Instead think about how many Muslims were protected then. If they were to be killed systematically, who would have been spared today?

SS: Indian Muslims are grievously hurt. They are suspicious and that's why they want to know the truth. Were your ministers present in the police control room?

Modi: It's all lies. All the facts are with SIT. The Supreme Court conducted an investigation. You should wait to learn what they have found.

SS: What did Atal Bihari Vajpayee tell you at that point? Did he tell you that you had failed to follow *Rajdharma*?

Modi: This is a lie. During his speech, Atalji said *Rajdharma* should be maintained and had always been maintained in Gujarat. But the media distorted it by reporting only a portion of the sentence uttered by Atalji.

SS: Rajiv Gandhi apologized after the 1984 riots. Sonia Gandhi and Manmohan Singh too apologized. Why did you not apologize for the 2002 Gujarat riots and express regret? As head of the government, it was your moral responsibility to do so.

Modi: First, you should see the statements I had made during that violent situation. In an interview in 2004, I had said the same thing: if my government is responsible for this, then it should be hanged in such a fashion that no administrator dares commit that sin again. And those who talk of forgiving them are in a way encouraging the crime. If Modi has sinned, then Modi should be hanged. But even after that, I tried sincerely to save many lives. If some people want to hurl abuses at me because of political reasons, I don't have anything to say.

SS: Do you feel hurt after what happened? Is there any sorrow in your heart and do you want to apologize as hundreds of people were killed? I am the editor and if a correspondent of mine gives me wrong information and I print it, then I apologize.

Modi: What is the point in apologizing now? I took full responsibility for what happened during that time, expressed sorrow and apologized. Please check what I said in 2002 after the riots. Now you should write that you (the media) have been doing injustice to me for the past ten years. You should now apologize to Modi.

SS: Would you like to send any message to Indian Muslims?

Modi: Brother, I am a small person and I do not have the right to send any message to anybody. I am a servant and will continue to serve. I would like to tell my Muslim brothers that they should not reduce themselves to being voters for others. Muslims have been reduced to mere voters in Indian politics today. Muslims should dream: their dreams and the dreams of their children should be fulfilled. They are voters and they must use their rights with an open mind. But before that, they should be treated as human beings and as Indians. There is also a need to understand their problems. If I can be of any help to them, I would surely love to assist them. But they too have to think and see with an open mind.

An interview to the *Wall Street Journal*

On 29 August 2012, one of the leading international dailies dealing with economy, trade, commerce, industry and development, namely, The *Wall Street Journal*, published an interview with Modi that explains a lot about his views on a wide range of subjects.

The interviewer, Amol Sharma, introduced Modi as one who was 'widely considered as a top contender for prime ministership' with the chief minister's loyalists pointing to Gujarat's sustained

10 per cent plus annual economic growth and investor-friendly policies, saying that he would 'bring to the table just what India needs'. And this is how the interview went:

WSJ: Can Gujarat sustain its fast pace of economic growth as it gets richer and as the nation's growth is slowing down to less than 7 per cent?

Modi: Going from 1 per cent or 2 per cent growth to 10 per cent isn't difficult. What is difficult is to sustain 10 per cent. But I'm confident that we can achieve it easily. I believe growth should be constant, sustained and inclusive. Its only meaningful if these three things are there. Otherwise, they're just economic figures.

WSJ: What was your reaction to India's massive electricity blackouts at the end of July (2012)?

Modi: The power and energy sectors are the biggest constituents of the infrastructure sector. If you ignore them, no development will happen. As far as the power blackout is concerned, I am embarrassed by it. This is a great loss for my nation. The situation was immediately compared to Gujarat. The world saw so much darkness that even a flicker of light caught their attention.

WSJ: Can Gujarat's electricity reforms be a model for other states?

Modi: Villages (in Gujarat) didn't use power at dinner time. They'd eat in the dark. Kids didn't have light to study for exams; if mother was sick and there was no electricity... it disturbed me. Then I got involved. God helped me. He gave me a technical solution: separating the network so there are different power lines for agriculture and domestic use. It became a huge success story – we completed it in 1,000 days. All the states of India felt that this should be replicated in their states too.

WSJ: Should India remove foreign investment barriers in the multi-brand retail sector, allowing in companies like Wal-Mart ... Would you support such a move?

Modi: When you bring in multi-brand retail items into the country, you're not just bringing the products, but you're also harming the local manufacturers. You must strengthen your manufacturing sector and put it on a level playing field in the world. Any kind of items manufactured globally – like small pens, pencils, notebooks – our manufactured goods need to be on a level playing field. Then let them come. Have competition. The biggest loss is going to be to manufacturers. Local traders will be fine. They will sell the stuff imported from outside and still earn profits.

WSJ: What are your plans in the auto sector?

Modi: For me as chief minister, my thinking about the auto sector is over. I will not spare a single second for the auto sector – it is already over. Now, naturally, people will come and they will do their business. What I am looking for is the next generation – and that is, we want to focus on defence equipment.

WSJ: Gujarat's malnutrition rates are persistently high. What are you doing to combat this?

Modi: Gujarat is by and large a vegetarian state. And secondly, Gujarat is also a middle-class state. The middle class is more beauty conscious than health conscious – that is a challenge. If a mother tells her daughter to have milk, they'll have a fight. She'll tell her mother: 'I won't drink milk. I'll get fat!' We'll try to get a drastic change in this. Gujarat is going to come up as a model in this also. I can't make any big claims, because I don't have a survey in front of me yet.

WSJ: What steps have you been taking to increase primary school enrolment, especially among girls?

Modi: Every year, in June, when it is 44°C, I personally go to those rural areas where there's minimum education. I stay there for three days and we go from house to house to say that all the girls must go to school. Then, for another two to three days in October, we go to assess the quality of education. I go myself to primary schools in villages. We ask the kids: 'Can you read, can you write?' We involve the teachers also. We made 60,000 toilets for girls in schools so that girls wouldn't stop going to school.

WSJ: How were you affected by the Emergency of the mid-1970s when you were an RSS worker and many of your group's leaders were arrested or forced into hiding?

Modi: I got an excellent opportunity to learn and understand democratic values. In the emergency, we came to know what it means to not have democracy. And it shook me. This played a significant role in making me what I am.

WSJ: Do you see yourself as a future prime minister?

Modi: I don't carry the burden of the past or the madness of the future. I live in the present. My present is my Gujarat, the 60 million people of this state, the villages, the poor families, the farmers, the children – to change their destiny. I can't think beyond that.

WSJ: Your critics say you should apologize for the 2002 riots. Why won't you?

Modi: One has only to ask for forgiveness if one is guilty of a crime. If you think it's such a big crime, why should the culprit be forgiven? Just because Modi is a chief minister, why should he be forgiven? I think Modi should get the biggest punishment possible, if he is guilty. And the world should know there isn't any tolerance for these kinds of political leaders.

WSJ: You're a very controversial figure. People who praise you often get into trouble. Does that bother you?

Modi: Anna Hazare (the anti-corruption activist) once wrote a public letter of appreciation to me. I saw it on TV. I wrote a letter to him. I said: 'You've made a big mistake and now people will harass you. Just don't get into the business of praising me.' In the next three or four days, everyone pounced on Anna Hazare. I always take it in jest.

WSJ: Some might accuse you of granting these sorts of interviews now for an image make-over. Your response?

Modi: If I wanted to make over my image, I could have given 10,000 interviews in the last ten years. I haven't done anything wrong that I need to make up for. I am what I am in front of the world.

In another interview, Modi laid stress on other issues. He suggested that the government should invest to support private-sector manufacturing to make the nation more globally competitive. The government, he insisted, had no business to be 'in business'. But, he added, the tragedy was that there was no liberalization going on.

As Modi saw it, he didn't have to think of the auto business any longer. His current interest would be in the manufacture of defence equipment.

The interviewer had some interesting things to say about Modi's style of working. As he put it:

> Mr Modi's governance style is an unusual combination of technological and personally accessible. His desk is empty; aides say he prefers information via Power Point presentations. To clamp down on corrupt or incompetent bureaucrats, he uses a custom-made online tool. Every third Wednesday, villagers go to regional centres around the state to air their gripes about a range of matters, including delays in getting food ration cards, widows' pensions or other benefits, and bribery demands from police. Local officials log complaints in the system. Issues that aren't resolved locally filter up to Mr Modi, who says he video conferences with local officials to assess the situation and dole out punishment.

Admirers and Detractors

In a strong editorial, The *Free Press Journal* (12 April 2012) said Truth had failed the secularists. The paper noted that even if Modi knew he was innocent, powerful forces – aided and abetted by the Central Government – were out to get him. 'But,' said the paper, 'he took the most vicious attacks on his character on his chin, displaying a remarkable sangfroid.' It also said: 'The so-called human rights activists, assorted busybodies and, of course, the NGO entrepreneurs, have actually hindered the process of healing by constantly targetting Modi as an ogre.' The Journal concluded by saying, 'The Congress Party has blessed these self-appointed human rights activists in the hope that what it has failed to achieve through the ballot box, it can achieve through other means. After the SIT report, this must stop.'

The Free Press Journal had the courage to take an objective look at Gujarat, Modi and politics in the country. However, there were many columnists and so-called 'experts' who lost no occasion to vilify Modi. As the state elections due in Gujarat in December drew closer, efforts to damn him became ever sharper. An article in The *Hindu* (9 May 2012) by Achyut Yagnik, described as a leading Ahmedabad-based sociologist, sought to belittle Modi. There were factors, Yagnik claimed, that could frustrate Modi's plans of winning the elections by a substantial majority. First was the rejuvenation of the Congress Party in Gujarat. According to Yagnik: 'In the last one year, the Congress has become proactive in the state and through various yatras and campaigns, has established new links with the people! The Congress Party's new aggressiveness is visible at many levels, as in the Assembly, in university campuses and in the local media.' Yagnik went on to say that the Congress leadership had also joined hands, though on a limited scale, with grass roots struggles carried out by farmers and tribals to protect their rights over local natural resources. Another factor, Yagnik reported, was widespread disaffection among poor rural communities such as pastoralists, fish workers and labourers. In the name of 'development', Yagnik protested, and to project himself as a *Vikas Purush*' (Man of Development), Modi had handed over vast tracts of coastal land and pasture land to big industries. Continued Yagnik: 'Mr Modi's personality, specifically the authoritarian and autocratic streak in him, is the third factor that can foil not only his plan to capture 151 seats in the 2012 elections but may even reduce the BJP's strength in the Gujarat Assembly.'

All these factors turned out to be untrue.

Then there was Kuldip Nayar whose hatred of Modi has few parallels. Writing in the *Deccan Herald* (29 June 2012), he noted that the Bharatiya Janata Party 'seems to have a tryst with doom'. It was unlikely, felt Nayar, that the BJP would make it to the Lok Sabha or that Modi could become prime minister. 'A person who has his hands tainted with the blood of Muslims cannot be projected as India's next prime minister,' he pointed out. For Kuldip Nayar, Modi's hands were red with the blood of Muslims.

It is quite common to come across Modi's critics in the English media; in fact, supporters of Modi in the English media are few and far between. However, Swapan Dasgupta, a well-respected journalist, described in an article in The *Telegraph* (7 July 2012), where Modi stood in relation to the Gujarat miracle. He stated: 'In the past decade, Gujarat has focussed on the upgrading of infrastructure ... in addition, the government has taken proactive steps to attract enterprise aggressively by laying down attractive facilities and terms ....' As Dasgupta saw it, 'None of this would have happened had the state not established a record of low corruption, quick decision-making and nurtured a civic culture that cherished entrepreneurship.' He went on to say, 'Had the chief minister been venal, unresponsive and mindlessly populist – as he easily could have been – would India still be talking of the Gujarat miracle?'

Dasgupta quoted Bibek Debroy who, also culling statistics from the Planning Commission, had shown that Gujarat's average growth rate had risen since the 1990s, but unevenly. The average growth was 6.1 per cent during the Seventh Five-Year plan (1985-90), 12.9 per cent during the Eighth Plan (1992-1997), 2.8 per cent during the Ninth Plan (1997-2002) and 10.9 per cent during the Tenth Plan (2002-2007). The estimated growth rate was consistent across sectors, including agriculture – India's most problematic sector. Agriculture had grown on an average by 10.7 per cent in the period between 2001-02 and 2010-11. Most significant was the rise in cotton production from 16.8 lakh bales in 2001-02 to 104 lakh bales in 2010-11. Noted Dasgupta: 'Although jumping to instant political conclusions would be rash, statistical evidence would bear out the belief that sustained double digit growth has coincided with Modi's tenure as chief minister. There are many in India who have genuine political objections to Modi. They believe, as Nitish Kumar does, that a future prime minister must be seen to be more compassionate and appreciative of the concerns of an India that can't cope with a market economy. There are others who say that a prime minister must have a more consensual and collegiate approach. But these concerns have nothing to do with claims that Modi is a fake.'

What we see from the above is a reflection of the 'glass half full, half empty' syndrome. Modi's admirers look at what Modi has genuinely achieved, while his critics point out to areas where he has not succeeded. What his critics don't realize is that Modi is not God and perfectionist though he is, perfectionism in all areas of human activity cannot be achieved overnight.

Kishore Rathod sided with Modi on the issue of why business-minded Gujaratis back him. Writing in *DNA* (19 Sept. 2012), Rathod had this to say:

> Never mind the sentiment of the secularists in Mumbai or the activists in Delhi, as far as the enterprising Gujarati is concerned. Modi is the best man to do business with. While those in Gujarat have endorsed their faith in Modi by giving him thumping majorities in the two elections since the riots, the Gujaratis – and their business partners outside Gujarat – are putting their money where their mouth is. Right from the Ambanis and Tatas, to the Shroffs and Godrejs, thousands of crores have been pumped into the industrious, industrialist-friendly neighbouring state in the ten years that Modi has helmed it.
>
> While Mumbai is stumbling from one deadline to another, Gujarat is not only growing by the year but is also simultaneously creating new infrastructure to sustain the growth in the years to come .... For every one job in the corporate office, tens of jobs are being created on the shop floor. And jobs are the harbingers of growth, drivers of economy. Thousands of industrial units have closed down in Maharashtra's industrial belts like Thane-Belapur and opened shop in the Daman-Vapi industrial belt of Gujarat.
>
> While the southern states are dominating the service sectors, there has been a steady flight of the brick-and-mortar business to Gujarat over the years and if things continue at this rate, the day may not be far off when the Gujaratis wake up to the benefits of shifting not only their manufacturing, but their entire base back home. They may well realize that instead of having just the best wishes of Modi, it would be much better to be part of his Gujarat with tan (body), man (heart) and dhan (money).

The Secular English Media and Modi

What is the matter with the English media? Why is a good segment of it so determinedly filled with hate where Narendra Modi is concerned? Tavleen Singh, a Delhi-based professional columnist has her own answer. According to her, those who portray Modi as a demon include leftists of varying shades of pink, Muslim intellectuals of varying shades of fundamentalist Islam, social activists of varying causes and political analysts whose intellectual development ceased when the secularism versus communalism debate died a natural death. As she put it: 'What united this motley crew is a deep fear that if Modi does become Prime Minister in 2014, their dominance of the natural discourse, their virtual monopoly on tickets to enter politics, get national awards, access government largesse and other forms of patronage like regular excursions to foreign lands, will end.'

But one suspects that there is more than that. There is a large body of 'intellectuals' whose origins go back to the British days when Hinduism was a No-No and to be anti-Hindu was fashionable. The more one laughed at Hinduism, the easier it was to gain easy entry into the privileged class. Independence merely made matters worse. Under the leadership of Jawaharlal Nehru, maintaining a discreet distance from practising Hinduism became the order of the day for those who wanted acceptability at certain societal levels. Such was Nehru's mindset that he wanted to have nothing to do with the renovation of the famous Somnath Temple and tried his best to persuade Dr Rajendra Prasad, then President of India, not to inaugurate the reconstructed holy place. Dr Prasad was not one to be dissuaded from performing this sacred task.

Partition had taken place, many argued, because of rampant communalism, and the only way to feel good was to decry Hinduism. Those who promoted such thinking perhaps had very little knowledge of Indian history! When the Shiv Sena raised the slogan: '*Garv se kaho hum Hindu hai*' (State with pride that we are Hindus), it obviously never occurred to our pseudo secularists that being proud of one's ancient *dharmic* heritage has nothing to do with the administration of the country. It is against this background that one must judge the prevalent attitude of our media.

There are other reasons adduced for the English media's attitude towards Modi. When asked to crawl, he does not even bend. When told he must apologize for the post-Godhra events, he asks: 'Why should I?' This hurts the ego of the media. Here is a man who cannot be browbeaten into intellectual submission, is clear in his mind on what is wrong and what is right, and has the courage to stand up to his convictions. This seems to have completely fazed the media, which is not accustomed to be told where to get off.

The Man of the Moment: Narendra Modi

Another reason for hating Modi is his connection with the RSS. Our left-leaning media just cannot accept the fact that no other volunteer organization in the country has rendered more and better social service than the RSS. After the Emergency, on 3 November 1977, Jayprakash Narayan addressed a huge RSS training camp in Patna. Does one have to remind readers that J P as he came to be known popularly, was for a long time a strong critic of the RSS? But this is what he said on that historic day:

'.... RSS is a revolutionary organization. No other organization in the country comes anywhere near it. It alone has the capacity to transform society and casteism, and wipe the tears from the eyes of the poor. Its very name is 'Rashtriya' – that is, national. I believe you have a historic role to play.... I am not saying this to flatter you ... There is no other organization in the country which can match you ... Think over how to bring about economic transformation ... I think more than myself, you can undertake this mission because you are competent to do it ...Your word has far-reaching effect ...You are in the forefront of transformation that is taking place before our very eyes ...You can accomplish a lot. May God give you the strength and may you live up to such expectations.'

When the country was invaded by the Chinese in 1962, our intellectuals were nowhere to be seen. But the RSS stood up for the cause of restoring self-respect of the people and no one acknowledged it more than a devastated Jawaharlal Nehru who invited RSS to participate in the Republic Day Parade of 26 January 1963. What greater tribute could the RSS get?

For most of his ten-year tenure, Modi has answered his critics with silence. He has let his work do the talking and allowed the law to take its course. It makes our media feel frustrated. Though hurt, Modi does not hit back at his critics, which puzzles them. As he once told The *Economist* (27 April 2012), 'I am telling you, the essence of democracy is criticism. I always welcome criticism ... But I am against allegations. What we hear is not criticism but allegations. We must differentiate between the two.' When he was asked whether he would like to be Prime Minister of India, his reply again was open. He said: 'Before I became Chief Minister, I never thought that one day I'd be one. My basic philosophy is: I don't want to be anything. I want to do something. Something for my country and the poor people.' He went on to say: 'I am not an ambitious person; there is no ambition in my life. I have a mission in my life and my mission is to serve my country.' In saying so he sounds like Mahatma Gandhi. His words baffle secularists. For our secularists, the very word *'Hindutva'* is offensive. To them it conveys everything negative and it drives them to desperation. But says Modi: 'I am a living example of casteless politics. I am an OBC and I come from the most backward caste. The fact that I have no caste base helps me because no one can say I take decisions based on caste.'

One of the most persistent critics of Modi has been Madhu Purnima Kishwar. Some time in December 2012, she wrote: 'As the Congress Party seems on the decline, there is increasing desperation in the air for all those who have arrived on the party's patronage. The possibility of Modi emerging as a winner has put them in panic. That is why the media in general and TV anchors, in particular, have gone overboard in demonizing Modi, so much so that even people like me who have been consistent critics of the BJP feel revolted enough to say : 'This has gone too far. Please do not manipulate us beyond our tolerance limit.'

Kishwar went further to remind the so-called secularists of 'the riots politically orchestrated by the Congress in Jamshedpur, Bhiwandi, Bhagalpur, Hyderabad, Bokaro, Meerut, Mumbai, Nellie and a host of other towns,' all under Congress rule, adding: 'Media collaborates with the Congress Party in trying to make the country forget that the guilty of all these massacres have not been punished.'

As Kishwar sees it: 'The demonization of Modi is so compulsive and thorough that no matter what he does, the media throws mud at him.' In many ways Kishwar agrees with Tavleen Singh whom I would like to quote once more because she is fearless and speaks with the benefit of inside knowledge. Tavleen Singh stated: 'What worries the intellectuals of Lutyen's Delhi is that Narendra Modi may not be as easy to seduce as Vajpayee was. He may find it easier to discern between cant and real culture and between courtiers and real loyalists, and this would inevitably lead to a total overturning of the patronage applecart. So, the demonization of Modi has been a joint project on a scale that has been quite unprecedented in the political history of modern India. It would be fair to say that no Indian politician has been demonized quite in this way and usually because the measure by which he has been judged has not been applied to anyone else.'

And finally one last piece of guesswork. Could it be, could it just be, that our intellectuals are in the same class as those involved in the Radia Scam? We have Paid News. May be we have Paid Views as well. Who can tell?!

Is Modi anti-Muslim?

According to Sanjay Singh, writing in *First Post Politics* (21 November 2012), till a few years ago, Narendra Modi didn't have a single supportive voice in the Muslim community. But by November 2012, he apparently had a few. According to Singh, they may not have been very vocal, but they were influential and managed to provide a bridge for Modi to address the community's broader concerns.

Among the names mentioned as being currently linked to Modi are an erstwhile protégé of Sonia Gandhi's confidant Ahmed Patel, called Asifa Khan; Zafar Sareshwala – a businessman who had filed many human rights cases against Modi in the International Court of Justice, and Ali Syed, a former Inspector General of Police in Gujarat. Syed was projected as a mayoral candidate in the last corporation elections in Ahmedabad but lost. He is now reported to head the state Waqf Board. Another visible face, according to Singh, is that of Baba Mehboob Ali a.k.a Sufi Sant who also heads the Haj Committee.

Zafar Sareshwala is not a politician and he and his family have been in the industrial valves manufacturing business and stock broking for a long time. Importantly, he has an exclusive BMW dealership in Gujarat and a showroom. As of 21 November 2012, he was in the process of opening a 1,00,000 lakh sq ft BMW showroom on the Sarkhej-Gandhinagar Highway.

In 2002, Sareshwala was in London when the riots took place and learnt that his business establishments had been targetted. Though he did not lose any family member in the course of the riots, three of his NRI neighbours were reportedly killed when they were on a visit to Gujarat. Sareshwala filed human rights cases against Modi and L K Advani in the International Court of Justice.

Then, some time down the line, Sareshwala changed his mind. Singh quotes him as saying: 'It was very tough then. After going through a prolonged churning of thought, consultations with family and friends, I decided to open a dialogue with Narendra Modi. After all, we live in a democratic system. I came to Ahmedabad from London in 2005. If he (Modi) was re-elected chief minister, who do we talk to? Dialogue is the essence of a democratic process. Some one had to hear our problems and we had to seek solutions from him. Now, can you shut the door and decide not to talk and then hope for a solution? Thus, we met Modi.'

There were many who did not appreciate the line that Sareshwala took. Singh quotes him as saying: 'But with the support of my family, I held firm. My point was, should we degenerate after the riots or move on? Modi gave me his number and told me to bring any or all such cases which came to my knowledge to his notice at any time, day or night. If someone tried to put a spoke in the wheel just because the person belonged to the Muslim community, corrective measures would immediately be taken. And he took action.'

As Singh sees it, things have changed for Sareshwala now. More people come to him for solutions. Name-calling from within the community and outside hurts Sareshwala, but, says Singh, 'He takes solace from the fact that the state administration has started taking corrective action and his community at large, too, has started benefitting'.

Suave, articulate and ambitious, Asifa Khan had been asked by Ahmed Patel, Sonia Gandhi's influential political secretary, to join the Congress in 2008. Ahmed Patel had known her as a journalist and they were both from Bharuch in Gujarat. In fact, she rose to become state Congress spokesperson and media cell convener of the All India Muslim Congress. But things did not work as well as Asifa thought they would. For every small thing, a decision had to come from Delhi – and that would take months. She was completely dependent on Delhi. For the Gujarat Congress, Delhi meant Ahmed Patel.

Asifa had a long list of anecdotes where meetings with a series of aggrieved Congress leaders, including MLAs, failed to result in solutions. And that applied to cases even when the leader concerned was from the Muslim community. She felt the BJP would be a better choice. Consequently, she joined the Modi bandwagon.

According to Singh, Asifa is full of praise for Modi about how he has changed the face of the state, locally, domestically and internationally. He quotes her as saying: 'There is one policy, one implementation in Modi's regime, without discrimination, without bifurcation on grounds of caste, creed and religion. There is clarity of sense and purpose.'

Rasheeda Bhagat has quoted Achyut Yagnik, who has been referred to earlier, as saying that the mercantile community among Muslims is now moving towards Modi. Rasheeda claims that several Muslims have told her: 'Our lives and businesses are safe when he (Modi) is in power'.

However, Singh says: 'The slow accretion of mercantile support for Modi does not mean all sections will warm up to him, but it is a beginning'.

VIBRANT GUJARAT 2013

The first of the Vibrant Gujarat Summits was organized in 2003 from 28 September to 2 October, barely two years after Modi became Chief Minister. At that summit, as many as 76 MoUs for 80 projects were signed worth ₹66,068 crore. That by itself was a mammoth achievement.

This success followed by more such achievements at the following summits:

- 2005 Global Investors' Summit: 226 MoUs worth 20 billion dollars were signed.
- 2007 Global Investors' Summit: 675 MoUs worth 152 billion dollars were signed.
- 2009 Global Investors' Summit: 8,662 MoUs worth 241 billion dollars were signed.
- 2011 Global Investors' Summit: 7,936 MoUs worth 462 billion dollars were signed.

Vibrant Gujarat 2013

The sixth Global Investors' Summit, Vibrant Gujarat, was inaugurated in Gandhinagar, Ahmedabad on 11 January 2013 in a style never before witnessed in India any time in the past.

More than 7,000 people attended the opening session, which was probably the largest such audience ever seen in India. Delegates came from 120 countries, including 225 from Canada, 170 from Japan and around seventy each from the United States and Britain. In his welcome speech, Modi especially welcomed partners of the event, particularly CII, JETRO, USIBC, UKIBC, AIBC and the ICCC, as also the Vice Minister of METI of Japan, the Ambassador of Japan, the High Commissioner of Canada, the High Commissioner of Britain, the Vice Governor of the Yunnan Province of China, the Vice Governor of Astrakhan, the Ambassador of Denmark, among many other celebrities.

Present at the Summit were some of the leading industrialists of India like Ratan Tata, Mukesh and Anil Ambani, Anand Mahindra, Adi Godrej, Chanda Kochar, Ratan Tata's successor Cyrus Mistry, Kumaramangalam Birla, Hari Bharatia, Shashi Ruia, Ajit Gulabchand, Pankaj Patel of Cadilla Healthcare, Baba Kalyani, Tulsi Tanti, Uday Kotak, Nimesh Kamopani of J M Finance, and Piruz Khambatta of Rasana.

Addressing the august gathering, Modi said that from a small beginning in 2003, the Summit had evolved into a truly international affair. He said that this had happened primarily because of the support and trust of investors and entrepreneurs. He stated that more than a thousand national and international companies were displaying their products at an exhibition close by. Speaking about the global slowdown, Modi said that the growth rate in Gujarat had not been impacted adversely. He maintained: 'We have acquired an element of resilience in the economy. It stands on all three important pillars: Manufacturing, Services and Agriculture. We have thus, not only been able to sail through but have also maintained a 10 per cent plus growth rate in all those three sectors.'

Modi said with pride that Gujarat's economy had sustained itself both in terms of jobs and livelihoods, had used the time for 'internal corrections' and because of this, the state had been able to withstand shocks without any labour retrenchment. Even more satisfying, he said, was the fact that the management and labour force had managed the situation in a collaborative manner. That was what Gujarat was known for, he averred. 'Togetherness is our biggest strength. We know how to get together. We know how to stand together. And we know how to grow together.'

Continuing, Modi said that today's world was characterized by two phenomena: the power of technology and the power of information. He said: 'We in India are further fascinated by the power of our youth. We have to harness this and put it to advantage. We in Gujarat have specifically made efforts to use all these three drivers of the modern world.'

Vibrant Gujarat 2013

Modi said that he was a 'firm believer' in the three pillars of progress in the modern world: Skill, Speed and Scale. Explaining this, he said: 'We are using technology to bring in speed in governance and in execution of programmes. We are focussing on skill development of our youth in a big way. We are also visualizing projects that are innovative, ambitious and futuristic. I firmly believe that this century is India's century. And to be realistically so, it has to be the century of the Indian youth.'

He proclaimed that he had drawn up elaborate plans for youth-led development in which women were going to be equal and active partners. He quoted Swami Vivekananda as saying: 'India will be raised not with the power of the flesh but with the power of the spirit'.

Modi claimed that Gujarat had evolved and implemented many innovative and far-reaching solutions to India's old and historic problems, whether it be water conservation or enrolling the girl child in schools: 'We are focussing on skill development of our youth in a big way'. Problems, he felt, were solved with peoples' participation. He added: 'We have also ensured that the solution becomes sustainable. We also ensure that they lead to measurable outcomes and visible change for the individual and society. Many of these projects have been recognized at the national and international levels. Many are being replicated by other states of India.' Giving an example of what constituted Gujarat's 'Global vision', Modi said its per capita consumption of electricity was double the average of India and two-thirds of the average of the developed world. 'We have.' he said, 'committed to make it on par with the developed world. Cooking gas will be made available to all urban households through pipe line. We have assured our people to construct five million new houses. We have committed to covering even the remaining 30 per cent of the households with piped water.'

Modi went on to say that his government had undertaken to modernize industrial clusters and make small and cottage industries stronger. 'Simultaneously, he said, 'we will be setting up world class investment regions and smart cities, world class ports, road, rail, logistics, health, education, transport, sanitation, environmental and tourism infrastructure.'

In conclusion he said:

> History has repeatedly shown us that the economic models based on exploitation will not work. There was a time when exploitation of labour was an issue. We tried to find a solution to it. Today, exploitation of nature and its resources is a burning issue. I will go a step further. Even exploitation of markets is not going to help. Unless the people living in those markets are empowered, unless the local capacities to produce are improved, unless the people are made partners in progress, their purchasing power would not sustain. Only such partnerships will be able to offer the sustainability we desire in our economic, social and personal lives. So, I reiterate that this event is not just about investments. It is not just about projects which give financial returns. It is about inducting togetherness in our socio-economic activities. It is about bringing global and local inclusiveness in our economic process. I will be happy with you in the march of our journey. I will be equally happy to see the realization of your dreams. I will be happier to see them realized at the earliest.

Towards the end, Modi received a huge applause.

Though none of the businessmen who were present openly backed Modi's political ambitions (the only speaker who did so was the regional politician from Russia), the implication was clear. They tended to prefer Modi's style of leadership to that of India's current government.

Ratan Tata spoke at the opening session. Tata credited Modi with making his state 'better than anywhere else' as an investment destination. 'Modi's government,' said Ratan Tata, 'executes what is promised'.

Mukesh Ambani hailed Modi as a leader with 'a grand vision'. He said: 'We began from Gujarat and we come back again and again to invest. We have committed investment of ₹100,000 crore in Gujarat.' He also committed a further investment of ₹500 crore in Pandit Deendayal Upadhyaya Petroleum University.

Anil Ambani, too, was lavish in his praise for Modi. He described Modi as a 'King among Kings' and added: 'Let me attempt to paint another picture:

- *2 October 1869, Porbander Gujarat*: the birth of Mohandas Karamchand Gandhi, the Father of the Nation;
- *31 October 1875, Nariyal, Gujarat*: the birth of Sardar Vallabhbhai Patel, India's man of steel;
- *28 December 1932, Chorwad Gujarat*: the birth of Dhirubhai Ambani, India's greatest entrepreneur;
- *17 September 1950, Vadnagar, Gujarat*: the birth of Narendra Modi.'

Anil Ambani stated that, 'Narendra Bhai has the Arjun-like clarity of vision and purpose. His skills have acted as a huge magnet for investors and entrepreneurs from India and across the world in the past decade. Narendra Modi dreams with his eyes open and has an open heart and mind.'

Cyrus Mistry, the successor and Chairman of the Tata group lauded the Gujarat Government and Modi. As Mistry's name was announced as a speaker, there was thunderous applause from the audience. Said Mistry: 'At the outside I would like to applaud the spirit and entrepreneurship of the people of Gujarat and spirit of the entire Gujarati diaspora ... it is important to recognize the infrastructure and enabling environment put in place by the Gujarat Government.' Promising to continue investing in Gujarat, Mistry said that the Tatas had improved the quality of lives wherever they had invested and would continue to do so in Gujarat. 'Our focus is on long-term value creation,' he said.

On the eve of 'Vibrant Gujarat 2013', Canada's High Commissioner to India, Stewart Beck, noted that leaders of both sides had expressed their commitment to increase bilateral trade to 15 billion dollars by 2015, and Canada's participation at the Summit would highlight Canada's advantages as a partner for India and the possibilities for strengthening business relationships between India and Canada.

The Japanese Ambassador said that his country had a 'natural win-win relationship with Gujarat' and Ron Somers, the President of a US-India Business Council, stated that Modi had set a new benchmark and proved that 'progress trumps politics'. Sir James Beven, the British High Commissioner, declared himself 'a son of

Gujarat' on the grounds that he was born in Leicester, which had the largest expatriate population of Gujaratis!

Even as the two-day long seminar came to an end, information came in that Gujarat had overtaken Tamil Nadu in 'economic freedom' in an index that ranked states based on how industry-friendly they were and the economic reforms they had implemented. Tamil Nadu, which had topped the previous two surveys in 2005 and 2009, had been pushed to second place in 2011, according to a report compiled by the Germany-based Friedrich Naumann Foundation, a watchdog for economic reforms across the world. Gujarat had thus moved from fifth place to the first in 2011: that was an indication that it now offered more investment freedom, good governance in terms of law and order, and minimal government interference.

'The index reflects a direct correlation between economic freedom and well-being of citizens,' the Foundation's Regional Director Siegfried Herzog was quoted as saying.

> 'The index has three parametres to determine a state's rank. The first is the size of the government: expenditure, taxes and enterprises. Thus, if a government has a high revenue expenditure and levies higher rates of sales tax, then it stifles economic freedom. The next is the legal structure and security of people. Here, the state should have a good justice delivery system, fewer pending cases and no judicial vacancy. Frequent lockouts and strikes are an indication that a state has fared poorly on this front. Tamil Nadu slipped in all three parametres, making place for Gujarat. For Modi it is a significant achievement.'

No wonder, then, that as many as 17,719 business proposals and investments worth ₹40 lakh crore – double the figure promised at the earlier Summit – were signed.

However, there were sceptics who did not take this figure seriously on the grounds that only a small percentage of MoUs signed had, in practice, been implemented.

There could be a variety of reasons for this: planning projects, one by one, can take months. Then, there is the non-availability of adequate technical staff, land and other facilities. It was acknowledged that in the previous five meetings of Vibrant Gujarat, many more MoUs for 18,029 projects with a proposed investment of ₹39.54 lakh crore were signed, but in reality, only 2,007 or 11.1 per cent of the projects had been completed, with another 1,710 or 9.5 per cent under implementation.

The other pertinent question is whether Gujarat has enough space for thousands of projects to be implemented and whether it would be wise for Gujarat to suspend future Vibrant Gujarat Summits. Available data suggests that in 1993-1994, the share of Gujarat's industrial sector (mining, manufacturing, electricity generation put together) was 7.99 per cent in the country's industrial GDP of ₹1.64 lakh crore, which increased to 14.03 per cent in 2003-2004, after which there had been a steady decline, standing at 9.27 per cent in 2007-08.

From the above comparison, it would seem unviable for Gujarat to take on large-scale projects with an investment of more than ₹10 crore. While in 2005, as many as 422 projects worth ₹16,500 crore had begun commercial production, the number had dipped to 75 projects in 2011.

It is quite possible that setting up new projects has found its limitation. But neither Modi nor the people of Gujarat need to feel let down. Foreign investors' faith in the credibility of Modi and his government stands unchallenged – the signing up of so many new projects shows that Modi must now ask himself whether the time has come to look for success elsewhere such as in the field of human development. Not just the people of Gujarat but India as a whole have reason to be proud of Modi's achievements.

Pinpricks

As 2011 turned into 2012 and elections to the state Legislative Assembly to be held in December 2012 began to draw closer, tension started mounting. Modi had won two elections post-2002 with a thumping majority. Would he be able to repeat that performance? Or would the UPA leader, Rahul Gandhi or the bête noire of his own party, Keshubhai Patel, win at the hustings? Were there others too who could put spokes in the wheel?

Rahul Gandhi – The UPA Leader

Would Rahul Gandhi, as leader of the Congress, beat him at the game? There was wide speculation in the media. Senior leader Mohan Prakash, in charge of Congress party affairs in Gujarat, told the media on 12 September 2012 that Rahul Gandhi would be visiting Gujarat shortly and would campaign there just as he had been doing in other states in the country. When media men asked him whether the assembly elections would be a Modi vs Rahul contest, Mohan Prakash said the question did not arise. 'Rahul Gandhi is a national leader while Narendra Modi is a state leader,' he said airily. Rahul Gandhi, Prakash added, would be leading his party whether it was in Uttar Pradesh, Gujarat or Maharashtra.

The Congress Party had already attacked Modi's Vivekananda Yatra on the grounds that there were no similarities between Swami Vivekananda and Modi. The Congress refrain was plain and simple. In effect it meant: The tussle between Modi and Rahul was imaginary and was being projected by Modi just to hide his shortcomings. Modi was not to take such insults lightly. Addressing a meeting at Rajkot on 17 September 2012, Modi said that Rahul was not just a national leader but an 'international leader as well', and could contest elections in Italy too. This acid response evoked loud laughter.

Modi recalled that in 2004, the Congress manifesto had promised to provide jobs to one crore youth. However, according to a report issued by the Government of India, Gujarat was the leader in providing jobs with a 72 per cent share.

On 24 September 2012, Z News.com shared some remarks made by a commentator. The commentator made the provocative declaration that the biggest political debate going on currently was whether the 2014 General Elections would witness a battle between 'Yuvraj' (Prince-in-Waiting) Rahul Gandhi and Bharatiya Janata Party's most charismatic leader Narendra Modi. 'But what is most surprising is Rahul's reluctance to challenge Modi in the Gujarat assembly polls due later this year,' teased the commentator.

Indeed, there had been reports that Rahul might not want to campaign in Gujarat. Provoking Rahul, Modi said in an address at a rally: 'Now Congress says Rahul is not coming to Gujarat. Why? People of the State and I want to know the reason.' Modi also challenged UPA chairperson Sonia Gandhi, Prime Minister Manmohan Singh and Rahul Gandhi saying: 'I am ready for any contest.' Congress came forward with a guarded but tepid respond to Modi's challenge. When AICC spokesperson Manish Tewari was asked whether Rahul would campaign in Gujarat as he had done in Uttar Pradesh, he said: 'Election is fought on the basis of local issues and all senior leaders who are given the responsibility to campaign there will do it. The Congress is ready for an electoral fight in the state'.

The observation was, as many people felt, that 41-year-old Rahul had proved to be nothing but a mute spectator in politics who came forward in a flash and disappeared the same way. Rahul had so far, had a number of failures in his short political career and had been at the receiving end not only from the Opposition but even UPA allies. At the same time, Modi had superbly projected himself as the 'messiah of development'. As was noted on Znews.com, Rahul's report card was certainly poor and he had got a drubbing not only in Bihar but in Uttar Pradesh as well – a state where his family had held power for four generations. His silence or at best rare remarks on important issues had arguably sent the message across that he was least concerned about the plight of crores of people who looked up to him. Not only had the Gandhi scion failed to impress voters during his campaign in state assembly polls, he also lacked knowledge in administration and foreign policy and had maintained silence on economic issues. His repeated silence on issues like the Anna Hazare movement, 2G Spectrum scam and the more recent coal blocks allocation had earned him only criticism, as the channel noted.

An exclusive survey conducted by TSI-Abacus Research on the State of the Nation (28 September 2012) showed that the two leading candidates for prime ministership were Narendra Modi and Rahul Gandhi. In a list of high profile political wannabes that included the likes of Nitish Kumar, Manmohan Singh and Sonia Gandhi, Modi and Rahul had emerged as clear favourites but Modi had trumped Rahul by a large margin. A sizeable 24.8 per cent had opined that Modi was the man to take India's growth story ahead, while a lesser 19 per cent thought it could be Rahul. Modi was unbeatable on any count. It was, said Swaraaj Chauhan, an international columnist, 'a battle between bachelors'. Whatever be the reality, noted Chauhan, Dr Manmohan Singh's cup of woes was running over.

Even his admirers in the United States were beginning to express serious doubts about Dr Singh's capabilities to deliver. An in-depth US Congressional Research Service (CRS) report was quoted as saying: 'Even before major corruption scandals broke in late 2010, Congress-led UPA was under considerable criticism for drift and ineffectiveness. Since that time, the decline of the Congress Party's standing has been precipitous. Less than two years after the party won a convincing 2009 national re-election victory, opinion polls showed a majority of Indians believe the UPA coalition has lost its moral authority to rule.'

The 94-page report was first released by the CRS for the American law makers on 1 September 2011. It further said: 'Over the course of the recent political upheaval, Dr Manmohan Singh's mild, non-political bearing, once considered part of his appeal, has become for many a liability, especially as the Indian leader has appeared slow-footed in reacting to national outrage over increasing evidence of high-level corruption. While Prime Minister Singh is not accused of personal wrong-doing, he has come under fire for an allegedly inattentive management style that, for some observers, facilitated an environment in which corruption spread.'

This was followed by a report from the well-known US Think Tank, Brookings Institution, authored by William Antholis, the Institution's Managing Director. It was made available on 16 March 2012. Said Mr Antholis:

> Meet India's most admired and most feared politician: Narendra Modi. The world's largest democracy, India, could elect him Prime Minister. And the world's leading democracy, the United States, currently does not issue him a visa.
>
> I spent 90 minutes with Mr Modi earlier this month at his Chief Minister's residence in Gujarat – a state of some 60 million people, about the same size as France, Britain or Italy, and practically twice as big as California. More than any other state leader in India, Modi is shaking up national politics.
>
> In person, Modi comes across as an effective administrator, a proud Indian nationalist, and a committed, if not zealous, Hindu. He is also a policy maven, introverted, precise and even passionate about the most technical of subjects. On almost all of these issues, his Gujarat is pushing, not following, New Delhi and India. Modi may be branded by the (2002) riots, but Gujarat's economic performance is without peer in India, growing an average 10 per cent each year for a decade. According to state published reports, pledged investments have grown from 76 MOUs amounting to 14 billion dollars in 2003, to nearly 8,000 MOUs signed in 2011 for 450 billion dollars. This is faster growth than any place on earth, including most of China.

That was a great tribute indeed.

The US Congressional Report, incidentally, had made a passing mention of the Nehru-Gandhi family, in which it was stated that 'many expect Rahul Gandhi to be put forward as Congress's prime ministerial candidate in the scheduled 2014 elections'. Said the report: 'Yet, this heir-apparent remains dogged by questions about his abilities to lead the party, given a mixed record as an election strategist, uneasy style in public appearance and reputation for gaffes.'

The Man of the Moment: Narendra Modi

And yet, the commentator was not quite sure that Rahul Gandhi could be written off. As he put it:

> 'It is too early to write off Mr Rahul Gandhi. The charisma of the Gandhi-Nehru family manages to hold together the Congress Party that presently does not have any broadly acceptable leader other than his mother, Ms Sonia Gandhi (who figures at 7th position in the recent Forbes list of world's most powerful women). Some speculate that Sonia, or her daughter, Ms Priyanka Vadra, may be the dark horse at a later stage. But then there is the mystery of Sonia Gandhi's unknown illness that could affect her performance. And Priyanka is unlikely to cope with the electoral battle if her name crops up late.'

The commentator gave a background of Rahul's educational qualifications and his winning the Amethi Lok Sabha seat in the May 2004 Lok Sabha elections, adding: 'Mr Gandhi retained his seat. Although the media keeps talking contemptuously about India's dynastic politics, Mr Rahul Gandhi has now emerged from his parents' shadow.'

So then, who, in the end, would win the 2014 general elections? The commentator, rather than provide his own answer, went forth to quote from a famous Chinese astrology book written by Suzanne White, that provided insight into the character of people born under particular Chinese birth signs:

According to Chinese astrology (based on animal signs), Modi happens to be a 'tiger', and Rahul, a 'dog'. Suzanne White felt that as a 'tiger', Modi was 'conservative and energetic', and while maintaining his charm, he was 'a power-house of energy and a doer of grand deeds'. Modi was not one to leave projects unfinished. He was a bulldozer with the engine of a tank and the scope of at least sixteen aircraft carriers. Modi shared his birth sign with Charles de Gaulle and Dwight Eisenhower.

As a 'dog', Rahul was one who wanted to change the world. He was brave, gallant, and one whose sole reason for being on this earth was to stalk the holy grail of perfection, not believing in violence or upheaval. In that sense, Rahul shared his birth sign with Mother Teresa, Akira Kurosawa, Andre Agassi and Jennifer Lopez.

Pinpricks

So, who would win? As Suzanne White put it: 'The Indian public could be treated to an exciting battle between India's two celebrated bachelors. The nation will have to wait with bated breath.'

There was a general belief that Rahul may not, after all, get into a fight with Modi. But he was obviously persuaded to visit Gujarat. Making his first appearance in Gujarat in the second week of December, Rahul attacked Modi for 'ignoring' the common man's voice and dubbed him as a 'marketer' who was hard-selling 'shining Gujarat', where people still faced problems like shortage of drinking water and crop failure. Addressing three back-to-back rallies in Jamnagar, Amreli and Sanand on 11 December, Rahul said: 'The government and your Chief Minster do not listen to your voice. He just cares about his own voice. He thinks only about his dreams, not of his people.'

Calling himself a follower of Mahatma Gandhi, Rahul said he was the true *Rajpurush*. 'A true political leader,' said Rahul, 'is the one who works to make dreams of others true and forgets about his own.' Attacking Modi's publicity campaign, Rahul said: 'Marketers say Gujarat is shining but here in Jamnagar, water is available only for fifteen minutes, that too on every fourth day. Is this Gujarat shining?'

To Rahul's allegation that the Gujarat State Legislative Assembly did business only for 25 days in a year, Modi replied: 'From May 2011 to May 2012, Rahul Gandhi's attendance in the Lok Sabha was 24 out of 85 sittings. From 2010 to 2011, it was 19 out of 72 sittings.' That, said Modi, showed Rahul's respect for the Lok Sabha.

As for Rahul's Gandhi's claim that he was a true follower of Mahatma Gandhi, Modi asked: 'If Rahul Baba is walking on Gandhiji's path, why is Bapu's first wish incomplete: to disband the Congress after Independence?'

While campaigning for the Gujarat Legislative Assembly elections in November 2012, Modi had more occasions to take on Rahul and the UPA. He took a dig at the UPA Government saying that three years had passed since an RTI application had been filed seeking details on the matter of disbanding the Congress but there had been no reply. 'When an attempt is made to hide things, one feels something is fishy,' Modi said. The Congress reply to this was predictable. Party spokesman Manish Tewari rubbished Modi's questions claiming 'these reflect the mind set and character of a person who had taken the low road and we do not want to dignify his lies by a rejoinder'. So, Modi's question went unanswered.

The entire election campaign consisted of charges and counter-charges. Sonia Gandhi, for instance, had said in one of her very few speeches that the Dial 108 emergency service was a project of the Centre. To this, Modi said it was the state's (Gujarat's) initiative to take people in emergencies to hospital, free of cost. Modi also raked up the issue of fake encounters. Addressing himself to Rahul, he said: 'Rahul Baba, if your family members have gone to jail in the freedom struggle, we appreciate it. But you cannot kill democracy with your family politics. Soniaji has used the CBI to put innocent people of Gujarat in jail.'

Responding to Rahul's allegation that he appropriated credit for everything for himself, Modi responded: 'I am the only person who says my Gujarat is shining due to six crore Gujaratis. But how individualistic are you? Five thousand schemes have been named only after your father, your grandmother and your great grandfather. You are *parivarvadi* (only for your family); you are individualistic and have crippled democracy ... Rahul Baba, *zaban sambhal ke bolna* (watch what you say!).'

And so it went. Admittedly, mud-throwing did no credit either to the Congress or to the BJP.

The Role Envisioned by Modi for the 2014 General Elections

With whatever views Modi and Rahul Gandhi lead their parties into electoral battle in 2014, there is no question that the former has clear views on the political scene and what his own role is. This came through in a detailed interview he gave to Saisuresh Sivaswamy and Nikhil Lakshman in May 2009 (Rediff.com), five years earlier. The views he held then still hold good, as far as one can see.

Pinpricks

Q: What do you think of Congress Party President Sonia Gandhi?

Modi: What? Is it my job to give an opinion on everything?

Q: No, but as a political personality.

Modi: *Arre bhai*, if she has any political experience or has made any contribution to the country, then a debate can happen in which the plus and minus points will emerge. *Bas*, she has the one party that she got from her in-laws as her legacy.

Q: Don't you think your party, the Bharatiya Janata Party, grew best when the dynasty's presence was waning in the Congress? And when the dynasty returned, the BJP's growth seems to have plateaued?

Modi: After P V Narasimha Rao formed the government (in June 1991), we won thrice from Gujarat. We were nowhere in the south, now we have a government there.

Q: Do you think Dr Singh's reputation as an economist and as a financial manager is overstated?

Modi: Look, when Dr Singh was Finance Minister (June 1991-May 1996), the Harshad Mehta scam happened. And when he is PM, Satyam has happened. The biggest shocks to the economy have happened in his tenure.

By virtue of him being the PM, there are expectations from him. If he were the chairman of the Planning Commission, the expectations would be different. If he was an economist, the debate would be different. A prime minister should be leading the nation differently. That's why he has to be answerable to the people for everything.

Q: Are you satisfied with this government's management of the financial meltdown?

Modi: What does my satisfaction have to do with it? They are not giving my state any funds. All over India, they adopted three projects as national projects, but not my Narmada project.

Q: And that is because Narendra Modi is the Chief Minister?

Modi: I don't say that.

The Man of the Moment: Narendra Modi

Q: Why would Gujarat then be discriminated against?

Modi: May be they feel the people of Gujarat don't help them. Politically, they are not useful to them. And they are taking it out on our people.

Q: You are making a direct allegation against the Government of India.

Modi: Yes, I am repeating it, that my state is being treated unjustly.

Q: Are there any other examples of this?

Modi: See, Gujarat has the maximum number of vehicles; petrol-diesel consumption is the highest here. You earn cess from it with which you build roads. But my state gets zero budget while their favourite state gets ₹13,000 crore. What will you call this?

Q: You are alleging there is a continuous pattern of discrimination?

Modi: I am saying exactly that. In my state, we want to take a water pipeline below the railway line; the expenditure is being borne by my government, but for the last two years, the Railway Ministry in Delhi has not given permission for this. In my state, in another place, we have this bridge that is complete on both sides: the railway line is on the river bank, so I have not been given permission to join the bridge. For two years, the bridge has been lying unusable after spending money on it … (Modi cites four other such instances.)

Q: You recently levelled a charge that ₹50,000 crore has gone missing from the government coffers?

Modi: The Comptroller and Auditor General's report is there on the basis of which I have asked this of the Indian Government. ₹50,000 crore is missing, where has it gone? And so far, the government has not answered.

Q: Do you believe Indian democracy is faulty?

Modi: It was not always like this, so we cannot say that there's something wrong with our system. The change may be on account of the individual or the system, but this is not good for democracy.

Q: Are there any three things you would change about Indian democracy?

Modi: One, make voting compulsory. There should be an option to reject our vote ... Two, the elected body should have a fixed five-year term ... Elections every two months, six months won't do for this nation ... by holding elections prematurely, it is not possible to showcase one's performance.

Q: When leaders like Sharad Pawar or P Chidambaram say something about you, you are the only leader to retaliate. Why do you feel the need to react to everything people say about you?

Modi: Please decide: is that an allegation or criticism? If it is an allegation, then it is my right to respond. If the criticism is wrong, then it is my right to issue correct information. This is also a right in democracy. Why do you take it amiss? Yes, I don't retaliate to an allegation with a counter allegation. That's not my style.

Q: How can Hindu-Muslim relations in this country be improved?

Modi: Get out of vote bank politics. Then everything will be all right.

Q: Why do you call it vote bank politics? Because what you call vote bank politics, others call it giving the largest minority a share in governance.

Modi: Why don't you read the Sachar Committee report? The Sachar Committee report says in Gujarat, everyone – Hindu and Muslim alike – are better off. And the Sachar Committee report was commissioned by the Manmohan Singh government. The report says everyone gets the same justice in Gujarat.

Q: You are seen – not only by news traders, to use your favourite phrase – but by many parts of Indian society as a divisive figure. Do you feel your achievements are not valued enough?

Modi: I don't know. I am not in it for myself. I am in for Gujarat. Shouldn't there be criticism in a democracy? The strength of democracy is in criticism. Yes, while criticism is welcome, allegations are not. If you don't criticize, where will the positives come from?

Q: Does it bother you when America denies you a visa?

Modi: For you it may be important. My thinking is, let us build a strong India that Americans will line up for a visa to visit our country. Your thinking reflects the slave mentality, not mine. I think let all of America stand in a queue to get our visa.

Q: People say you are too polarizing a figure to lead India.

Modi: Those who say so, please discuss with them why they think like this, what proof do they have? In all of India, Narendra Modi is the only chief minister who speaks for five crore Gujaratis.

Q: There is a belief in some political circles that you are trying to retreat on *Hindutva*.

Modi: What is your definition of *Hindutva*? The Supreme Court of India has said *Hindutva* is a way of life. Those who have associated me with *Hindutva*, please ask them what they mean. I am devoted to Bharat Mata. I am a *poojari* (worshipper) of her culture. From our Vedas to Swami Vivekananda, all our ancient rishis, Gandhi, Buddha – we should be proud of them all. And we do feel proud. If you don't agree, you are welcome to criticize.

One of Modi's strengths has been his easy access to people. A group of young people from Parbani who had visited Gujarat as a part of the *Prakash* Yatra had a scintillating discussion with Mr Modi. Their observation was that the former Prime Minister, Mr Atal Bihari Vajpayee, had made development a 'national issue'. Going ahead in that direction, Modi had stated that he wanted to make development a 'basic need'. He wanted development to be a people's movement. A question was asked about the 'sustainability' of the Gujarat model. He immediately clarified: 'Modi may or may not be there ... but the development of Gujarat shall not stop.' Thus, his effort would be to institutionalize every idea, every development activity. Another question asked was how the system of government in the 21st century should be? He instantly replied: 'Maximum governance, minimal government'! The group was able to get to know about a few innovations such as the Jyotigram plan, Karmayogi programme, annual chintan shibirs for the officers, Nirmal Gujarat plan, URBAN Plan, Chief Minister Fellowship Plan, e-city, *Sadbhavana* Yatra, 'Vidyadeep Plan' and the *Rakhsha Shakti* University. However, that was the tip of the iceberg.

The Nitish Factor

During and after the elections, one issue often raised its head: Was Modi aiming at the prime ministership of India if the NDA came to power in Delhi? Many opined that that indeed was Modi's aim, and in spite of claiming that he was committed to Gujarat all the way, there was no way he could hide his ambition.

It is well known that Modi has his supporters as well as his detractors, and among them, one man stands out – Nitish Kumar, Chief Minister of Bihar. Nitish Kumar's dislike of Modi has led him to state that should Modi be the NDA's candidate for the prime ministership of India, he would dissociate himself from the BJP. And judging by the vigour with which he has expressed himself, it is clear that he means to stand by his word.

What is unforgettable is that Nitish Kumar owes a great deal to the BJP. In the early 1990s, when the United Janata Dal began splintering into small outfits, Nitish Kumar went along with George Fernandes and benefitted from electoral alliances with the BJP in the 1996, 1998 and 1999 parliamentary elections. In all those elections, Nitish Kumar won his parliamentary seats with support from the BJP – the same party that had been dubbed communal by him and his party colleagues in the past.

In March 2000, when Nitish Kumar became Chief Minister of Bihar, Modi was General Secretary of the BJP and was to remain in that position till he was dispatched to Gujarat in October 2001.

It is not so well known that Nitish Kumar had a sneaking admiration for Modi at that time. Reference has been made to this by a leading Hindi writer, thinker and political activist, Premkumar Mani.

In a published report, Premkumar Mani recalled an incident, sometime in 2004, when he had a long chat with Nitish. It was a year when, in the Lok Sabha elections, the NDA, led by George Fernandes and Nitish Kumar, had been badly mauled. Premkumar Mani told Nitish that the NDA had to bite the dust because of Modi and the events of 2002. Mani apparently had no respect for Modi and told Nitish so. Nitish Kumar's reaction came quite as a

The Man of the Moment: Narendra Modi

shock to Premkumar. As the writer put it, Nitish was unwilling to concede Mani his point. He told him: 'Narendra Modi is the new face of the BJP. He comes from a backward class: he is a Ghanchi, – a minority backward caste. The BJP's Brahmin lobby is out to defame him. He comes from a very poor family. He is extremely simple and very diligent.' According to Mani, Nitish seemed to be in a trance and was unstoppable. He went on to tell Mani: 'Modi is a dynamic man. Meet him once and you will become his admirer. He comes from a very poor family. I have become his fan.'

Nitish Kumar and Modi's backgrounds were very different: Nitish came from a *kulak* Kurmi family of Bihar, while Modi hailed from an extremely poor and most backward class Ghanchi family of Gujarat. Nitish's father was an ayurvedic *Vaidyraj* (doctor), while Modi's father was a small-time tea vendor. Modi spent his childhood in his father's tea shop, while Nitish was studied engineering. Whatever Modi learned, he learned in the school of 'hard knocks'.

Nitish's accusation has been that Modi did not work towards stopping the 2002 riots. He turned against Modi. When Bihar became a victim of floods and suffered a great deal and Modi magnanimously offered financial help, Nitish brusquely refused to accept it.

During the 2012 state assembly elections, Modi was reported to have made a reference to Bihar saying that at one time Bihar was 'a spiritual and political leader of the country', but had slipped into socio-economical backwardness ever since casteist leadership took over the stage. Nitish greatly resented that comment and reacted by saying that Modi should keep his own house in order and make no comments on others. Modi was expecting Nitish to come to Gujarat during the canvassing for the 2012 polls to lend him support, but Nitish did not oblige. Indeed, when it became clear that Modi and the BJP had won handsomely, Nitish even refused to send a word of congratulations to his Gujarat counterpart.

Keshubhai's Machinations

Call him a frustrated politician, call him a casteist with high ambitions, call him a failed chief minister – whatever epithet may best suit him, Keshubhai Patel has been one of Modi's worst opponents. True, after Keshubhai was eased out of power, it was Modi who was asked to replace him as chief minister. One can hardly blame Modi for that. The offer of chief ministership had come to him too as a surprise. But right from that time, it seems that Keshubhai was just not able to forgive Modi. Early in 2012, Keshubhai started attacking Modi saying that he was a demon and people were living in fear of him. At a public forum, Keshubhai declared that the Patidars (Patels) were living under the shadow of fear. On 13 May, he went one step further by saying: 'Gujarat is ruled by *pindaris* and thugs and people live under fear, including IAS and IPS officers.'

A week earlier, on 6 May at a meeting of the Somnath Temple Trust, he had said: *Dar ke agey jeet hai* (victory is yours if you overcome fear). The person who had allegedly put fear in everybody's heart was Modi.

In the previous assembly elections in 2007, Modi had sailed through despite a rebellion of sorts by Patidar leaders within the state BJP. Reports suggested that Modi had done so by sharpening the divide between the Leuva and Kadva Patels.

But in 2012, Keshubhai was seen as a power centre that could hurt Modi a great deal. At massive community gatherings, Keshubhai was hailed as Bapa, meaning Respected Elder. According to one report, in April 2012, in Surat, few people attended a meeting addressed by Modi. In contrast, at a community gathering at Jamkandorma in Saurashtra held two days later, some 60,000 people were present at an address by Keshubhai. One reason for the anti-Modi angst reportedly was the fact that many Patels were being targetted in court cases relating to the 2002 riots. Word was going round, especially among anti-Modi circles, that the 'political isolation of Modi had begun in the party'.

Determined to displace Modi, Keshubhai had floated his own party, the Gujarat Parivartan Party (GPP). On 9 August 2012, Keshubhai's party was to merge with BJP's second rebel Gordhan Zadaphia's Mahagujarat Janata Party. Yet another former RSS functionary, Jagdish Damji Desai of Palitana who had been denied a BJP ticket, joined Keshubhai. Many sincerely believed that Modi was going to be in real trouble. What should have worried Modi was that in addition to these rebels, another former BJP Chief Minister, Suresh Mehta, was giving Keshubhai company, along with Kashiram Rana, a former state BJP chief.

But not all cadres of the media were pleased with these developments. The *Free Press Journal* (2 July 2012) was unmoved. It wrote:

> *The reported move by the disgruntled elements in the Gujarat BJP to go their own separate way ought to be welcome. If former Chief Minister Keshubhai Patel is unhappy at his growing marginalization under the Narendra Modi dispensation, he should be welcome to explore other alternatives. For, pursuit of power has become the sole objective of today's politicians. It is unlikely that Modi will share power with Patel. It is another matter that by floating a so-called third front in the state, supposedly equidistant from both the BJP and the Congress, it can only succeed, if at all, in spoiling the electoral prospects of their former party. Power will still elude them. But consumed as they are with jealousy and resentment against the rise and rise of Modi, their real motive would be not so much to gain power but to deny it to Modi. Therefore, it would not be a surprise if they get generous help in their misadventure from the Congress which on its own is bereft of a credible leader in Gujarat ....*

The paper said that surprisingly, Patel did not seem to be deterred by the sorry plight of the dissidents who had deserted the BJP on the eve of the previous assembly elections. The paper said that they had failed to make any impression on the Gujarat voters last time around. It added: 'And given the growing political awareness of the *aam aadmi*, it would come as no surprise if the BJP dissidents led by Patel too were rebuffed in the coming assembly poll.'

That is exactly what happened. Modi was expected to win as many as 135 seats, but he managed to win 115, only two less than what he had won in 2005. The *Free Press Journal* opined: 'The voter is clear enough to realize that the dissidents hanker after no loftier objective than the leaves and fishes of political office.'

The Sanjay Joshi Angst

Sanjay Joshi, a fellow RSS worker who had started his political career along with Modi, had come to Ahmedabad in 1988-89 from

Maharashtra to work for the BJP. In 1990, Modi was the General Secretary of the state unit of the BJP while Joshi was Secretary. Both had worked together for about five years along with other leaders; that was the crucial phase of the state BJP when the party had come to power for the first time in Gujarat with Keshubhai Patel as Chief Minister in 1995.

However, in 1995 itself, after a revolt by then party leader Shankarsinh Vaghela, Modi was shunted out of the state and Joshi became the powerful general secretary of the BJP state unit. To cut a long story short, with Vaghela out, Keshubhai returned to power in 1998 only to be eased out in 2001 and be replaced by Modi.

Joshi took it badly. In 2012, Joshi decided to take on Modi. Hoardings began to appear in Ahmedabad supporting Joshi. The hoardings and posters with Joshi's pictures stated: *Chote man se koi bada nahi hota, tute man se koi bada nai hota* (nobody becomes big with a narrow mind). The billboards also said: *Kaho dil se ... Sanjay Joshi phir se* (Say with all your heart, Joshi once again).

A PTI report (6 June, 2012) mentioned that the hoardings apparently targetted the Gujarat Chief Minister though his name has not been written anywhere on them. Modi reportedly threatened to quit the national executive, if Joshi was allowed to continue as its member. The BJP central leadership asked Joshi to resign from the national executive following which Modi went to Mumbai to attend the national executive meeting.

The Elections of 2012

Modi launched his poll campaign on 11 September 2012 and it raged with increasing bitterness as the days passed. Congress leaders were unsparing in their criticism of Modi and the language used reflected poorly on the competing parties.

Modi accused the Congress of 'misusing' the Central Bureau of Investigation (CBI) to target him. Signalling that he would fight the coming polls on the plaint of 'injustice meted out to Gujarat', Modi appealed to the people to work towards a 'Congress-free Gujarat' on the lines of the '*Gutka*-free Gujarat'[1]. Addressing a meeting in Mehsana, Modi said that he had faced multiple probes but demanded that it was time for the Prime Minister to face an SIT probe on the coal block allocation scam that was darkening the country's image. 'To corner me, they form an SIT whenever they want to. I appeal to Manmohan Singh and the Congress to come forward and have a competition in facing probes. Let us see who has more prowess in facing such probes,' Modi challenged.

Modi alleged that the Congress had a habit of targetting constitutional authorities by creating an atmosphere of anger against the institutions that did not toe its line.

Many in the media might have wondered whether Modi would really capture legislative power in Gujarat. Keshubhai was a power to reckon with among the Patel community. Prime Minister Manmohan Singh may have thought that one light push and Modi

---

1 *Gutka* is a preparation made from crushed betel nuts, tobacco and othe flavourings. Consumed like chewing tobacco, it is one of the major causes of oral cancer and other health disorders. Narendra Modi launched a campaign for '*gutka*-free Gujarat' and ordered a state-wide comprehensive ban on sale and consumption of gutka on 11 September 2012.

would be out. He was likely to have been briefed by the haters of Modi within the Congress and there were many. Singh's address in Vansda (Navsari) on 9 December 2012 showed that he had been taken in by party propagandists. For Dr Singh to get into active politics itself was something of a novelty; for him to voice anti-Modi views in public strongly indicated the severe pressure he must have had from the party's top leadership. Rahul and Sonia also did the same.

Stepping up the party campaign, Dr Singh told a large audience that minorities, including some government officials, were feeling 'insecure' under Modi's government. He also accused the BJP of indulging in 'divisive politics' – something that he himself was unconsciously doing in his speeches. As The *Indian Express* (10 December 2012) reported, he said: 'It is the responsibility of any government to make minorities and weaker sections feel secure. The Gujarat Government is not giving any attention to this. There have been repeated complaints from this state that minorities and some sections are feeling insecure; even some government officials have complained about this. It is very sad that such an environment persists in the land of Mahatma Gandhi. Our opposition party plays politics to divide sections of society on the basis of religion and caste. The time has come to liberate Gujarat from this type of politics and to not let those people come back to power who have been trying to get votes by dividing our society and country.'

Contesting the Modi Government's development claims, Dr Singh said: 'The development of Gujarat is focussed among a few sections of people; a major part of the population is left behind .... We just want to know who are the beneficiaries – whether the development reaches villages, minorities and other poor sections of society.' Dr Singh also said that 41 per cent of the state's women were victims of malnourishment and the enrolment of minorities in schools had gone down.

The same approach was adopted by Home Minister Sushil Kumar Shinde. Addressing a meeting in Vadodara on 9 December 2012, Shinde termed the BJP as a party 'which orchestrates riots', and as having too many prime ministerial candidates. He added: 'The BJP and Shiv Sena once came into power in Maharashtra. However, whenever they have come into power, they have orchestrated riots. The people of Maharashtra realized this and taught them a lesson in 2004, by throwing them out of power.'

Taking a pot shot at Modi, Shinde said that they (Modi and the BJP) spoke of better law and order, but 13 lakh cases had been registered in the last 10 years. He said: 'Children who go missing are not returning. Poor women who go missing are not found. I am the Home Minister and I get all the intelligence reports.'

Luckily for Shinde, nobody asked him how many cases had been registered in courts of Congress-ruled states, how many missing children had not returned and how many missing women had not been found!

The vilification was indulged in not just by Congressmen but also by a large section of the English media to the point that the BJP senior leader L K Advani was moved to complain. Writing on his blog on 8 July 2012, Advani said that no political leader in India's history had been so 'systematically and viciously maligned' as the Gujarat Chief Minister. But there were exceptions. For example, Arvind Panagariya, a Professor of Economics at Columbia University, writing in The *Times of India* (22 September 2012) said that 'critics who insist on viewing everything related to Modi through the 2002 lens and thus, failing to separate their economics from politics, have fallen short of 20/20 vision.'

Prof Panagariya said that based on the per capita Net State Domestic Product (NSDP) in 2009-2010, Gujarat ranked third, behind Maharashtra and Haryana but ahead of Tamil Nadu, Kerala, Punjab and Karnataka, in that order.

Panagariya said that while the performance in agriculture had received the greatest attention, perhaps 'the most exceptional feature of Gujarat's success has been the performance of manufacturing. Compared with the national average of 15 per cent, manufacturing in Gujarat accounted for 27.4 per cent of the Gross State Domestic Product (GSDP) in 2009-10.'

He went on to say that while 'critics might say that this proportion has risen only one percentage point since 2002-03, given the uphill battle manufacturing faces in India, even maintaining the share at this high level is a challenge.'

And he added: 'Based on the Tendulkar poverty lines and methodology, overall poverty in Gujarat fell by only six percentage points during 11 years between 1993-94 and 2004-05. But during just five years between 2004-05 and 2009-10, it fell by an impressive nine percentage points. In 2009-10, the poverty ratio in Gujarat at 23 per cent was almost seven percentage points below the national average. The decline in poverty has been observed across all major social groups.'

As Panagariya saw it, the critic's case was particularly weak in education, considering that Gujarat added 10 percentage points to the literacy rate during 2001-2011, more than any other comparative state.

'While one can selectively poke holes in nearly every success story, taken as a whole, it is difficult to remain unimpressed by what Gujarat has achieved,' he said.

Then there is Swapan Dasgupta who, writing in The *Free Press Journal* (13 July 2012), pointed out that the Modi miracle was no fake. He conceded that Modi may have played to the pre-existing strengths of Gujarat but asked: 'But had the Chief Minister been venal, unresponsive and mindlessly populist – as he so easily could have been – would India still be talking of the Gujarat miracle?'

Dasgupta was back again supporting Modi in The *Telegraph* (14 September 2012) saying that 'there is a feeling in some circles that the coming months could witness a growing momentum in favour of Narendra Modi.' Dasgupta said that 'since 2009, Modi has emerged as the favourite son of BJP-inclined voters' and 'in terms of popularity, he has eclipsed all other BJP notables'. Opinion polls suggest, said Desgupta 'that the Gujarat Chief Minister has broadened his appeal considerably to embrace a vast section of urban India, the middle classes and the youth. Today, Modi's appeal is far wider than the support for the BJP, a development that both excites the rank and file of his party and leaves a section of its leadership deeply worried.'

Mona Mehta, Assistant Professor of Political Science at IIT, Gandhinagar, noted in The *Indian Express* (11 December 2012) that 'despite his (Modi's) rhetoric against the UPA, Modi's political makeover from *Hindutva* to development is a response to the larger story of Indian economic growth. The Gujarat elections in 2007 launched the first Modi makeover campaign to match the changed political agenda in Delhi ... *Hindutva* slogans which had a significant impact on Gujarat voters in 2002 were now replaced with slogans about Gujarat's economic growth and global investment in the state. Development became the central theme and the sub-texts of Gujarati pride, and *Hindutva* was pushed into the background .... The implications of this election's outcome will be important not just for Gujarat but also for India. If the Modi makeover strategy succeeds spectacularly in Gujarat, the BJP may be tempted to use this Gujarati model at the national level ....'

But there were others who felt that Modi had become a disaster. Atul Sood, a teacher at Jawaharlal Nehru University, New Delhi, wrote in The *Hindu* (30 November 2012) that he found many things wrong in Modi-ruled Gujarat. The biggest casualty of the 'successful' growth in Gujarat, said Sood, was employment, though he was quick to add that 'the stagnant employment growth in the last five years in Gujarat was better than the decline in employment experienced at the national level'. The loss in rural employment had occurred along with reduced participation of small farmers in the fast-growing, high-value crops and reduced access to cultivated land because of changes in the norms for sale and purchase of land. Gujarat, wrote Sood, 'provides a window to understand the limits of market-led growth and an insight into a police regime that does not attempt to mitigate the most brutal consequences of this specific mode of production.'

A prime example of the extent of anti-Modism, was an article in *Economic and Political Weekly* (8 December 2012) by Neera Chandoke, Director of the Developing Countries Research Centre, University of Delhi. According to Chandoke, 'If today Gujarat appears peaceful, it is because the minorities have been banished to the spatial margins of the ghetto and bludgeoned into acquiescence by a muscular ideology that has tamed both political and civil society.' The people of Gujarat, according to Chandoke, 'have paid a heavy price for buying into demagoguery'. She added: 'Let us hope they understand that growth without human development is hollow and democracy without minority rights in tyranny.' Ironically, the 2012 elections vindicated Modi.

The *Hindu* (20 December 2012) has never been a great admirer of Modi, if one believes Smita Gupta whose article proclaimed that 'the selective images of progress that have cast a spell on many, do not represent a progressive world-view, but an evolved *Hindutva*'. As she saw it, 'From the man to the mask to the hologram, Mr Modi's political journey as Chief Minister has grown progressively delusional.' Her attack, at one level, was personal. In her opinion, Modi no longer resembled the RSS *pracharak* he once was. 'His wardrobe, customized by Jade Blue, an expensive chain of menswear stores, patronized by the likes of Gautam Adani, has given him a new whole image. The sleek appearance, set off by a range of turbans, *bandi* (a kind of sleeveless jacket commonly worn by men in Gujarat) and traditional shawls, is a far cry from his earlier frill looks.' She went on to add: 'As the great impresario of Gujarat, he has used official machinery to showcase himself as Father Bountiful, with district magistrates playing event managers for an unending series of melas, blurring the line between party and government.'

Gupta's criticism of Modi in the field of administration was stronger. A sample: 'Those making flying visits to the state, whether NRIs or home-grown industrialists, are so dazzled by the glitzy glass and chrome malls of Ahmedabad, Surat and Rajkot and the network of super highways, that few among them care to look beyond at the pockmarked roads and the swathes of poverty in the interiors.'

Gupta even challenged Modi's sincerity. Commenting on his approach to Islam and Muslims, her assessment was summarized thus: 'At the much-hyped *Sadbhavana* rallies, Mr Modi posed with Muslims, but refused to wear a skull cap – even for a few seconds – lest it alienate his core *Hindutva* base. His object was merely to help his acolytes tell those who care to hear them that he is not anti-Muslim.' It just didn't occur to Gupta that it is wrong in principle for any caste, creed, religion or community to distinguish itself as a separate entity through styles of dress and department. Where was it mandatory for a Muslim to wear a skull cap all the time?

The Man of the Moment: Narendra Modi

What is significant is that when Modi began his first fast, priests of various religions – Hinduism, Islam, Christianity, Sikhism and Zorastrianism – and sects such as Swaminarayan, sat alongside Modi. If our secularists are to be believed, all those priests were hypocrites! Before beginning his fast, Modi had clearly said that he had 'suffered' more than anyone realized, at the sufferings that the riot victims had undergone. As chief minister, he averred, he was a representative of each and every one of the six crore Gujaratis, irrespective of their caste, creed, culture and religion.

Modi's critics came in various shapes and forms. Thus, Parsa Venkateshwar Rao Jr, Editorial Consultant to *DNA*, writing in his paper (16 December 2012) said that the 'mistake that Modi and his liberal *"frenemies"* (friendly enemies) make is to think that Gujarat is the stepping-stone to success.' That, claimed Rao, was not the case. Among other sharp comments, he said that while the BJP might retain power for many years, the fact was 'Gujarat is the bastion of right-wing communal politics masquerading as an economic success'. To that he added:

> *The underlying thesis of the fear of Modi's possible poll success is this: that Mr Hyde who turned Gujarat into a shining laboratory of Hindutva would want to take the experiment forward in the rest of the country. Interestingly, Chief Minister Narendra Modi seems to share the same prognosis of his army of liberal detractors. He and his coterie of admirers believe that a hat-trick of success in Gujarat will catapult him on to the national stage and that he will take a pot shot at being the Prime Minister in 2014. Ambition is not a bad thing and Modi can dream about better things for himself and his party. Modi has shown himself to be quite shallow and at times even callow ... He has grown up to be a Chief Minister in the distorted Gujarat political situation, but he has a long way to travel to make sense of national issues. The learning curve has not even begun ....*

Other newspapers too showcased how much hatred Modi evoked.

Writing in The *Hindustan Times* (11 September 2012), Ajaz Ashraf, a Delhi-based journalist said that while the judgement of the Special Court in Ahmedabad convicting 32 people for their role in the Naroda-Patiya 'massacre' should help heal the wounds of the Muslim community, the verdict was neither likely to diminish

The Elections of 2012

the fear the community had about majority communalism nor persuade it to believe that the horror of Gujarat would never revisit them.

He presented his case thus: The massive mandate 'Modi received in two successive assembly elections perplexes Muslims into asking: why hasn't the violence of 2002 repulsed the Hindu supporters of Modi?'

Like many secularists and Modi-haters, Ashraf too, it was obvious, did not want to think of how some 55-odd innocent women and children were roasted alive in a coach of the Sabarmati Express by a Muslim mob in Godhra, raising uncontrollable anger against this horrendous atrocity. Ashraf's blinkers merely induced the belief: 'The endeavour to project him (Modi) as a possible PM consequently persuades Muslims to believe that there is as yet no social consequence that the riots violated the nation's collective conscience, particularly as he has adamantly refused to apologize for them.'

What is interesting to note in this connection is why the Muslim community has not apologized for the slow and deliberate roasting of the innocent Sabarmati Express coach travellers! The reaction of many indicates that they do not want to face reality or to be reminded of the roasting of women and children which one newspaper casually dismissed as 'an incident' that provoked the subsequent rioting.

Even when Modi sought to use a three-day fast as a sign of deep regret, the Muslim mood outside Gujarat was one of hostility. Thus Mufti Muqarram Ahmad, the Shahi Imam of Fatehpuri Masjid in New Delhi, was to say that there was nothing in the fast that could be said to be a genuine effort by Modi towards communal harmony. The Mufti thought the fast had an ulterior political motive. As he told The *Deccan Herald* (18 September 2012): 'This fast by Mr Modi has political motives. It has nothing to do with establishing communal harmony. If he is so concerned about the issue of communalism, then why didn't he apologize for the post-Godhra carnage in his fast?'

Muslims alone were not involved in the damning of Modi. Of all people, Mahatma Gandhi's great grandson, Tushar Gandhi, dismissed Modi for indulging in 'self-publicity'. The fasting, according to Tushar Gandhi, was an example of 'me and myself'.

Another critic was a one-time RSS ideologue, K N Govindacharya, who was quoted by The *Sentinel* (12 September 2012) as saying that the Sanjay Joshi episode had shown that Modi lacked tolerance and was personal in political matters. In Govindacharya's opinion, Modi was not a suitable candidate for the prime ministership of India, and claimed that the NDA convener Sharad Yadav was a better candidate. Damning Modi's alleged claims, Govindacharya said that 'continuous speculations and aspirations by leaders is demeaning the office of the prime minister'.

According to *DNA* (19 December 2012), what was happening in Gujarat was a 'subtle *Hindutva* wave'. According to Shekhar Gupta in The *Indian Express* (19 December 2012), 'By choosing fury over fact, delusion over reason, passion over politics, Modi's enemies – beginning with the Congress – make Gujarat politics a one-horse race.'

In fact, Shekhar Gupta has a very interesting story to recount the mood in Gujarat, which must be taken as totally independent of Modi. One suspects that even if there was no Modi, a sense of disquiet with the Muslims has always been present in the Gujarati Hindu psyche. This was the story:

Shekhar Gupta was once working for *India Today*. The latter was planning to bring out its Gujarati edition in the *Navaratri* month of 1992. Shekhar did a good deal of travelling within Gujarat during that period. Once the Gujarati edition came out, it immediately began to pick up circulation and soon touched the one-lakh mark. Then came the Babri Masjid demolition. *India Today* responded editorially with what Gupta calls 'entirely justifiable anger'. The English edition's headline was: 'A Nation's Shame'. In Gujarati it was *'Deshna Maathanu Kalank'*. As the cover was going to print, the marketing head of the weekly warned the publishers that if the Gujarati edition carried that headline, 'the edition would soon shut down'. He was overruled by the publishers. But the reaction in Gujarat vindicated the marketing head. The *India Today* office in Delhi started getting an 'avalanche' of letters, post cards, inland covers – everything. Readers brandished

The Elections of 2012

India Today with defamatory titles as *Islam Today, Pakistan Today* and, as Shekhar Gupta notes, 'worse titles'. Agents and vendors refused to pick up the magazine. Circulation declined and the edition was finally shut down, 'the only language edition of *India Today*' to be so closed.

It is easy to point out that in 1992, Modi was nowhere in the picture. How does one explain Gujarati anger? To quote Shekhar Gupta because it is so relevant:

> *Is there something about Gujarat that makes it so angry? In a recent pan-Indian opinion poll conducted by NDTV, one of the questions was if India should have better relations with Pakistan. In Punjab, 72 per cent people said Yes, and in Haryana, 80 per cent. In Rajasthan the number was 42. And in Gujarat – it was just 30, amongst the lowest in the country. What is it that makes Gujarat our angriest border state?*

Shekhar Gupta is very sceptical of our secularists. He has a question to ask them:

> *If you say that all his (Modi's) claims of growth and development are rubbish, then why are Gujaratis voting for him? Can you then go on also to hail the same people for the religious tolerance and liberalism that is said to have ruled their land pre-Modi?*

> *One accusation against Modi is that he is only a marketing person. But his rivals also need to realize the essential principles of marketing, that nothing fails more disastrously as an obvious lie, no matter how passionately you say it. That is why, as we saw ... the Congress questioning of Modi's claims on power supply and industrial growth falls flat and works in Modi's favour.*

Needless to say, there are some 'intellectuals' who just do not want to understand or cannot understand either Gujarat or Modi. Such a one is Amulya Ganguli who, writing in The *Sentinel* (16 December 2012) went to great lengths to run down Modi, as 'the grumpy head of a patriarchal household', whose appeal is 'confined primarily to the communal-minded Hindus of the urban middle class'. Ganguli's explanation for Modi's 'switching over' to industrial development' is that Modi had realized that the 2002 riots would remain the main stumbling block against the dream he had been entertaining – that of wanting to be the

The Man of the Moment: Narendra Modi

prime minister. As Ganguli saw the situation, Modi had to win more than 117 out of the 182 assembly seats if his desire to become prime minister had to be strengthened.

The fact remains that though Modi won the assembly elections by capturing only 115 seats – two less than in the past elections – he seemed to have been nervous about scoring his target. But how was it that he won only 115 seats when many exit polls said that he could win as many as 135 seats? The answer was provided after the elections were over when Keshubhai Patel was interviewed by The *Times of India:*

Q: Your campaign focussed on bringing about change in Gujarat's leadership. But Modi is still the CM with the possibility of becoming PM in future.

Patel: It is wrong to believe that Modi's victory is complete. Some of his prominent ministers lost this time. Even his party president could not win.

Q: But Modi is obviously doing something right if he got 115 seats and you got only two.

Patel: A number of factors are responsible for our defeat, but most importantly, we were not able to appeal to the youth who voted in large numbers because of the Election Commission.

Q: How would you evaluate the performance of your newly-formed Gujarat Parivartan Party?

Patel: We did not win as many seats as we expected but we succeeded in reducing Modi's majority by two seats, compared to 2007. Our vote share was 3.63 per cent, which ate into BJP's vote share by 1 per cent. We won only two seats, but we damaged BJP's chances by at least 15, especially in Saurashtra. Can you imagine Modi's overall tally had we not been in the race? He would easily have pocketed 130 to 135 seats ....

Much was made of Keshubhai Patel by Modi-haters. But the truth came out in an *India Today* Group-ORG opinion poll published in the weekly on 5 November 2012. Both Leuva and Kadwa Patels were interview and the results were as follows:

Q: Will you vote for Modi, if the election is held today?

The Elections of 2012

A: Yes (72%); No (25%); Can't say: (3%)

Q: Has Modi been fair to your community in the last five years?

A: Yes (62%); No (27%); Can't say: (11%)

Q: Will you vote for Keshubhai Patel?

A: Yes (10%); No (77%); Can't say: (13%)

On other issues, too, Modi came through with flying colours. Voters across the country were also questioned:

Q: Was Narendra Modi responsible for the Gujarat riots?

A: Yes (28%); No (58%); Can't say: (14%)

Q: Has industrialization in Gujarat created jobs?

A: Yes (67%); No (18%). No industrialization has happened (7%). Can't say (8%)

Q: Who would you prefer as a BJP prime minister?

A: Narendra Modi (56%); Sushma Swaraj (9%); Nitin Gadkari (3%); Arun Jaitley (3%), None of them (13%); Can't say (16%)

Q: Between Rahul Gandhi, Narendra Modi and Nitish Kumar, who would you prefer as PM?

A: Narendra Modi (56%); Rahul Gandhi (35%); Nitish Kumar (2%); Can't say (7%)

Q: What is Modi's greatest achievement?

A: Development (43%); Improved Power Supply (15%); Created Employment Opportunities (14%); Reduced Corruption (10%); Improved Irrigation Facilities (5%); Can't say (11%).

Said *India Today*: 'Modi at the stumps came out with an agenda that he knew would outsell his opponents' rage against the horrors of the riot. He marketed himself as fighter of the endangered nation and introduced a theme larger than Gujarat Terrorism. He won. In 2007, it was altogether a re-modified Modi: the can-do development man, the *Vikas Purush*.'

The Managing Editor of *India Today* S Prasannarajan, interviewed Modi:

The Man of the Moment: Narendra Modi

Q: So you are set to come to Delhi?

A: No. I won't answer any hypothetical question.

Q: You have a very clear idea about what's to be done in Gujarat. What's the most important thing you think needs to be fixed in India now?

A: India does not have a *neta*, *niti* and *niyat* (leader, policy and commitment).

Q: You won't become that *neta*? Most opinion polls project you as India's most eligible prime ministerial candidate.

A: I'm focussed on Gujarat. My commitment at the moment is to 60 million Gujaratis. My real dream is to take the growth indexes of Gujarat above the world's most developed countries. And I can do it. There are so many possibilities. For instance, there are 52 islands along the coast of Gujarat. I want to make them tourist attractions of international standard. I'm always thinking out of the box. Also, remember this: Historically, the Nehru *parivar* (family) doesn't like any Gujarati leader. They treated Patel badly. They treated Morarji Desai badly. Now it's my turn to be targetted by them.

Q: You have this image of the modernizer, and you get corporate India's endorsement. Yet you oppose foreign investment in retail.

A: It's a state subject and its imposition infringes on the federal structure of the country. More than that, after agriculture, small shops even affect our manufacturing potential. FDI won't help Hindustan's economy. Even President Obama doesn't want American jobs to go out of America. I read his tweet on that.

Q: I thought your role model would be Mrs Thatcher or Mr Reagan?

A: Obama is right on this point. Anyway, FDI in retail is not good for Hindustan's economy.

Q: It doesn't look that you have regained the Muslims' trust.

A: I don't believe in vote bank politics. For me there is no Hindu vote bank or Muslim vote bank or minority vote bank. The 60 million

The Elections of 2012

Gujaratis are my family. Of course, I'll get the BJP vote. But those who vote against me are also my family.

Q: You seem to be a leader who earns more admiration than affection among your voters. Some even tell me you are emotionally opaque.

A: That's not the impression I get from the people. There are different layers of emotions. Can't you see from the rally that they love me? They love me so much that I have to fulfill the sentiment of my people. And that is the challenge I see for myself.

Q: You are also seen to be arrogant.

A: Perception is not reality. The image of an arrogant Modi is created by a clique of the super-arrogant.

Q: Are you a loner?

A: I'm always with the people. There's no time to be a loner. I have dedicated myself to the nation since I was 16.

Q: Maybe you are a loner within your own party?

A: Whatever I'm today is because of the BJP and the party's central leadership.

The Press Post-Mortem after Election 2012

Many conjectured that in the 2012 elections, Modi banked largely on the urban connect to win a third term. The younger generation was drawn to his agenda of 'governance'. On Twitter, Modi had 9 lakh followers. A total of 2,05,77,532 or 54.51 per cent of the state's electorate belonged to the age group of 18 to 39 years. Modi had an excellent connect with the young. The election results proved it.

Out of the 182 seats, BJP won 115 seats, two less than in the last elections and Congress won 61, two more than in the previous elections. It would be appropriate at this juncture to recall Keshubhai Patel's admission that had he not set up his own party and fought against Modi, the latter would have won 135 seats. But even 115 turned out to be good enough!

Speaking in Hindi outside the BJP headquarters in Khanpur after the victory was finally announced, Modi mocked 'poll pundits for getting it wrong', and asked people to 'forgive him for any mistake that he might have made', even as the crowd that had gathered roared 'NM for PM'.

Repeatedly crediting the voters for his victory, Modi called the six crore Gujaratis 'God' and asked them to 'bless' him so that he did not make any mistake in the future.

He added that the BJP was his '*maa*', and went on to thank the 'mothers and sisters' and 'youth' who comprised the BJP's loyal vote bank. He also especially thanked the *karmayogis* (government employees), maintaining that 75 per cent of the postal ballots had been in the BJP's favour.

Interestingly, BJP won even in some areas where the Muslims had a strong presence. It scored a victory in Vejalpur (35 per cent Muslims), Bapunagar (28 per cent), Vagra (44 per cent), Bharuch (38 per cent), Jamalpur-Khadia (60 per cent), Jambusar (52 per cent) and Limbayat (27 per cent). The Congress had fielded seven Muslim candidates of whom only two won. Gayasuddin Sheikh from Dariapur in Ahmedabad won by a narrow margin securing 60,967 votes against his BJP rival Bharat Barot who received 58,346 votes.

Narendra Modi won by a large majority of 86,373 votes. Significantly, Sonia Gandhi's political advisor, Ahmed Patel, who belongs to Bharuch and Narmada – areas mostly dominated by a loyal Congress vote bank of Muslims and tribals – was not able to bring home a single of the seven seats. He had camped and campaigned there aggressively for five consecutive days before Phase I of the polls and briefly even for Phase II. Clearly, the BJP had made a dent in Congress electorates not only in central Gujarat but all over the state.

Reactions from the Indian Press

One explanation provided for Congress failure was that it had 'shot itself in the foot'. According to The *Hindustan Times* (23 December 2012), 'internal sabotage and squabbling has emerged as one of the major factors behind the Congress party's poor show'. According to the newspaper, in Ahmedabad city, the Congress lost the two Jamalpur and Bapunagar seats by slender margins because the local leaders worked against the party candidates. In Jamalpur, a sitting MLA had been denied a ticket, so he contested as an Independent and won. Writing in *DNA* (26 October 2012) columnist Seema Mustafa also blamed 'a section of opportunist mullahs' who sought to make light of the violence 'in which thousands were killed, maimed and raped'.

According to The *Hindustan Times* (25 December 2012), 57 of the elected MLAs were facing criminal charges and 134 were *crorepatis*. Among the 134 *crorepati* MLAs, 86 belonged to the BJP and 43 to the Congress. It was a sign that, in the end, money mattered in politics.

The Man of the Moment: Narendra Modi

What did the English media think of Modi's success? Given below are some post mortems and opinions:

The *Economic Times* (21 December 2012) opined that the fact that Modi had dropped a couple of seats as compared to the 2007 tally, did not take away from the magnitude of his achievement. The paper reminded its readers that in the 1930s, Stalin, Hitler and Roosevelt had all promoted vigourous development in their own countries, to legitimize a different kind of politics and associated values. Said the paper: 'Modi and the BJP have sought to legitimize the exclusive politics of Hindu majoritarianism which offers Muslims security, conditional on their suitable conduct, rather than as a right devolving from their citizenship. This is what makes the rates of growth political rather than mere matters of economics and arithmetic. Unless this politics is explicitly disowned, development cannot serve as a passport to power at the centre ....'

The *Times of India* (21 December 2012) said that 'the plank of governance, development and stability made for a package deal generating pro-incumbency.' However, the paper said, the RSS-led saffron family appears divided on giving Modi top rank in the BJP central leadership, since, viewed as an abrasive lone ranger, he isn't quite the team player. The paper blamed Modi for not making his development agenda 'more inclusive of Muslims', and added that neither, 'can he claim to have healed the wounds of the post-Godhra violence by providing speedy succour to the victims'.

The *Deccan Herald* (21 December 2012) said Modi's 'hat trick' of victories 'has significance beyond the boundaries of the state' because 'it propels him to the national stage of politics. The BJP, said the paper, won in eight of the 12 Muslim-dominated constituencies, showing that Modi's development and good governance plank could not be dismissed as mere hype. At the same time, the paper drew pointed attention to the fact that within his own party, Modi had detractors who would have liked to see Modi merely scraping through the elections.

The *New Indian Express* (21 December 2012) reminded everyone that Modi's 'substantial sway in Gujarat was essentially an urban phenomenon'; it also said that 'a section of Muslims, especially those who had benefitted from his reforms did endorse him'. That he had won on a development agenda and not on a communal or caste divide, said the paper, 'is an endorsement of Modi's model of governance'.

Very critical of Modi, The *Hindu* (21 December 2012) said that 'the real issue at stake in the polls was not the electoral map of Gujarat but the political future of Mr Modi.' Mr Modi said the paper, had 'stoked the fires of Gujarati *"asmita"*, treating the state's "six crore" people – whom he had polarized in 2002 – as if they were an undifferentiated whole'. However, it added, 'not every Gujarati is willing to buy into this kind of rhetoric.' The paper said the BJP's rank and file was pushing Modi to take the long march to Delhi though the party's second rung – not to speak of its key allies – seems not too enthused by this project.

The *Asian Age* (21 December 2012) said that 'while Mr Modi's achievement in this election remains noteworthy, many high-ranking national BJP leaders should be breathing a sigh of relief that the Chief Minister didn't win in a spectacular manner as was being widely prophesised'. 'Were that the case,' stated the paper, 'they might have had to line up behind the Gujarat Chief Minister in the party leadership stakes'.

The *Telegraph* (21 December 2012) said that numbers were important in the outcome of any election, but in the case of Narendra Modi's triumph – a victory foretold – 'what fetched him the numbers are perhaps much more significant'. The paper pointed out that conventional wisdom has it that development is not a vote catcher in India, but added that Modi's win 'goes against this wisdom'. Throughout his election campaign, Modi never uttered a single word against foreign direct investment in retail trade which only provided 'eloquent testimony to Mr Modi's commitment to economic development'.

Earlier on 21 December 2012, The *Hindustan Times* had said that the next step for Modi 'could be' Delhi. The election victory, stated the paper, 'belongs solely to Mr Modi for not raising any divisive issues, whether of caste or religion during his campaign, focussing solely on his development record'. In contrast, the paper said that the Congress seemed 'directionless, even agenda-less. There was no single Congress leader in the state capable of countering the Modi judgement'. However, said the paper, despite his creditable showing, 'no one knows better than Mr Modi how difficult it will be to cover the distance from Gujarat to Delhi'. Like some other newspapers, The *Hindustan Times* too, drew attention to the fact that 'many in his own party are fearful that a resurgent Mr Modi at the Centre, were the BJP to come to power, would marginalize them within the BJP ... However, it will be very hard put to ignore Mr Modi's claim, were he to make one, for the top post.' In conclusion, the paper maintained that 'whether anyone likes his *Moditva* brand or not, Narendra Modi cannot be described as just another regional leader anymore'.

It is in this connection that the views of Yogendra Yadav, National Executive member of the *Aaam Admi* Party make significant reading. Yadav said that the fact remains that Modi had won and won a clear mandate. 'It may not be a historic win but winning a third consecutive election with a comfortable margin is no joke. Clearly, this victory catapults him as the principal leader of the BJP in the next Lok Sabha elections.' Yadav conceded that it was a vote for good governance and development sans politics of caste and community and no doubt 'an endorsement of the record of economic growth in the last decade'. However, he said, the verdict could not be seen as a verdict on the government's record on education and health that left much to be desired. Summing up the situation, Yadav said: 'In his victory speech, he (Modi) offered an apology but not for the one thing he should have apologized for. Modi's inevitable and now unstoppable rise to national leadership of his party invites us to think if what is popular is also democratic.'

The general belief is that all industrialists are in Modi's favour. Media reports, however, have showed that this is not true. Anu Aga, Chairperson of Thermax Ltd, has been quoted as saying that development cannot be at the cost of secularism. As reported, she said: 'We need development but not at any cost. Development is important but so are a host of our issues. One of the most important things is secularism and we can't ignore that.'

To balance that, one can go to Santosh Desai, Managing Director of Futurebrands India Ltd. According to Desai, Modi is what he is, attracting people not by changing his message to suit them but by appealing to those who believe in his way. As Desai put it: 'To

The Press Post-Mortem after Election 2012

be sure, Modi has to broaden his focus from Gujarat to the rest of the country, but there is enough strength in his brand to resonate with the mood in the country today.... he emits a strong aura of clarity and authority. In a sea of leaders that reek of political expediency and in a political culture that thrives on ambiguity and obfuscation, Modi stands out for his uncompromising positions and his ability to deliver what he promises.'

In a way, criticism of Modi has been sharper in India than abroad. For every positive development, India's Modi-critics have been quick to point out the Modi government's alleged deficiencies.

A good example is an article by Sanjukta Pathak in *Firstpost* (24 September 2012). Warning that people should not be taken in by what Modi's spin doctors have been saying, Pathak draws attention to 'farmers' suicides, cases of big ticket corruption, tribal discontent, malnutrition and resentment against the aggressive, some would say reckless, industrialization drive of the Chief Minister'. Pathak's point is that it has been the 'obsession with the 2002 riots that has virtually made everything else about Gujarat irrelevant and invisible.' She pointed out:

- Thirty-seven farmers have committed suicides this year in the drought-hit Saurashtra region alone. According to NCRB data, Gujarat has shown a rising trend of farmers' suicides since 2004. It has been the highest in 2012 since 2000 ....
- The current government has finished the state's coffers in two activities – waiving off taxes for industrialists and political activities of the chief minister.
- Nearly half the population in the state is undernourished. The prevalence rate is more than 61 per cent among scheduled tribes and 55 per cent among scheduled castes ....
- Gujarat ranks 18 in the country in literacy; it is a poor performer on other human development indices ....
- The Comptroller and Auditor General (CAG) report has detected irregularities worth ₹16,700 crore in various transactions of the state government.

- The process of gifting away land to big industrialists has made the once massive land bank of Gujarat a rare commodity for the poor ....
- A wave of discontent is brewing among the fishermen too. The much-publicized ₹11,000 crore Sagarkhedu Sarvangi Vikas Yojana, aimed at development of 3,000 coastal villages just before the elections is going nowhere. The scheme was expected to benefit 60 lakh people. So far, only a minuscule fraction of the amount ₹235.68 crore has been spent and the number of beneficiaries is just a little over 76,000.
- Another pocket of protest involves the state government employees who were denied payment terms and medical and other perks as per the Sixth Pay Commission. Employees on a fixed pay ware denied upgradation .... This comes from the same government that has waived ₹31,000 crore of tax amount for automobile majors to come and operate in the state ....

Should we say Gujarat is a normal state now?

Pathak got some of her information from outsiders whom she has quoted – people such as Gujarat Pradesh Congress Committee President Arjun Modhwadia, noted danseuse and social activist Mallika Sarabhai, and a senior Congress leader and former deputy Chief Minister, Narhari Amin.

One problem of malnutrition concerns tribals and Dalits who have been traditionally undernourished because of their low social and financial status and are likely to remain undernourished, one suspects, until they are drawn out of their low social status and lack of employment. No chief minister can possibly change this system overnight – a point often forgotten.

But there is a no way facts can be ignored and one can understand Modi's dilemma. One can't re-order a highly caste-ridden society overnight, a fact which Modi's critics are unwilling to face.

At a personal level, among Modi's critics is a scholar, the sociologist Ashish Nandy, one of India's foremost public intellectuals, who interviewed Modi sometime in the late 1980s when the latter was 'a nobody, small-time RSS *pracharak* trying to make it as a small time BJP functionary'. Why on earth Nandy wanted to interview a 'nobody' is not clear, but the interview apparently was long and rambling. Writing in a journal called *Seminar*, Nandy had this to say:

> It left me in no doubt that here was a classic, clinical case of Fascism. I never use the terms 'fascist' as a term of abuse; to me it is a diagnostic category comprising not only one's ideological posture but also the personality traits and motivational patterns contextualizing the ideology. Modi, it gives me no pleasure to tell the readers, met virtually all the criteria that psychiatrists, psychoanalysts and psychologists had set up after years of empirical work on the authoritarian personality. He had the same mix of puritanical rigidity, narrowing of emotional life, massive use of the one defence of projection, denial and fear of his own passions combined with fantasies of violence ....

These days, Modi's legions of admirers would scornfully not pay much heed to such a report!

Modi's record as an efficient and capable administrator is undeniable. He appears to prefer power over money, which is a particularly appealing proposition for voters who regard most politicians as corrupt, ineffective and weak ... and those who admire him profess their adoration with an unusual intensity.

Reactions from the Western Press

What does the Western world think about Modi? An article in The *Economist* (20 December 2012) provides an answer.

As The *Economist* saw it, Modi's victory for a third successive term in itself was no surprise, though his emphatic margin of victory was striking. Nobody, said the weekly, should be in any doubt that Modi would now want to push on to become prime minister. Modi's strengths, as the weekly explained were: a hat trick of electoral victories in the state, competent administration, a steady flow of investment by locals and foreigners, gradually warmed international ties as typified by Britain's decision in October to engage him.

Though, as the weekly saw it, national opinion polls in India are 'probably less reliable then they are in other countries', for what they were worth, they constantly showed that Mr Modi was the single-most popular man to be the next prime minister. Importantly, too, he had energy and a hunger for power. As the weekly noted: 'Sit with him for an interview and he appears composed; his eye gleam with ambition and he is on top of his material. Unlike the Congress (who dares not talk to journalists or indeed almost anyone beyond a cloistered circle of advisors), he is the likelier to show vigour and vim.'

The weekly, however, also opined that this was not enough for Mr Modi or indeed the BJP, to look forward to national office with any confidence. The weekly reminded the reader that Mr Modi was a 'controversial figure, especially beyond Gujarat because of his behaviour in 2002'. In most other recent state elections, he had either refused to campaign on behalf of his party or had been discouraged from doing so. Stated the weekly: 'Mr Modi is such a divisive figure that if he dominates the BJP in the coming year or two, there is a chance that the next national election becomes a referendum about his suitability to rule and his brand of Hinduism, rather than a discussion of Congress's record in government.' And that, said the weekly, 'might suit Congress rather well'.

The weekly said that 'it is notoriously hard to draw convincing lessons from any state election results and apply them to national voting.' There remain immense uncertainties, not least the question of Mr Modi's dominance of the BJP. Stating that Modi was not good at holding together coalitions and making compromises, the weekly added:

> Broader questions remain about the BJP, for example, what are its policies? The Opposition's confused and mistaken opposition to new rules on foreign investment in retail in India and its bungled efforts in forcing a vote on the issue in Parliament, make it look hostile to pro-growth measures, just as India's economy slows to less than 6 per cent GDP growth .... It is unclear that Mr Modi would bring any broader national appeal for the BJP.... In building alliances and holding them together, it is still Congress that has shown the greater skill in recent times. Mr Modi and the BJP will have to learn some new skills if they are to turn state election successes into national ones.

The Press Post-Mortem after Election 2012

The Western media, by and large, has been balanced in its approach towards Modi though two important points can still be raised: Why was reference made only to Muslims killed in the 2002 riots and not to the number of Hindus killed? Secondly, nobody seemed to care about the anger that had been aroused by the way in which some fifty-odd innocent women and children were literally roasted alive in the Sabarmati Express coach. One can understand death by shooting. But it is hard to visualize the slow and immensely painful roasting of people in a coach that was set on fire by a huge mass of Muslims, with deliberate intent.

A friend in Chennai

Tamil Nadu's Chief Minister Jayalalitha has maintained the most friendly relations with Modi. Jayalalitha was among the handful of chief ministers present at the swearing-in of Modi when he reassumed office in December 2012. Similarly, Modi was among the few chief ministers who attended Jayalalitha's swearing-in in May 2011. In January 2012, when Modi went on a fast, Jayalalitha sent her representative to Gandhinagar to participate in Modi's *Sadbhavana* fast. In February, Modi, in turn, sent warm birthday greetings to Jayalalitha. Noticed has been the fact that over the last few years, the two have been engaging constantly on political platforms with obvious warmth.

Modi was all praise for Jayalalitha when he visited Chennai to participate in an annual event organized by Cho Ramaswamy in January 2012. Present on the occasion was L K Advani who was also full of praise for the Tamil Nadu Chief Minister. Speaking on the occasion, Advani said that it was not merely ordinary cooperation but much more than that which made him feel that AIADMK was a 'natural ally' of the BJP. 'There are so many things in common between us,' he said.

Will He or Won't He? 26

When exactly did the talk of Narendra Modi becoming a likely candidate for the prime ministership of India start? Prior to the State Assembly elections of 2012, all his enemies were gunning for him with vicious intent. An NGO, Jan Sangarsh Manch had petitioned the Supreme Court seeking a direction to be given to the Nanavati Commission, inquiring into the 2002 Gujarat riots, to summon Modi for his alleged role in the carnage. The Supreme Court refused to entertain the petition. On 26 March 2012, the Bench firmly stated that it could not monitor the working of the Commission and interfere at every stage with the impugned order of the High Court.

But the agenda of the secularists to get Narendra hanged by hook or by crook continued. The Supreme Court had appointed Raju Ramachandran as the *amicus curiae* to look into the matter of the Zakia Jafri case. In his report, Ramachandran argued that a case could be made against Modi for various offences committed during the 2002 riots, including promoting enmity among different groups. This was subsequently rubbished by the Special Investigation Team (SIT) appointed by the Supreme Court. Arguing point by point, the SIT exonerated Modi of all the charges made against him. It said that Modi had taken all possible steps to control the 2002 riots and questioned the motive of the NGO. On 12 May 2012, The *Free Press Journal* said that 'it is to the credit of Modi that in spite of a relentless examination of his conduct, he has come out unscathed. The *amicus curiae's* 'search for truth seems to have been marred by his desire not to be unacceptable to the loud and quarrelsome secularist brigade.'

The total clearance by the SIT undoubtedly showed up the beleaguered Modi in a different light.

It was then that the country started buzzing with the question: Could one think of Modi as the face of BJP for the Lok Sabha elections in 2014?

Writing in *Hans India* (24 June 2012), Anita Saluja expressed the opinion that 'after the crucial BJP National Executive meet in Mumbai, the RSS has picked up one flower from the bouquet – Narendra Modi.' She stated:

> The RSS, in fact, has not much of a choice for Lok Sabha elections in 2014. Among those who are in the race, Advani has been tested twice; Arun Jaitley has never himself contested elections though he is a good media manager and a backroom boy; and Sushma Swaraj, though a good orator, does not match the skills of Modi; and Gadkari lacks the political experience and the maturity to head the government.

As the state elections drew closer and Modi started to launch a number of yatras, The *India Express* ran a story saying: 'Message Clear as Modi Begins Poll Yatra: It's Gujarat vs Centre' (12 September 2012).

Was The *Times of India* thinking the same? It would appear so. In its 23 September 2012 edition, a report stated, 'As Modi emerges as the BJP's prime ministerial candidate for the 2014 elections, he feels he has been able to pacify sections of Muslims through his *Sadbhavana* mission, which was flagged off on his birthday 17 September last year (2011).' By then, the possibility of Modi becoming a prime ministerial candidate was becoming a matter of open discussion among the public.

A report in The *Indian Express* on 3 October 2012 noted: 'No politician stirs as much anger or grudging admiration as the burly Mr Modi. He leaves little doubt about his wish to become Prime Minister.' Modi was quoted as saying: 'I am interested in doing something for my country.' The report added: 'Polls show him to be the most popular figure to lead the country, outshining Congress's indecisive Rahul Gandhi. The rank and file of his Bharatiya Janata Party love him.'

Among other things the report said: 'Courts have found him guilty of nothing .... Other BJP leaders are wary of Mr Modi. When he talks of seeing himself as destined to triumph, his eyes burn with determination ...If the party wants to campaign on the economy and its efficient government, Mr Modi is its likeliest candidate .... Mr Modi's time could come if the BJP got a big victory in 2014 .... It would then be in a good position to impose its choice of Prime Minister on its coalition partners ....'

As the state elections in December moved ever closer , Neerja Chowdhury writing in *DNA* (12 December 2012) said: 'It goes without saying that the Gujarat election is no longer just about Gujarat. If Modi wins convincingly, he will hit the road that could take him from Gandhinagar to Delhi.'

Writing in The *Free Press Journal* (21 December 2012), Kalyani Shankar said: 'Modi may have crossed the first hurdle race of winning the state for the third time, but there are many more in the hurdle race ahead. For the past one year he (Modi) had done nothing but placing himself as the front-runner for the country's top job ... Modi is not Advani or Vajpayee for the allies to accept him without a murmur ... Besides, Modi is a loner. He does not like to share power ...'

The *Times of India* (21 December 2012) asked: 'Is it now "*Dilli Chalo*" for Modi? If yes, the transition to the national stage won't be easy ... The RSS-led saffron family appears divided on giving Modi top rank in the BJP central leadership. Viewed as an abrasive lone ranger, he isn't quite the team player ... Modi's image as a *Hindutva* hardliner remains and it can't but impact his national ambitions. His rivals in the faction-ridden BJP will lay claims to greater all-round acceptability ... His hat-trick in Gujarat is no mean feat. But taking strike beyond Gujarat will be a tougher challenge.'

By the third week of December 2012, of course, it was clear that Modi had emerged victorious in the state elections and media comment was becoming more and more Modi-focussed. Thus wrote The *Indian Express* (21 December 2012): 'He (Modi) has not been coy about his prime-ministerial pitch, addressing his campaign exclusively to the national stage ....'

In the aftermath, as he delivered his victory speech in Hindi, his gaze appeared riveted on Delhi. After his emphatic win,

Will He or Won't He?

therefore, the BJP may no longer be able to evade or delay the question of his capacity to lead the party in the next general election.... The central BJP, already in unceasing turmoil over the leadership question, will now have to deal with the formidable claimant from Gujarat who disdains not just the opponent across the political fence but also the opposition within ....

In that same issue and on the same day, Pratap Bhanu Mehta, President of the Centre for Policy Research and a contributing editor to the *Indian Express* pointed out that 'Modi's path to a greater national role is still fraught', considering that 'no Chief Minister has been able to make an easy transition to national politics'. Pointing out that Modi is now 'the pre-eminent face of the BJP', Mehta wrote: 'Modi is not so much a three-dimensional character, as an idea. He represents a longing for centralization in an age of dispersion, decisiveness in indecision, growth amidst stagnation and government in raucous democracy. He may still prove a rallying point against a decaying plutocracy.' Writing two days earlier in the *Indian Express* (19 December 2012), its Editor-in-Chief Shekhar Gupta asked: 'What gives Narendra Modi such invincibility?' Providing his own answers, he wrote: 'Shall we call it a self-defeating conspiracy of the faithful? The entire community of Modi-haters and baiters, political rivals and ideological questioners has driven itself into a hole, creating its own delusions and believing them. The only beneficiary in the process is Modi ... By choosing fury over fact, delusion over reason, passion over politics, Modi's enemies, beginning with the Congress, make Gujarat politics a one-horse race ....'

The *Economic Times* (21 December 2012) warned Modi and the BJP against legitimizing 'the exclusive politics of Hindu majoritarianism', saying that 'the magnitude' of his election success did not give him 'unstoppable political momentum', and that unless his politics of Hindu majoritarianism 'is explicitly disowned, development cannot serve as a passport to power at the Centre'.

Writing in The *Times of India* (21 December 2012), Ashok Mitra, a well-known political commentator said, 'If there were a primary in the party, a majority of office-bearers and adherents outside of a small cabal at 11 Ashoka Road, would vote overwhelmingly for Modi. What is remarkable is that Modi's stature and moral authority vis-à-vis the party are entirely his own making (and) these are not the result of a family inheritance.' Mitra said Modi 'represents India's urging for an authoritative leader though not for an authoritarian one and that 'difference is crucial and needs to be appreciated by his friends and foes alike. The Modi that excites India is the one who has made Gujarat's India Shenzhen, who has converted a trading society into a manufacturing economy and who has sold his voters the dream of becoming India's first middle-class state, besides which he has till the spring of 2014 to conclusively demonstrate he is also the man India awaits.'

But before going on to 2013, it is worth remembering what *India Today* (5 November 2012) had to say – and this was much earlier than the elections that showed that Modi's hold on the electorate has in no way lessened. The Editor-in-Chief, Aroon Purie, then made the following points that are valid to this day:

- For many, especially outside Gujarat, Modi is the ultimate icon of *Hindutva* politics (and) is one chief minister who can claim that he has delivered on his promises.
- That there are no serious allegations of corruption against Modi or his administration is an added feather to his cap.
- In our opinion poll, the people of Gujarat are clear that they would like to see Modi as prime minister. His own ambition to move to Delhi is hardly a secret.
- Development isn't just a number in Gujarat. It means 24 x 7 electricity supply to all cities and villages.

And what did the *India Today* poll say? Here are some answers:

- *Was Narendra Modi responsible for the Gujarat riots?* No (58%); Yes (28%); Can't say (14%)
- *Would you like to see Modi as the next Prime Minister?* Yes (56%); No (33%); Can't say (11%)
- *Who would you prefer as a BJP Prime Minister?* Narendra Modi (56%); Sushma Swaraj (9%); Nitish Kumar (3%); Arun Jaitley (3%); Can't say (16%)

That Modi had the full and practically unqualified support of leading Indian industrialists became evident in talks held in

Gandhinagar on 10 January 2013 during their meeting at the Vibrant Gujarat Summit. Anil Ambani said that for the past twelve years, Modi had been practising whatever the Mahatma had taught. Modi had sacrificed personal gains for a greater national good. Gautam Adani stated that it was just 'a matter of time' for Modi's elevation to national leadership.

Reporting how those who attended the Vibrant Gujarat Summit 'outdid each other in their praise' for Modi, Neerja Chowdhury questioned in The *Times of India* (15 January 2013): 'Could Modi, with his tough image, no charges of corruption and focus on development step into the vacuum of leadership that exists today?' Among those who attended the Vibrant Gujarat meeting was Swapan Dasgupta who, writing in The *Telegraph* (18 January 2013), made the point that 'much of what Gujarat has achieved has been due to the single-minded determination of Modi to circumvent political opposition through exemplary economic growth. It is Modi's no-nonsense style of functioning and his ability to pick the right team and motivate it that has made all the difference'.

It was about this same time that top leaders among the many in the BJP came out openly to propose Modi's name for the candidature of the prime ministership of India. The first to do so was Yashwant Sinha, on 28 January 2013. A day after he announced his support, Ram Jethmalani followed suit, with the words: 'According to me, Narendra Modi is the best prime minister for this country. Nothing has happened to change my mind ... Modi is my definition of secularism and he is 100 per cent secular.'

AT CLOSE QUARTERS: THE MAN AND HIS PERSONA

The common man and the media have attributed a number of epithets to Narendra Modi, describing him as a tough administrator, shrewd politician, fearless and forthright, unafraid to stand alone – the list goes on and on ... However, what is the man, Narendra Modi, really like? For the less informed, Modi's persona unfolds like a kaleidoscope of talents, old-world courtesy and a zest for life that few can match.

Master of Words

Many have heard Narendra Modi speak. Even his detractors admit he is an excellent orator and a master of rhetoric. He speaks fluently without even a piece of paper to refer to. People like to hear him over and over again and say that 'Ma Saraswati' (Goddess of Wisdom) resides on his tongue. But very few know that Ma Saraswati resides on his fingers too when they hold a pen! At different times, he has been a writer, editor, compiler, translator, short story writer and even a poet. Recently, he penned the hit lyrics for a 'garba' (Gujarati folk song and dance) at the time of the Navratri festival. A few years ago, he was invited as the chief guest at a gathering of Gujarati language humourists. His address was so full of humour that the conference declared him to be the best humourist of Gujarat.

Narendra Modi has mainly written in Gujarati though he knows Hindi, English and Marathi as well. He wrote his first book *Sangharsh ma Gujarat* (*Gujarat in Conflict*) at the age of 25 years. The book deals with Gujarat during the Emergency when it was the only non-Congress state. Narendra was underground at that time and carried out multiple responsibilities. The book recounts the relentless fight carried on for 30 months for the sake of democracy. It is a documented history of underground activities. Although this was his first attempt at writing a book, Modi completed it at a stretch in 23 days, solely out of his memory, because he did not keep any notes!

In the 1970s, he wrote short stories for the *Indian Express* Group's Gujarati magazine named *Chandni*. He also wrote a short novel during this period along with contributing to another magazine called *Aaram*. All these are compiled in a book titled *Prem Teerth (Pilgrimage of Love)*. The central idea of the stories is Motherhood and one can feel how deeply he is absorbed by the sentiment of Motherhood. He translated Dattopant Thengdi's book in Marathi titled *Samrasta sivay Samajik Samata Ashakya* (Without Similar Interests, It is Impossible to have Social Unity) into Gujarati. Shri Guruji, second *Sarsanghchalak* (paramount leader of the RSS) had written hundreds of letters in Marathi, Hindi and English, that Narendra translated into simple Gujarati. It is not a word-to-word translation but captures the emotions. These edited letters have been published as *Patra rup Shri Guruji* (Respected Teacher in Form of Letters).

Lakhmanrao Inamdar a.k.a. Vakilsaheb was an RSS *pracharak* in Gujarat for 43 years. He guided hundreds of RSS workers. For Narendra Modi, he was a mentor. His life and work is described in the book *Setubandh*. Though a biography, it reads more like an eulogy on him. Another *pracharak* Rajasaheb Nene is the co-author of this book. It has been translated into Hindi and even today, Vakilsaheb's sense of commitment and the quality of perseverance inspires many workers.

Shree Guruji: A Swayamsevak was published in Hindi and Marathi. It describes Guruji's life as a *swayamsevak*. Shri Madhavrao Sadashuvrao Golwalkar, popularly known as Guruji never ceased to be a *swayamsevak* despite being the head of the RSS.

Narendra was fond of reading right from childhood. The library of Vadnagar was like his second home. When he was in the VIII standard, he wrote a play called *Peelu Phool* (Yellow Flower). The theme was the sensitive subject of Untouchability, and promoted the message that it was a great sin. Narendra also directed and acted in this one-man play. The play proved to be very appealing and his friends and teachers still remember it.

When Narendra was a *pracharak* for about 18 months, he wrote a diary in the form of a letter to Mataji. For example he would write, '*Hey Ma, Pranam Tane* (Mother, respectful greetings). Today I did ... it was my mistake ...' Modi says that the diary gave him great pleasure.

During the Emergency, he compiled and published a small newspaper called *Satywani* (The Truth) to keep people informed of the goings-on. He regularly wrote a column under the pen name Aniket for *Sadhana*, a weekly. He wrote on politics, political strategies, culture, personalities and other topics.

Narendra was always interested in people. He had a knack for writing about various personalities. His verbal caricatures bring out salient features of common and uncommon people about whom he writes. A book of his titled *Jyotipunj* (Cluster of Light) caricatures various unusual people whom he has known closely. Their love, warmth, affection and feelings have always inspired him. With many he has worked as a colleague but while writing about them, he has been objective. From the innumerable personalities he has come across, he has included a few in this book. To sacrifice life without any expectations is one of the most unusual traditions of our society. There are people who are ready to sacrifice their lives for the nation. They rarely go down in the annals of history, but when remembered, they inspire. Modi's *Jyotipunj* brings to light such architects of society, revealing the extent of faith and devotion that inspired his protagonists. The language too is very powerful. The book takes the reader on a journey from tradition, society, community and culture to values, dedication and deep convictions.

Modi's inspirational words on education are compiled in a book titled *Kelve te Kelavani* (One that Educates is Education). *Samajik Samrasta* (Social Unity) is a collection of 45 articles that invokes meditative thought about building bridges with society and within society.

Narendra's sensitivity is evident in his poems. *Aankh aa Dhanya Chhe* (These Eyes are Fortunate) is a collection of his poems. It reflects his nature and love for Gujarat.

Modi's latest book is in English titled *Convenient Action: Gujarat's Response to Challenges of Climate Change*. Though primarily a coffee-table book, richly and appropriately illustrated, it not only picturizes the steps taken by the Government of Gujarat to handle climate change, but also throws light on the thoughts and feelings of Modi on what he calls 'a complementary relationship between Man and Nature'. He maintains that he first began to understand and appreciate nature when he studied the *Prithvi Sukta* of the Atharva Veda during his college days. He notes, 'The sixty-three *sutras* composed thousands of years ago, contain a whole spectrum of knowledge that is now being propounded under various scientific, academic and analytical banners during discussions on global warming.' It is very touching to learn that he grew up in an atmosphere that was more in harmony with nature and so embedded was the respect for nature in his own home, that he was told by his mother to fold his hands and ask for Mother Earth's forgiveness, after getting up in the morning but before putting his feet on the ground. The images in the book are so well chosen; the language used is so expressive – indeed, in a way, so emotive, that to read it is sheer joy. In a brief foreword to the book, Steve Howard, CEO of the Climate Group, London, describes it as 'a Green Autobiography of Narendra Modi who has shown a definite path and determined strategy to meet the challenges of Climate Change'.

Insights into Modi's Personality (as seen by the authors)

Initially, we authors had three extensive interviews with Narendra Modi, lasting for nine to ten hours each. Subsequently, they were followed by short ones as and when necessary. We always found him in the same frame of mind – cool and collected, well-groomed, cordiality personified, courteous and ready. His thinking was clear; his speech was succinct and devoid of any ramblings.

We take pleasure at this point of our book to introduce Narendra Modi, as we judged him, to you, our readers. When he meets you, he is fully with you. His heart and mind are both involved in interacting with you. He does not mince words, is relaxed and not disturbed by any staff or phone calls. He is a good host and takes care to offer the appropriate snacks and drinks, though he himself does not touch anything as he is disciplined about his dietary habits. He speaks fluently and talks in chaste Hindi and Gujarati (our interviews were carried out in English and Hindi, and occasionally in Gujarati). He neither makes pretences nor any efforts to 'impress' as some claim. In fact, he comes through as a transparent person. After every interview, he would see Dr Randeri and me to the door to wish us goodbye.

Most of the discussions with him reaffirm his human values and love for the country. He comes through as a person who is totally dedicated to the task of building the society and nation. We never got the impression that he ever bragged about his achievements. However, he was certainly proud and joyous about them.

During the interviews, we often asked him 'direct and inconvenient' questions but he was never ruffled and answered them with exemplary equanimity. Talking to him was like reading an open book. He never dodged any questions. His memory was fantastic. He could talk about events chronologically without any hesitation. He could remember details about personalities and conversations at events. He could create a clear verbal picture by describing it in a few words. He never showed any feeling of superiority.

After every interview, he would come out of his bungalow to see us off. After the second interview, Mr Kamath opined: 'Over the years, I have interviewed princes and presidents, prime ministers and dictators all over the world but have never met any one like Narendra Modi. He has vision, dedication, enthusiasm and intelligence, and is not greedy. It will be interesting to see how he shapes up.'

Modi has not forgotten the people with whom he was in close touch during his *pracharak* days. They too remember him fondly and feel good that he has not forgotten them. He was like a family member for some of them and though they rarely meet now, the bond is so strong that they do not feel differently. Modi is spotted more often at condolence meetings or to pay his last respects

At Close Quarters: The Man and His Persona

at funerals but seldom at weddings. After becoming the chief minister, he once invited 25 of his good school friends with their spouses for dinner. They were pleased to know that he had not forgotten them and commented that he mixed with them so freely that for a while, they forgot that their host was the chief minister! On another occasion, he organized a function to felicitate all his teachers and acknowledged how indebted he felt to them.

Besides literature, Modi has many other interests, though increasingly, he finds less and less time for them. Many remember the time when he was spotted entering a theatre unobtrusively to watch plays or quality movies. At that time, he did not have Z class security. Few people perhaps know that he is a good photographer and sometime in the 1990s, he actually organized an exhibition of his photographs. A regular visitor to photographic exhibitions, he was once asked by the Ahmedabad Photographers' Club to give a talk on the subject, using a slide show. It was greatly appreciated and Modi, apparently, spoke like a professional.

Another incident demonstrates Narendra Modi's love for sports and encouragement to sportspersons. Lajja Goswami, a girl from Gujarat, had won the silver medal in the 50 metre centre rifle event at the 2010 Commonwealth Games. That very night, Modi called to congratulate her and later visited her home in Jitodia village in Anand on 19 October 2010. He sat on the bed in the most natural manner, discussed Lajja's needs and presented her with a cheque for ₹5 lakh as a mark of appreciation. He said, 'It is for the first time that a sportsperson from Gujarat has won a medal in CWG. Preserving the core spirit of Gujarat with immense passion and commitment, Lajja has really turned out to be a shining star. Lajja has made Gujarat proud. She is a role model for the young sportspersons of the state.'

Narendra Modi has often been admired for his 'detachment' towards his family in the sense that no family member has ever been favoured for anything. However, the credit for this goes to his family members too who have never taken undue advantage of his position. Obviously, this is a reflection of his family values! The only member of his family that he meets is his mother. She is now very old, and every now and then, he drops by to see her. This would be an appropriate time to recall the five words with which his mother blessed him when he went to seek her blessings after becoming CM. Her words were *'Beta, kadi laanch naa laish.'* (Son, never indulge in bribery). This teaching has always been practised by Modi and even his worst detractors have never been able to accuse him to the contrary! Modi possesses an exceptional ability to detach himself from accusations and abuse. He has often been quoted as saying that detachment is something he believes in and practises. This may explain how he is able to pursue his goals single-mindedly and purposefully.

Once, after an interview, Kalindi asked him rather audaciously if she could *see* his bedroom. He consented with a smile and directed her how to go there from his office. He admitted that he himself had not yet seen the entire CM's bungalow that had been allotted to him as he confined himself to a few rooms for his personal residence and office. His personal abode consisted of a passage with a sofa, and a room with no furniture, as he used it for exercise and yoga. His bedroom contained an ordinary bed and a few pictures/statues of Shiv, Ma Saraswati and Vivekanand.

Modi once visited Udupi and Manipal. The car he was to take from the helipad to Manipal was about a hundred yards away and the terrain was marked with stones and potholes. Mr Kamath had gone to receive him and escort him to the car. When Modi saw that Mr Kamath was finding it hard to walk, he held him firmly by his hand 'as caringly as a son would do to his father', an observer later said. Mr Kamath then realized that respect for elders was ingrained in Modi.

Varying Perspectives

Aakar Patel, a writer, columnist, and an erstwhile editor of a daily, described Modi in an article he wrote for The *Hindustan Times* (21 December 2012). He said:

- Modi has a sense of style and would not be seen in public without being turned out perfectly. For Modi being turned out perfectly means a trimmed beard and hair, and clothes that are stylishly cut, even if they are traditional.
- His clothes, especially the iconic half-sleeved kurtas, might seem like khadi and often they are, but they are

not inexpensive. His designer used to be the Ahmedabad store Jade Blue, the most expensive couture store in the city. The perfect fit over his shoulders suggests a few hours spent on trials.

- He is single ... but he has no personal life outside of his work, so far as I know.
- He is uninterested in money. I don't know why precisely I am writing this other than the fact that this is what I believe, based on what I know of him. I think the idea of power excites him, but the idea of money doesn't.
- He has a sense of humour and he is playful. I know this from personal experience. If Modi did not take himself as seriously as he does after becoming chief minister, he would be pleasant company. He is warm and confident with people.

Gujarati women absolutely adore him. Modi, though he may not acknowledge this, is a sex symbol in his home state ... He has the aura of a king or emperor, someone who exudes absolute power and authority and is, therefore, someone irresistible to women.

He is a vegetarian who doesn't smoke and doesn't drink.

Paras Chauhan described him in *Planet Satire* as having an optimistic personality and aggressiveness in his body language.

In his article 'India's G-7: Local Leaders with Global Interests,' William J Antholis, Managing Director of Brookings, listed India's seven largest economies and seven chief ministers who led them. Identifying Gujarat as one of the newly emerging industrial engines of India in GDP matters, the author wrote, 'Narendra Modi, from mid-sized Gujarat (a mere 60 million people), leads the pack. Modi combines machine-like efficiency with charismatic (and many say destructive and divisive) nationalism.'

In *One India News* (15 February 2012), Kishore Trivedi described some outstanding qualities of Narendra Modi. He quoted Narendra Modi: 'Dream big, Aim for the best. "Dreams are not seen when you sleep, dreams are those that don't let you sleep."

Trivedi described him as a workaholic to the core and quoted Modi as having said: 'An opportunity to work is good luck for me. I put my soul into it. Each such opportunity opens the gates for the next one.'

Trivedi believed Modi was a 'True Mass Leader' as his words indicated: '... Individual efforts can bring excellence but only collective efforts can deliver effectively ... Our goal is Gujarat's growth for India's growth ...'

Time and again Modi has talked about Inclusive Growth – where no one is left behind. He says, 'People's participation is the essence of good governance.'

It is interesting to note how the people on his staff see him. They say **Shri Narendra Modi** is a great dreamer, who has the remarkable ability to transform his dreams into reality. He is a hard taskmaster and strict disciplinarian, but at the same time, he is an embodiment of strength and compassion. They affirm that Modi has great faith in education as a means of integral human development and progress to take society far beyond the encircling darkness, gloom and poverty.

Modi is seen as a big believer in people, has skillfully led half a million strong team of government employees into new realms of a proactive work culture through 'continuous learning'.

He is considered both a realist and an idealist with robust optimism. He has imbibed the noble view that not failure but low aim is a crime. He values clarity of vision, sense of purpose and diligent perseverance as essential qualities for achievement in any walk of life. Concern for his land and people is uppermost in his mind.

The staff perceives him as an intelligent, strong leader with brilliant decision-making ability and a good listener.

Major General I S Singha of the Golden Katar Division in Ahmedabad, stated in The *Indian Express* (14 March 2011): 'Chief Minister Modi has all the qualities of a successful Army Commander. His programmes are aimed at development of both the state and the nation. Like in the Army, he (Modi) keeps a deadline for completion of work, and ensures that the target is achieved by the set time.'

At the end, and for the record: As per a report in *India Today Online* (Gandhinagar, 1 December 2012), Narendra Modi's income in the latest I-T return was ₹1,50,630. The value of the assets of the Gujarat Chief Minister stood at ₹40 lakh in 2007. His assets at that time included a plot in Gandhinagar Sector-1, bought for ₹1,30,488, and valued at ₹30 lakh. The market value of this plot has been shown as ₹1 crore in the present affidavit. The development work on the plot is worth ₹2,47,208, it says.

Afterword

At the outset, the first thing that we, the authors, want to aver is that this book is not an 'authorized' biography. True, both of us had lengthy interviews with Narendra Modi, prior to bringing out the original text published in 2009. Dr Randeri, herself a Gujarati, understands the Gujarati psyche well. While conducting her research, she interviewed several fellow Gujaratis, including many who were critical of Modi, to gain a wider-based, more objective approach. The earlier book was a look at Modi's life from childhood to 2009.

This book, *Narendra Modi: The Man of the Moment* is a thoroughly revised edition of its earlier avatar and takes a huge leap forward in bringing the reader up to date with the protagonist – his political life, the guiding forces that motivate him to be what he is, his standing in India today and the worldview of his stature in India. In updating the earlier text, we have taken extensive recourse to material downloaded from various websites on the Internet, newspaper reports, articles and interviews. We ourselves have had our differences with Modi but we decided our approach towards him should be positive and not contaminated with personal considerations.

We consider Narendra Modi as a leader with exceptional and rare qualities. His achievements, especially in the fields of industrial development, agricultural growth, village empowerment and women's development have transformed Gujarat in one magnificent decade. We have written this book in a fair and objective manner, even if Modi's professional detractors find it hard to accept him as one of the greatest achievers of our times.

Modi has no claims to sainthood. In many ways, he reflects Gujarati sentiments, in all their verisimilitude. Professional secularists may have a blinkered view of Hindu-Muslim relationship, but the

The Man of the Moment: Narendra Modi

major factor that all must consider is that Hindus and Muslims, not just in Gujarat but all over India, have yet to come to terms with India's turbulent history. The riots that have taken place in India for decades prior to and following Independence reflect that truth. Many tend to see Modi strictly in terms of the post-Godhra riots, but if one examines the genesis of communal riots in Gujarat in the past, one may see him in the right context.

The reason for such demonization not merely in Gujarat but in an all-India context has been sought by an American scholar, David Frawley in his classic study *Hinduism and Clash of Civilizations*. Frawley has noted that 'there is no other country in the world where it has become a nationalist pastime among its educated classes to denigrate its own culture and history' and 'there is no other country where the majority religion, howsoever enlightened, mystical or spiritual, is ridiculed, while minority religions, howsoever fundamentalist or militant, are doted on'. Among the elite, it is especially fashionable to run down *Hindutva*. Our study of Modi and the history of Gujarat in the last one decade is made in this context. For us, it was a sad day when the United States, in consonance with this anti-Hindu mindset, refused a visa to Modi. It was an even sadder day when Wharton School, part of the University of Pennsylvania, cancelled an invitation to Modi to participate in a scholarly event on the ground that he had abused human rights.

If truth be told, the US has arguably been the worst violator of human rights. Whether it was in Vietnam, Iraq or more recently in Afghanistan, the US has been responsible for more abuse of human rights than any other country in the world's history. The saddest part of it is the fact that those who encouraged Wharton in its questionable stand include many Indian scholars, giving Frawley's assessment of the Hindu elite's mindset full credit.

It is against this background that this book was written. Modi needs to be defended. America will never understand Modi or for that matter India, because it has never experienced what India and Hindus in particular, have gone through in centuries past from the likes of Mahmud of Ghazni, Mohammad of Ghori, Babar, Aurangzeb and their ilk.

400

Afterword

Millions in India today believe that they want someone like Modi to become the Prime Minister to uphold India's self-respect, to convey to countries like the United States, China and Pakistan not to take India for granted and to provide governance that delivers. This book is in line with that assertion.

Annexure I

International Awards Won by Gujarat State

2001: The Green Award from the World Bank to Gujarat State Disaster Management Authority (GSDMA) for Reconstruction and Rehabilitation Programme (GERRP) for promotion and maintenance of environmental concerns in the implementation of the projects funded by the World Bank.

2002: Excellent Health Care Facilities Award from the World Bank for availability, utility, reliability and satisfaction of patients.

2003: Sasakawa Award for Disaster Reduction from the United Nations for outstanding reconstruction and rehabilitation work done by the GSDMA following the earthquake in Gujarat in January 2001.

2004: CAPAM Gold Award for Best Public Administration and Management from Commonwealth Association for Public Administration and Management (CAPAM).

2004: CAPAM Award for Innovation in Governance from CAPAM to GSDMA for initiatives taken for owner-driven reconstruction, the role and involvement of the community, the transparency and equity procedures and rehabilitation and reconstruction programmes launched post the earthquake.

2004: Recognition by Commonwealth Telecommunications Organization and University of Manchester Institute for Deployment Policy and Management for e-Transparency and SWAGAT Scheme.

2005: ICLEI (International Council for Local Environmental Initiatives) Local Governments for Sustainability Award to Vadodara Municipal Corporation for commitment towards climate protection campaign.

2006: CAPAM International Innovations Award to Rural Housing and Rural Development Department of Gujarat for 'Citizen Engagement and Service Delivery' for farm ponds constructed in rural areas.

2006: Asian Innovation Award from Singapore Economic Development Board and the *Wall Street Journal* to the Department of Health and Family Welfare, Government of Gujarat for the 'Chiranjeevi Yojana' (for reduction in mental mortality and provision of health care with equity and dignity to the poor and the marginalized).

2006: Dubai International Award by Dubai Municipality in UAE to Ahmedabad Municipal Corporation for its slum networking programme.

2007: Sasakawa Award for Best Performance in Leprosy Eradication by International Leprosy Union, Pune and Sasakawa Memorial Health Foundation, Japan to Government of Gujarat for excellent work done to reduce the prevalence rate of leprosy, reconstructive surgery and rehabilitation of leprosy patients.

2007: INMEX (International Maritime Exhibition) Excellence Award to Gujarat Maritime Board for 'multiple business models that changed the mindset of the maritime population towards ports and shipping'.

2008: Stockholm Challenge Award from The Royal Institute of Technology, Stockholm for 'Jan Seva Kendra' project of Gandhinagar for 'Exemplary ICT-driven e-Governance Public Service Delivery Mechanism'.

2008: CAPAM International Innovations Award by Ministry of Public Service and Administration, South Africa to Rural Housing and Rural Development Department, Government of Gujarat for 'e-Gram and Vishwa Gram Mission' for 'Driving Digital Inclusion in Gujarat'.

2008: KPMG Infrastructure Today Award from KPMG, a global network of professional firms operating in 148 countries to Gujarat Alkalis and Chemicals Ltd for being the 'most admired state level PPP agency'.

Annexures

2011: Sabre Award by The Holmes Report to Vibrant Gujarat Global Investors' Summit (2011) for the 'Best Communications Campaign in the Indian Subcontinent' conferred at an international conference held in Lisbon, Portugal.

2011: Sabre Award by the Holmes Report for the 'Best Government/ Public Sector Communications Campaign in the Asia-Pacific' conferred at an international conference held in Singapore.

Annexure II

Awards For Narendra Modi

Narendra Modi emerged as **the Best Chief Minister** according to the India Today Opinion Poll for 2005, 2005 and 2007.

In October 2005, Readers of the Gujarati weekly *Chitralekha* rated Narendra Modi as **'The Person of the Year'**.

In 2009, Narendra Modi was presented with the **Asian Winner of the fDi Personality of the Year Award** by *fDi* magazine, a London-based English-language bimonthly owned by the Financial Times Ltd.

SWAGAT (State Wide Attention of Grievances by Application of Technology), an innovative initiative of Narendra Modi, won the prestigious **United Nations Public Service Award** in 2010 for 'Improving Transparency, Accountability and Responsibility in Public Service'.

In 2010, eGov magazine, (the India eGov 2.0 Awards) presented the official portal of Chief Minister Narendra Modi (www.narendramodi.in) with the prestigious **eGov 2.0 Award** for the 'Most innovative use of social Media'.

The Computer Society of India conferred on Narendra Modi the award and the title of **'eRatna'** in 2011 for his contribution in the field of e-governance.

The Information and Communication Technology (ICT) initiatives at the Chief Ministers office won the **'Award of Excellence – Departmental Level'** at the CSI Nihilent e-Governance Awards, 2011.

SWAGAT won the **CXO Award** in 2011 for 'improving public services.' It also won **Nation e-Governance Award**.

Annexures

Narendra Modi appeared on the **cover of *Time* magazine** in its issue of March 2012, one of few Indian politicians to have achieved this feat. His leadership was described as 'strong and businesslike, one that could guide India towards honesty and efficiency'.

The eGovernance strategies and ICT enabled initiatives at the CMO were awarded the **'Best Government to Citizen Initiative of the Year Award'** at the eIndia Summit held in 2012.

In the year 2012, Narendra Modi was awarded the **CNBC TV 18 Award** for 'Outstanding Contribution to the Cause of Indian Business'.

Bibliography

Books

Varadrajan, Siddharth, *Gujajrat: The Making of a Tragedy*. New Delhi: Penguin Books, 2002.

Malhotra, Inder, *Dynasties of India and Beyond*. New Delhi: Harper Collins, 2004.

Sanghvi, Nagindas, *Gujarat: A Political Analysis*. Surat: Centre for Social Studies, 1995.

Varshney, Ashutosh, *Ethnic Conflict and Civic Life: Hindus and Muslims in India*. New Haven: Yale University Press, 2002.

Modi S K, *Godhra: The Missing Rage*. New Delhi: Ocean Books Pvt. Ltd, 2004.

Kulkarni, Atmaram, *Portrayal of a Charismatic Leader*. Mumbai: Leelavati Publications, 1998.

Malhotra, Inder, *Indira Gandhi*. New Delhi: National Book Trust of India, 2006.

Newspapers

Business Line

Business Standard

Deccan Herald

Free Press Journal

Gujarat Times

Hindustan Times

Pakistan Link

Sunday Express
The Asian Age
The Hitavada
The Indian Express
The Pioneer
The Statesman
The Telegraph
The Times of India
Janmabhoomi Group of Papers

Magazines and Journals

Chitralekha
BJP Today
Express
India Today
Outlook
The Week

Websites

Business Week Online
India Observer

Index

2nd Backward Class Commission, 27
20-point programme, 21
2001 Agra Summit, 50
2002 communal riots in Godhra, 63

A

Abdullah, Farooq, 48
Accident theory, 150
Adani, Gautam, 387
Advani, Lal Krishna, 15, 34, 108, 116, 181, 192, 333
Aga, Anu, 376
Ahmedabad riots, 1969, 30
Ahmedabad riots, 2001, 29
Aiyar, Swaminathan, 126, 197, 209, 223
Akbar, M J, 71
Akhil Bharatiya Vidyarthi Parishad (ABVP), 14
Akshardham temple, 112
Alleviation of water problem, 141

Ambani, Anil, 339, 387
Ambani, Mukesh, 138, 278, 338
Anti-Muslim conflagration, 27
Anti-reservation agitation, 27
Antholis, William, 345, 395
Ashraf, Ajaz, 364

B

Banu, Saira, 77
Banerjee Committee, 95, 97, 146, 149
Best Bakery, 106
Bhagavatacharya Narayanacharya High School, 4
Bhankar, Mukundraoji, 175
Bharatiya Lok Dal (BLD), 17
Bhatt, Ashok, 173
BJP Today, 55, 128
Bharatiya Janata Party, 26, 40, 49, 111, 121, 145, 149, 190, 343, 372
Bharatiya Jan Sangh, 15
Bhatt, Sheela, 105

Bhosale, Nanubhai, 11
Bus Rapid Transport System (BRTS), 268

C

Chandrashekhar, 36
Chandod conference, 26
Chandoke, Neera, 362
Chaulia, Sreeram, 285
Chintan shibirs (brain-storming sessions), 164
Chiranjivi Yojana (Long Life Scheme), 163, 276
Chowdhary, Amarsinh, 28
Chowdhury, Neerja, 384, 387
Chhatra Sangharsh Samiti (CSS), 16
Clinton, Bill, 48
Commonwealth Association for Public Administration and Management (CAPAM), 147
Commonwealth Heads of Government Meeting (CHOGM), 49
Congress (O), 17
Congress (I), 11, 28, 40, 111, 121

D

Dalai, Suresh, 173
Dasgupta, Swapan, 128, 198, 207, 215, 269, 326, 361, 387
Das, Sohini, 279
Dave, Gopal, 173
Dave, Rasikbhai, 5
Dayal, Prashant, 193
Debroy, Bibek, 327
Desai, Hitendra, 29
Desai, Makarand, 23
Desai, Morarji, 17, 25
Desai, Santosh, 376
Deshmukh, Nanaji, 18
Development yatra, 132
Dholakia, Amit, 208
Dutt, Barkha, 85

E

e-grams, 162
E-GRAM Vishwa Gram Yojana, 231
Ekta Yatra, 179, 324
E-Mamta, 232
Emergency, 17, 19, 20, 22, 52, 276, 305, 330, 390
Engineer, Asghar Ali, 112
Fernandes, George, 18

G

Gajendragadkar, Vasant, 15, 23
Gandhi, Indira, 15, 25, 27, 71, 209, 319

Index

Gandhi, Mahatma, 10, 73, 113, 161, 184, 275

Gandhi, Rahul, 201, 316, 342, 383

Gandhi, Rajiv, 27, 73, 104, 128, 185

Gandhi, Tushar, 365

Gandhi, Sonia, 67, 72, 110, 191, 194, 348

Ganguli, Amulya, 204

Swagat programme, 231

Gau-raksha, 15

Gaurav yatra, 107

Ghanchis of Godhra, 64

George, T J S, 124

Gill, K P S, 101, 103

Global maritime security, 300

Godhra riots, 27, 65, 69, 76, 83, 106,122, 183, 215

    2002 communal riots in, 63

Godse, Nathuram, 73

Goebbels, 99

Governance, 221

    earthquake and rehabilitation, 222

    farm water management, 227

    panchayati raj, 232

    rural development, 230

    samras grams, 233

    strides in agriculture, 223

Govindacharya, K N, 366

Gram sabha, 166

Gram SWAGAT programme, 231

Gujarat Alkalis and Chemicals Ltd (GACL), 169

Gujarat Chamber of Commerce and Industry (GCCI), 78

Gujarat State Fertilizer Company Ltd (GSFC), 169

Gujarat State Petroleum Corporation Limited (GSPCL), 169

Gujarat day, 154

Gujarat Institute of Disaster Management (GIDM), 61

Gujarat Lok Sangharsh Samiti (GLSS), 17

Gujarat Parivartan Party (GPP), 355

Gujarat *Sammelan* (convention), 13

Gujarat State Disaster Management Authority (GSDMA), 58

Gupta, Shekhar, 366, 385

Gupta, Smita, 363

Gupta, Sudhir, 99, 205

Gutka-free Gujarat, 358

Guzdar, Cyrus, 271

Gyan Rath Yatra, 145

H

Hegde, B M, 219
Herzog, Siegfried, 340
Hindutva, 20, 184, 189, 196, 33, 362
Hindutvawadi, 20

I

Indian Mujahideen (IM), 94
Integrated Child Development Services (ICDS), 162
International awards won by Gujarat, 403

J

Jaitley, Arun, 106, 117, 121, 190, 288, 304
Jaitley, Jaya, 66
Janmashtami, 7
Jan Sangh, 14, 16
Jan Sangharsh Manch (JSM), 97
Janata Chhapu, 22
Janata Front, 17, 21, 21
Janata Party, 25, 26
Jatti, BD, 23
Jayalalitha, 381
Jha, Prem Shankar, 206
JP movement, 16
Joshi, Manohar Murli, 34

Joshi, Sanjay, 356, 366
Joshi, Sudhir, 5
Jyoti Gramodyog Vikas Yojana, 159, 168
Jyotigram Scheme, 159, 225

K

Kalpasar Project, 142, 258
Kamath, 392
Kanya Kelavani Nidhi, 160, 238, 239
Kar sevaks, 64, 67, 71, 74, 97
Karmayogi Maha Abbhiyan, 140, 249
Karmayogi scheme, 164
KHAM, 26
Khan, Asifa, 333
Khurshid, Salman, 116
Kishwar, Madhu Purnima, 331
Krishna, Srivastva, 261
Krishi Mahotsav, 155, 167, 228
Kisan raths, 155
Kisan Mazdoor Lok Paksh (KMLP), 17
Kulkarni, Atmaram, 31, 41
Kumar, Nitish, 353
Kumar, Virendra, 124
Kutch earthquake, 57
Kite flying carnival, 138

Index

L

Lakshman, Nikhil, 348

Laxman Jnanpeeth, 38

Lyngdoh, J M, 106, 114

Lok kalyan melas, 56

Lok Sevak Sangh, 18

Lok Shakti Rath Yatra, 34

M

Madhok, Balraj, 14

Mahurkar, Uday, 222

Maha Gujarat Janata Parishad (MGJP), 14

Maha Gujarat movement, 6

Mahakumbh, 511

Makwana, Kishor, 176

Malhotra, Inder, 73

Malhotra, V K, 159

Malik, Iffat, 125

Mander, Harsh, 77

Mani, Prem Kumar, 353

Masani. Minoo, 208

Matri shakti, 239

Mehta, Chhabildas, 40

Mehta, Mona, 361

Mehta, Pratap Bhanu, 149

Mehta, Suresh, 44

Mehta, Tarak, 176

Mehta, Tarun, 221

Mitra, Ashok, 385

MISA, 21

Misra, R K, 189, 196

Mistry, Cyrus, 339

Mission Mangalam, 240

Mitta, Manoj, 104

Modi, Narendra, 3, 28, 40, 72, 98, 100, 108, 116, 132, 181, 192, 316, 399

    awards for, 406

    Britain and, 283

    childhood of, 3

    education of, 4

    vision for the 2014 general elections, 348

    family background of, 3

    friendly circle of, 4

    holy man's prediction about, 7

    Japan and, 295

    Keshubhai's machinations and, 354

    Nitish factor and, 353

    personality of, 391

    poor financial condition of, 6

    press post-mortem after election 2012 and, 372

    Russia and, 286

spiritual matters of, 9

Swami Vivekananda's impact on, 8

visit to China, 287

meeting with CPC Politburo members, 291

visit to Israel, 282

Modi, S K, 65, 68

Mookerjee, Debraj, 122

Musharraf, 50, 113

Mustafa, Seema, 373

N

Nagarik Swatantra Sammelan (NSS), 22

Nanavati Commission, 95, 187, 313, 382

Nandy, Ashish, 378

Narayan, Jayaprakash, 6, 16

Narmada Bachao Andolan, 39

National Democratic Alliance (NDA), 49, 282

National Human Rights Commission (NHRC), 87

National Labour Party (NLP), 17

Nair, Arvind, 229

Navnirman, 15

Nayar, Kuldip, 189, 326

Ninan, Sevanti, 85

Nyay Yatra (Journey for Justice), 34

P

Pakistani Islamic terrorists, 112

Panagariya, Arvind, 360

Panchamrut Yojana, 244

gyan shakti, 244

jan shakti, 245

jal shakti, 245

raksha shakti, 246

urja shakti, 245

Panchvati yojana, 231

Pandya, Vishnu, 19

Parekh, Deepak, 271

Parmar, Chandrika, 201

Patwari, Prabhudas, 17

Patel, Aakar, 394

Patel, Chimanbhai, 28, 35

Patel, Harish, 5

Patel, Babubhai Jashbhai, 17, 21

Patel, Kadwa, 368

Patel, Keshubahi, 17, 26, 41, 42, 150, 181, 355, 368

Patel, Leuva, 368

Pathak, Sanjukta, 377

People's War Group (PWG), 135

Phanshikar, Vijay, 99

Index

Phillipose, Pamela, 118
Port development, 264
Pracharak, 9, 12, 15, 41
Praant padadhikari (regional head), 24
Praant pracharak, 24
Praja Socialist Party (PSP), 14
Prasad, Navin, 222
Purie, Aroon, 386

R

Raghavan, R K, 85
Raghu, Sunil, 118
Ramanbhai, 172
Rama Rajya, 184
Ranade, Eknathji, 12
Rana, Kashiram, 43
Rane Commission, 27
Rao, Parsa Venkateshwar, 364
Rao, P V Narasimha, 39
Rashtriya Swayamsevak Sangh (RSS), 6, 172, 330
Rath yatra, 27, 105
Rathore, kishore, 328
Railway Protection Force (RPF), 64
Rocca, Christine, 102
Roy, Arundhati, 77
Reddy, Sanjiva, 25

Report of the Justice Jagannath Reddy Commission, 31
Reservation Policy, 26
Rice, Condoleezza, 151

S

Sabarmati Express, 33, 63, 65, 71, 92, 115, 125, 281, 365
Sabarmati Riverfront Project, 267
Sadbhavana, 303
  mission, 304
  yatra, 309, 352
Saluja, Anita, 383
Samras Yojana (Harmony Scheme), 161
Samskardham, 37
Sagar Khedu Scheme, 202, 262
Sanghavi, Nagindas, 27, 28, 39
Sanghavi, Vir, 151
Sareshwala, Zafar, 332
Sardar Patel Awas Yojana, 231
Sardesai, Rajdeep, 85, 117
Sarna, Navtej, 152
Sarsanghchalak, 23, 389
Sarvodaya, 11
Satyagraha, 11, 18
Shaikh, Sajid, 68
Shankar, Kalyani, 384

Sharma, Amol, 321
Shinde, Sushil Kumar, 359
Siddiqui, Shahid, 317
Singh, Ajay, 114
Singh, Charan, 17, 25
Singh, Onkar, 50
Singh, Rajnath, 54
Singh, Sanjay, 332
Singh, Tavleen, 328, 331
Singh, V P, 36
Singha, I S, 396
Sivaswamy, Saisuresh, 348
Shah, Amit, 45, 98
Shah, Harshad, 175
Shourie, Arun, 183
Sohrabuddin's killing, 191
Solanki, Madhavsingh, 21, 26, 28
Somnath Yatra, 179
Sood, Atul, 362
Special Investigation Team (SIT), 313, 382
State Level Bankers' Committee (SLBC), 158
Sujalam Suphalam Yojana (SSY) project, 140, 142
Swachch Gram Swasthya Yojana (Clean and Healthy Villages Scheme), 231
Swami, Parveen, 94

Swarup, Harihar, 114
Swatantra party, 29
Swayamsevak, 10, 18, 172

T

Tata, Ratan, 213, 278
Tehelka tapes, 187
Tehriq-e-Kasa, 112
Terrorist and Disruptive Activities (Prevention) Act (TADA), 106
Tewatia, D S, 88
Tewatia Report, 90
    facts that need verification, 91
    indisputable facts, 90
    information that appears to be untrue, 91
    some mysteries, 92
Thapar, Karan, 185
Thottam, Jyoti, 315
Total revolution, 16
Trivedi, Kishore, 395
Tuomioja, Erikki, 102

U

Umerji, Maulvi, 97
Umarji, Vinay, 279
United Progressive Alliance (UPA), 145

Index

US Congressional Research Service (CRS) report, 344

Uttarayan, 139

V

Vaghela, Shankersinh, 19, 36, 42, 108

Vajpayaee, Atal Bihari, 15, 44, 50, 7, 101, 104, 129

Vanbandhu Kalyan Yojana, 244

Vande Mataram, 127

Varadarajan, Siddharth, 64

Varshney, Ashutosh, 30, 31

Vembu, Venky, 288

Verma, J S, 88

V-Governance, 140

Vibhaag pracharak, 24

Vibrant Gujarat, 136, 335

    global investors summit 2003, 136

    global investors summit 2005, 136

    global investors summit 2007, 137

    vibrant Gujarat Summit 2003, 273

Vishwa Gujarati Parivar Mahotsav (Worldwide Gujarati Family Festival), 139

Vishwa Hindu Parishad (VHP), 13, 74

Vision for Gujarat: Address to NRIs – 2012, 275

Visvanathan, Shiv, 201

Vittal, N, 309

Vivekananda, Swami, 9

Vivekananda *Yuva Vikas* Yatra, 308

Vora, Rustum, 279

W

Wadi Yojana, 156

Women's welfare programme, 236

    Balika Samruddhi Yojana, 237

    Kanya Kelavani (education of girls), 238

    Virat mahila sammelan, 237

World Health Organization (WHO) report, 82

Y

Yadav, Lalu Prasad, 149, 158

Yadav, Yogendra, 376

Yagnik, Achyut, 325

Z

Zakia Jafri case, 382

Zinzarde, Gopalrao, 11